Advance Praise for
SHANDA

"In her revealing memoir, Letty Cottin Pogrebin, widely known for her intelligence, style, generosity, and boldness, admits the heavy burden of secrets including her own which she has long carried. *Shanda*, her clear-eyed look at one immigrant family's habit of secrecy and fear of shame reveals why a lifetime of trying to uncover hidden truths has informed her insightful books and articles on topics many are afraid to tackle."

— **Ruth J. Abram,** historian and founding president, Lower East Side Tenement Museum

"Secrets are costly—heavy weights to carry around. In *Shanda*, Letty Cottin Pogrebin takes aim at shame, the factory where the costliest secrets are made. She dismantles the machinery of shame, and she does it with stories that are vivid, emotional, and unforgettable."

— **Alan Alda,** actor, author, director

"The richness of Pogrebin's stories, the complexity and beauty of her storytelling, and her devastatingly honest soul-baring make *Shanda* a powerfully stunning piece of life and art."

— **Mayim Bialik,** actor, author, neuroscientist, co-host of *Jeopardy!*

"Pride may be a deadly sin, but shame is simply deadly. With her trenchant wit and generous heart, Letty Cottin Pogrebin explores the theological and historical imperatives that drove her family to conceal pain and bury truths in service to misguided ideas of propriety and perfectionism. *Shanda* is a bracing book: both liberating and exhilarating."

— **Geraldine Brooks,** journalist and Pulitzer Prize–winning novelist

"With unflinching honesty, Pogrebin takes on the defining role of shame in her family, helps us name our own vulnerabilities, and reframes humiliation and secrecy into a powerful reckoning with our hidden truths and by extension, our humanity. *Shanda* is amazing, relatable, her bravest book yet."

— **Angela Buchdahl,** senior rabbi, Central Synagogue (NYC), first Asian-American to be ordained a rabbi

"Pogrebin has written much about family, politics, revolution, and evolution. Now she brings her fulsome attention to private and public shame, the personal secrets that are ever-haunting, and the national shame that causes brutal conflicts and global disasters. *Shanda* is a memoir about secrets that can paralyze us or, when released, help us fly."

— **Judy Collins,** singer, author, activist

"From its opening lines, *Shanda* captures our universal feelings about secrets and shame, and never lets us go. In this emotionally deep, often profoundly funny memoir, Letty Cottin Pogrebin confronts the darkness, shrinks it, and brings us out into the light. Her literary voice is one-in-a-million."

— **Tovah Feldshuh,** Tony and Emmy-nominated actress, writer, and playwright

"As Pogrebin reminds us, Jews remember and writers write, yet rarely has anyone brought such honest scrutiny to the question of what we reveal to others and what we keep hidden about ourselves. *Shanda* is a book about shame and secrets, it is about the lives and the lies of an immigrant Jewish family in a century where for Jews, hiding could be life-saving. But it is also about the process of discovering what had been kept hidden. The surprise is that in coming to know the secrets that others considered shameful, we not only become more compassionate and forgiving toward them but also come to know them more vividly—not for who they thought they had to be but for who they are. In the end then, *Shanda* is a meditation on love."

— **Carol Gilligan,** author of *In a Different Voice* and co-author, most recently, of *Why Does Patriarchy Persist?*

"Pogrebin divulges her own family's astonishing array of secrets and delves into the annals and anthropology of Judaism and feminism, fat shaming, sexual shaming, and more. *Shanda* is a book for anyone who has ever felt or feared shame, which is to say, this is a book for everyone."

— **Ellen Goodman,** Pulitzer Prize–winning journalist, columnist, and author

"This beautifully written memoir spoke volumes to me. As a proud feminist, Jew, and member of the LGBTQ+ community, I can't thank Letty Cottin Pogrebin enough for confronting her family's shandas with such brutal honesty and humor, and for unmasking shame-based fears that have destroyed innumerable lives for generations."

— **Judy Gold,** Emmy Award-winning stand-up comic, actress, TV writer, and producer

"This is a memoir wonderfully grounded in the vibrancy of Jewish-American life, circa mid-20th-century. Its warmth and affection are contagious."

— **Vivian Gornick,** literary critic, essayist, memoirist

"Every writer knows that the best stories are those that cannot be written. But in *Shanda*, Letty Cottin Pogrebin breaks the rules and reveals some of the deepest secrets her family tried to keep hidden. The result is a beautiful meditation on the mysteries that families carry, and that, cumulatively, help shape a people."

— **Yossi Klein Halevi,** senior fellow, Shalom Hartman Institute, author of the *New York Times* bestseller, *Letters to My Palestinian Neighbor*

"Pogrebin has written a brilliant, fun, wicked memoir that drills down into the pain of humiliation and fear of exposure in ways that readers of every age will recognize as true. *Shanda* is a brilliant memoir and a must-read."

— **Molly Jong-Fast,** contributing writer, *The Atlantic*

"With wit, erudition, and searing honesty, *Shanda* unfolds like a riveting mystery novel—you can't stop reading until the very end. A powerful subject, treated with sensitivity and grace."
— **Francine Klagsbrun,** author of *Lioness: Golda Meir and the Nation of Israel*

"Pogrebin tells personal stories that, despite their particularity, speak to everyone's experience, and the wisdom she draws from Jewish teachings speaks to readers of any faith tradition or cultural heritage. Like all great memoirs, *Shanda* is an intimate reflection of the human in us all."
— **David Kraemer,** professor of Talmud and Rabbinics, library director, Jewish Theological Seminary

"Letty Cottin Pogrebin's work has changed lives everywhere. In *Shanda*, she does it again, giving us inspiration and strength to resist the chilling effects of shame and secrecy. This is a brave, beautiful book of reckoning."
— **MK Merav Michaeli,** Israeli government minister and member of parliament, leader of the Labor Party, and former journalist

"The authenticity of Letty Cottin Pogrebin's voice is what sets *Shanda* apart from a shelf full of memoirs. She is brave, she is brilliant, she is funny, and she is warm, but above all she is real, and because of that, her exploration of her own family history and her relationship to the universal feeling of shame and its particular applications to Jewish America hits deep. This is a remarkably memorable memoir because of the way Pogrebin tells her eminently relatable memoir. She is the mother you long to learn from, the friend you reach to confide in, the feminist writer who serves as a generational role model, the woman you just want to be close to."
— **Jodi Rudoren,** editor in chief, *The Forward*; former *New York Times Jerusalem* bureau chief

"You don't have to be Jewish to love *Shanda*. (I grew up a Congregationalist Christian.) You will marvel at Pogrebin's always compassionate, often funny descriptions of the astounding family secrets kept by those nearest and dearest to her. (My language would not have been quite so wonderful!)"

— **Patricia Schroeder,** former U.S. Congresswoman (Colo.)

SHANDA

A Memoir of
SHAME AND SECRECY

LETTY COTTIN
POGREBIN

Post Hill
PRESS

A POST HILL PRESS BOOK
ISBN: 978-1-63758-396-8
ISBN (eBook): 978-1-63758-397-5

Post Hill Press
New York • Nashville
posthillpress.com

Published in the United States of America
1 2 3 4 5 6 7 8 9 10

Dedicated to the memory of my immigrant grandparents
Jenny and Nathan Halpern
Yetta and Max Cottin
and their children's struggle to become "real Americans."

BOOKS BY
LETTY COTTIN POGREBIN

How to Make It in a Man's World
Getting Yours
Growing Up Free
Family Politics
Among Friends
Deborah, Golda, and Me: Being Female and Jewish in America
Getting Over Getting Older
Three Daughters
How to Be a Friend to a Friend Who's Sick
Single Jewish Male Seeking Soulmate
Shanda
Stories for Free Children (editor)
Free to Be You and Me (consulting editor)

Everyone has three lives: a public life,
a private life, and a secret life.
—Gabriel García Marquez

There is no agony like bearing an
untold story inside you.
—Zora Neale Hurston

You've got to speak your shame.
—Brené Brown

AUTHOR'S NOTE

"Shanda" means shame or disgrace in Yiddish.
(It's pronounced Shahn-da.)
[This is not a biography of Shonda Rhimes.]

CONTENTS

II
PRIVATE SHAME

III
GUILTY SECRETS

IV
PUBLIC SHAME

A GOOD NAME

People often ask writers why we write. Flannery O'Connor famously responded, "I write because I don't know what I think until I read what I say." For Joan Didion the answer was, "I write to find out what I'm thinking, what I'm looking at, what I see and what it means, what I want and what I fear." Junot Diaz doubled down, melding the universal and the particular: "Writing helps me answer my own questions about what it means to be human, or, in my case a Dominican human who grew up in New Jersey." With adjustments to gender, ethnicity, and geography, his reply most closely approximates my own. Writing helps me answer my questions about what it means to be human, or, in my case a Jewish human who grew up female in New York in the middle of the twentieth century in an immigrant family torn between loyalty to their own kind and longing for American acceptance. I wrote this book to make sense of that world, that family, and its secrets.

The relatives they left behind in the Old Country were a nameless blur, so for all intents and purposes, this history of my family begins with Jenny and Nathan Halpern, my mother's parents, and Yetta and Max Cottin, my father's mother and father, who came to the United States from Eastern Europe in the first decade of the 1900s. Those four Jews produced a combined fourteen offspring, who, in turn, birthed twenty-five children, including me, a cast of characters with enough secrets to fill this book twice over. But I couldn't create a coherently meaningful narrative around their stories until I recognized the force that bound them together and connected our family to the larger immigrant experience. That force, I realized, once I'd done some research into their lives, was an abiding, sometimes goading, sometimes galvanizing, fear of shame. Besides figuring out how to thrive in the New World, my grandparents, aunts, uncles, and cousins learned through bitter experience that nothing could overcome the ruinous impact of public disgrace, and any act, fact, person, or circumstance with the potential to humiliate them had to be circumvented at all costs or converted into a secret. Their need to avoid scandal was so compelling that, once identified, it provided the lens through which I could see my family with fresh eyes, spotlight their fears, and, in so doing, illuminate my own.

The recent flood of intimate memoirs—about addiction, infidelity, closeted homosexuality, sadism, masochism, depression, incest, infertility, bigotry, and spiritual crisis—makes it almost impossible for younger people to fathom what an anathema it used to be, and for some of us still is, to share anything, let alone a messy personal struggle or an ugly family secret. Likewise, social media's rampant hyper-sharing—not just of people's career crises or honeymoon itineraries but also their sexual fantasies, prenatal ultrasounds, anxiety meds, and gender-reassignment surgery—makes it hard for millennials and Gen Xers to understand how sacrosanct privacy once was. So, let me contextualize the world in which I grew up. There was no internet; no Facebook, Twitter, or Instagram; no cyberbullying, cancel culture, sexting, or trolling; nor was it possible for a person to search for and find an online archive of another person's most intimate, cringeworthy bloopers, benders, and bad trips. In my youth, all it took to destroy one's "good name" was a shanda, the Yiddish word for shame, scandal, disgrace.

I'm obsessed with secrets because I grew up with so many of them. Byzantine cover-ups hid my parents' failures to meet the Jewish community's omnipresent pressure to be a credit to one's family, faith, and people. I knew the high bar I was expected to meet and the perils of falling short. Intelligence, reliability, and ethical probity were the qualities I was sworn to uphold and model in the world, and if I did not measure up, or do a good job of concealing my imperfections, I knew they would reflect badly on my family and The Jewish People, an entity so exalted in the world of my childhood that all three words still demand initial capital letters. I memorized vital statistics about The Jewish People: that we comprise a scant 2 percent of the US population and an infinitesimal 0.2 percent of all humanity; that we're a tiny but tenacious remnant of God's Chosen People, dispersed across the globe, hounded in ways large and small by every possible permutation of anti-Semitism, but united by our history, our sacred texts and traditions, and our fealty to one another. The Crusaders tried to slaughter us, the Inquisitors tried to convert us, the Nazis tried to exterminate us, *but we're still here.* Or, as comedian Alan King famously put it when asked to summarize the holiday of Passover: "They tried to kill us. We survived. Let's eat."

Because The Jewish People survived, I had to do us proud. Because we're "the people of the book," I had to be literate and well-educated. Because we were commanded to be "a light unto the nations," I had to blaze a trail of excellence and live an exemplary life. I've both carried that burden and defied it. As a child, I learned what was valued and what had to be denied or censored, which walls could be spackled and which had to be torn down and rebuilt. And I learned how to keep a secret. It wasn't just cultural mores that clamped my mouth shut, it was the ever-looming fear of the shanda.

My mania around secrecy and shame was sparked in 1951 by the discovery that my parents had concealed from me the truth about their personal histories, and every member of my large extended family, on both sides, was in on it. Years later, as tongues loosened, I learned that the original dissemblers in our family were none other than my maternal grandparents, Jenny and Nathan Halpern, who, until they died, hid a seismic event that occurred in 1898, before they came to America. Between those two brackets— the exposure of Mom and Dad's sins of deception and Grandma and Grandpa's sins of omission—lay dozens of buried secrets about a slew of folks I thought I knew. In the process of exhuming their stories and disentangling their deceptions, I came to understand how indelibly my family had imprinted upon me its template for shame and secrecy.

Shame is not unique to Jews, to be sure. In *The Twelve Tribes of Hattie*, the African American writer, Ayana Mathis, writes, "When I was a little girl, I played a secret game...I would bobby pin one of my grandmother's yellow towels over my own hair. I would swing the towel and flick it over my shoulders, my lovely blond mane.... Somehow, at the age of eight, I already understood that the white world, which was then for me the whole world outside of the confines of my family, thought my life less valuable, less precious, than that of my blond, blue-eyed alter ego. I was ashamed of this reality, though certainly I had no fault in it. Black children play games of race shame and race-switching to this day...already beset by a sense of unworthiness they cannot name."

Dr. Mona Hanna-Attisha, an Iraqi American physician who played a key role in exposing the lead in Flint, Michigan's water supply, writes in *What the Eyes Don't See* that had she been wrong about the water's toxicity, she would have been painfully, permanently humiliated in front of her extended family, medical residents, professional colleagues, and friends. "There is an Arab concept called 'aeb,' or shame. I always did my best to banish it from my brain because it's wrong and stupid and shouldn't be in my mind, but at the same time it had been planted there so long ago, it was like a tumor that couldn't be completely excised. It had cells that kept mutating and replicating." Like the Jewish shanda, the Arab aeb is bigger and broader than a wound to the ego; it's the dishonor one brings upon one's family, ancestors, and entire community by speaking wrongly or acting badly.

Annabelle Tometich "spent fifteen years pretending to be a White guy" whose identity she assumed when she was writing restaurant reviews for a newspaper in Fort Myers, Florida, under the name Jean Le Bouef. "The name's power and privilege had consumed me," she confessed in a *Washington Post* opinion piece, but the power she acquired masquerading as a French White guy "came at a price: my identity." By hiding her real name, gender, and biracial ethnicity, this brown-skinned daughter of a Filipina mother and White father went "from never being enough, to being no one."

To my mind, the most haunting shame stories are those told by Korean, Chinese, Filipina, Taiwanese, Burmese, and other so-called "comfort women," 400,000 of whom were tortured, sexually abused, and serially raped by their Japanese captors during World War II. One survivor, who was seventeen when she was abducted and enslaved, testified, "The first day I was raped, and the rapes never stopped.... I was born a woman but never lived as a woman...I feel sick when I come close to a man. I shiver whenever I see a Japanese flag.... Why should I feel ashamed? I do not have to feel ashamed." In 1945, at the end of the conflict, the male prisoners of war returned to their home countries where they were honored by their governments and countrymen while the women who survived Japanese brutality were treated as if their shame was their fault. Ostracized, shunned, stigmatized as whores, they were revictimized and made to feel as if their debasement by the Japanese had sullied the image of their respective nations. For more than seventy-five years, most of the women suffered these indignities in silence. But a courageous few protested and sued for redress. Now quite elderly, their ranks thinning fast, they're demanding financial reparations and a formal apology from Japan. However, their children, grandchildren, and great-grandchildren, who've also been stigmatized all these years, are deathly afraid that revived media attention to the case will further intensify *their* disgrace and extend the black mark of shame to *their* descendants, so the younger generations are begging the old women to quit seeking justice.

If humiliation can be inherited by the relatives of innocent victims, it's no wonder that shame adheres like superglue to the relatives of a certifiable villain. The late Bernard Madoff, for example. His massive financial fraud destroyed the lives and financial security of an estimated 37,000 people in 130 countries, bankrupting the faceless and famous alike (among them, Steven Spielberg, Kevin Bacon and Kyra Sedgwick, former New York Mets owner Fred Wilpon, Hall of Fame pitcher Sandy Koufax, and Nobel laureate Elie Wiesel). It emptied the coffers of hundreds of charitable foundations and put a stop to their good works. A few of his duped clients committed suicide. His son Mark, who denied knowledge of the Ponzi scheme, became so overwhelmed by stress and shame that he looped the leash of the family dog around a ceiling pipe in his living room and hanged himself. Mark left behind two toddlers and an estranged wife, who changed her last name to Morgan. To escape humiliation, Madoff's wife, Ruth, and her five grandchildren all changed their names. Another son, Andrew, attributed the relapse of his rare lymphoma to the impact of the scandal, telling *People* magazine that it "killed my brother very quickly. And it's killing me slowly." Andrew died in 2014 at the age of forty-eight. Madoff's younger brother Peter pled guilty to conspiracy and falsifying records and told the court he was "deeply ashamed and terribly sorry." He served nine years of a ten-year sentence and was released in August 2020. Madoff's wife Ruth, besieged by death threats, shunned by friends, neighbors, even by her hairdresser, hid from the paparazzi and the public behind designer sunglasses. In 2008, on Christmas Eve, she attempted suicide. In 2012, she sold her sprawling apartment on the Upper East Side and moved to a one-bedroom condo in Connecticut. At this writing, Ruth has not spoken publicly in ten years. The Wall Street fraudster's shame, the tragedy that keeps metastasizing, produced yet another coda in February 2022, when his sister Sondra and her husband Marvin Wiener, were found dead of gunshot wounds in an apparent murder-suicide.

Bernie Madoff's religion rarely escaped notice in the press. Jewish pundits worried out loud and in print about the long-term effect of his ignominy on the image of The Jewish People. Already catnip for the anti-Semites, his crimes might have been even more of a shanda for us had the media not mentioned, along with his religion, the fact that nearly all his victims were Jews or Jewish institutions, a notation that carried the subtext, to me at least, that sparing Christians from financial ruin was Madoff's saving grace. I didn't lose a penny with him, but I, too, felt his swindle to be a blight on the Jewish collective. You might say, I generalized him, a phenomenon common to most minority populations in this country. Having participated in several years-long intergroup dialogues, I can attest that my Black, Brown, and Muslim friends have similar reactions when one of their members brings shame to their cohort. Guilt by association is our cross to bear.

Without knowing which boxes these men checked on their census forms, you can probably identify the race or ethnicity of Richard Ramirez, Sirhan Sirhan, Bill Cosby, and David Berkowitz (alias "Son of Sam"), whose antecedents are, respectively, Mexican, Palestinian, African American, and Jewish. According to human rights monitors, when those criminals were making international headlines, America saw a dramatic increase in racist, Islamophobic, or anti-Semitic incidents. Yet nothing comparable happened when the notorious wrongdoer was a White Anglo-Saxon Protestant. I'd be surprised if a single Welsh, English, German, Norwegian, or Irish American felt personally sullied when Jim Jones poisoned more than 900 people in Jonestown, a third of them children. Or when Jeffrey Dahmer, the "Milwaukee Cannibal," murdered and dismembered seventeen men and boys. Or when Timothy McVeigh, the domestic terrorist, blew up the federal building in Oklahoma City, killing 168 innocent human beings, nineteen of them children. And it's a safe bet that their White ethnic sisters and brothers were not collectively shamed by the horrific crimes of these White men or harassed on the streets in wake of their disgrace.

Whenever news broke that someone had done something terrible, my mother would say, "Please God, don't let him be a Jew," and she would search the story to see if the police had a suspect with a Jewish name. I've become my mother. The minute I hear about another mass murderer, I say, "Please God, don't let him be a Jew." (It's always a man.) And I know that my Black, Brown, and Muslim friends are inserting their own identity label at the end of the sentence and saying the same. We've learned that one bad apple can rot us all.

I was raised by Ashkenazi Jews in Queens, New York. J. D. Vance was raised by evangelical Christians in Appalachia, yet his memoir, *Hillbilly Elegy*, spoke to me because it opened an aperture I recognized. His people's struggles with poverty, violence, and addiction mirrored my people's struggles with fear, secrecy, and the belief that imperfection must be met with deception or reinvention. Every family has its underbelly. Mine was fat with pretense, the denied, the obscured, the unsaid. A timely discovery of letters from the 1930s, '40s, and '50s, as well as documents, photos, and yearbooks that I had not encountered in years, helped me write my way out of my childhood and into my parents' marriage. Their revelatory correspondence gave evidence that shame-avoidance dictated many of their decisions, and fear of the shanda explained events that had confounded me for years: why my father refused to discuss his two brothers who died mysteriously before they were thirty. Why my paternal grandfather would banish his youngest son for refusing to attend an elite yeshiva. How a radio show made one of my uncles persona non grata in my mother's family.

The poet Adrienne Rich coined the word "revisioning" to describe the act of "looking back, of seeing with fresh eyes, of entertaining an old text from a new critical direction." In the process of revisioning my family and its secrets, I came to understand the sizable dimensions of my inheritance from them—fear of shame, dread of powerlessness, need for control, the pursuit of perfection. Their secrets differed from mine but our motives to conceal were the same: we hid what made us feel deficient. We lied to forestall humiliation. Camouflaged our flaws and papered over our missteps to spare our families pain, indignity, or derivative shame. Revised our origin stories or erased entire chapters of our lives—illnesses, financial strain, religious hypocrisy, youthful mistakes—so we could present an ideal image to the world, keep the goyim (gentiles) from thinking ill of us, or pass muster with our fellow Jews.

More than two thousand years ago, Ben Sira, a revered Jewish sage, wrote this prescient warning.

Have regard for your name
For it continues with you
Longer than a thousand great treasures of gold.
A good life has its number of days,
But a good name continues forever.

Thirteen centuries later, Shakespeare put similar sentiments into the mouth of Iago.

Good name in man and woman…
Is the immediate jewel of their souls:
Who steals my purse steals trash…
But he that filches from me my good name
Robs me of that which not enriches him
And makes me poor indeed.

Either quote could serve as advertising copy for Reputation. com and other online services that, for a price, will scrub the internet of every statement, image, affiliation, criminal proceeding, photograph, news report, or reference that might discredit, defame, shame, humiliate, or destroy an individual, company, or corporation. Not so easy to eradicate, however, are guilt and dread, the intractable, ungovernable fear of being found out. This is a memoir about shame and secrecy, what we do to cover stuff up and what happens when we can't.

I

FAMILY SECRETS

CHAPTER 1

BRAIN STORM

First mistake. Taking my neurologist's call on my cell phone. At Whole Foods. In the produce department.

"We have the results of your MRI," the doctor says, adding, before I can stop him. "It shows a growth in your head."

I freeze, knees buckled, grab my shopping cart for support. "How big?" I ask. I'd already survived breast cancer. Where tumors are concerned, I know from experience that size matters. Stage matters. Type matters. Location matters. Everything matters.

"About the size of a small plum."

Fate's whimsy had stopped me at a bounteous display of apricots, nectarines, peaches—and plums, some deep purple and no bigger than a ping-pong ball, some red and speckled with the circumference of a Macintosh. The importance of tumor fundamentals had been made clear to me four years before when a mammogram revealed that I had one in my right breast. After follow-up tests and a week of petrified waiting, I learned that my tumor was malignant but small enough to be excised with a lumpectomy and treated with six weeks of radiation. It had a name, "tubular carcinoma," which in Cancerland, is one of the "good tumors" since it seldom requires a mastectomy or chemotherapy. But in the land of the Jews, at least when I was growing up, there was no such thing as *good* cancer. Siddhartha Mukherjee, an Indian American oncologist, called cancer "the emperor of all maladies." My family called it "the C-word." Cancer was the one affliction that did not speak its name, and every Jew who received that diagnosis knew enough to expect the worst, an outcome for which centuries of Jewish history and Jewish humor had prepared us.

> *The Russian says, "I'm thirsty. I must have vodka."*
> *The Frenchman says, "I'm thirsty. I must have wine."*
> *The German says, "I'm thirsty. I must have beer."*
> *The Mexican says, "I'm thirsty. I must have tequila."*
> *The Jew says, "I'm thirsty. I must have diabetes."*

For those unfamiliar with our tribe's subgroups, I should clarify at the outset that Jews come in many forms and flavors. Those whose ancestors hailed from Spain or North Africa are called Sephardim and tend to have different habits, tastes, and practices than do Jews called Ashkenazim, who came from Eastern Europe, as did all four of my grandparents. Ashkenazim, in turn, are subdivided into Litvaks (from Lithuania and Latvia) and Galitzianers (from Ukraine and Poland), the former being self-defined as cool, rational, and intellectual, the latter as warm, emotional, and funny. (Think Leonard Nimoy as Spock in *Star Trek* versus Fran Dresher as Fran Fine in *The Nanny*.) Born to a Litvak dad and a Galitzianer mom, I should be a balance of both, but I definitely lean Litvak. For us Litvaks, the brain is not just the body's neurological control panel but also the beating heart of the Jewish soul. And the worst place to get the C-word is in the B-word, meaning the brain, which is to say, the mind. In my family, "Jews live by our brains" was as much a truism as "Jewish husbands don't beat their wives," "there are no Jewish alcoholics" (because we'd rather eat than drink), "as long as a Jewish man is smart, funny, and makes a living without getting dirty, he doesn't have to be tall, dark, and handsome," and, "as long as a Jewish woman is smart, talented, and feminine she doesn't have to be blonde, blue-eyed, or big-breasted."

The plum in my brain also has a name: pituitary adenoma. It, too, is one of the "good tumors," and the best thing about it is what it is *not*: malignant. Not something that metastasizes to other organs. Not *cancer*. That litany loops through my skull like the earworm commercial for Kars for Kids. Unfortunately, however, the plum happens to be situated perilously close to my optic and facial nerves and were it to press on them, it could deform my face and leave me blind. So, it's gotta go.

Cue the nightmares. Shaved head. Skull cracked open with a hammer and chisel. Accidentally nicked nerve. Grotesque scar. Deep furrow. Permanent bald spot. Thankfully, a different reality unfolds. My neurologist refers me to a brain surgeon who specializes in extracting pituitary adenomas, bit by bit, through the nostrils. Called "trans-sphenoidal endoscopic endonasal surgery," the procedure leaves no visible scars, though it does alter the interior architecture of my nasal passages and leaves me with a partially open septum (the wall separating the two nostrils). After surgery, the nose on my face, never my best feature, looks none the worse for having been used as the turnpike to my brain. But I'm not out of the woods. I have double vision, so I can't drive. My husband sees two lines running down the middle of the road, I see two sets of double lines going off in opposite directions. I can't smell anything—coffee, garlic, a pie in the oven. My French perfume, Madame Rochas, may as well be Windex. I can't taste anything either, including my A-list edibles, lamb chops, four-cheese pizza, walnut brownies. The aftereffects of the procedure are disorienting and distressing. Food and beverages have no flavor, only texture (wet, crisp, dense, hard) and temperature (warm, cold, tepid). This too shall pass, my doctors promise, but being someone who expects The Worst, I'm convinced my sensory losses are permanent.

When we were kids, my friends and I used to torment each other with hypotheticals: "Suppose a bad guy was threatening to kill you unless you sacrifice one of your five senses, which would you give up: smell, taste, touch, sound, or sight?" Never a fan of forced choices, I struggled mightily before opting to sacrifice touch. Now, a month post-surgery, touch and sound are my only fully functional senses until, one astonishing morning, I open the coffee canister and literally smell the coffee. I get off on the fragrance but when I brew a cup, it has no taste. Days later, again with no warning, a sip of fresh orange juice explodes in my mouth and tastes the way Beethoven's "Ode to Joy" sounds. A few weeks after that, the double lines reunite on the West Side Highway. The scent of lilacs growing in profusion along a path in Central Park overwhelms me with its intensity and the peachiness of a perfect peach almost brings me to my knees. Gratitude has long been my default, but once all five senses are in working order, I'm freshly awed by the miracle of the ordinary and the fact that each new dawn takes me further away from that surreal moment in Whole Foods when I heard the words "brain" and "tumor" in the same sentence.

What, you may be wondering, does this have to do with a memoir about shame and secrecy? A lot, it turns out. I wanted to understand why my instantaneous reaction to the brain tumor was to hide it, whereas a few years prior, my first reaction to the breast cancer was to tell the world about it. Since cancer was what killed my mother, you'd think the breast cancer diagnosis would have freaked me out. But rather than conceal that I had a malignant tumor in one breast I wrote a book about *it*. I wore a pink ribbon, gave speeches about it, and kept my buddies abreast (sorry!) of every detail of my tests, prognosis, surgery, and treatment. In contrast, when I found out about the *noncancerous* tumor in my brain, I told no one but my immediate family and a few close friends. Why was I so determined to keep it a secret? More to the point, why would a *benign* tumor register as scarier and more life-threatening than a *malignant* tumor?

As with many of life's riddles, the answer came to me in the form of a joke.

Question: "What are the top three factors that determine real estate values?"

Answer: "Location, location, location."

In short, my reactions to the two health crises depended on where each tumor was located and what that part of my body meant to me. A breast I could live without and still carry on with my normal life. An impaired brain would be the end of me as a thinking person. The tubular carcinoma in my breast posed a graver health threat than the pituitary adenoma in my head, but the importance I assigned to the brain made its tumor more perilous. Even after I had the surgery and regained all five of my senses, I felt it necessary to keep the pituitary adenoma a secret, convinced as I was that people would treat me differently if they knew something was awry in my head, by which I meant, my mind. Were I to say benign tumor, I was sure they would hear *cancer*, and it would warp their view of me from then on, change the ease of our interactions, skew the symmetry of our friendship, and make me feel even sorrier for myself than I already did. To correct my friends' misperceptions, I would have to explain the medical details of my condition to each person, one by one. They would say something well-meaning that I would experience as overly solicitous or tone deaf. Something like, "How *are* you?" "Did they get it all?" Or, "Are you okay?"

I'd say, "I'm fine. It wasn't malignant."

"But it had to be removed, right?"

"Yes, but it was no big deal."

"Come on! It was *brain* surgery!"

"Not the kind you think. They took it out through my nose."

"Your nose?!! Eww! Why?"

"Because the pituitary gland is located at the base of the brain behind the bridge of the nose and directly below the hypothalamus and surgeons now have a way of extracting an adenoma—which is a benign growth formed from glandular structures in epithelial tissue. They take it out through the nose so they don't have to chisel into the skull, and…"

I had imagined this conversation countless times and enduring one in reality was about as appealing to me as root canal. I also imagined that once people knew what I had, they would surreptitiously stare at my skull, sneak a peek up my nostrils, and monitor me for signs of cognitive deterioration. They'd see me as "the woman with the brain tumor." I'd become terminally self-conscious, forever doubting myself and dissecting my behavior: Did I slur that sentence? Is my vocabulary as fluent as it used to be? Am I expressing myself coherently? Names and movie titles elude people half my age and eluded me before I had the tumor. But were I to forget a name or title now, my friends would trade knowing looks and think, Uh-oh, she's losing *it.*

In *How to Be a Friend to a Friend Who's Sick*, the book I wrote when I got breast cancer, I posit illness as the proving ground for friendship. Part guidebook, part memoir, it recounts my feelings and those of the more than eighty people I interviewed (formerly sick folks who'd had all kinds of ailments and all kinds of friendships) about what people said to us or did for us when we were sick, which remarks we'd found comforting, helpful, or nurturing, and which were annoying, hurtful, or devastating. My goal in that book was to impart practical, patient-tested advice to anyone who cares for, or about, someone who's ill in body, mind, or spirit. But after the tumor was removed from my brain, my writer-self wanted nothing to do with it. Candor, truth-telling, sense-making—the reasons why I write—vanished from my wheelhouse. Nouns and verbs shut up shop, and each time I faced the blank screen intending to disclose the plum in my head and how it had threatened my life, my fingers froze on the keyboard. What stopped me wasn't writer's block, it was identity tremors. And the specter of the shanda.

Identity is another word for the story we tell ourselves about ourselves. Since adolescence, I'd been telling myself I don't give a fig about what other people think, I'm a nonconformist. Comfortable flouting convention, going against the grain, and speaking truth to power. Not someone who follows trends, reads a book because it's a bestseller, gives Good Will her white tennis sneakers when the fashionistas declare them uncool. And I didn't quit ordering vodka martinis when "everyone" started drinking cosmopolitans. Once the tumor exposed vulnerabilities I'd been unwilling to acknowledge, my self-constructed identity underwent a radical change. Now, the story I tell myself is this: I'm deathly afraid of losing my mind, becoming cognitively impaired, and having anyone see me as anything less than smart. I equate human worth with intellect. I ridicule people who care about how they're viewed by others, but

I'm one of those people, indentured to the same fear of imperfection, humiliation, and shame that afflicted my parents.

Two things happened to make an honest writer of me: Alan Alda, one of America's best-loved actors, went on network television and told the nation he had Parkinson's disease. And Blu Greenberg, the founding mother of Orthodox Jewish feminism (a thriving movement, not an oxymoron), said some magic words that got me off the dime. (Leaving the dime, according to the dictionary of idioms, means taking action, "especially following a time of indecision or delay.")

My husband, Bert, and I have been friends with Arlene and Alan Alda since 1972, when he was a writer, director, and performer and I was the editorial consultant on Marlo Thomas's acclaimed children's record, book, and TV special, *Free to Be…You and Me*. In the fifty years since, the Aldas and the Pogrebins, sometimes with our combined six kids, have celebrated birthdays, weddings, and anniversaries together, shared uncountable dinners, and slept over in one another's homes. So, that day in the summer of 2018, after watching Alan confess his condition on *CBS This Morning*, I had no compunction about calling him to praise his candor and ask him a few questions.

"Is the Parkinson's affecting your mind?" was the first. Alan answered that, and all my other queries, with his trademark wry humor. I recognized many of his fears in mine, but twenty minutes went by before I confessed to him that I'd had a brain tumor.

Here's my recollection of where the conversation went from there.

"Why the hell didn't you tell us? Arlene and I could have kept Bert company in the waiting room."

"Don't take this the wrong way, Alan, but my people tend to be touchy about threats to our brain power. For a Jew to have a brain tumor is different from a Catholic getting Parkinson's."

"Hey! Who do you think you are, calling me a Catholic?" rebounded the parochial school kid who'd left the faith decades ago. "And by the way, for an actor to get Parkinson's is different than for a regular person to get Parkinson's. We're supposed to *act* sick, not *get* sick."

I remembered when Alan had a health crisis in Chile while he was on location taping a science show. "You almost died then. But almost as soon as you came out of the anesthesia you were talking about that experience to anyone who said, 'How ya doin'?' Yet you kept your Parkinson's a secret for more than three years. What's the difference?" I almost told him my location theory, but he proffered one of his own.

"In Chile, I had a crimped intestine that stopped the blood supply to the rest of my body. I needed surgery to cut out the dead part of the intestine and connect the two live ends together. There's no cultural stigma about intestinal surgery like there is about Parkinson's, about all brain disorders for that matter. When people hear you have Parkinson's, their first reaction is, 'Oh my God, it's all over.' I was afraid I wouldn't get any acting work if people knew. I thought everyone would see me differently."

"Tell me about it," I said, sardonically. "Still, it's a big leap from hiding the disease to announcing it on national television. What made you go that far?"

"I was watching the rushes for a film I'd just made, and when I saw my hand tremors on the screen, I knew I needed to get the word out ahead of the gossip columnists. I decided to do it on TV because I could control how the information went down. I didn't say, 'Hey, here's this huge secret that I haven't told anyone.' I deliberately talked about it very calmly. I said things like, 'I'm doing all I can to fend off the disease, boxing for instance, and I feel good about that.' I explained all the little tasks I have to solve every day, like how to button my shirt in less than three minutes when it used to take me thirty seconds. I said these days I look at each physical challenge as a puzzle to be solved.

"Because of my tone and attitude, the interview had an overwhelmingly positive effect on people who saw it that day or heard about it on social media. The response on Twitter wasn't, 'Oh my God, that's so awful.' It was, 'Good for you, Alan! You're working on it. You're inspiring me to do the same.' I'm glad I told the truth because it takes a lot of work to hold a secret. The relief was enormous. I refuse to let the disease define me or stop me from working. It's just something I got. Like I got bald."

My talk with Alan convinced me that the only way to free myself from the heavy labor of hiding the tumor was to admit I had it and do so without shame. "It was just something I got. Like I got wrinkles," was the line I practiced saying for days. But before I could start writing about it, I felt the need to talk about it first to a small, friendly audience—my Rosh Hodesh group, ten or so women who've been meeting in different permutations every month or so for the last thirty years. "Rosh Hodesh" is Hebrew for the first day of the month on the Jewish calendar, and that's theoretically the night we're supposed to meet, but we're not rigid about the date. Our rules are flexible and simple. Each session is two-hours long and facilitated by a different member of the group, who leads the discussion on a topic of her own choosing and brings whatever reading materials she feels will jump-start our conversation. Our topics, broadly defined as "anything relevant to our lives as Jews and/or feminists," have ranged from racism, anti-Semitism, sexual politics, midlife transitions, the generation gap, gender mutability, family traditions, BDS (the Boycott, Divestment, and Sanctions movement), the 2017 Women's March, and any number of passages from the Torah, Talmud, and Siddur (daily and Sabbath prayer book). When it's my turn to facilitate, I announce in advance that my topic will be "the power of the shanda" and I ask everyone to come prepared to confide something about herself that the rest of us don't know.

The night of my session, I open with a quick review of how secrecy and shame figure into the lives of so many of our biblical forebears. (See Chapter 3.) Then, summoning every soul-fortifying metaphor in my quiver of clichés, I grit my teeth, gird my loins, woman up, brace myself, steel my spine, and speak my secret. Shock ricochets around the room like a pinball. "A *brain* tumor?! *Chas* v'chal*ilah* (God forbid)." "Oh, shit!" and "Oy-oy-oy!" give way to, "How do you feel?" "Is it gone?" "Are you okay?" I assure everyone that I'm fine. Except I can't seem to write about this experience and if I can't make myself reveal my *own* secret in a memoir about shame and secrecy, I'll be a hypocrite and the book will be a sham.

"What do *you* think is stopping you?" A.B. asks. (Since we long ago promised to protect each other's privacy, I'm making alphabet soup of the women's real names.)

"Fear," I reply. "I'm afraid readers will react the way you guys just did. I'm afraid knowing my secret will affect how all my friends see me. I'm afraid editors won't give me assignments and publishers will lose interest in my work. And my worst fear is…" (I'm glad we're all Jews because I'm about to say something that could sound like a Jewish stereotype.) Pause. Beat. Deep breath. "…My worst fear is losing my mind." Everyone laughed until they saw I was dead serious. "All sorts of human qualities were appreciated in my family, but we knew the trait that took the gold would always be a 'Yiddishe kop.' ('Jewish head,' which translates to mental agility, common sense, and good scholarship). Descartes said, '*Cognito, ergo sum*' (I think therefore I am)." I tell my friends that "*unless* I can think, I can't *be*. My existence would cease. With my cognitive ability compromised, how could I reason, remember, analyze, come up with ideas out of the blue? For me, brain equals being, which is why, when alien cells invaded mine, I imagined The Worst. And panicked."

C.D. nods and leans forward. "If it happened to me, I'd feel the same," she says, giving me an affectionate pat on the knee.

"Jews have always been hugely outnumbered and vulnerable," E.F. adds. "If my ancestors didn't have their smarts, they would never have survived and I wouldn't be here today. I'm not ashamed to say it: intelligence ranks near the top of my hierarchy of needs, immediately after food, clothing, and shelter."

"Mine too," says G.H. "You're saying if your brain was destroyed, *you'd* be destroyed because you wouldn't be *you* anymore. I get that. But I don't get why you can't write about it. What's the worst thing that could happen? People know you from your writing, but they don't know you personally, and you don't know them. Why do you care what they think?"

"It's the people I *do* know I care about. When they see 'tumor,' they'll think cancer, and when they read 'brain,' they'll think slippery slope, cognitive dysfunction, dementia, and they'll start looking at me in weird ways. I know that look. I've seen it on the faces of a couple of friends I *did* confide in."

I.J. suggests that I stop obsessing over how I look to others and reframe this as an opportunity to help my readers break free of *their* secrets.

Mention of *their* secrets reminds me that I had asked members of the group to bring a secret of their own. Reclaiming the facilitating role, I ask, "Who's willing to start?"

K.L. takes the floor. When she was six, her parents woke her out of a sound sleep to tell her that the man she'd been calling Daddy wasn't her real father; her real father was killed in World War II when she was a year old. The man she calls Daddy was that man's best friend in the Army and he'd always liked Mommy very much, so he married her. K.J. says she wasn't upset by that revelation since the man she'd been calling Daddy was the only father she'd ever known. What upset her was that her parents warned her never to tell the secret to her four siblings or anyone else in the family, but they didn't explain why it had to be kept hidden, which suggested there was something shameful about her being the child of another man. For years, she was terrified that her siblings might find out and she would become the family outlier.

M.N., the eldest of our members, admits feeling, all her life, that her mother didn't love her. When a relative told her that she'd had a brother, an infant who died before she was born, M.N. was able to sympathize with her mom's persistent depressions rather than resent them or blame herself for causing them.

O.P., a dynamic woman in her forties who was adopted as a baby, confesses that she's always felt secure in her parents' love but can't shake the feeling that she's their lesser child because her sister, their biological daughter, looks like their mother and she doesn't.

Q.R. appears to have the perfect blended family. She has a wonderful second husband and a pack of great kids (his, hers, and theirs), but tonight she reveals that they've been struggling with intrafamily tensions for some time. Much as she would like to unload her anxieties and confide in us, she doesn't feel right about sharing the information because it might get beyond our group and cause a shanda.

Refreshed by everyone's insights and honesty, I came home raring to make a first pass at the chapter that had been so problematic. But before opening my manuscript, like everyone else with access to the internet, I opened my email. Amazingly, I already had a message from one member of our group, Blu Greenberg, who subsequently gave me permission to fish her name out of the alphabet soup and identify her here.

> *Dear Letty,*
>
> *I want to thank you for facilitating such a stimulating discussion tonight at Rosh Hodesh. I just feel bad that we were not able to give you support during and after your diagnosis and treatments for brain cancer.*
>
> *Love,*
> *Blu*

I couldn't press Reply All fast enough.

> *Dear Shvesters,*
>
> *I see that I need to repeat this, in writing: I do NOT have cancer. Though obviously inadvertent, Blu's error has revived my fears of misperception. I'm now reconsidering whether to disclose my secret in the memoir. Meanwhile, I'm counting on each of you to keep my BENIGN brain tumor confidential. Please confirm receipt of this message.*
>
> *Letty*

Seconds later, Blu emailed her apology, along with this request.

I strongly urge you to "out" yourself in the book since, among other things, you'll be teaching others the important distinction between a benign and malignant tumor. How else can we learn it unless you correct us?

Love from your friend who made the mistake fifteen minutes after you drove home the message.

I called her on the phone. She told me it's understandable that I might feel paralyzed by the pressure to tell the truth about something I'm still trying to understand. But withholding my secret would be antithetical to the main message of the book, and my lack of transparency would invalidate the memoir at its core. Unless I confront whatever it is that's making me hide the tumor, I'll be writing under false pretenses. "What's more," Blu said, "revealing your true feelings in print would be a mitzvah [a great good deed]. It would normalize everyone else's *mishigas* [craziness]. We're all hiding *something*, you know."

Subsequent to my friend's gentle pushback, several chance literary encounters helped me "unpack" the tenacity of my resistance. One was this passage from *Surprised by Joy: The Shape of My Early Life*, by C. S. Lewis, whose mother died when he was a boy.

With my mother's death, all settled happiness, all that was tranquil and reliable, disappeared from my life. There would be much fun, many pleasures, many stabs of joy; but no more of the old security. It was sea and islands now; the great continent had sunk like Atlantis.

I've never read a more precise description of the impact of maternal loss. My mother's death when I was fifteen left me out to sea, unmoored, unparented. My father loved me in his detached fashion; my sister, fiercely and deeply, though our relationship was second to her obligations to her young children and hobbled by fifty miles of geographical separation not to mention our fourteen-year age gap. My aunts had kids of their own and, though unfailingly kind, seemed less "there" for me after Mom was gone. I was no one's priority. Every kid deserves to be first in someone else's life. I had lost that someone. Lost control of my childhood, the intimacy of daily family life, and all the material things that anchored me in the world. From fifteen on, I had to chart my own course, write my own narrative, create the life I wanted, the career satisfaction that had evaded my mother, a marriage unlike that of my parents. Bereft of security and guidance, I reared myself. And once I felt secure, once I came ashore and felt solid ground under my feet, I refused to let it shift or quake ever again.

In the weeks after the Rosh Hodesh meeting, I spent a lot of time vacillating, wrestling with myself, and reading more randomly than I ever had, as if guided by a Ouija board to the writers whose words I needed. In Gabrielle Union's 2021 interview in the *New York Times Book Review* these words resonated in a big way: "I always looked at vulnerability as my kryptonite, something to be ashamed of, not something to lean into." Ditto! Vulnerability has always been the tenderest spot on the skin of my psyche, and the tumor had rubbed it raw, disrupting the roadmap I'd set out for myself in my teens. Terrified by the prospect of yet another loss, I cowered behind the façade of the strong woman I had been pretending to be. I became the child of my mother, who had concealed from me the cancer that eventually killed her. I hid my tumor to protect that little girl.

A line from Jenny Offill nailed it for me: "[W]hen you're going through any kind of extreme or difficult experience, there's that shame that you're falling apart." *Exactly!* I thought. But then I read her novel, *Weather*, in which her protagonist, Lizzie, "goes to a dermatologist who examines every inch of her body and says that each mark is: 'Exceedingly unlikely to be cancerous! Exceedingly unlikely to be cancerous!' Lizzie thinks: 'I wanted every day to be like this, to begin in shame and fear and end in glorious reassurance.'"

I did *not* want to begin each day in shame and fear. Been there. Done that. I would not be Lizzie.

Finally, out of nowhere, another adage germane to my dilemma, this one from George Orwell, popped up one day on my Facebook feed: "Who controls the past controls the future. Who controls the present controls the past." By endangering my cognition, the tumor threatened my triumph over a past disconcerted by bereavement and family dissolution, aroused my terror of a present defined by disintegration, and predicted a future of depletion and loss. No wonder I was a wreck. The question was, what to do about it—succumb to passivity or find a way to reveal my secret without ceding it the power to derail my well-ordered life?

Somehow, in concert, those incidental literary encounters and the wisdom imparted to me by my friends—one a lapsed Catholic, the other an Orthodox Jew—and the wise words of C. S. Lewis, an Anglican, moved me to a conclusion, obscure before, trite sounding now, but persuasive nonetheless. The doctors had repaired me, radiated me, and reassured me that I was not going to end up brain dead. My job was to internalize their prognosis, quit mucking things up with What-ifs, and take control of the one thing I *could* control. Simplistic as it sounds, that tautology felt epiphanic. If my fears were self-generated—if *I* was the one who could not square the advent of a brain tumor with the possibility of longevity, intellect, and health—then I was the one who could convert the tumor into something incidental: a thing I just got, like I got wrinkles. But first, I had to divest my secret of its power to shame me. I had to shrink my tumor down to size. The size of this chapter.

CHAPTER 2

BRIGHT THINGS KEPT IN THE DARK TEND TO TARNISH

Whenever I see *Fiddler on the Roof* (it's probably been twenty times), I feel like Anatevka is my Pylypets. A tiny village in the Carpathian Mountains, which sometimes appears as a dot on the map of Austro-Hungary, sometimes Czechoslovakia, now Ukraine, Pylypets was the shtetl my maternal grandparents abandoned at the dawn of the twentieth century, carrying nothing but their traditions and leaving behind everyone who knew their secret.

In the entry hall of my apartment on the Upper West Side hang twenty-six antique family photographs. One of them, a somber studio portrait taken in 1919, shows my maternal grandparents, Jenny and Nathan Halpern, and their seven children, all of whom look surprisingly elegant for a brood of immigrants barely a decade and a half off the boat. My mother, Ceil, the eldest, then in her late teens, wears her Mona Lisa smile and a fashionable dress of the period, most likely one she'd made herself. The youngest child, five-year-old Milton, sits front and center in a starched white sailor suit, arms crossed, suggesting that his appearance was cajoled under protest. A landscape mural shares the background with a side window whose gauzy light illuminates everyone's faces and renders the contrast between Nathan and the four blue-eyed members of the family, and Jenny and the three brown-eyed kids, as arresting as if the sepia-toned photograph was a Kodacolor print.

The original Halpern family, circa 1919. Jenny and Nathan seated with Herbert standing between them, and Milton, the youngest, arms folded, front and center. The other five children are (standing from left to right) Ceil, Lou, Tillie, Sadye, and Rona, in a white dress.

Growing up, I saw quite a lot of my grandparents, yet I can't say I *knew* either of them, they were just two little old Jews with weird eating habits and not much to say. Jenny was a short, plump *balabusta* (homemaker), her unibosom terminating in an undifferentiated waistline, her hips permanently encased in an apron. I see her in the kitchen, stirring *cholent* (Jewish stew), shelling peas, plucking chicken feathers, scrubbing Grandpa's shirt collars against a corrugated steel washboard, soaking her swollen ankles in a pan of soapy water after a day on her feet. I remember her as a kindler of Shabbos candles, a maker of blintzes and strudel, a whisperer of Yiddish—the lingua franca spoken by Jewish immigrants when they didn't want their American children to understand what they were saying—a melancholic figure with a sad, soft smile, her salt-and-pepper hair twisted into a knot and secured with wire hair pins that stuck out of the back of her head like needles in a pincushion; a quiet presence easily effaced by more commanding women. Jenny appeared ancient in my eyes when she was fifty. The charmer was her husband, Nathan.

When I conjure my grandfather, he's reading *The Forvertz* and smoking one of his many well-seasoned briar pipes. Or he's building a dollhouse for me and my cousin Prissy, which we play with to help activate our invented family narratives. Or I see him creating a diorama inside an empty glass gallon jug—a domestic *tableau vivant* of a Sabbath dinner scene in an observant Jewish home. I used to love watching him insert tiny objects through the neck of the jug with tweezers as long as chopsticks, every handmade item, from the rug to the chandelier, a miniature replica of the real thing—the Lilliputian dining table blanketed in lace, napkins the size of postage stamps, a silver vase filled with teensy-weensy flowers, a mini-decanter of wine, itty-bitty kiddush cups and Shabbos candlesticks, a diminutive braided challah, and seated across from each other in tiny wooden chairs, two wee figures, husband and wife, dressed in clothes befitting a festive Jewish meal. When the scene was complete, Nathan would stuff a cork in the neck of the jug and top it with a crown of crystal beads.

I'm able to describe his "Shabbos jugs" in such granular detail because I own two of them and right now I'm looking at a photograph of another. The picture appears in a 1956 article from the *New York Times* about an exhibit at the American Museum of Natural History showcasing crafts made by senior citizens. What's intriguing about the picture is its caption, which, for me at least, raises larger questions about the *Times* and its journalistic integrity, religious and class bias, Jewish shame and institutional secrecy. The caption under the picture of Nathan with one of his Shabbos jugs describes the piece as "a complete old-fashioned table setting with figures of a man and woman about to start eating." Not a word about the ceremonial objects on the table or the fact that what they were "about to start eating" is a traditional Sabbath meal. Am I supposed to attribute these omissions to innocent editorial error or ignorance of the caption writer? Or was the substitution of the generic adjective "old-fashioned," for words like challah, kiddush cup, and Shabbos consistent with *Times'* policy in those years of hiding, ignoring, downplaying, or censoring anything its Jewish publishers deemed "*too* Jewish?"

In *The Trust*, a book about the family behind the *Times*, Susan Tifft and Alex Jones write that Adolph Ochs, the son of German-Jewish immigrants who became publisher of the paper in 1896, understood that his Jewishness presented a problem to members of New York society and was determined "not to have *The Times* ever appear to be a 'Jewish newspaper.'" The subsequent publisher, Arthur Hays Sulzberger, whose tenure coincided with two monumental events of the twentieth century, the Holocaust and the founding of the State of Israel, bent over backwards to avoid privileging Jews or looking like an advocate for Jewish causes, a policy that spawned reprehensive acts of journalistic malpractice. One notorious example was its 1944 story about a confirmed report that the Nazis had exterminated 400,000 Hungarian Jews and planned to kill 350,000 more within the week. The paper devoted a paltry four column inches to the piece and ran it on page twelve.

Let me be clear about this: I am not equating the paper's downplay of the horrors of the Holocaust with its incorrect description of my grandfather's tableau. I'm merely putting in historical context this uncharacteristic disregard for accuracy by the paper of record. The Jewish ceremonial objects were central to Nathan's work. The cup, challah, and candlesticks were visible in the photograph of the jug. The man in the tableau is wearing a yarmulke. Most educated readers, especially its New York readers, Jewish or not, were familiar with those ceremonial objects. So why weren't they named? Did the caption writer settle on the innocuous "old-fashioned" because he (*Times* staffers were all men in those years) or his editor didn't know what they were? Or because, in 1956, a dozen years after shamefully underplaying or underreporting the slaughter of three-quarters of a million Hungarian Jews, the owners of the *New York Times* were still embarrassed to be Jewish and afraid of being tarred as a "Jewish newspaper?"

It's too late to fact-check what happened behind the scenes, but if you worked there in 1956 and witnessed this little episode, please email me to either confirm or rebut my speculations about the paper's motivations. In fairness, I'll allow that the omission of the "too Jewish" identifiers could conceivably be Nathan's fault. My family's immigrant generation tended to be proudly Jewish among Jews but prone to ethnic shyness and self-effacement among gentiles. What I'm saying is, my grandfather may have been so thrilled by the opportunity to display his work in the magnificent museum on Central Park West, that *he himself* downplayed the Jewish content of his tableau to make it less Jewish and more universal.

Nathan has been gone for more than sixty years, but I still have a sense memory of his pipe tobacco, its maple-syrup/woodsmoke/leathery fragrance baked into the wallpaper in the ramshackle farmhouse in Shrub Oak, New York, where he and Jenny spent their summers in the 1940s and early '50s. It was basically a box with a basement and a couple of porches. Every room was smaller than you'd expect yet accommodated a remarkable number of people. I don't remember a single modern appliance in that house, but I know there was an icebox in the kitchen serviced by an iceman who always arrived with a fresh block of ice before the old one finished melting. And I remember a butter churn because Grandma always made her own butter, though I don't know how she found the time. Not only was she always cooking for a crowd, but she had to take naps because of her frail health. A picnic table and four long benches filled the entire back porch. On nice nights that's where everyone usually had supper, all crammed in and happy to be together. Grandma and Grandpa's bedroom was downstairs, also the kitchen, dining room, and parlor. There were four spare-looking bedrooms upstairs, one in each corner, and each had a coil of insect-speckled flypaper dangling from the ceiling and two windows at the level of the trees so you could see the foliage from your bed and fall asleep to the click of the cicadas.

The property also consisted of a barn, a garage with an attached tool shed, a goat, a chicken coop, a trellis threaded with flowering vines, a shady spot with a white glider, a dollhouse that Grandpa made for me and my cousin Prissy, and an outhouse. The adults had first dibs on the one indoor bathroom, and there were enough grownups to keep it occupied most of the day. We kids were relegated to the outhouse, which smelled like a porta-potty, and in lieu of toilet paper we were supposed to wipe ourselves with sheets from the Bronx telephone book that had been strung up on cord nailed to the wall beside the open latrine. Sometimes I remembered to bring a couple of tissues with me, sometimes I didn't.

When I think of Grandpa Nathan, I think of Shrub Oak, and vice versa. I see him hunched over a trowel, planting, watering, weeding, or harvesting vegetables from his garden, which was surrounded by a border of empty green glass prune juice bottles that he had sunk into the soil, bottoms up with several inches of glass visible above ground so when the sun hit the bottles they looked like emeralds. I thought they were great. Mom thought they were an embarrassment. My uncle Herbie, an amateur ventriloquist, who came to Shrub Oak in his army uniform straight from World War II, said we may as well post a sign on the house: Constipated Jews Live Here.

To provide Grandpa with enough Sunkist prune juice bottles for his border, our family must have consumed an ocean of prune juice. I hated the stuff. And almost everything else that my parents and relatives considered delicious—*kasha varnishkes* (buckwheat groats, bowtie noodles, and onions) *kishka* (stuffed derma), *schav* (sorrel soup), *borscht* (beet soup), chicken feet fricassee, *p'tcha* (meat jelly), tongue (from a *cow*, ugh). To say I was a picky eater is a colossal understatement. Mom would offer me six alternatives to a meal she'd made, none of which I would eat, until, at her wit's end, she would send me to bed with no supper at all. If this happened in the summertime, when we were staying in Shrub Oak, I could always count on Grandpa to sneak upstairs with a couple of *mandelbrot* (Jewish biscotti) when my mother wasn't looking.

Here's the thing that gets me: all those years when they were looking mild and innocuous, eating strange food and padding around the house in their slippers, my grandparents were guarding a humongous secret. Tillie was the one who let it slip. The closest of my mother's three sisters, and the aunt I'd spent the most time with growing up, Tillie Kahn had a tummy-jiggling cackle contagious enough to make people laugh even if they hadn't heard the joke that elicited it. She wore rimless glasses, kept her hair in a blondish upsweep, and at four-feet-nine never left her house without stepping into cork-soled mules that raised her height to five-feet. For ten years in the 1940s, my parents and I lived next door to Tillie, Ralph, and their three kids, Judy, Danny, and eventually little Joel, in a small, semi-attached brick house in Jamaica, Queens. But it wasn't until many years later, when she was peeling potatoes at her cracked tile countertop and I was sitting at her kitchen table smoking a cigarette, that the words "Grandma's first marriage" dropped from her lips like babka crumbs and the look on her face said, "Uh oh!" and I realized that she knew something about my grandparents that no one was supposed to tell me. And it was radioactive.

Born in 1879 in Pylypets, the shtetl with the ever-changing national borders, Jenny was a teenager (think Tzeitel in *Fiddler*) when she was forced into an arranged marriage with a much older man (think Lazar Wolf, the village butcher in the same play). After the wedding but before their union was consummated, she fashioned a rope of twisted bed sheets, jumped out the window of the bridal chamber, and raced to her true love, Nathan (think Motel, the tailor), the man who would become my grandfather.

"You've got to be kidding! *Grandma was a runaway bride*!?"

"Shaa! It's a shanda!" From the urgency of Tillie's tone, you'd think the chief yenta of Pylypets was eavesdropping at the kitchen door. Any Jew who was raised to dread public humiliation more than anything (except cancer) would have understood why. I was shocked and confused. I asked my aunt which part of the story was shanda-worthy? Jenny being a rebellious bride, brazen enough to defy her parents, reject her Lazar Wolf, and shinny down a rope of bedsheets on her wedding night? Or running off with another man?

Tillie said her mother had not only pulled off something unheard of for a woman of the 1890s, she'd committed the heinous sin of publicly shaming a man. He wasn't a bad fellow, just too old for her, but she'd clearly humiliated him and since a Jew was never supposed to do anything that made The Jews look bad, and

Pylypets was home to a hundred Jews but also to a thousand gentiles, all of whom knew that a Jewish girl had deserted her groom an hour after they left the altar, the stench of scandal clung to Jenny for some time.

"Which was terrible enough, Tillie said. "But the shanda was...I mean the *real* shanda was..." She looked skyward, as if her mother might cause a bolt of lightning to strike her through the kitchen ceiling if she uttered one more word, then busied herself at the sink, filling a large bowl with water, adding the peeled potatoes, washing her hands.

"Quit stalling," I nudged my aunt. "We're talking about something that happened in *1898*! Go on! The shanda was what, for heaven's sake?"

"The man never gave her a *get*."

"Oy!" Now, *that* was a problem I could understand. Halacha (Jewish law) does not recognize the termination of a marriage unless the husband literally places a get (an official Jewish divorce decree) into his wife's hand, or the hand of an appointed agent). Needless to say, Jenny did not pause on her way out the window to ask the man to hand her a document. She ran to her beloved Nathan, he found a rabbi in his hometown of Skole (then in Poland, now Ukraine), and they got married. Romantic, for sure, only their story didn't end as happily as its boffo beginning would suggest. After Jenny gave birth to four children in Europe, Nathan sailed to New York to open a store that sold loose teas and coffee beans, intending to earn enough money to send for his family. I never knew this until Tillie dropped her bomb, but soon after he settled in on the Lower East Side, he took up with another woman and stopped responding to Jenny's plaintive letters. After two years without word from him, Jenny turned for help to her brother, Will, who put all manner of pressure on Nathan (even tried to bribe him) but couldn't get him to bring Jenny and the kids to America. In the end, it was Will, a successful New York clothing manufacturer, who financed their journey, in steerage, and when Jenny stepped off the boat in Manhattan, Nathan told her he wanted a divorce.

In the early '50s, my grandparents came to live with my parents and me in the pine-paneled basement of our house in Jamaica. They were in their seventies by then; I was a callow adolescent who winced at the sight of Nathan's false teeth floating every night in a glass of water or Jenny gumming a slice of Wonder Bread soaked in warm milk. It was hard to believe that this little Jewish woman had once been a nineteenth-century Wonder Woman and this muted old man was the reason she broke all the rules.

After learning their story, I asked two Judaic scholars if the absence of a get from the first man might cast doubt on the legitimacy of my grandparents' marriage. Both were quick to dismiss that idea, and each, independently of the other, gave me a crash course on the halacha of Jewish marriage, which decrees that one or more of the following acts must take place in order for a marriage to be legally binding: a ring must be placed by the groom on the bride's forefinger in the presence of two kosher witnesses (two people unrelated to either bride or groom). A *ketubah* (Hebrew marriage contract) must be signed, also in the presence of two kosher witnesses. And, after the wedding, the couple must seal the deal with sexual intercourse.

"Did your aunt witness her mother's first wedding?" one of the scholars asked me.

"Of course not. Tillie wasn't born yet."

"Therefore, she couldn't know if the wedding ring was placed on your grandmother's finger, right?"

"Right."

And she couldn't testify that the witnesses to the signing of the ketubah, assuming there was a ketubah, were kosher, could she?"

"She couldn't."

"The only thing your aunt knew for sure—because her mother told her so, face-to-face—was that your grandmother's first marriage was never consummated. Correct?"

"Correct."

"Therefore, your grandmother did not need a get, and her marriage to your grandfather was legal. No worries, no shanda, case closed."

Much later, it occurred to me to ask my aunt why Jenny never told her other five kids about the first marriage. "How come she only confided in you and my mom?"

"Maybe because we were the eldest," was Tillie's guess. "Or we were girls and girls know how to keep secrets."

I still didn't understand why Jenny expunged this incredible, endearing chapter from our family chronicle. Granted, she had broken the rules established by hundreds of years of custom: Jewish girls were supposed to marry the men their parents picked out for them, and when she ran away, the gossip brigade undoubtedly had a field day. But escaping from a non-marriage is not a violation of Jewish law.

"Maybe she was afraid that someone who had a gripe against her or my father, or any of us, could use her previous…umm… non-marriage against them," Tillie conjectured. "And by the time she got some rabbis to clear her name, every Jewish parent on the Lower East Side would have banned their kids from marrying a Halpern. We should only be glad that her secret got buried with her."

Viewing this story through a feminist lens, I wonder if our family dynamic would have been different had we been aware of that buried incident in our grandparents' past. Bright things, kept in the dark, tend to tarnish. Exposed to the light, Jenny's revolt against convention might have been burnished into a cherished family heirloom and everyone would have been as proud of her leaving a bad match as we were of Nathan leaving the Old Country to make his way in America. At the very least, we would have understood that the only reason any of us exist at all is because more than a century ago, in a shtetl in the Carpathian Mountains, a young Jewish woman jumped out the window and took control of her life.

CHAPTER 3

HIDING IS MY HERITAGE

Secrecy has always felt Jewish to me. Initially, I traced that impression to the dinner tables of my childhood and lessons learned from the stories and silences of a raft of relatives who frequented each other's homes for Shabbos or Sunday supper. Memory gilds the past, I know, but here's how I remember those gatherings. No matter how small the table or large the crowd, whoever was hosting always seemed to fit everyone at the table; extensions were added, benches pulled in from the porch, and bridge chairs brought up from the basement, and the more we scrunched together, elbow to elbow, kids, grown-ups, babes in arms, the more energy coursed through the room. Memory tells me we sat down at the table to eat before anyone asked for a drink, though that may be the twenty-twenty hindsight of a child who had yet to discover the emollients of a cocktail. Booze was an afterthought, at least in our house. Food and talk were the main events; disputes, like bread, were chewed on and savored. Conversation was salted with laughter and peppered with commentary. Arguments were not merely tolerated but relished, especially when they concerned politics, sports, or religion. For one Jew to interrupt another in the middle of a sentence—what my father called "getting a word in edgewise"—was considered normal interpersonal behavior. Unless the Jew was in the midst of telling a joke. Punch lines were as uninterruptible as prayers.

Only in Jewish homes of my acquaintance did a person have to explain why he or she was not talking. "What's wrong? You feel sick?" someone would ask if too much time had elapsed without someone at the table expressing an opinion. As they lingered over Mom's roast beef and crispy potatoes and squinted through the wafting smoke of Dad's mid-meal Lucky Strike, my loquacious family members bickered about everything: Best bridge to Queens— Whitestone or Triborough? Best blintzes—cherry or cheese? Best department store—Alexanders or S. Klein? Baseball team: Dodgers or Yankees? Matzah balls—firm or fluffy? Candidate for president in the 1948 election—Truman or Wallace? (Dewey out of the question.) Then there was the weighty dispute about how to pronounce kugel. Was it COO-gul or KEE-gul (spelled *kigel*)? The Litvaks (Dad's people) said it the first way and preferred their kugel savory. Mom's side, the Galitzianers, called it kigel and preferred it sweet. I don't remember who won, but I remember laughing like crazy because what they were arguing about was noodle pudding.

Humor and self-mockery were my relatives' defense mechanisms against weakness and fear. Unseen by the naked eye was the filter through which they strained their banter, the sieve of self-censorship that took careful account of topics known to be off limits and skeletons meant to stay entombed. Should a shanda surface, it would be quashed on the spot with the same sound Tillie made when I asked too many questions about Grandma's non-marriage. "Shaa!" appears in no dictionary, but we all knew what it meant: "Shut up! Don't disgrace us."

If not the shaa!s hissed at our family dinner tables, I thought the calamities of Jewish history might explain why secrecy feels so Jewish to me. Millennia of hatred and persecution have honed the uncanny ability of our people to masquerade or vanish if necessary. During the Inquisition, as Spanish and Portuguese rulers were forcing Jews to convert to Catholicism or face exile or death, some of us disappeared by blending into the gentile population (the analogue for people of color is "passing"); others submitted to a public conversion while continuing to practice their faith surreptitiously.

Variously referred to as "hidden Jews," "secret Jews," "Conversos," "Crypto-Jews," or "Marranos" (the latter a derisive term meaning swine), they were hunted down by church authorities or turned in by faithful Christians who'd been ordered to report suspicious heretical behavior.

In her eye-opening, mouth-watering article in *Lilith* magazine, Susan Barocas, an expert on Sephardic cuisine who was a guest chef for three seders in the Obama White House, wrote "that no Jews were ever more marked by the food they grew, cooked, served, and ate, than the Jews of Spain. This was food closely related to a history that twisted and turned from persecution to prosperity and back again many times, according to who ruled Spain…Christians or Muslims." When anti-Jewish riots and mass killings broke out during the fourteenth and fifteenth centuries, how a family cooked and ate—for instance, avoiding pork (a mainstay of Christian cooking) and fish without scales; keeping meat and dairy separate and preparing special dishes for Shabbat and holidays—could expose them as reliably as the circumcised penis on a baby boy. In a 1570 case, Barocas writes, a maid testified that she had "witnessed her mistress cooking 'mutton with oil and onions,' which she understands is the Jewish dish adafina." (Similar to the Ashkenazi dish, cholent.) Other telltale signs of illicit Judaic observance during that medieval period included changing to fresh table linens on Friday nights, buying certain vegetables before Passover, blessing one's children without making the sign of the cross, refraining from work on Saturdays, and fasting on Yom Kippur.

The Enlightenment enabled European Jews to live and work among their country's majority population, though not always in comfort or safety. Their social status and religious liberty continued to depend on the whims of the powerful and the kindness of their neighbors. In good times, they could display their Hanukkah menorahs in their windows as tradition decrees; in bad times, they lit their candles behind closed doors. In good times, they could affix a mezuzah to their doorpost without fear of inviting vandalism and harassment. In good times, Jews were able to celebrate

Passover freely and joyfully; in bad times, they had to conduct their seders with their front doors open to public view or risk accusations of "blood libel."

(Culinary note: Christians who promulgate this ancient blood libel—the charge that Jews murder gentile children to use their blood to make matzahs—are betraying their ignorance of our religious practices. Jewish dietary laws prohibit us from consuming so much as a drop of blood. Kashrut demands that observant members of the tribe must drain, wash, and salt a piece of steak or chicken then soak it for a minimum of half an hour before it can be cooked. If we go to such ends to avoid eating blood in our meat, why would we *add* it to our matzahs?)

Many descendants of hidden Jews were raised with an awareness of that history. Alexandria Ocasio-Cortez, the youngest woman ever elected to Congress, revealed at a 2018 Hanukkah candle-lighting ceremony in her district that she had Converso ancestors who were expelled from Spain in 1492 and escaped to Puerto Rico, where they've lived as Catholics ever since. I've learned from other Hispanic Catholics that family members of theirs still practice ceremonies at home that are recognizable holdovers from Jewish tradition. An elderly Mexican acquaintance told me about the mystifying rituals he'd witnessed in his Catholic family when he was a child. His grandmother lit two candles every Friday night with a cloth draped over her hair. His great aunt always bought a box of matzahs on Easter. An uncle of his would eat anything in a restaurant but not allow pork or shellfish in his home. None of his relatives would discuss the source or significance of those customs; however, in deference to their Converso antecedents, they continued to perform them.

A Lutheran woman I met at an interfaith conference said she'd always had a special affinity for Jews and, though she couldn't put the feeling into words, she often "felt Jewish" herself. After an analysis of her DNA yielded seventy Ashkenazi matches on chromosome 7, she was able to trace her lineage to Nuremberg, Germany, where, in 1499, John of Capistrano incited bloody anti-Semitic pogroms and forced the entire Jewish population to convert. Those Jews who refused were burned at the stake. She told me she felt awful for her ancestors but vindicated in terms of her inchoate feelings of inner Jewy-ness. When I met her, she had just begun a serious course of Jewish study with the goal of undergoing a formal (re)conversion.

These days, a gift certificate for "23 and Me" makes a dandy birthday present and disclosing the fact that one has Jewish ancestry sparks many a lively conversation. I thought recent eruptions of violent anti-Semitism all over the world might have made newbie Jews think twice before advertising their discovery. Instead, most of them revel in it. They tell politically incorrect, Jew-flattering jokes— "Now I know why I got so many As in school," or, "Tomorrow, I'm going to invest in the stock market!"—which, based as they are on positive attributes (Jews are smart and skilled in money matters), get laughs. We're inclined to accept with grace wisecracks linked to stereotypes that make our group look good; those based on negative stereotypes we call anti-Semitic. Had a gentile, upon discovering a bit of Jewy DNA, come out with, "Now I'll have to get a nose job," I wouldn't have cracked a smile.

Journalists have sunk their incisors into several celebrities who turned out to be less than 100 percent WASP, the implication being that they'd been purposely hiding the Jewish part of their background because they were ashamed of it. Exuding the sour smell of "gotcha," journalists grill the newbies into the ground, as if, now that they've been "found out," the world needs to know the truth. "Who told you?" they ask. "How did you feel about it?" In Madeleine Albright's case, it was, "You *must* have known. Why didn't you know? What were you trying to *hide*? "Shortly after she was named secretary of state, the *Washington Post* reported that Albright was born in 1937 to Czech Jews who converted to Catholicism in 1941 and three of her Jewish grandparents and at least a dozen of her Jewish relatives perished in the Holocaust. Raised Catholic, Albright became an Episcopalian when she married and never knew that her parents had concealed the religion of their birth and hers. In an interview at the 92nd Street Y, she told Christiane Amanpour that she was "completely stunned" by the news. When reporters suggested Albright was lying, she insisted, again and again, that she'd had no idea. Since I know from experience how adept Jewish parents are at keeping secrets from their daughters, I never doubted that she was telling the truth.

In 2003, another secretary of state, John Kerry, was informed, also by a journalist, that he had Jewish grandparents on his father's side. It seems Fritz and Ida Kohn converted to Catholicism in 1901 and changed their names to Frederick and Ida Kerry. The reporter also unearthed the fact that Ida's brother and sister were killed in Nazi concentration camps. Kerry's Jewish connection became big news during his 2004 presidential campaign. As happened with Albright, some of the coverage of the Kerry revelation implied that he'd hid his Jewish connection, thinking it an impediment to his government career, and got caught trying to put something over on us. But flip the facts and ask yourself if our current secretary of state, Antony Blinken, a Jew, were to suddenly discover that his grandparents were Congregationalists, can you imagine a comparable brouhaha? I can't. Which, I submit, proves that hiddenness, especially hiding one's true identity, is associated with Jews in particular and explains why I think of shame and secrecy as quintessentially Jewish issues.

One Saturday morning, I was in synagogue listening to the reading of the Torah portion, when it hit me that I needn't look to my secretive family, or the Conversos, or Madeleine Albright, to figure how I came to feel that way. The Ur-origin stories of The Jewish People taught me to feel that way. Even before I was old enough to think analytically about anything, the Jacob story presently being chanted up there on the bimah was just one of many bible tales that taught me secrecy is intrinsically Jewish. Then too, children's bible stories were read to me at bedtime. Children's services at the Jamaica Jewish Center included abbreviated Torah readings and child-friendly sermons about whatever story had just been chanted in Hebrew. I attended three-times-a-week Hebrew

School from age three to fifteen, so I've probably read or discussed the story of Jacob thousands of times in my life; I did not need to hear today's Torah reading to know that the poor guy was bamboozled, promised the hand of Laban's beautiful daughter, Rachel, but tricked into marrying his plain daughter, Leah, whose face had been hidden behind the bridal veil. What struck me about the story that day was how unconsciously I had taken for granted the incredible number of top-drawer biblical characters who are enmeshed in a moral or ethical dilemma or a dramatic conflict that gets resolved by hiddenness, concealment, secrecy, or acts of trickery, such as was perpetrated on Jacob by his father-in-law, Laban. And the more I unspooled that realization, the more it led back to the one who started it all: God.

In Exodus, God explains the deal to Moses in no uncertain terms:

> *...you cannot see my face, for man shall not see me and live.... I will put you in a cleft of the rock and I will cover you with my hand until I have passed by. Then I will take away my hand, and you shall see my back, but my face shall not be seen.*

Not only is *hester panim* ("divine hiddenness") central to Jewish theology, it's the original model for secrecy, the primal archetype for the Jew who hides or is hidden. Many biblical heroes conceal themselves behind veils or disguises. They plot, they cheat, they pretend to be what they aren't, yet end up as exemplars of morality and piety. With their stories, the Torah establishes that human duplicity may sometimes be necessary for the fulfillment of God's plan. Consider the evidence (my italics for emphasis):

» Adam and Eve *cover up* their shame in the Garden, not for being naked, for disobeying God.

» Abraham and Isaac *pretend* their wives are their sisters to avoid being killed.

» Lot's daughters *trick him* into having sex with them.

» Leah is *disguised* as her sister, and Laban makes Jacob work seven more years to win Rachel.

» Rachel *hides* her father's idols from her husband, Jacob.

» Jacob and his mother *trick* his father, Isaac, and cheat his brother Esau of his birthright.

» Joseph's brothers leave him to die in a pit and then *lie* that he was killed by wild beasts.

» Joseph *hides* in plain sight when his brothers come to Egypt begging for food.

» Tamar *tricks* Judah into having sex with her.

» Baby Moses is *hidden* in a basket, found by the Pharaoh's daughter, and raised in the palace.

» Moses kills an Egyptian and *hides* the body in the sand.

» Esther (whose name derives from the Hebrew word *hester*) *conceals* her Jewish identity from King Ahasuerus and becomes the Queen of Persia.

On one hand, the Torah condemns falsehood, on the other it affirms the "legitimacy and occasional necessity" of premeditated lies, writes Yael Shemesh, associate professor of Hebrew Bible at Bar-Ilan University. Even after Moses descends from Mount Sinai with the Ten Commandments, the ninth of which forbids giving false testimony, God's chosen people continue to make stuff up. Justifying this contradiction with some dazzling hermeneutics, Professor Shemesh notes that "nowhere in the legal literature of the Bible is there any general injunction to refrain from telling lies. The commandment 'You shall not bear false witness against your neighbor'...refers solely to the judicial context, while the verse 'you shall not deal deceitfully or falsely with one another'...is concerned with business dealings, and the next verse, while forbidding one to swear falsely in God's name, does not prohibit lying in itself."

If the Almighty is willing to excuse, facilitate, even mastermind duplicitous behavior and, if humans are supposed to "*Imitatio Dei*," it stands to reason that we would deduce some practical, real-world lessons from these sacred texts, namely that God's plan sometimes requires doing the wrong thing for the right reasons, and when utilized in the service of a higher good, deception and subterfuge can be divinely forgivable and ultimately redemptive. But if we misperceive God's plan and do the wrong thing for the wrong reason, shame and dishonor will fall upon our house.

According to Jewish teachings, the ignominy of shame can't be overstated. The Talmud is unequivocal: to shame someone is tantamount to shedding their blood or defeating them in war. "A person would rather experience physical pain than shame." Shame is among God's most fearsome punishments. After Job passes every test of faith, God assures him, "They that hate thee shall be clothed with shame." Conjuring shame's power to destroy everything dear to the Israelites, their work, flocks, herds, sons, and daughters—the prophet Jeremiah assumes the divine voice to warn that committing profane speech and false prophecies "will bring an everlasting reproach upon you, and a perpetual shame, which shall not be forgotten." The prophet Obadiah curses Esau's descendants: "For thy violence against thy brother Jacob, shame shall cover thee, and thou shalt be cut off forever." The prophet Hosea, also speaking for God, says the people have "sinned against me, therefore will I change their glory into shame." When the Israelites are laid low, the prophet Isaiah reassures them, "Do not be afraid, for you will not be put to shame; don't be humiliated, for you will not be disgraced." The Book of Psalms is full of declarations regarding shame. "When pride cometh, then cometh shame." "Let mine adversaries be clothed with shame." "Poverty and shame shall be to him that refuses instruction."

My mother, as you'll soon see, took instruction well. Psalm 25, verse 1 ("O my God, I trust in thee; let me not be ashamed, let not mine enemies triumph over me") spoke to her hunger for respectability and her fear of the exposure of a shanda that might allow other people to triumph over her. Her fears became my instruction. Shame feels Jewish to me, not because other people or groups don't feel it, but because it's coded into the DNA of my family and ABCs of my faith.

CHAPTER 4

THE PLASTIC SHOPPING BAG

I couldn't have been more excited had the Dead Sea Scrolls turned up in my backyard. And I didn't need an archeologist to excavate this treasure; I just had to pull it out of a cupboard in my own apartment.

Faith leaders call coincidences "God's way of remaining anonymous." The Swiss psychiatrist Carl Jung used the term "synchronicity" to describe "the simultaneous occurrence of related events." I was reminded of this phenomenon when, in 2019, by accident or divine intervention, I received a phone call from my granddaughter, Molly, then a college sophomore, who told me she was taking a seminar on biographies and her professor, John Gaddis, himself a Pulitzer Prize–winning biographer, had assigned his students to write a fifty-page biography and the person she'd chosen as her subject was *me*. Before launching into the project, though, she explained that I had to understand exactly what it would entail: she would interview me, my relatives, friends, former colleagues, and classmates; visit my archival collection at Smith College and go through my correspondence, speeches, articles by, and about, me, reviews of my books, my notes from political conferences, women's liberation meetings, consciousness-raising groups; and she'd need unfettered access to my home office files, no matter how personal.

"This can't be an 'authorized' biography, Grams." I could hear her air quotes over the phone. "It has to be warts and all, no matter what I dig up or how it shames you. Can you promise you won't edit stuff out?"

My spine registered a frisson of fear; my brain, an instinct to negotiate a trade—full cooperation in return for veto power, red lines, a zone of privacy. Instead, I said, "Of course, darling. I promise."

At that, Molly hung up and went off to do her thing. She powered through my books and articles. Drove up to the Sophia Smith Collection in Northampton, Massachusetts, and pored over my archives. Interviewed me for hours. Spoke to Bert, our kids, friends of mine from all arenas of my life, tracked down my colleagues at *Ms.* magazine, as well classmates I hadn't seen in years, which wasn't easy since the internet didn't exist when I was last in touch with most of those people; I had no email addresses for them, only phone numbers, many of which were so prehistoric they appeared in my handwritten address book without area codes. After months of outside research, Molly arrived at our apartment and made a beeline for my study, a room filled with antique wooden file cabinets, floor-to-ceiling bookshelves, and a rolltop desk, and asked where I keep my personal files, childhood mementos, family memorabilia, photo albums, and the like. I pointed to the double doors of one of the deep lower cabinets, and Molly scooped up what stood front and center on one of its shelves—four of my teenage diaries, small leather-bound volumes secured by tiny brass locks, which she immediately and effortlessly opened. Then, bending over and tilting her head sideways, she peered into the jam-packed shelves. "What else is in there?"

"Damned if I know. Grandpa and I have lived here for fifty years." I kneeled down and reached into the bottom shelf. Synchronicity! Had my granddaughter not taken a biography course and chosen me as her subject, I never would have found the overstuffed plastic shopping bag. It looked like a cliché—the thing that fell off the back of a truck. But the minute I saw it, I remembered what was in it and how it ended up in my possession. My sister Betty had discovered it at the bottom of our mother's closet in 1955 when Mom died. Fifty-eight years later, a few days before Betty herself passed away, she gave it to me.

~~~

We're in Newton, Massachusetts, at the assisted living residence where she has spent her last years as a widow and an intrepid battler of the ovarian cancer that has spread through her body. My beloved, sallow-skinned, pain-ravaged sister is stretched out on her recliner in a cotton nightgown, a paisley shawl draped over her shoulders. We've been talking about her life, looking at pictures, reminiscing. She points to a large plastic shopping bag near the door and tells me I should take it with me when I leave. "Old letters," she says. "Someday, you'll want to read them." I ask if she wants some strawberry ice cream, the only food she was able to tolerate during the chemo. She shakes her head emphatically, reminds me that she hasn't eaten anything for weeks; it's the first part of her exit plan. No more chemo. No more food. No more pain. She's done, determined to die in her own way by her own devices. Tomorrow, she'll stop drinking liquids. Three days later she'll be dead. I understand. I don't fight her. My sister has always been a planner, strong-minded, clear-headed, resolute. She deserves a dignified death.

We both know this visit is our last. The summer sun, which had poured through the slats of her venetian blinds most of the day and buttered us with warmth, is gone now, taking most of Betty's energy with it. Streetlights cast amoebic shadows on the rug. It's getting late.

"Gotta go," I say, leaning down to embrace my sister one more time. The shawl falls away as she reaches toward me, exposing arms bruised purple from countless needles. Her hug lasts long enough for me to memorize it.

"I can't believe this is happening," I murmur through my tears.

"You'd *better* believe it, kiddo. I'm not starving myself for nothing." She lets herself fall back against the recliner. "I love you, Letty. Always have. Now go home and take the bag with you."

In the taxi to Back Bay station, I was going to pull one of the letters out of the bag, but it was too dark to read. I intended to pull one out in the Amtrak waiting room, but I couldn't stop sobbing. After settling myself in a window seat of the nearly deserted quiet car for the four-hour trip to Manhattan, I intended to sample a bunch of letters. Instead, I nod off and don't wake up until the conductor strides through shouting, "Penn Station, Nooo Yawk!" It's past midnight when I get home. I drop the bag on the floor of my study thinking I'll get to it in the morning but I wake up with a million things to do, and the morning after that, the same, and the next morning, I get the call that my sister has died, and I shove the bag into the depths of the cabinet.

Six years later, thanks to my granddaughter and the goddess of synchronicity, the bag is in my hands. Upending it on my dining room table disgorges a blizzard of letters, onion skin stationery, letterheads from hotels and cruise ships, synagogues and civic organizations, faded fountain pen ink scrawled on envelopes studded with three-cent stamps and penny postcards, sky blue Aerogrammes rimmed in patriotic stripes and ornate foreign stamps; yellowing legal documents, calendars, birth certificates, death certificates, newspaper clippings, handwritten lists. Molly has no interest in memorabilia from before I was born, but I'm writing a memoir of my family, people who existed three and four generations before *she* was born. For me, the blizzard is paydirt, a buried treasure unearthed. The letter on top of the heap is filled margin to margin with my father's cramped, spidery script. It's dated 1939, the year I was born. I sit down at the table and start reading.

CHAPTER 5

THE PALESTINE LETTERS, SPRING 1939

He had me at, "Dear Sweetest Thing in the World." That was the salutation my soon-to-be father, Jack Cottin, wrote to my soon-to-be mother, Ceil Halpern, in one of the dozens of four-, five-, and six-page missives he sent her in the spring of '39, while she was home in the Bronx pregnant with me and he was traveling to and from Palestine, today's Israel. Without the contents of the shopping bag, I could not have cracked open the marrow bones of my parents' secrets, decoded their conflicts, their zizagging passions, the craggy map of their marriage. Their letters to one another answer questions I didn't know enough to ask when I began writing this book; for openers, why would my father spend eight weeks traveling across the globe when my mother was only three months from giving birth to me?

Dad often claimed that, had he *not* gone to Palestine when he did, he would have lost his share of the estate of his father, who died the year before in Tiberias. I knew my Grandpa Max had been killed in an Arab raid but was unaware of the gory details until a few years ago when my Israeli cousin, Wendy Bar-Yakov, researched that history. It seems that our grandfather had been asleep with his second wife (name unknown) in a small Jewish tent colony when a marauding band of Arab militants slit open their canvas with machetes, cut their throats, and set the compound on fire, killing seven. Wendy located a mass grave in the Tiberias cemetery and found the Cottin names on the marker. She'd also found them listed in an Israeli registry I never knew existed called "Former Americans Who Were Victims of Arab Terror Prior to the Establishment of the State."

During his trip to Palestine, Jack wrote to Ceil nearly every day, addressing her as "Darling Mine," "Sweetheart Mine," "Honey Mine," "Baby Doll," "Sweet Doll," and "Mommy Gorgeous." After admonishing her for not answering him more promptly, he would repeat how much he missed her and sign off with "I love you" in multiple languages. She called him, "Dearest Husband," "Darling," "Beloved," "Sweetheart," and "My handsome Lothario," and frequently noted how lonely she was and how empty their Bronx apartment felt without him. Their tender romanticism struck me as entirely appropriate, given that I now know my parents had only been married for two years in 1939. By the same token, the fact that they'd *only* been married for two years made the blinding flashes of hostility in their correspondence unsettling and, in hindsight, prophetic. Laid bare were their long-festering issues, some familiar from the arguments I overheard as a little girl hiding at the top of the stairs, others new to me and freshly searing. Unmediated, their voices traveled across eight decades and pierced my heart even as I marveled at the plenitude and regularity of their exchanges. Almost daily during his eight-week absence, the two of them recorded their every activity, thought, and feeling, posting not to five thousand "friends" as many of us do now, but to a readership of one. Who *does* that anymore? Soul-baring, long-form letter writing has become extinct, a fatal loss for future lovers, biographers, and memoirists. Without the trail of emotional breadcrumbs they left behind on paper, I could not have perceived as clearly as I do now my father's insensitivity, gall, or whatever else it was that allowed him to leave my thirty-seven-year-old mother to fend for herself when he knew that her "geriatric pregnancy" put her at risk for late-term complications and a premature birth.

When I was a child, the album Jack had put together of snapshots from his trip made it seem glamorous and exotic. I loved seeing my dashing dad sitting astride a camel in Alexandria, posing at the port of Marseille, tipping his hat to Vesuvius, or being dwarfed by the Pyramids. It never occurred to me to ask why he took time to sightsee rather than cut short his ill-timed journey and rush straight home to his pregnant wife. In the letter she wrote to him the day he set sail from New York harbor, Ceil made plain how unhappy she was after his departure.

> Dearest Jack,
>
> You looked very sweet and handsome on the boat. It was very becoming, this nonchalant air of a seasoned traveler. But coming home and not having you with us was an awful shock. I was overwhelmed with loneliness. I'm sure I could never expose one I love to that experience. The sun went down when you left and it's been gloomy ever since. I know it won't shine for me until you come back.

The snide remark sandwiched between her flattery did not escape Jack's notice:

> Were you bawling me out diplomatically when you stated you "couldn't expose one you love to such loneliness?" I don't think that's fair. You know I didn't run away from you. I felt this trip had to be made. Anyway, my darling, I love you and always will.

Ceil's next letter plaintively inquired, "Do you miss me a little? You probably have so many diversions and so little time to remember me. Your terribly lonely wife." A week later, she backtracked from that timorous tone with a full out blast of despair.

Darling,

I felt so miserable after you left. I was frantic. I couldn't sleep nor eat until I realized the harmful effect my behavior would have on the baby. Finding I had no control over myself, I blamed you and I felt very bitter about your trip. It seemed to me then as before that nothing can justify your leaving me at this time, knowing how much I worry about you, about the dangers you are exposed to every minute you are there.

Jack responded with affection and reassurance, sending, "Oodles, bunches, bundles, crates, large packages, small packages, briefcases, overnight bags, suitcases, and trunks full of love," and promising to change his departure date, "in order to get home sooner and take you in my arms. (Will I be able to get them around you?)" Charming, endearing, adorable, to be sure. But he did not advance his departure date.

Her plea for him to behave better upon his return was a frequent refrain, though rather than be explicit, she'd wedged it between two fawning sentences:

One of the things I can boast about that few wives can is your very interesting and loving letters. How nice it would be if when you come home you would express your love in our daily contacts as you do in your letters. They thrill me deeply and make me feel so homesick for you.

Again, seesawing between praise and recrimination, she alluded to Jack's prior transgressions while begging him to be his best self:

You are getting into a very good habit of thinking of me often. Will you do that when you're home? Your letters are poetic and sentimental, and I love you for it. I always knew there was, hidden somewhere in your nature, an appreciation for the aesthetic things in life, only you've been suppressing it. I'm glad this trip has awakened these hidden qualities and I hope it will also have some effect on one or two little faults of yours and will modify them a bit. Perhaps I shouldn't expect you to be the perfect husband, but I have so much confidence in you and love you so much that any little thoughtlessness toward me hurts me deeply. And I hope that when you return, we will be as happy as we should be, and have been (except on a few occasions).

She ends that letter with a reference that nearly knocked off my reading glasses: "I miss you desperately, my darling, and trust in God that you will hurry back to us soon. Like a Catholic counts the beads of her Rosary, I'm counting the days, praying that each will pass quickly."

My mother was a *very* Jewish Jew, so how did she come up with the rosary image or have the audacity to analogize it to her feelings toward her very Jewish husband? Did she see someone praying the rosary in a movie? Read about it in a book? Did she ever attend church with one of our Irish or Italian neighbors? I doubt that. Jewish law forbids us from entering a church, not because we might be seduced into abandoning our faith but because Judaism considers the whole idea of the Trinity to be offensive to our One God, and the sight of a Jew standing among those who pray to the Father, Son, and Holy Ghost, might convey to a gentile observer the appearance of Jewish impropriety. In other words, it would have been a *shanda far di goyim*. (A shameful act witnessed by a non-Jew and therefore even more scandalous than one committed inside the fold.)

For the better part of a week, I read every letter my parents wrote to each other, riveted by their clashing personalities and contrasting expectations, their ongoing strife, all the hope-filled pain that my mother had concealed from the world, the disappointments she'd papered over, the insults she'd endured because the truth about his unfeeling ways and their chronic bickering, had it been revealed, would have been unbearably humiliating. In public, Ceil ignored her husband's carping, her warm smile and gracious conversation covering for his rudeness. On the page, she begged him to change his habits but hedged her words, tempering her entreaties with heavy doses of love and longing.

The letters offered no clue to the mystery of the rosary reference, but they helped me understand the turbulence beneath the surface of Ceil's seemingly enviable marriage to her seemingly impressive husband. They also demystified his inscrutable relationship to money and how it played out in his interactions with Mom, me, and everyone else.

I never knew my father to fail at anything, never heard him fret about his law practice or worry about his finances. A respected attorney, homeowner, president of his synagogue and a half dozen other Queens County Jewish organizations, Jack Cottin was the guy who, when dining out with another couple, picked up the check; the one the family could rely on to pull out a wad of crisp new dollar bills or a sack of jangling silver dollars and hand one to every kid at the seder table so we could ransom the *afikoman*. To my eyes, he was always the snappiest dresser with the neatest car, a man of means, successful, decisive, confident.

The Palestine letters torpedoed that image. A complaint here, an anecdote there, occasionally an outright confession, exposed an alternative reality that still astounds me. They revealed that my father frequently ran short of cash. Got stiffed by small-time clients. Made bad investments, struggled to keep up appearances, and constantly waged an internal tug of war between his generous impulses and his penchant for penny-pinching.

En route to Palestine, his ship, the S.S. *Excalibur* made a stop in Sorrento, where he disembarked for a stroll through the market district. "I wanted to buy a few colorful scarves of heavy silk at ten lira each, but I didn't because the shopkeeper rated ten lira as equal to fifty cents and I know I can buy lira cheaper when we get to Alexandria." From Jerusalem, he wrote, "I don't buy everything I'd like to buy. But I can get silver bracelets, brooches, necklaces, and rings set with real stones, amethyst, coral, sapphire, lapis, onyx, etc. dirt cheap—seventy-five cents for an item easily worth three dollars in New York." When he finally broke down and purchased gifts to bring home, none were made of silk, silver, or precious stones. Yet, seemingly delighted by his largesse, he enumerated what he'd bought for whom: "One large carved wooden camel for us; five smaller ones for Dotty, Lou, Tillie, Sadye & Rona [his sister, brother, and sisters-in-law]; three still smaller ones for our bridge group; four camel caravans for Betty, Rena, Judy, Danny [a few members of the younger generation]; a siddur for Mom; a machzor [High Holy Day prayer book] for Pop; a challah cloth, fancy yarmulke and shofar for Al [his sister Dotty's ultra-Orthodox husband]. Hooray!" His enthusiasm seemed excessive until I realized he was trumpeting his conquest of a secret parsimony I had never known existed.

Likewise, Ceil's letters revealed traits of hers that she'd kept hidden. They show her stiffening Jack's spine, urging him to hang tough during negotiations with other relatives who also claimed pieces of Max's estate. "Don't let them soft pedal you, sweetheart. Stick to your original demands. You may have to make quick decisions. I know you can be firm, but your heart is too charitable. Please don't yield. Remember charity begins at home where it's needed so badly." I had not known my mother to be so strategic.

I also learned through their letters that Ceil was the political engine in their marriage. While she was well-versed on a variety of domestic and international affairs, Jack was almost entirely focused on the Zionist cause. By March 1939, Hitler had already annexed Austria and Sudetenland, overrun Czechoslovakia, delivered the bombastic Reichstag speech in which he predicted "the annihilation of the Jewish race in Europe," and signed the infamous Munich Agreement with Chamberlain. Yet when Ceil wrote, "I'm really worried. Dark clouds are gathering everywhere. War talk is even more dramatic now than during the Munich crisis," Jack, writing from Jerusalem, naively reassured her, "The war scare is definitely past."

Business aptitude was another of my mom's heretofore unknown talents. In his absence, she managed two small Bronx buildings—one on St. Ann's Avenue, one on Bathgate—that were jointly owned by my father and grandfather, a surprising fact in itself. (I never dreamed that anyone in our family had enough money to dabble in real estate.) Ceil writes, almost joyfully, about collecting rents in both buildings, negotiating leases for the vacant street-level stores—"one to a cider maker, the other to a man with a moving van"—making the unilateral decision to get the three empty apartments in the Bathgate building painted before showing them to prospective tenants so she could justify listing them for slightly higher rents. Her report closed with, "I also persuaded the painting contractor to reduce his bill by $44. How am I doing, honey? aren't I substituting well for you? Though I'd rather you did it."

In light of her impressive managerial accomplishments, that last line sounds insincere. Did she really prefer that Jack do it? Or was she walking back her enthusiasm on the chance that he might take her deft management of the two buildings as a threat to his male ego. Based on the patronizing tone of his reply, that, indeed, was how he took it. "You're doing swell," he wrote, reclaiming the patriarch's right of approval and the power to delegate. "I think I'll appoint you to take care of the buildings. I knew you could do it only I figured it would be too much work for you. When I'm back, I'll relieve you. Otherwise, you can continue with it and make some pin money."

Had my parents known their words would end up under their daughter's microscope I doubt that they would have expressed their sore points and vulnerabilities in such unguarded prose. When they were alive, Dad hid his weaknesses, Mom her strength. Their letters exposed the nakedness of her feelings and the architecture of his manipulations. Their sudden segues from an impassioned salutation to a brain-deadening weather report, from anguished cries to insulting accusations gave me whiplash. Same for their dizzying transitions of tone—scolding, adoring, beseeching, forgiving, all in the same paragraph.

Honey Sweet Ceil,

I ought to be really sore at you. I finally get a letter, so what do I find in it? I find you're like an elephant, never forgetting a wrong—true or fancied. However, I've missed you so much that I'm going to make it my business to forget about that whole business regarding the Chinese dinner and all its appendages and ramifications and say, "to hell with them."

I'll never be able to deduce what happened at the Chinese dinner, or which wrong the elephant refused to forget. But the eroticism that flowed from Jack's pen onto the stationery of the S.S. *Marco Polo* on his crossing back to New York needs no simultaneous translation.

Sweetheart love,

I'm getting into bad habits. I go to sleep at 10 and by about 6, I'm all slept out… I know what'll fix that. All I need is to wrap my arms around you and put your head on my shoulder and then I'll be all right. I'll be able to sleep till at least 7. I'll be home soon so make sure that you're feeling well and looking well, or else you won't get all those beautiful things I bought for you, and besides, I'll give you a licking—I'll lick you all over—lips, eyes, nose, and beyond.

After that romantic, albeit transactional, reverie, it was jarring to read his disingenuous references to the ship's fine wines and luxury smoking rooms, as well as his forays on the dance floor. "With all the activities on board, life is pretty boring and the graceless inability of the young females I've danced with makes dancing not so much fun. But who cares? I'll be home soon, and I can dance with you."

That, in a nutshell, was my father—charming, flattering, tone deaf, hurtful. For weeks, he'd been rhapsodizing about the wonders of French ports, Italian ruins, Alexandria, Cairo, Jerusalem, all of which his pregnant, homebound wife had missed out on. So why would he paint a picture of himself cruising the high seas in grandeur and fraternizing with young women unworthy of his fox-trots? My mother's reaction to that letter is lost to history. Maybe she was frosty when they met at the pier in New York. Maybe she swallowed his double-edged sword (ship boring but luxurious; girls young but graceless) with a smile of forbearing. I, for one, would have been fuming.

His postscript would not have pleased me, either: "Bring enough money to pay for a cab 'cause I'll probably be broke." Clearly, Jack's negotiations in Palestine did not end well. His share of his late father's assets—the upshot of his eight-week absence from his seven months pregnant wife—was two hundred British pounds, the 1939 equivalent of $1,000.

CHAPTER 6

SHE COULD HIDE A HIPPO IN A HATBOX

Sometime in the early 2000s, a letter surfaced that never made it into the shopping bag, and I think I know why. It turned up in a slot on the inside back cover of the album of snapshots that Jack took during his travels in the Middle East, a pocket I'd never noticed during all the years when, as a child, I'd obsessively paged through the album. Assuming the secret compartment contained a loose photo or a hotel brochure, I was overjoyed when I pulled out a letter Ceil wrote to Jack in 1939. A dozen years would pass before I came into possession of the plastic shopping bag, and I had not yet read any of my parent's private correspondence so finding this one, which was long and newsy, was a thrill. Until this line, appended in Betty's round teenage hand.

> *P.S. Mommy is okay, and the twins are*
> *still kicking.*

Flabbergasted, I dove for the phone. "I'm sitting here looking at a letter Mom wrote to Dad when he was in Palestine…"

"And?" Betty prompted.

I kept staring at her postscript. "And there's this weird thing you wrote on the last page."

"How weird can it be? I was fourteen."

I read her the line.

"Come again?"

"You wrote, 'Mommy is okay, and the twins are still kicking.' That's what it says, Betty. And you didn't put quotation marks around the word 'twins.'" I paused, dry-mouthed, then croaked, "Is it true?"

"Is what true?"

"That I had a twin?"

"Don't be ridiculous! You were the only baby Mom gave birth to in 1939."

"What makes you so sure?"

"I was in the car when Dad picked Mom and you up at the hospital. I was in the back seat. A nurse put you in my arms and I held you the whole way home."

"You weren't with Mom in the labor or delivery room. Maybe that's where the other baby died."

"Impossible. They would have told me."

"Not necessarily. You were a kid. They were great liars, remember? Mom could hide a hippo in a hatbox. Maybe the other one died and they hid it from you. And you made yourself forget it because you were traumatized."

My sister's reply came out in snorts. "I. Would. Not. Forget. The. Death. Of. A. Baby."

"Why would you write 'the twins are still kicking' if Mom didn't have two babies bashing around in her belly? Twins aren't something you'd make up."

"I don't know!" she snarled. "I must have been joking."

"To me, it's no joke. Tell me *exactly* what you remember about that day." I heard myself talking to my sister, who was in her mid-seventies at the time, as if she were a recalcitrant witness or a child refusing to say who threw the first punch in the playground. Switching the receiver to my other ear, I took a breath, and softened my interrogatory tone. "Sorry. Let me restate: Can you please tell me what you remember? I'm really curious."

"Okay, okay!" She sounded halfway between bemused and irritated. "Dad went into the hospital to get Mom and you. I was waiting in the back seat of the car in the parking lot. When they finally appeared, Dad had his arm around Mom's waist and she was walking slowly and a nurse wearing a white uniform with a starched white cap and white shoes and stockings was following close behind cradling you in her arms. You were swaddled in a pink and white striped bunting and you had a lot of straight black hair, and you were adorable. I was desperate to hold you and after Dad settled Mom in the front seat, he opened the back door and told the nurse to place you in my arms. Which she did. And, as I've told you a million times, it was one of the happiest moments in my life. I'll remember it as long as I live."

Frankly, my sister's memory was a shallow pool. Plumb her past for details and you'd hit bottom after two, maybe three, questions. Her life story, like our mother's, showed wide gaps in the telling. When the truth was too hard to bear, she and Mom did the same thing: buried it. Despite my dogged grilling, Betty remembered nothing else about the day she and Dad picked Mom and me up in the hospital. I let up on my interrogation and soon forgot all about Betty's P.S.—until she died and left me the shopping bag, and two *more* twin mentions appeared in the letters: another P.S. from Betty to Jack—"The twins miss you as much as Mommy and I do"—and a P.S. from Jack to Betty in one of the letters he penned from the ship back to New York, the same letter in which he told Mom about his having danced with graceless women: "Well, Bets," he wrote, "I didn't win the Captain's ping-pong or bridge tournaments but I don't care because you love me and so does Mommy and so do the twins."

Now I had three proof texts corroborating that Mom had been pregnant with twins—two in my sister's handwriting, one in my father's. But what happened to the other baby between the last P.S. and the day when Betty saw my parents leave the hospital with only one baby? Did the second infant die of some terrible malady or congenital flaw, which Ceil, in her habitual quest for normalcy, if not perfection, might have felt compelled to conceal? Even if it died of an "ordinary" complication of labor or delivery, Ceil may have been loath to admit she'd lost one twin because of the stigma that seems to attach to parents of dead children.

I'm thinking of what journalist Jason Green wrote some years ago when his two-year-old daughter was killed in a freak accident—a loose brick fell from a building's eighth floor, striking her on the head while she sat on a bench with her grandmother. Greene said he experienced the "pall of societal shame" that "hovers over everyone in this club." (The parents of dead children club, the saddest of all memberships.) He noted how many people recoiled from him as if his tragedy was contagious, as if it were possible to ward off the randomness of fate by turning one's back on those who suffer.

If I did have a womb mate, my mother might very well have kept its death a secret rather than admit to being a member of the club of bereaved parents. She'd already had enough occasions of shame to last a lifetime. As for Jack, I can imagine him cooperating in her cover-up, not because of the shanda factor, but because of Jewish law, which he knew from A to Z, or aleph to tav, according to which infants do not become fully viable until they are thirty-one days old and if they die before that day, it is as if they "had never lived." That sounds heartless until you remember that these strictures date back to a time when newborns died early and often. Rather than parents having to endure round after round of ritualized grieving—funeral, burial, shiva (first seven days after burial), *shloshim* (full thirty days of mourning after burial), and so on— they are prohibited from traditional public mourning for the dead infant in order to redirect them to their living children and their continuing obligation to "be fruitful and multiply." Jack, respecting the halacha, would have allowed the baby's death to go under the radar and refused to mourn it. Ceil, who followed his lead on religious matters, would have welcomed those religious prohibitions, because in this case, the law aligned with her propensity to bury her misfortunes as quickly as possible and to deny painful truths, even to herself. Their separate but equally compelling motivations, Mom's to avoid the "pall of societal shame" and Dad's to observe the letter of the law, would provide reason enough for them to hide the loss of my twin from everyone, including me.

However, women's emotions don't always obey men's laws. For my mother to act as if the baby "had not lived" would have been easier decreed than felt. And for me to dismiss those three mentions of twins without playing out the possibility that there *was* another baby, was, at this point, impossible. Reasoning by deduction, I sifted through what I knew about Mom's beliefs and ruled out conclusions that did not jibe with them. To begin with, if my twin died, few people would have been the wiser since almost no one would have known that Ceil was carrying twins in the first place. Why am I so sure? Because my mother's Judaism was one-part supplication, one-part gratitude, and eight-parts magical thinking. Her actions were dictated, first and foremost, by the vagaries of the Evil Eye, alias the devil, whose primary objective on earth was to destroy a Jew's best-laid plans. Mom's pregnancy-related shtetl superstitions made a deep impression on me when I was a child, and years later, when I became pregnant, they became mine.

I, too, believed it was bad luck for a pregnant woman to be photographed, choose her baby's name before it was born, decorate its nursery or buy its bassinet or layette in advance, or broadcast any boastful, immodest, or self-congratulatory specifics about her pregnancy, such as the fact that she gained only twenty pounds and never had morning sickness. *Or that she was carrying twins.* Such statements or acts were forbidden because they suggested that the woman took for granted a normal delivery and a healthy child. This was exactly the sort of hubris that attracts the devil's attention and inspires him to zap the offender with extremely bad luck, such as a miscarriage, a breech birth, or worse. Given my mother's caution in such matters, the likelihood that she'd told no one beyond her immediate family about being pregnant with twins, and the halachic prohibition about mourning an infant who doesn't make it to thirty-one days old, hiding the death of my intimate other could have, no, would have been relatively easy to conceal. What occurs to me now with the confirmation provided by the three P.S.es is the possibility that my baby self may have suffered a preconscious trauma of which I am unaware but which has been influencing my personality and behavior ever since.

In her book, *One and the Same: My Life as a Twin and Everyone's Struggle to Be Singular*, my daughter, Abigail Pogrebin, writes about the "vanishing twin syndrome," which happens when one fetus is miscarried in utero and its tissue is absorbed by the mother or the surviving fetus. Since this phenomenon occurs in around 30 percent of multiple pregnancies, I thought it might explain my missing twin, but Abigail reminded me that the miscarried fetus usually vanishes before the twelfth week of pregnancy and at the point when "the twins" appear in my sister's and father's letters my mother was already in her twenty-seventh week.

⚬⚬⚬

Since May 17, 1965, when Abigail and her sister Robin were born one minute apart, people have been asking me if twins run in our family. "They do on Bert's side," I tell them, referring to my husband's identical redheaded cousins. "I'm not sure about mine."

Though unable to definitively determine whether "me" was once "we" I'm inclined to believe I had a gestational companion not just because of three mentions in the Palestine letters, but because a missing twin would explain the otherwise unexplainable sense I have whenever I'm alone, that I'm not. I've experienced it countless times through the years, this thing I insist on calling "a sense" because it doesn't take the form of a supernatural interloper, ghost, poltergeist, or apparition; it's more like the scent that lingers in a room after a perfumed woman has vacated the premises. It's not a physical sensation; it's an ineffable, quiet, disembodied, protective, serene thing that's just there when no one else is.

Three years after Mom died, I wrote to my sister and did my best, at age eighteen, to get a handle on that ethereal feeling and our mother's indelible influence on us both:

> *I don't think this life which you and I are shaping for ourselves, the decisions we make and the values we hold dear, can fully be credited to our own judgments. There is a greater wisdom that lives deep within us and guides us every moment and that is our mom. I do many things with her in mind, and I often imagine her advice or approval. When I'm alone, I feel her beside me, an ever-present companion and guardian of my safety.*

> *I make sorry note of the elusiveness of memories that were once so sharp and poignant. My thoughts of her are fewer and hazier, not separate items of recollection but a composite, a mood of soft remembrance. It's as though she never was, only because she always is.*

Lately, while attempting to solve the secret associated with my birth, two new possibilities lodged in my mind. What if, all these years, my ethereal companion was not my mother but my vanished twin? And, since the cosmos has been known to deliver reparative justice, what if my having had twins myself—in effect, birthing an extra baby—was God's way of replacing the sibling I lost?

CHAPTER 7

THE FLORIDA LETTERS, WINTER 1940–41

Whenever I'm in the Miami area, I try to make time to visit South Beach, the historic Art Deco district where so many of the original low-rise, bleached-white buildings built in the mid-twentieth century have been restored to their former glory. That's where, at my father's insistence, my mother and I spent three months so the sun could dry up my incessant coughs and colds. Our family album is thick with photos of me at eighteen months posing like a child model under the lollipop palms and cascading bougainvillea or wading in the surf in my teensy-weensy bikini, and of Mom looking cool in a floral halter top and flowing wide-legged pants, her teeth white as Chiclets beneath the brim of a floppy straw hat. We look like we're luxuriating among the hoi polloi, but Mom's Florida letters tell a different story. Contrary to her Palestine letters a year and a half earlier, her grievances that winter are even more explicit and excruciating.

She hadn't wanted to go; Dad had insisted. According to him, he was the magnanimous paterfamilias who'd generously indulged us for the benefit of my health. "Rockefeller's not the only guy who can send his wife and kids to Florida for the winter!" he would boast, though Mom and I certainly weren't living in the lap of luxury. He put her on a tight budget, demanded that she account in her letters for every purchase (which she dutifully did, listing "$1.50 baby's bathing suit, $1.30 sneakers, $3.00 doctor visit, $1.85 medicine, 30 cents stationery"), and reprimanded her if he felt she'd overspent.

In February 2020, when I was last in South Beach, now called "the playground of the glitterati," an Armani Exchange stood on the corner where more than eighty years ago, my mother and I moved into one of the sparsely furnished garden apartments that were rented by the month, mostly to middle- and working-class Jews from up North. Upon our arrival in December 1940, Ceil wrote, "I found us a little bungalow for $300 for the full season on lower Collins Avenue. It's surrounded by gorgeous shrubbery and bright flowers, everything so colorful and enchanting. But just five blocks away from here you can see real beauty, wealthy homes and expensive hotels so exquisite they are indescribable. You wonder how people must feel living in such posh surroundings." She sounded like Gatsby, as if the impoverished little girl she used to be could never stop gazing across the bay at the blue light and fantasizing about the habits of the rich.

While her letters testify that she missed Jack terribly, she also spilled a lot of ink ruminating on his bad behavior and the state of their marriage. Most of what I learned about my father's casual cruelty and my mother's reactive misery came from their correspondence during those ten weeks we spent in South Beach. Consider this missive, written on December 31, 1940, in which Ceil resumes her pattern of wavering between hope and regret, anger and supplication.

> *Please dear, make one New Year's resolution for my sake never to repeat that scene you made at the Foxes before I left for Florida. And I'll make any resolution you have in mind for me. OK? I don't know why I annoyed you. You never told me the reason…that's your way. But I refuse to give up hope that someday we can live harmoniously together. I have said this before*

and gotten no response from you, so I guess there's no use in feeling optimistic about your ever changing your ways. It's a pity. The time we're wasting. The years slip by, but can we honestly say that we are happy or that we are as one? isn't that the definition of an ideal marriage? I can see the bored look on your face as you read this: that is the cross I have to bear—your refusal to understand me or to try to improve our relationship.

Before we were married, I had a beautiful picture of what we would be and do together. I still cling to it. And I still believe that if you sincerely loved me (and knew the meaning of love) we could make our life an enjoyable one.

Rather than soften his heart, Ceil's poignant longing for "the ideal marriage" and her "beautiful picture" of what they "would be and do together" made Jack more combative:

I don't mind taking your criticism if it isn't harping and carping, but I hate when you shut up like a clam, then my stubbornness makes me do the same thing and ignore you. If I have faults, it's pretty late to cure them and they're not as bad as you make them out to be.

To that, Ceil responded with a cri de coeur as piercing as an ice pick.

In our four years of marriage, I've never heard you apologize for something you've done, or to say a word of regret for an inconsiderate act. There's not a drop of humility in you. You are always right even when you insult me, as when you told me to shut up, or when you say something embarrassing, belittling me, as you did that time in front of my family at the housewarming. I could mention dozens of such humiliating experiences. I don't want to go through life like this.

The in-person battles I witnessed throughout my childhood were never as blistering as the crossfire that blazed off these sheets of stationery and left me with contact burns. In writing, my largely self-educated mother could organize her thoughts and express her feelings with candor, coherence, and a touch of acid; face-to-face she was easily crushed by the steamroller of my father's postgraduate vocabulary and disdainful rebuttals. "Sweetheart," she wrote in one of her agonized letters, "it's nice to hear that you haven't borrowed any money or disgraced me."

Did Jack deserve such unalloyed contempt? Based on her description of his rude "card habits," it appears that he did. Yet her complaint was honeyed with hope and garnished with a compliment.

> *Dearest Jack,*
>
> *I'm glad you had a nice bridge game with your friends on Saturday. I hope and pray that you were a modest and quiet winner. Maybe when I get home, I will happily find your card habits have changed. Then I will be a truly proud wife. My ambition is not to have to watch you slam cards on the table or listen to you ridicule, correct, or blame others for some play that you disdain. Here's hoping my beloved husband is a gentleman at the card table as he is elsewhere.*

That got a rise out of him.

> *Don't worry so much about my gentlemanliness. If you didn't have a phobia on the subject, it wouldn't be so bad. I didn't bawl anyone out on Saturday. I didn't raise my voice except to have everyone hear my bids, and I took my winnings like a gentleman. I'm sure the impression I made on our friends won't cause you any disgrace.*

It was a typical response. Jack's letters made plain that, when confronted by Ceil's criticism, no matter how tempered by love and praise, he would defend, deny, or deflect the blame, in this instance, insisting the fault lay in her "phobia," other times accusing her of being thin-skinned when the original problem was his behavior and his imperviousness to her pain or discontent. Reading her pleas, I suffered along with her as she chronicled his callousness and made plain her relentless, ultimately futile, efforts to reform the complicated, seductive, brusque, maddening man she loved. Why did she stay with him? I've been searching for the answer to that question all my life.

⁓⁓⁓

If his Palestine letters gave me my first inkling of my father's secret penury, the Florida letters doubled down on the evidence and introduced a new thought, heretofore unimaginable, that his tight-wad leanings were the result of actual financial stress. For the first time, I entertained the idea that the man who'd always appeared to live large was hiding serious money troubles. One of Mom's letters indicates that she, too, was grappling with that possibility. Fed up with his constant nagging about picayune expenditures, she zeroed in on the disconnect between the big spender image Dad liked to project and the truth of his skinflint behavior.

> *You frighten me now with your attitude. You have always acted as if you have a limitless supply of money, and expenses should never bother us. Fortunately for you, I have never taken advantage of that outlook and have been careful of how I spend money, even though I'm not familiar with your office income.*
>
> *I'm sore at you because you're not consistent. You tell me to go ahead and spend, and then you get worried or angry when I do. Didn't you know how you stood financially three weeks ago? I suppose, as usual, you*

talk first and think afterwards. I've been very econom-
ical in my purchases since we got to Florida, and I
hope to make the remaining money last for the rest of
the season.

But I need you to tell me the truth about our
finances.

Jack's penny-pinching reached new levels of absurdity in his
letter of March 11, 1941. Conflicting emotions buffeted me as I
read his ridiculous reprimand.

You wasted 3 cents in sending your letter. If it required
double postage because it was overweight, you should
have put on 12 cents to send it air mail or 6 cents reg-
ular mail. The rate is 3 cents an ounce regular and 6
cents an ounce airmail. It weighed less than an ounce
and 6 cents would have carried it to me. The letter I
wrote today, as you can see, weighed about 2 ounces
and I put 12 cents stamps on it.

While I recoiled at the pressure he'd put on Ceil, I also felt
sorry for Jack, who had boxed himself into a prosperous, munificent persona that he could neither sustain nor relinquish. Their
letters make abundantly clear that both of them were pretenders,
constantly struggling to live up to their billing: Ceil carefully nurturing her image as a happily married woman; Jack shaping his into
a Jewish American male success story.

CHAPTER 8

THE DAY I LEARNED MY PARENTS WERE LIARS

My obsession, my "Rosebud," if you will, is not a children's sled moldering in a press baron's basement but a family tree that my father drew in the sand, a few months before I turned twelve. Over the decades, I've revisited that scene in many genres; it appears in different incarnations and reconstructed dialogues in my nonfiction book, *Deborah, Golda, and Me*, and my first novel, *Three Daughters*; in interviews, articles, and speeches; in therapy sessions and dreams. By now, that day on a beach in Winthrop, Massachusetts, should have loosed its hold on me, but only the passage of time and the frankness demanded by this memoir—which impelled me to "re-vision" it here—have brought me to a place where I can acknowledge its indelible impact and finally let it go.

It's a cold, blustery day in early spring of 1951. My parents and I are spending the weekend in Winthrop, a seaside community on the north shore of Boston Harbor at the home of Esther and Ben Sargon, my father's younger sister and her husband, to celebrate the bar mitzvah of their son, Simon.

After sabbath services at their synagogue, a dozen or so friends and relatives have strolled back to the house, where they've congregated in the steamy kitchen, talking, laughing, slathering bagels with cream cheese and piling on lox and whitefish. The bar mitzvah boy huddles in his room with his pals while the littlest kids are running around upstairs. I'm feeling cozy and content, seated at a card table in the parlor across from my cousin Rita, a short, chubby-cheeked woman about ten years my senior. Salt spray streaks the windows, a stiff breeze whistles off the ocean and through the eaves, but if there's a draft, I don't notice it because I've just won another hand of gin rummy and caught my cousin with thirty-three points.

It's my turn to deal but Rita gathers up the cards before I can grab them. She licks her stubby fingers, cuts the deck, shuffles it, and deals, slapping each card against the table as if it needs a spanking. She doesn't enjoy losing, especially to a kid half her age; that I can see. Her face is flushed, and she's chewing gum harder and faster than gum is meant to be chewed.

"I was supposed to be the dealer, so you can go first," I say, magnanimously.

She makes a show of fanning her cards. "To hell with you and your whole goddamn family!" she shouts. Her outburst shocks me but demands a rebuttal. My riposte is an all-purpose seventh-grade counterpunch. "You're just *jealous*!"

"Of *you*?" She sneers. "Don't make me laugh!"

"No, of Betty," I say, a plausible claim since I consider my sister the ideal woman. I wish she was here right now, but she and her husband, Bernie, are home in Peekskill, New York, taking care of their toddler, Steven, and Betty is pregnant with their second child. "You're jealous of her 'cause she's smart and beautiful, and she has a wonderful husband." I pile on, "And they have an adorable little boy. And she's pregnant. And you're not…"

"No one gives a damn about Betty. I'm the first *real* grandchild in the Cottin family. I'm the oldest and always will be."

I realize she's mad at me for trouncing her at gin, but she's plainly wrong: Betty is twenty-six; Rita is twenty-two. Can't she do simple arithmetic? "You're crazy!" I yell back, more puzzled than angry. "My sister's four years older than you. *She's* the oldest grandchild."

"Your sister isn't even your whole sister, you little twit. She didn't exist in our family until my Uncle Jack married your mother."

Sparks flash in Rita's round brown eyes. "I should know! I was at their stupid wedding." With that, she flings down her hand and upends the table, sending the deck flying. The cards skitter down my flat chest to the floor. A thought starts to slither toward the light: *My cousin just told me a secret. A big one. About my sister...my parents...*I'm trying to stay focused on the light, but my arms have gone numb. *It's important...I need to understand it...*the light is dimming, I'm sliding off my chair. I can't hold on...

The queen of hearts is still in my hand when I wake up. I haven't traveled through the looking glass. I'm flat on my back on the rug in my aunt and uncle's parlor. My cousin Rita is nowhere to be seen. Crouched beside me are my parents, one on each side. Mom is trembling, the whites of her eyes webbed with wiggly red tendrils, her freckled cheeks streaked with tears. She's pressing a damp washcloth to my forehead. "It's okay, sweetheart, it's okay," she's murmuring again and again. Dad has a Lucky Strike clenched between his mustache and lower lip, the smoke clouding my view of his pale blue eyes.

"I shouldn't have listened to you, Ceil. We should have told her years ago."

Mom flinches, smooths my hair, says she never meant for me to find out like this. Dad stubs out his cigarette in the Pernod ashtray on the coffee table and tells me to grab his neck.

"Come, *bubeleh,* you'll feel better when we get outside; you need fresh air, that's all." He slides his hands between my back and the floor, hoists me to my feet and steadies me against his chest. "We're going to take a nice long walk on the beach, the three of us, and Mommy and I will explain everything." My mother folds the damp washcloth and wipes her face with it, then leans on the coffee table to push herself upright. I watch her steady herself and head to the hall closet for our coats. Somehow, the two of them maneuver me into my loden green parka and, bracketing me like bookends, guide me out the door, across the narrow coastal road, and down some cracked concrete steps to the deserted beach. A brace of gulls squawk and screech beneath the slate-gray sky. It must have rained earlier; the sand is thick and moist, the surf thundering against the howl of the wind. My father's baritone cuts through the racket, imploring me to keep an open mind, not be judgmental, just listen to the facts, which, he admits, are complicated, but if I pay attention to the dates and names, everything will make sense. He leans forward so he can see Mom and she can hear him, and slingshots his question across my chest. "Should I start?" She nods. He begins. Though obviously not verbatim, here's my best recollection of what my parents told me that day.

<hr>

Each of them was married before. To other people. After some years, they became intensely unhappy with their partners, and they both got divorced. That was in the late 1920s when a failed marriage was as shameful as a felony conviction, doubly so for Jews, and, for Jewish women compounded by blame since our tradition considers the wife responsible for maintaining *shalom bayit*, peace in the home, and if there's friction, it's her fault. No one cared that Mom's first husband was a reprobate and a brute. They censured her because she was a divorcée and, adding pathos to the shanda, she had a fatherless child.

Dad is talking too fast and too fancy, as he does when he's explaining one of his legal cases or a tractate of Talmud. I can't follow what he's saying. The sand is sludge and the shoreline slants toward the sea and the berm is littered with shells and driftwood and the wind is stinging my face and I don't understand. Felony? Reprobate? Censure? Stigma? Pathos? Brute? And a child, whose fatherless child?

Mom is talking now, telling me how excruciating it was to be considered damaged goods. She knew what people were thinking: Jewish women are supposed to stay married; why couldn't she? The gossip was humiliating. She had a little girl. No man wants another man's reject, especially if she comes with a child sired by the other man. People wouldn't believe Mom was abused by the first husband. Everyone knows Jewish husbands don't hit their wives, at least that's what they say. And if her husband *did* beat her, she must have done something really bad to deserve it.

"Women shunned me, pointed at me in the street, whispered about me in shul. The only men interested in me were widowers who wanted someone to take care of their motherless children. Or old men who wanted me to take care of *them*."

"Who you callin' old?" Dad yells across my chest in a jocular tone. "I didn't want you to take care of me, honey. I wanted you for your body."

Mom doesn't crack a smile. Neither do I. How could he joke about this when she's so upset? Her tears have blown dry on her cheeks, but her mascara is smudged, her lips are cracked and parched. I feel like saying, *Never mind, Mommy, you don't have to explain.* Except I *want* her to explain.

"Who abused you?" I ask, finally.

"Joe. I just told you."

"Who's the little girl? Dad said you had a little girl."

My mother stops, turns, and cups my face in her gloved hands. "Your sister, sweetie. I'm talking about your sister. I'm telling you Betty is my daughter by my first husband, not by your daddy."

I grab her last line by the tail. My daddy isn't my sister's daddy. Betty and I have different fathers! And she never told me! Snapping my head away from Mom, I break into a run until I'm so far ahead that my parents have to jog to catch up with me. My mother trips on a sand mogul, lurches sideways, and grabs my father's arm to stop herself from falling. "Dammit!" she cries, wincing as she kicks off her black suede pumps and bends over to massage her stockinged feet. I know those shoes. She only wears them to weddings, bar mitzvahs, testimonial dinners, and dressy occasions when, as she always puts it, "Beauty requires women to tolerate torment." I hate that axiom; it makes me dread growing up. I also know that those pumps always inflame her bunions, pinch her pinky toes, rub holes in her nylons, and raise angry blisters on her heels. Poor Mom has been wearing these tormentors since early this morning.

She walked to services in them, then back to Esther and Ben's place. For the last half hour, she's been slogging down the beach in them. Now, shaking the sand off each foot, she puts the pumps back on, and hobbles forward, picking up the story where she left off. She tells me Joe was a dreadful man. Hot-headed. Mean as a snake. Lazy. Never made a living. Lost their nest egg in a shady land deal. When Ceil insisted that Joe go out and find a job, he bloodied her lip. After that, he'd hit her the minute she dared to complain about anything. She'd married him to get out of her parents' house. It was a terrible mistake, she said, but once Betty was born, she felt every child deserves to have a father, even a lousy one, and divorce was such a shanda in those days, so she stayed with him for Betty's sake. Until the day she couldn't. She remembers that day, grimacing. Joe was napping. Betty, who'd been toddling around the apartment, accidentally knocked over a standing lamp. It crashed to the floor and Joe woke up yelling, and Betty was terrified and wouldn't stop crying. "When he went for his belt," Mom says, trembling beside me, "I scooped her up and ran out with nothing but my purse and the clothes on our backs."

She stops, face crumpled, shoulders racked with sobs. Dad steps in front of me and wraps Mom in his arms. "That's all past," he says, stroking her back. The curly pelt of her Persian lamb coat flattens under the press of his palms. "You're fine, honey. Betty's fine. Nothing to cry about." He pulls me into his embrace. "We're all fine, right *ketsileh*?"

By now Dad ought to know how much Mom hates those nicknames. Usually, when he calls me ketsileh, which means little kitten in Yiddish, she reminds him that I'm not a cat, I'm a girl, an *American* girl, and he should speak to me in English. Today, she just extracts a lace-trimmed hankie from the pocket of her Persian lamb coat and wipes her cheeks for the tenth time.

"I'm *not* fine." I shake my head and jerk my body out of their circle. It's getting dark. The wind is fierce. I'm cold, I want us to turn back, but I won't be the first to say so.

"*Look* at me," Dad commands. I nail my gaze to his mustache. "What Joe did to your mother has nothing to do with you. All you need to know is Rita was dead wrong. Your sister *is* your real sister, understand? I adopted her. She's as much my daughter as you are."

Mom nods energetically. "And she adores you, sweetheart. You know that, don't you?"

Young Betty

How could she ask me such a question? Of course, I know that. I couldn't wish for a better sister than Betty. Even when she was a super-cool teenager and I was a royal pain, she never shooed me away or treated me like a burden. She taught me to tie my shoes, tell time, read, set my hair in pin curls, apply nail polish without getting it on my cuticles. She made me her flower girl and let me scatter rose petals ahead of her as she walked down the aisle. After she and Bernie got married and moved up to Peekskill, she told me I should call her collect whenever I feel lonely or scared—which is often. And no matter what's happening in her life, she always stops everything and lets me talk or cry and gives me good advice and stays on the phone with me until I feel better. When she comes to the city to buy stuff for her house, she takes me with her and asks my advice on wallpaper, fabric, and bathmats. She says I have good taste. She makes me feel smart. I used to think Betty was perfect, but she lied to me about herself and our parents. She didn't tell me what Mom and Dad were hiding. A sister can't be perfect if she keeps secrets from her sister.

"I don't mean to rake up all that misery," Mom offers. "I just think it's important for you to understand why I left Joe, what he was like, what he did—"

Dad, ever the clarifier, interrupts. "Joe's not the issue right now, honey. Let's just stick to the facts, okay?" He turns to me and runs through the chronology, promising it will help clarify the facts. The facts are my mother and father ended their first marriages in the late 1920s and married each other in 1937. He adopted her daughter Betty in '38. I was born in '39. The four of us moved to Jamaica in '41. And since they were starting a new life in a new place with new people, they took the move as an opportunity "to start a new life with a clean slate."

Mom tells me why the slate needed cleaning. "You know how grown-ups are. When they first meet another couple and they want to make friends, they ask each other questions like, 'How long have the two of you been married?' We decided that from then on we would tell people we got married in 1923 because that covered Betty being born in 1925, which made it plausible for her to be the daughter of both of us. Nobody had to know about our previous divorces. Nobody had to know that she wasn't Dad's biological child."

"One little lie—a backdated wedding—put an end to people giving Mom the fisheye," Dad observes, with a wry smile.

"Not just me, Jack. Nobody gives *either* of us the fisheye anymore. Nobody asks us embarrassing questions. Everyone sees the two of us as a normal couple with a normal past, a past like theirs. Friends, neighbors, my hairdresser, the rabbi, our bridge group, my canasta ladies, your organizations, they take us at face value. They accept us for what we seem to be." Mom is limping now. She must be in agony. I am too. The wind is stabbing through my parka and I'm ready to turn around, but we keep walking away from the bar mitzvah house, moving ahead, and Mom keeps talking, as if she's reassuring herself, not just me. "They accept us for who we *are*— Ceil and Jack and their two lovely daughters. A nice Jewish family. A normal American family."

"Period. The end," Dad declares. I fix my gaze on the blade of the horizon. A ghostly mist has rolled in from the sea. Mom's gimpy gait is more pronounced, but her face is almost radiant, the worry lines erased from her brow, the creases from her cheeks, as if truth-telling is a youth potion.

"Didn't anyone ever comment on the age difference between me and Betty? Isn't a fourteen-year spread between siblings pretty unusual?"

Mom says it is, but most people are polite; they don't ask such personal questions. When someone does, she tells them she and Dad had been trying to conceive all those years and had just about given up hope when God gave them their little Bunny. Mom tilts her head coyly and leans against me, forgetting I'm the one who needs propping up.

"Who else knows?" I ask. Dad answers. Facts are his domain.

"Betty knows, of course. The aunts and uncles on both sides, the whole family, actually, since they witnessed our courtship."

"My cousins?"

"The older ones, since they were at our wedding. But we swore them all to secrecy. Even though we didn't know a soul in Queens, we didn't want anyone to blow our cover unwittingly if they ever happened to meet one of our new friends. We drilled all the relatives—"Remember, we met each other when I was in college not when our girls were in boarding school, we got married in 1923 not 1937, and so on. We made them promise never to mention divorce, or Joe or my—" Dad stops abruptly and coughs into his hand.

Mom jumps in. "None of our relatives lived in Queens, so they were unlikely to run into any of our new friends. But just in case they happened to drop in when a friend was visiting, we didn't want a family member to commit a faux pas." That's a new word for my mother. She seems pleased with herself for using it in a sentence.

All of a sudden, an old memory drops anchor amidst the rolling waves: the night Uncle Ben committed a faux pas in front of me. And I didn't notice.

~~~

It's 1948. My parents' anniversary is coming up on February 12, their Silver Anniversary. I ask Dad how they plan to celebrate. "Not going to make a big deal of it," he says. "It's just a number." I'm only eight years old, but I've seen friends of theirs make a big deal about *their* twenty-fifth anniversaries, so I'm disappointed until, out of the blue, I get this brilliant idea. *I'll* make a big deal of it! Instead of giving them one of my handmade creations—a clay ashtray, matching lariats, woven potholders—I'll get a store-bought present, the set of tiny liqueur glasses that Mom had gushed over the last time we were at Gertz' department store shopping for a gift for one of her friends. I'd stolen a peek at its price tag and was silently thrilled to see that the set had been marked down from $14.98 to $9.99! I'll give Aunt Tillie ten singles from my allowance and an extra dollar to get the glasses gift-wrapped, and she'll buy the set for me and keep it in her house, and my parents will never know until the big night.

Ceil and Bunny in front of the two-family house on 167th Street in Jamaica. The entry to our house, 82-22, is on the left. Aunt Tillie, Uncle Ralph, and their three kids entered their house, 82-20, on the right.

On February 12, I tell Mom I'm going across the street to play with my friend, Sue. Instead, I sneak next door to Tillie's and she helps me make a chocolate layer cake with vanilla frosting and, since I'm bad at piping icing through a pastry bag, I use Nestle's chocolate bits to write a number two and a number five so big that you could read it across the room. Then I sneak back to my house, run up to my room, and put on a fancy blouse under my sweatshirt so Mom won't get suspicious. That afternoon, when Mom starts preparing supper, I tell her not to make dessert. I have something special planned. At eight o'clock, I shepherd my parents next door for the celebration. Aunt Tillie and Uncle Ralph are dressed very nicely, and there's a bottle of bubbly wine in a cooler on the dining room table. Aunt Rona and Uncle Ben have already arrived from the Bronx (one of the surprises I arranged by myself). I steal away into the kitchen and carry the cake into the dining room, and we all sing, "Happy Anniversary!" and everyone gathers around my cake. Uncle Ben looks at it quizzically. "Already it's their twenty-fifth? Gee, time flies."

"Ben! It's their Silver Anniversary! How could you forget?" Aunt Rona grabs her husband's hand and explodes with, what must have been fake, laughter. "He never remembers our anniversary," she says to Mom. "Why should he remember yours?"

"Oh, right! Of course!" Ben raises his glass to Mom and Dad. "Happy anniversary to the happy couple! Now please cut the cake. I'm salivating."

In 1948, that family scene played out without raising my suspicion. Why would I notice my uncle's near "faux pas," my aunt's quick cover-up? I was too focused on retrieving the gift-wrapped box from its hiding place in Tillie and Ralph's linen closet. Only now do I piece together what was going on. And, staring at the razor-sharp horizon, I do the math. On February 12, 1948, my parents had been married for eleven years.

I feel my face flush, hot with humiliation. "How could everyone *lie* to me?!" I shout into the wind. "At that little anniversary party I arranged at Tillie's house a couple of years ago, all of you must have been laughing behind my back. How could you lie to your *own* child?!"

"We did not lie!" my lawyer father protests. "We just hadn't gotten around to telling you the truth."

"I insisted we wait until you were old enough to understand why we did what we did. What it was like back then; the social pressure, the shame…" Mom's voice trails away; she looks pleadingly at my father.

"It was our secret," he says. "We didn't want to burden you with it. Keeping a confidence is a heavy responsibility. Kids don't mean to but they blurt things out; they can't help themselves."

I'm stunned to hear my father condemn children who tell the truth instead of parents who don't. The temperature has plummeted since we set off on our trek. Mom and Dad seem frozen in place, looking at one another, or trying not to. Neither seems ready to leave the beach. I'm shivering in my parka, but inside I'm on fire.

"You wanted to spare *me* the burden of your secret? I think you were only thinking of yourselves, protecting yourselves from being found out. Same with Betty. She went along with your lies because they made her feel better about herself."

As if to prove my claim, another vivid memory helicopters in from the past. Betty is still living at home. I'm in her room looking up a word in her dictionary, a habit she'd taught me when I turned five. But for the first time since I'd been consulting her dictionary, I notice the name scrawled on its flyleaf. "Who's Betty Holtzman?"

"Oh, that!" She waves me away with a chuckle. "I had a crush on a boy named Holtzman in junior high. It sounds silly now, but I was testing how my name would look if I married him." That makes sense to me at the time. By then I was six. Now, under a glowering sky, I ask, "What's his last name?"

"Who?"

"Your first husband."

Mom starts to answer but her voice sounds like mine does when I gargle. "It's Holtzman," she croaks. "Joe Holtzman."

"Wait a minute, ladies, I'm going to make this easy for Letty." As if mimicking Rumpelstiltskin, Dad stamps his feet on the ground until he's produced a patch of sand as big as a bed sheet and flat as an artist's canvas. "I'm going to draw a family tree so you can see where everyone fits in." He plucks a sharp stick from the detritus washed up on the shore and carves a long horizontal line with a big circle at each end. It looks like a barbell, not a tree, but he writes "Ceil" in one circle, "Joe" in the other, and pointing at it, says, "There's Mom's first husband." From the center of the

Ceil-Joe barbell, he drops a vertical line that ends in a circle he labels "Betty."

"Are you with me?" My father looks up, eyebrows arched; always teaching. I'm with him, following the stick as he extends a horizontal line from the opposite side of Ceil's circle and ends it with a new circle, this one marked Jack, then drops a line from the Ceil-Jack barbell and adds a circle marked "Letty." That's clear enough: Ceil married Joe and had Betty, then married Jack and had me. I assume he's done, but there's more, a new horizontal line from the opposite side of Dad's circle, a bar that leads a new circle that he fills with the name, "Paula." I follow the stick. A vertical line materializes at the center of the Jack-Paula barbell, then, lips firm and tight, teeth clenched, he draws a circle and stares at it, transfixed, before filling it with block letters, "R-E-N-A."

That's how my father tells me he has another daughter.

He says Rena was two years younger than Betty, but you'd never know it since Rena was so precocious. She and Betty met in boarding school and became fast friends.

I conjure the sadistic headmaster of Dotheboys Hall in *Nicholas Nickleby*. "You *both* sent your daughters to boarding school?" I exclaim in disbelief. "How horrible!"

"There was *nothing* horrible about it," Mom says, emphatically. "It was the best Jewish boarding school in the East. Lucky for me, they took three-year-olds."

Of all the revelations hurtling at me today, that's the most shocking. How could this woman, who rarely lets me out of her sight at age twelve, have sent my sister miles away from home when she was *three!* I'm reeling, but my mother, increasingly defensive, says the wealthiest Jewish families sent their daughters to that school. Why shouldn't her little girl go there? Grandma and Grandpa were in no position to look after Betty all day, and Mom didn't want them to. Her parents are good people, but they had three or four kids still living at home. Besides, what could Betty learn from them? They can barely speak English. They don't listen to music. They don't read books, just Yiddish newspapers—the *Forvertz, Der Tog*. They put *schmaltz* on everything. Why would she expose her daughter to their Old World ways when Ceil could live with Nathan and Jenny, save her earnings, and pay her daughter's tuition to a wonderful school that turns little Jewish girls into refined young ladies.

"Your sister loved boarding school," Mom says with a half-smile. "She'll tell you, just ask her."

"You bet I will," I mutter under my breath.

"Rena loved it, too. You can ask her...someday." Dad's voice, already not his own but tremulous and raspy, suddenly goes quiet. The wind is salted with sand; is that why his eyes are teary?

I study the barbells, the circles, names I've never heard before of people I never knew existed—Joe, Paula, Rena—when a thought lands with the force of a fist: if Rena is my father's daughter, and Betty is my mother's daughter, *both* of them are my half-sisters. The difference is, I've grown up with Betty, but cousin Rita was right: my sister isn't my full sister. All I have is half-sisters, and when it comes to sisters, two halves don't make a whole. Especially when I never even knew Rena existed. What happened to her? Did Dad reject her? Did she leave? Is she dead? I point a toe at Rena's circle in the sand. "Where is she?"

"I wish I knew." Dad stabs his stick into Paula's circle. "She cut off my visitation rights when Rena was fourteen. I haven't seen my daughter since. I can hardly remember what she..." Nearly as stunning as today's revelations—the discovery that my parents were both divorced before they met, and got married two years before I was born, not two years before Betty was born, and my sister is really my half-sister, and I have a secret sister somewhere out there in the world—is the sight of my fiercely proud, stubbornly unemotional father, weeping. Usually steel-spined, impeccably groomed, his straight brown hair tamed by Brylcreem and a side part, right now, crouched over his diagram, the hem of his overcoat scalloped with muck, his brown hair wildly disheveled, he looks more like a rheumy-eyed vagrant than like Clark Gable, the movie star he's been mistaken for more than once (mostly because both share protruding ears and a trim mustache).

Mom rescues him again, deflecting me from the shock of his tears. "I know you have no memory of her, but once Dad and I got married, Rena used to spend time with us, a couple of weekends a month, an overnight during the week, school vacation days. She was as crazy about you as your sister Betty was. And no wonder. You were such an adorable baby, with a thatch of silky dark hair, always smiling and agreeable. I'd have to wrestle you away from Rena so you could take your naps. Then one day, as Dad said, Paula suddenly put a stop to her visits and threatened to hurt her if Jack tried to see her again. It was awful. He had to give her up."

He gave up his little girl and left her with a crazy lady!? That's even worse than Mom putting hers in a boarding school. Who *are* these people? "How could he abandon his own daughter? How could he just walk away?"

Mom says he did not *just* walk away. He fought for Rena in court, but most judges favored the woman in divorce cases, at least in the 1920s, so Paula was awarded full custody and Dad only got visitation rights.

He cracks his writing stick across a raised thigh and flings both pieces into the sea. I thought they would sink but they float. All three of us watch them bob in the waves while my father struggles to regain his composure and resume the narrative. He tells me Rena's visitations were going well until I came along and she told Paula she wanted to spend more time with Betty and me. That's what sent Paula into a jealous rage. She accused Jack of alienating their daughter's affections and swore she would rather see Rena dead than living with us, and if he ever tried to see her again, Paula said she would kill her.

Dad combs his fingers through his hair a few times. He had good reason to believe her, he tells me, largely because Rena once called him in tears complaining that Paula had stomped on her glasses and broken them when she made the mistake of saying she liked Ceil's cooking. Another time, Paula had pushed her halfway out the window five flights above the street and said she would push Rena all the way out if she didn't stop talking about Jack and

Ceil or Betty and me. Dad says after that, Rena stopped coming and he was afraid to contact her or call the police or social services on the chance that her mother might flip out and harm her before the cops got there. "I had to give her up to keep her safe."

To me, that sounds completely ridiculous. He's a lawyer, for God's sake! Always bragging about cases he won against all odds. How could he not win custody of his own daughter and save her from that violent woman? Why couldn't he convince a judge that his ex-wife was an unfit mother? Or is *this* story yet another one of their lies? The diagram on the flat-packed sand contains basic facts, my father's specialty. Ceil and Joe had Betty; Paula and Jack had Rena; Ceil and Jack had me. We are three daughters, three circles, on the same plane. Yet my circle is the largest and most central, as if I'm the fruition of some complex genetic experiment, the culmination of each of my parents' previously imperfect attempts to create a family. So why do I feel like an orphan? Because if Betty's father could leave her, and Rena's father could trade in Paula for Ceil, and Rena for Betty, couldn't he leave me?

"I want to go back to the house. I'm cold." Without waiting for them to respond, I tighten the cords on the hood of my parka, shove my hands in my pockets, and start walking in the opposite direction.

"Me, too, sweetie," Mom says. "And my feet are killing me."

Dad shakes the gritty sand off his topcoat, and they both turn and follow me. "I hope the bar mitzvah boy didn't eat up all the lox," he says. "I'm hungry."

In 1808, Sir Walter Scott wrote, "O, what a tangled web we weave, when first we practice to deceive." A century and a half later, Ogden Nash, who must have been eavesdropping on my child-hood, riffed on that famous couplet, "Oh, what a tangled web parents weave when they think that their children are naïve." Trouble is, I was naive; spectacularly, abysmally so. I'd never questioned what my parents said or did. I'd lived under their roof for more than a decade but missed all the clues hidden in plain sight. Never noticed there were no pictures of my father with my sister when she was a baby or small child, only after she was a young adolescent. Never doubted my mother when she said the girl with the braids standing next to Betty in the photo was "a distant cousin." Kids accept the reality they're born into, and why shouldn't they? Trust in their parents is supposed to be children's birthright.

When I woke up this morning, had you asked me to describe myself, I would have said I was a daughter, sister, and granddaughter happily embedded in a warm-hearted, admirable, honorable family; the niece by blood of twelve adoring uncles and aunts, twenty-four closely bonded cousins, and assorted relatives by marriage, none of whom I imagined to be remotely capable of suborning perjury. Yet I'd just learned that those same people were collaborators in an elaborate set of falsehoods about my parents' prior lives and had hidden the existence of my secret sister. After their tortured confessions on the beach, I saw myself as a fool and a dupe. I saw my parents and relatives as perpetrators of every conceivable colloquial metaphor for double-dealing and subterfuge. They'd pulled the wool over my eyes. Sold me a bill of goods. Put one over on me. Pulled a fast one. Built me a Potemkin village. Mom and Dad were supposed to be good God-fearing Jews. How could they be so devious? Betty was my closest confidante. How could she have lied to my face? And how could everyone else in the family have been in on it without slipping up on the charade?

∼⚭∼

Our family's social hub was my childhood synagogue, the Jamaica Jewish Center, a large building on Goethals Avenue and 87th Road, now modernized, expanded, and repurposed as the Queens Gateway to Health Sciences Secondary School. Back in the day, the JJC was among the most vibrant Jewish institutions in New York. It's where we attended services, holiday celebrations, weddings, and funerals. The building housed a beautiful, serene sanctuary but also a swimming pool and a bowling alley, a grand ballroom, library, offices, conference rooms, and a Hebrew School that served hundreds of kids from pre-K through high school. The JJC is where I went to after-school religious classes, got confirmed, became a bat mitzvah, and graduated from Hebrew High School. It's where meetings were held by Temple Sisterhood, Hadassah, WIZO, Pioneer Women, and National Council of Jewish Women. It's where my mother became a dedicated (i.e., selfless) volunteer, while my father, the consummate "macher" (big shot), became active in, and eventually assumed leadership of, virtually every Jewish communal organization in the borough of Queens.

His crowning glory was his multiterm presidency of the Jamaica Jewish Center, which, in 1949, hosted a gala testimonial dinner to honor his devoted service. The journal they produced for that event describes his background at some length and includes this sentence: "While Jack Cottin was still at college, he met the charming Cyral Halpern, affectionately known as Ceil." Today, this would be called fake news. Ceil and Jack did not meet when he was in college. They met nearly twenty years later at the boarding school where each of them had separately enrolled their respective daughters. It took some doing, but they'd successfully reinvented themselves into a long-married couple with a placid past. Imagine how triumphant they must have felt sitting side by side on the dais at that gala, elbowing each other under the table as the emcee read the lie Jack had planted years before in his biography. Picture them at home later that night, congratulating themselves on every step of their brilliantly executed masquerade. In the nine years since they'd migrated from the Bronx to Queens, Jack Cottin and his charming wife, Ceil, had been transmuted into prominent members of their Jewish community, unsullied by gossip or rumor, the shame of their failed first marriages expunged along with the disgrace of her twelve years as a divorcée and his child abandonment; their secret safe, as it would remain for the rest of their lives.

During the 1970s and '80s—when I was busy co-founding *Ms.* magazine, feminist organizations, women's foundations, Black-Jewish dialogues, Torah study groups, and Palestinian-Jewish dialogues—I used to fantasize about starting a group for people who'd been lied to by those they'd trusted. Anonymous support groups exist for alcoholics, drug addicts, overeaters, gamblers, and shopaholics; why not a Dupes Anonymous for children of deceit? I think we should be able to connect with one another anywhere in the world, meet in church basements, nurse weak coffee in Styrofoam cups, and help each other understand why, since being lied to as children, we always seem to feel, on some primal level, that we're on shaky ground.

Learning the truth about my family on the beach in Winthrop reordered my world. Betrayal became my burden, gullibility my shame. If those closest to me could lie without conscience or consequence, then anyone could misrepresent anything, and everything was up for grabs. I'm not saying I became pathologically suspicious, just inclined toward doubt. I ask a lot of questions—too many for some people's comfort—so many that my grown children used to accuse me of "interrogating" their friends. A psychologist friend once overheard my conversation with a new acquaintance and likened it to "an intake interview." If that's an insult, I'll cotton to it rather than be blindsided ever again.

CHAPTER 9

PAPERING OVER MARITAL MISERY

Hillary Clinton famously said, "Every marriage is a mystery to me, even the one I'm in." The mystery of my parents' marriage will never be solved to my complete satisfaction, but one thing is crystal clear: spousal disenchantment was an occupational hazard for the Halpern women. The saga of their marital misery opens with Grandma Jenny, who escaped from the bridal chamber to marry her passionate suitor, only to be betrayed and humiliated by his decades-long affair with another woman. Jenny's four daughters fared little better. Ceil's infatuation with Jack curdled under the hot sun of his outsized ego. Tillie's storybook romance with Ralph—compelling enough for them to have married in secret and then lived apart for two years—went sour somewhere along the way. Their vivacious sister, Sadye, married Herman, a refugee who spoke English with a thick Yiddish accent that made her ashamed to be seen with him. Rona, the youngest, raven-haired and glamorous, appeared to have found an ideal match in Ben, a handsome artist and jewelry designer, until you witnessed one of their fiery flare-ups around money. Because we spent much less time with my father's family—and his sisters, Dottie and Esther, didn't confide in my mother the way her own sisters did—I can't testify reliably to the conjugal dynamics of the couples on my Cottin side. However,

I do remember lots of carping and bickering between my Aunt Dottie and Uncle Al Schwartz whenever we ate at their table, and my Sargon cousins have described their parents, Esther and Ben, as fundamentally incompatible and their relationship as rocky.

Celebrating the Darvies' anniversary, 1944. Standing on left: Dottie and Al Schwartz, Tillie and Ralph Kahn, Herman Chester. Seated on left: Rona Darvie, Pris Darvie, Nathan Halpern, Faith Chester, Marvin Chester. Standing on right (left to right): unidentified man, Bertha and Lou Halpern, Ceil and Jack Cottin. Seated on right: unidentified woman, Judy Kahn, Betty Cottin, Joan Halpern, Jenny Halpern, Ben Darvie.

Today, I'm listening to Tillie's earliest memories, captured on a cassette tape when she was in her eighties in an interview conducted by her grown children. She said Jenny and Nathan, fearing a pogrom and anticipating the forced conscription of their sons, realized there was no future for them in Pylypets; they decided to build a new life in Di Goldene Medine, the Golden Land. Nathan sailed for New York on June 27, 1907, intending to earn enough money to bring the rest of his family over as soon as possible. Jenny and their four young children stayed behind in "a little house across from a church and near a small bridge over a stream."

At that point on the tape, Tillie fluidly recites how old she and her siblings were when, in 1909, they finally set off with their mother to join Nathan in America.

Ceil was eight, I was six, Louis, four, and baby Sadye, full of life and full of love, was two. We traveled on a big wooden sleigh with no brakes, pulled by a pair of horses who went galloping through the narrow passes and down the Carpathian Mountains. I've been afraid of mountains all my life and that's why. For two weeks, we sailed across the ocean with hundreds of other people in the bottom of a huge ship. Mama, being strictly kosher, had brought along pickled herring, boiled potatoes, and kuchel, those flakey bow tie cookies we all loved. Everyone was throwing up except me. I ate everything with no problem. When we landed at Ellis Island, a man met us with oranges and bananas. I'd never seen those fruits before. I thought they were wonderful. It took me a while to realize that the man was my father.

On the tape, Tillie describes the reunion between her mother and father as "far from cheerful." Jenny quickly learned that Nathan had been "squandering money on other women and having a high old time." What's more, he hadn't paid for their voyage; it was Jenny's brother, Will, then a successful New York garment manufacturer, who sent her the steamship tickets once it became clear, after two years of silence, that Nathan was in no hurry for his wife and kids to join him. As if that weren't enough of a shanda, the day she arrived, Nathan informed her that he wanted a divorce. With four children under the age of eight, no English, no education, no skills, no friends, not even the first idea about how to use the subway, Jenny was not just devastated but completely helpless. Once again, she turned to her brother Will who managed to strong-arm Nathan into a secret arrangement that saved face for the family. With zero leverage, Jenny agreed. Anything was better than a shanda. She did it for her children.

Ceil (nee Sarah) in Pylypets, a shtetl in Hungary, age three, circa 1904

"It was an arrangement of convenience that allowed Pop to do whatever he wanted outside the house as long as he continued to live with us and support us financially," Tillie's voice explained. "Momma told me about it when I was eighteen. From the outside, their marriage looked normal. At home, Pop used to say hurtful things that upset her so much she would go into the bathroom and cry. He kept company with his lady friend whenever the spirit moved him. One Saturday night when Ralph and I were dating, we ran into Pop and his girlfriend in Coney Island, and I must admit I could see the attraction. She was so different from my mother, happy and merry where Momma was quiet and serious. It never crossed my mind to snitch on Pop. Knowing we met his girlfriend, it would have hurt Momma more."

Despite Nathan's brash betrayal, Jenny had three more children with him—Rona, Herbert, and Milton (who prided themselves on being "born in America"). Tillie's vivid memories of life on the Lower East Side unspooled on the tape with crystalline clarity: "I went to P.S. 15. We lived at 313 East 4th Street until I was in the fifth grade when we moved to a cold-water flat at 246 East 4th Street. Mama rented out a couple of rooms to boarders, single men who came from the Old Country. She did all the cooking and cleaning for us and the boarders and got so tired that she sometimes neglected us children. Ceil and I slept together in a narrow bed near a window that opened on an air shaft. There was only one toilet for each floor so I couldn't blame the boys who lived upstairs for urinating down the shaft. Many times, I woke up wet. I also remember the roaches. I graduated from eighth grade in 1919 and got a job in a factory where I earned six dollars a week for six twelve-hour days clipping loose threads off coats and dresses."

Listening to my aunt's reminiscences brought back the decade of my early childhood when my parents and I lived in Jamaica at 82-22 167th Street, and Tillie and Ralph and their kids lived, separated by a plasterboard wall, at 82-20. A minute ago, I wrote that Tillie and Ralph's marriage had "soured," yet I can't recall witnessing a single moment of dissension between them. Though I do remember what happened at the party Tillie gave Ralph on his eightieth birthday. "It was a terrific gathering," I wrote to Betty who was living in Yugoslavia that year. "Lots of long-lost cousins and great enthusiasm. The classic moment was when Tillie called everyone to order and read a statement that began, 'To my dear husband on his 80th birthday,' after which she told anecdotes about her children and grandchildren but never said another word about Ralph."

I asked Tillie's daughter, Judy, now in her nineties and the oldest living member of my generation of cousins, if she saw tension in her parents' marriage. She laughed. "You could cut it with a knife.

They fought all the time, sometimes explosively. I can't believe you never heard them through the wall. Maybe your parents out shouted them." (That was possible.) "Once I was so scared, I ran next door and made your father come over and calm them down. Momma told me she would have left Pop if she had a high school degree and some job skills, but she had neither." With no leverage and no options, Aunt Tillie, like her mother, Jenny, stayed married unhappily ever after.

The Halpern women put on a cheerful facade in front of their friends but confided their marital grievances to one another on a regular basis. Mom also gleaned monthly counsel from "Can This Marriage Be Saved," the advice column that ran for years in *The Ladies' Home Journal*. Though it seldom addressed problems that mirrored her complaints, the case histories it described reassured her that she wasn't the only unhappy wife in her adopted country. Knowing that "real" Americans were also having domestic troubles normalized her misery and brought a kind of comfort. Jack was her second bet on wedded bliss. If *this* marriage couldn't be saved, the only off-ramp on the road ahead would take her over a cliff and into the abyss of the shanda.

My parents' problems could have been predicted based on their roles in their families of origin: Jack, the cherished first-born son in a household ruled by a stern Jewish patriarch (Max) who lorded it over his docile, compliant wife (Yetta), had no model of a caring husband and no patience for the needs of a woman with high expectations of her own. Meanwhile Ceil—the eldest child in a family where privation forced her to sacrifice her own aspirations, and shame made her desperate for respectability—grew up determined to create a life of refinement and mold her mate to fit her dreams. A union of two people with such different histories and fundamental incompatibilities was destined to fail. Had my mother found herself in such an unsatisfying marriage in the twenty-first century, I like to think she would have bailed out after a year. There would have been recriminations. Regret. Pain. But no shame.

CHAPTER 10

"JUST PUT A PILLOW OVER YOUR HEAD AND TURN UP THE RADIO"

Almost every night of my childhood, my parents had a fight after supper. It would start when Dad got up from the table and said he had to go to a meeting, which signaled Mom to ask why he had to be a big organizational macher before he could feel important—before he could feel like a man. An audience, a group to preside over or lecture to, a panel discussion, conversations to moderate about serious matters, like the future of Zionism, or the best way to cut the synagogue's budgets, those were what animated him. Mom and I never seemed to be enough.

The truth is, Ceil needed more too. She had hated being a divorcée but being married wasn't enough, she wanted to be *happily* married, and happiness was togetherness with a man whose first priority was his wife and child, a family man who relished exchanging intimacies with his wife, lingering over coffee after supper, leisurely walks, family outings on weekends. But that wasn't the life Mom was living because that wasn't the man she married.

Jack in his Jewish War Veterans uniform, with me, "Bunny" circa 1944

They met in their thirties, already set in their ways. She was a homebody. He thrived on outside activities and many organizational affiliations. Sitting on the porch with him, listening to classical music on the radio was her idea of a perfect evening. He needed a crowd, applause, recognition from his peers. The Jewish War Veterans claimed the lion's share of his time, especially during the years when he served as the JWV's county commander, first of the Bronx post, then after we moved to Jamaica, of the post in Queens. Two of his dark-blue garrison caps, embroidered with his title, turned up in that lower shelf in my study, along with a photograph of Dad and me posing on the small patch of lawn in front of our house, he in his full dress JWV uniform, me, age four or five, in a white dress, white shoes, and socks, with white ribbons entwined in the hair Mom had braided at the top of my head.

The Queens chapters of the Jewish National Fund, Israel Bonds, United Jewish Appeal, B'nai B'rith, the American Jewish Congress, the Zionist Organization of America (no resemblance to the right-wing incarnations of the AJC and ZOA today) were my father's main preoccupations, as attested to by dozens of clippings, bulletins, and flyers I found in the cabinet that identify him as those organizations' president or chairman. Anti-Semitism, raising money for Jewish settlement in Palestine, and building support for Jewish nationhood were the issues that fueled his activism during the '40s and '50s. Once Israel became a State in 1948, he fund-raised to make the desert bloom, equip the fledgling Israeli army with weapons, and secure US aid and congressional support for the fledgling nation. However, it was the Jamaica Jewish Center he served the longest and most dutifully, a statement well documented in the aforementioned journal from the 1949 dinner dance honoring his "sheer devotion to the JJC," which provides contemporaneous proof that Mom's complaints about his absences were not exaggerated.

> *Jack Cottin has been a working president—not just a "show window" president (even though he is good to look at). Come down to the Center any night and you will find him counseling with some committee, straightening out an administrative problem, planning the next big Center function, resolving a conflict, encouraging a project manager, wrestling with the budget—and everywhere harmonizing a diversity of temperaments.*

The writer of that paragraph, not being privy to my parents' suppertime disputes, goes on to applaud Mom for sharing her husband with the synagogue community and makes offhand note of her talents: "Kindly, gentle-hearted and a devoted helpmate, Ceil is Jack's right hand. We owe a great deal to her, not only for sparing so much of him for our Center's work, but for her own time and effort in many Center projects. Besides being a good homemaker and hostess, she makes time to do oil painting as a hobby. And the Cottin home is carried on in the finest Jewish tradition." The journal does not thank me for sharing my father with an institution and getting the short end of the stick. On an average weekday, I got a glimpse of Dad at breakfast while he read the *Herald Tribune*, a kiss when he left for the office, a hug when he came home at seven, a few questions at the supper table about my day at school, then a view of his back as he hurried out the door to a meeting.

Should you suspect that I'm going overboard on the father-deprivation front, here are my *only* memories of us spending any protracted time together. They're easy to enumerate because there are so few of them, and they live in my mind because they were special. There was one outing to Coney Island where we had a ride on the huge Ferris wheel and a Nathan's hot dog with sauerkraut. Two outings to Jahn's, an ice cream parlor in Jackson Heights that had stained glass chandeliers (imitation Tiffany's), a mechanical player piano that you could sing along with, and a fabulous sundae called The Kitchen Sink. My most unforgettable memory dates back to the weekend of the 1944 Jewish War Veterans national convention, which was held at Grossinger's Hotel in the Catskills. At the Saturday night dinner, Dad, then the Queens County commander of JWV, was seated on the dais along with other officers from around the country, all of them in full regalia, and I was seated on my father's lap. A shriveled old man hobbling on a cane took the chair beside us. I thought he looked like a rag doll so lost was he in his dark-blue jacket and light-blue pants, a uniform unlike everyone else's.

"Lucky us," my father said, brightly. "Our seatmate is the last living Jewish veteran of the Civil War!" I had no idea what war the Civil War was, but Dad looked at the ancient soldier with such gentle awe that I absorbed his wonderment. "Sir," he said, "I'd like to introduce you to my daughter Bunny."

The man's grip was bony but firm. "Honored to meet you, young lady," he said, pumping my arm. "And how old might you be?" I told him I was five. "Well now," he replied, smiling, "that makes you ninety-three years younger than I am. You have a long life ahead of you, Bunny. But I bet you'll never forget that you just shook the hand that shook the hand of Abraham Lincoln." I never have.

Other experiences with my father were not as vividly memorable, yet they all felt special. He taught me to ride a two-wheeler without starting me off on training wheels. He taught me the crawl, backstroke, butterfly stroke, and swan dive in one afternoon at Lake Mohegan. But I don't remember us bike-riding or swimming together. He had no time for such frivolities. The pleasure was in the pedagogy, the reward in the result.

In February 1952, I became one of the first girls in Conservative Judaism to have a bat mitzvah. Back then, girls read from the haftarah (selections from Nevi'im, the book of Prophets) not the Torah (the Five Books of Moses). My haftarah portion was the story of the prophet, Deborah, and my father, who was my bat mitzvah tutor, made clear from the start that there would be no shortcuts for me, no memorization, no phonetics. He was going to teach me the way he taught bar mitzvah boys years ago. I would learn cantillation, the system of melodic tropes with which the words of the sacred text are chanted, each sound denoted by a tiny symbol above or below the Hebrew word. And only after I'd gotten that entire alphabet under my belt would I learn to chant my assigned text. To appreciate the integrity and thoroughness of his method, imagine having to translate *Les Misérables* from the French and learn the rudiments of music theory before you could sing "Frère Jacques." Because he was such a rigorous taskmaster, a compliment from my crusty father lifted my self-esteem like nothing else. Studying my portion under his rigorous tutelage made me feel I was more than his pupil, or his daughter; I was his substitute son.

Some of his teaching methods bordered on bonkers, for instance, the way he taught me to drive. At the time, New York State law barred anyone under sixteen from operating a vehicle. Over sixteen, you could drive legally if you had a learner's permit and were supervised by a licensed driver sitting in the passenger seat. However, with these conditions: you couldn't drive at all within the five boroughs of New York City, in Nassau and Suffolk Counties, on bridges, through major tunnels, and on five highways in Westchester County. I was fascinated by cars and desperate to drive, so one weekend while we were upstate in Phoenicia, visiting the country house belonging to my mother's sister and brother-in-law, Rona and Ben Darvie, Dad put me behind the wheel of our Dodge sedan. In no time at all, I'd mastered its three-speed manual transmission, depressing the clutch and shifting gears like a seasoned pro. The two of us were tooling along the dirt roads, chatting away as casually as if I'd been chauffeuring him for years, when he shrieked, "*Bear ahead! Bear! BEAR!!*" I slammed on the brakes. I looked around for the bear. There was no bear. Dad said he was just testing my reflexes.

Most of my driving lessons took place inside the forbidden boundaries of the five boroughs. He taught me to parallel park on the street in front of our house in Queens (illegal). He had me ferry us on the Van Wyck Expressway (illegal) to Idlewild Airport (now JFK), where we watched a number of planes take off and land (still a futuristic sight in the early '50s). I didn't have a learner's permit. He was a lawyer but had no use for laws (secular or Jewish) that made no sense to him. "The best way to learn to drive in city traffic is to practice in Times Square," he said, as I made a left onto Broadway. I was fourteen.

Those scenes are frozen in my memory like chunks of fruit suspended in a Jell-O mold. I attribute that to Mom asking me so many questions when Dad and I came home from one of those outings: where did we go, what did we do, see, eat, buy? I thought she was curious about what she'd missed. Thinking about it now, I suspect she wanted him to hear my excitement fresh from the experience in the hope that it would make him want to spend more time with me. Her strategy had no effect on him, but it did magnify and reify those experiences for me. Recounting them to her fixed them in my memory. After she died and before I left for college, I lived alone with Dad for five months in the house on Wareham Place. That's when his fathering deficits became apparent. I didn't fault him for not knowing how to cook or sew or clean. I was my mother's daughter; I could handle all of that. What he didn't know was how to simply *be* with me, on an ordinary day, in an unremarkable place. Those five months exposed him as all headline, no text.

Mom was text and context. The command post of my childhood, she devoted nearly all of her waking hours to my care, amusement, and well-being. Yet, it shames me to admit, I have few Jell-O mold memories of what she and I did together. Hers was an everyday presence, and Mom-time was just life. Plumbing my past, what rise to the surface are quotidian images of her braiding my hair for school, giving me bubble baths, reading to me before bedtime—*Little Women, The Five Little Peppers*, Charles and Mary Lamb's *Tales from Shakespeare*, Robert Louis Stevenson's *Kidnapped, Treasure Island*, and "A Child's Garden of Verses." She sang me to sleep with "Old Lady Moon," and "Ofyn Pripitchik," the Yiddish lullaby whose opening bars still have the power to bring me to tears. She taught me how to separate the yolk from the white of an egg with my hands; wrap Scotch Tape over my knuckles with the sticky side out and use it as a lint brush; pluck feathers off a chicken with an eyebrow tweezer. When I was sick in bed, which was often, the two of us listened to her favorite radio soap operas—*Backstage Wife, Our Gal Sunday, Stella Dallas, The Romance of Helen Trent*—and Mom would explain the plot points that went over my head. We made Calderesque circuses, spiny sculptures of giraffes, lion tamers, and tightrope walkers, out of the thin wires that used to be twisted around the cardboard cap of every milk bottle. When I got better, we smooshed the circus figures into ball and contributed them, along with used tin foil and razor blades, the silver paper from chewing gum wrappers, and big balls of rubber bands, to the war effort. But I see now that the dailiness of her constant, unsung mothering was eclipsed by the fanfare of Dad helicoptering in, now and then, lights flashing, propellers whirring, to give me a good time. She kept me alive and growing. He flew me into the clouds for a few hours of exhilaration, bought me a sundae called The Kitchen Sink, and reaped all the glory.

What I remember most about my childhood, sad to say, is the sound of my parents fighting. How it felt to listen to his rising fury and her sobbing supplications, and sense my own escalating fears, which often sent me to the phone to call my sister and beg her to come home and make them stop. I knew it was unfair to ask her to drop everything, leave her husband and children, and drive fifty miles from Peekskill to Jamaica every time Mom and Dad had a scary argument, but I also knew I could count on her to sympathize with my misery, calm me down, and dole out the right advice. "Don't get between them, sweetie; it'll only upset Mommy more." "Don't worry, Daddy would never hit Mommy." "Don't be silly, Mommy would never leave Daddy." "Just stay in your room. Close the door. Put a pillow over your head and turn up your radio."

My pillow couldn't stifle their voices any more than I could stop myself from eavesdropping. Our first house in Jamaica had thin walls, three rooms downstairs, three rooms up, with an open stairway in between. When they fought in the living room, I listened at the top of the stairs. When they fought in their bedroom, every word traveled through my bedroom wall. When he roared out of the house, I worried that he might never return, or if he did, she might not let him in. Their arguments colored the canvas of my childhood with a dark dread that they might break up and everything in my life would disintegrate. Long before I knew about their previous marriages or met anyone whose parents were divorced, I had nightmares about mine splitting up. Betty promised me they wouldn't, and they never did, so it took my breath away when I found this letter that peels back the curtain to the moment when Ceil *did* end their relationship and Jack responded the next day with this letter:

December 26, 1935

Darling Honey,

I had a premonition that you were going to leave me, but I refused to let myself think of it. Our friendship was too wonderful to be spoiled by those thoughts. Now that it has happened, I promise you, dear, that I won't make it any harder for you than it is. I'm trying to be philosophical and I'm not even going to state in this letter how I feel about it, this one thing only: I sincerely hope that what you have done will bring you more happiness than I could have given you. And if I can do anything in the future to contribute to your well-being, suffice it to say, I'll be ready and willing.

Thoughts, thoughts, thoughts! They're chasing each other through my mind. I won't write them here for fear that reading them may cause you additional hurt, and that I don't want to do. Physical pain I caused you through carelessness. I hope you believe I'm grievously sorry for that. Additional heartache I have no desire to cause you.

My Darling, your kisses will never be forgotten nor will you. No one can take from me these last two years. The thought that during that time, you were mine will always be enough to bring joy to my heart even at the most painful times.

Darling, of all the good wishes for the New Year that you will no doubt receive, none can be more sincere and fervent than mine. May God bless you and guard you and give you all the good things on earth and above all, supreme happiness permanently and constantly.

Yours,
Jack

P.S. I hope the enclosed will cover your financial loss.

The dateline above establishes that she left Jack in 1935, two years after they met and more than a year *before* they got married. The man who wrote that letter was someone I never knew—apologetic, open, vulnerable. I can't imagine what he did that caused her "physical pain." Equally opaque is his postscript about her "financial loss." But his behavior must have been bad enough to make her leave him after two years' investment in the relationship. I'll never know what made her take him back. Maybe his letter did the trick. Maybe, being thirty-four, divorced with a child, she thought Jack might be her last best chance. The point is, dear, reader, she knew what she was getting into when, fourteen months after she left him, she married him.

I thought the breakup of 1935 was shocking until another of my father's letters floated to the top of the pile. This one dated a week after my bat mitzvah is addressed to me, but I have no recollection of ever receiving it.

> *February 15, 1952*
>
> *Letty Darling:*
>
> *Last night you said something which caused me great concern. I refer to your remark to Mommy that you'll hate her forever if she leaves me.*
>
> *Even if she does leave our marriage, you must understand that she has no desire to hurt you, she just feels that she can't go on as things are, that our fighting will cause her permanent harm, and that she'll be happier being apart from me. You can't argue with feelings! If she does leave, your place is with her. You are her daughter and daughters are closer to their mothers than they are to their fathers. That's natural.*
>
> *I will be very sorry and sad if Mother leaves me. I love her, even though she may not think so. However, since she feels as she does, I don't know what I can do except to agree to whatever she decides.*

I think you understood that the millions of wrongs of which she accuses me took place when we were angry with each other, not in a vacuum. I'm writing this letter to you because Mommy didn't let you talk to me last night before you went to bed, although you wanted to. I expect she will do everything she can to prevent another conversation between us.

Whatever happens, remember, Sugar, that Mommy loves you and I'm sure you love her. I love you too (you know it, don't you?) and always will—even after I'm dead.

Daddy

I was not a little girl in February 1952. I was almost thirteen. Yet, there's a hole in my head where that scorching memory should be, a willful amnesia induced, perhaps, by the trauma of having witnessed the fight that finally sent my mother over the edge. It must have been a doozy, and the only way to survive it was to repress it, which, obviously, she did, as did I. And, just as she had done fifteen years before, she gave him a pass for whatever he did that enraged her in 1952.

Her reasons for *not* leaving him—both times, and maybe other times that were never recorded in writing—died with her. But, today, nearly seventy years later, I find Dad's letter so infuriating that I feel compelled to deconstruct it.

My rash statement during their argument the previous night—that I would hate my mother forever if she left him—appears to be the impetus for his writing to me. I see it as his opening gambit to get me to intervene and change her mind. He begins with a loyal defense of Mom ("she has no desire to hurt you"), and asserts his rationality and fairness ("can't argue with feelings!") Then, wily in its subtlety, comes his coup de grâce: he lets me know that *my* fate is in the balance. If Mom holds to her decision, she'll take me with her because "daughters are closer to their mothers than they are to their fathers." And, though he expects that "she'll do everything she can to prevent another conversation between us" (shades of crazy Paula preventing him from communicating with Rena), he will abide by "whatever she decides" (shades of his bowing to the judge's decision to grant Paula full custody). The subliminal message, the message I can't possibly miss, is that he won't fight for me, so if I let Mom leave him, I'll lose him. After that bone-chilling possibility, comes the closer: flattery. I may be a kid but I'm the one who understands that his "millions of wrongs" weren't wrongs, just Mom's accusations, and anyway, she's equally at fault because it "didn't happen in a vacuum," they were "angry at each other."

Parse that letter and you'll have an inkling of my father's insidious style of combat. He does something thoughtless or says something insulting, she gets angry or hurt, he shifts the focus from his actions to her overreactions, she feels frustrated by his manipulation, he becomes the blameless husband, the hapless victim of a wife who "interrupts and gets excited." Everything was always her fault.

I've mined my memory to bedrock, but I cannot recall ever receiving that letter. Which doesn't mean I didn't get it. Like so many members of my family, repression and denial are my strategies of last resort. If I *did* get the letter, I'm sure it revived my terror of divorce and goaded me to do exactly what my father was counting on me to do: beg my mother to change her mind. And if I *did* beg her, I'm sure she took him back for my sake, just as she stayed with Joe for too long for Betty's sake.

Three years later, Ceil was dead, but had she lived, I'm equally sure there would have been more insults, more fights, more frustration, hostility, and rage. She would think about leaving, threaten to leave, maybe stay with Tillie or Rona for a few days, but she would never go for good. The shanda brigade would not forgive her another divorce. Her misery would remain her secret until her cancer put an end to their battles.

CHAPTER 11

IT WAS EASIER TO FIB THAN TO FAIL

More of my family's secrets skulk out of the past every day, some that shake me to the core, some that appear trivial but speak volumes, especially regarding Ceil's obsession with what people might think and how things might look.

Date discrepancies, for instance. I found her 1954 driver's license application—not the license itself, so the entries were written in her hand—and in the space for DOB, she had printed Nov 8, 1905. This was odd, to say the least, since she always said she was born in 1903. Indeed, I remembered the family celebrating her fiftieth in November 1953, because that's the month I acquired my first serious boyfriend, not something a girl forgets. So which date of birth was correct—1903 or 1905? Neither, it seems. The shopping bag yielded this list, scribbled in pencil on a homely shred of foolscap paper, again in Mom's own hand:

Sarah [Ceil] November 8, 1901
Tillie April 17, 1904
Louis October 15, 1905
Sadye September 8, 1906
Rosie [Rona] November 19, 1911
Herbert August 11, 1913
Milton September 21, 1915

Why would Ceil need a list of the birth dates of the seven Halpern siblings, including her own? My guess is, she made the list to remind herself of everyone's DOB should it be requested by those with power over her family's life—school authorities, government agencies, doctors, and so on. Given this proof of her true birth year, there had to be a reason why she shaved off either two or four years. I look to my own past for clues. When I first applied for a Social Security card, I added a year because the summer job I wanted required applicants to be sixteen and I was fifteen. The drinking age in New York was eighteen back then. I had not yet turned sixteen but I was a senior in high school and most of my classmates were already eighteen, so one of them got me a bogus driver's license that made me two years older. Today's kids use fake IDs in bars and X-rated movie houses to pass for twenty-one. But why would Ceil change her date of birth in her adult life? Based on her chameleon-like history, I suspect she adjusted her age depending on how old she felt she needed to be in order to meet the demands of a particular situation.

Dad always crowed about having been "born with the twentieth century." Given that his birth year was 1900, were Mom to admit that hers was 1901, she may have feared that their age difference was too negligible to conform to the gender orthodoxies of her era, which decreed that a husband should be considerably older than his wife (as well as taller, richer, and smarter). When they met, she was in her thirties. Maybe she considered eighteen months an insufficient age spread, so she made herself two years younger. But after years of claiming 1903 as her birth date, why in 1954 did she write 1905 on her driver's license renewal application? My guess is that she'd lied so often, she forgot what she'd written on her last application (the way I forgot which friends I'd told about my brain tumor). When you're juggling a number of secrets, it's hard to keep track of the truth.

Mom's age discrepancies came to mind when I read the *Times'* obituary of the clothing designer, Karl Lagerfeld, who "rewrote his story so often that even the year of his birth remained a migrating plot point." Though born in 1933, he long claimed his birthdate was 1938, then changed it to 1936, and years later to 1935. "He created up to seventeen collections a year for fifty-four years, but his greatest invention may have been himself...[his] preference for personal myth over reality might have had something to do with where and when he was born: in Germany, just as Adolf Hitler came to power.... Even when unpleasant truths entered his world, Lagerfeld was able to repurpose them for personal renovation.... Imagine a man who can reinvent through sheer will. 'Simplify your life,' he [wrote]. 'Avoid complications unless you derive some pleasure from them. In a word, don't let yourself suffer.'" He could have been describing the philosophy of Ceil Halpern Cottin, born in Pylypets, Austro-Hungary, a designer who never became famous or successful but likewise lied about her age when she thought it mattered, and years before he did, artfully repurposed unpleasant truths for personal renovation.

Before recounting another of Ceil's date-related deceptions, I want to credit her as the person who imbued in me a veneration for the electoral process. She was a leftie *and* a patriot who believed the first Tuesday in November was as sacred as Yom Kippur. On national holidays, Dad put on his Jewish War Veterans uniform, hoisted the Stars and Stripes up the flagpole on our tiny front lawn, and saluted. For Mom, being a "real" American meant memorizing the Pledge of Allegiance, learning the national anthem, and voting every election day. Voting was payback to the country that welcomed her impoverished refugee family and never punished them for being Jewish.

In 2020, in celebration of the one-hundredth anniversary of women's suffrage, I wrote a piece for *The Forward* about my first time in the voting booth. It was November 1945. I was six. And my mother and I were going to the polls to vote for the mayor of New York City. When we got to the polling place, she led me behind the curtain and picked me up so I could reach the levers. She asked if I could find the name William O'Dwyer on the voting machine, and when I did she let me do the honors. But first, she told me why "we" wanted O'Dwyer to be the mayor: because he was a Democrat (like everyone we knew, except for a few scattered Marxists); he was an immigrant (like Mom, though he was Irish-Catholic); and he was a lawyer who had represented Jews caught smuggling weapons to the Haganah, the paramilitary force of pre-state Israel. (Any friend of the Zionist cause was a friend of ours.)

Ceil came to this country eleven years before American women won the right to vote. She always claimed she'd become a citizen at eighteen, the earliest age at which an immigrant could apply, and that she'd cast her first vote at twenty-one, the legal voting age at the time. But like a dead hand reaching out of the grave to correct the record, her Certificate of Naturalization emerged from the commodious shopping bag and it was dated, April 14, 1938. In 1938, my mother wasn't eighteen, she was thirty-five or thirty-seven, depending on that year's lie. Bottom line: she pretended to be a citizen for nearly twenty years before she actually became one. Since finding her naturalization papers, two questions have had me stumped: Why would a woman who so fervently aspired to be a "real American" wait twenty years to become a *real* American? And what finally set the process in motion?

Both questions can be answered in three words: fear of failure. She lied because she waited so long. She waited so long because she only had an eighth-grade education and believed herself incapable of passing the citizenship test, which, according to flyers in the post office, required "a basic understanding of U.S. history and government." Unable to conquer her anxiety and fear, she didn't even try to take the test, simply *called* herself a citizen and acted like one. She followed politics, formed opinions about candidates, talked about them knowledgeably, but never voted because she couldn't. As for what set the process in motion, it had to be her biological clock, which by 1938 must have been ticking full blast. Being seriously superstitious, and hypervigilant about warding off the Evil Eye, she must have felt it important, before getting pregnant, for her to resolve some of the disparities between truth and invention. Were she to give birth to an American baby without being a real

"real American" herself, it would be a shanda. In keeping with her clean slate policy, she couldn't raise a child to exercise the rights and freedoms she valued so deeply unless she became a citizen and participated in the democratic process herself.

When I try to imagine how her journey to citizenship played out, two scenarios unspool before me. In the first, Jack proposes to Ceil and she says yes but admits that she may not qualify for a marriage license because she was delivered by a midwife in her mother's bed in Pylypets and has no written proof of her identity.

"No problem," Jack says. "Just bring your naturalization papers." Ceil admits that she's not yet a citizen because she's been too intimidated to take the test. Jack comforts her and helps her acquire "a basic understanding of U.S. history and government." Ceil passes the test. Jack accompanies her to the US District Court in Lower Manhattan carrying something in a brown paper bag. Ceil recites the Oath of Allegiance to the United States after which (cue the sparklers), he takes her to the park across from the courthouse, serenades her with "You're a Yankee Doodle Dandy," tears open the bag, and presents her with a box of Drake's Yankee Doodle cupcakes.

Uplifting. Romantic. Cinematic. However, Ceil's habit of papering over her inadequacies argues for a sadder, sorrier denouement. In this second scenario, she's too ashamed to admit that she's not really a citizen. She keeps postponing the trip to the marriage license bureau. She signs up for the exam without telling him and secretly attends a night school adult ed class in US history. She passes the test. Goes to court by herself. Takes the oath. Gets the certificate with its telltale date, flashes it at the clerk at the marriage license bureau, then hides it in some obscure place, never to be seen again until Betty finds it after Ceil dies and sticks it in the shopping bag.

I've invented those little dramas because I really can't fathom what took my mother so long to become an American citizen. All I can tell you is, more than eighty years later, when I found the certificate, I wept.

The remaining questions would require a three-act play to answer. Why would a woman as protective of her image as Ceil was retain letters and documents that attest to all her prevarications, humiliations, and discontents? Why did Betty save all that old stuff and pass it to me as if family secrets were heirlooms to be transferred *l'dor v'dor*, from generation to generation? And why, strangely enough, has it been so uplifting to unravel all the struggles and stratagems it took to create a new life in this new world? In a 2016 online essay in stuff.co.nz, entitled "The unbearable burden of carrying secrets," Olivia Clement, a playwright and filmmaker, tells the story of her eighty-five-year-old French grandfather having given her the key to a locked cabinet containing a sealed envelope on whose face, he'd written, "In the case of my death, to be thrown in the River Seine without opening," and made Olivia swear she would do as he wished. When her grandfather died, she asked her mother what she should do with the envelope. Her mother said she should keep her promise, so Olivia walked to the nearest bridge and threw the envelope in the river. "That was that," she writes. "His secrets were gone."

I would have followed his instructions *after* I stole a peek in the envelope. But Olivia didn't struggle, ponder, or vacillate. She understood why the envelope "needed to exist in the first place. It wasn't enough for him to hide his secrets in the dusty corridors of his mind; they had to be physically stored away, in the real world." Presumably, so they could be destroyed.

Was that what Mom hoped Betty would do with the plastic bag when she found it at the back of our mother's closet? Maybe. Was it what Betty thought I would do when I dragged the bag home? Not a chance. I'm sure she knew that someday I would read every shred of paper and I would write about what I found and learned. Why? Because I'm a Jew and a writer. Because Jews remember and writers write.

CHAPTER 12

"ALL MY LIFE I LED A DOUBLE LIFE"

The above words jumped off the pages my mother had torn out of a Fidelity Insurance datebook—June 15 through June 24, 1955, days Mom would not live to see. I had no idea that she had written a deathbed note to my sister until fifty-eight years later when Betty herself was dying and I traveled up to her assisted living residence for a visit we knew would be our last. The summer sun poured through her windows and spilled across the recliner chair where my sister, chemo bald, cancer thin, sat with an afghan spread across her knees and the shopping bag in her lap.

Years later, when I found Mom's deathbed musings among the papers unloaded on my dining room table, I wept my way through it. Even now, whenever I reread it, my eyes smart, and my throat tightens. Laid bare by her soft penciled script, is my mother's doleful struggle for refinement and respectability, her capacity for self-reflection, and her clear-eyed recognition of the arc of her journey from shame to cover-up to reinvention.

> *Dearest Betty,*
>
> *It's 4 AM. I can't sleep. I've read some and don't have patience for more. I do a lot of thinking these days, much in retrospect of the long ago, a lot about my life.*

Left behind in Europe by a beloved father when he went to America for 4 tortuous years, while we were beholden to relatives for support. Two weeks in steerage crossing the Atlantic, on dried bread. Landing here at 8-years-old and again, worry and poverty. Loving my world in school but being snatched out of it at 14 to go to work in a horrible sweatshop, an artificial flower factory.

I worked that first year under the foremanship of a cousin of mine who was a Simon Legree if ever there was one. Many a night I would come home and drop off to sleep, without nourishing food, in a pool of tears. At sixteen, I got a job at Hattie Carnegie's and came into my own. Life looked promising and good despite the hectic chaos at home, the crowded quarters and confusion. Then my Uncle Will & Aunt Mary asked me to come and work for them in their dress factory and I did so without question in appreciation for his generosity to Mom and his devotion to all of us children. But it put an end to my wonderful future at Carnegie. Then there was marriage—and you know the rest.

Looking back, I realize a strange thing: that all my life I led a double life.

In Europe I concocted stories about why my father was away for so long. In NYC when we lived in a slum neighborhood and I was ashamed of it, I gave my suitors Uncle Will's fancier address. Then, for ten years, though hating myself for doing it, I hid the fact of my divorce and lived among my friends as a single girl, never admitting to anyone that you existed. For ten years! Even now I'm trying to keep my illness secret. Maybe I should have come out with it, but the truth was always too hard to bear and a big burden to me.

Still, I had many compensations socially, great friends, the tops in any group. Doors were opened to me in the nicest homes, and I was always welcomed in all inner circles. In business, too, I can really say I was successful and had wonderful opportunities and I always tried to make the most of them.

It's interesting how the early years have a way of coloring one's adult life. I remember how impressed I was by the close and harmonious relationship of the families in "Little Women," "The Five Little Peppers," and many other books.

I always envisioned having an American family full of love, courtesy, and charm—behavior I didn't see in my European surroundings or on the Lower East Side where everyone was always harassed and too preoccupied with their needs to think of the niceties.

A nice family became the dream I could never achieve. As you know, Dad is impatient and short-tempered and as a result I could not be what I wanted to be, the patient, pleasant mother.

I behaved badly many times toward my children. And as an older sister I made some mistakes in my judgment of my younger brothers and sisters. Due to my hard work life and many frustrations, I sometimes lashed out at them and interfered when I should have minded my own business, as when my brother Herbert wanted to be a ventriloquist and I insisted he get a regular job instead. He was a very good ventriloquist. Why didn't I keep quiet and let him decide?

I guess I thought of life in terms of the bare essentials.

Ceil's note ends there, as if reviewing her mistakes had exhausted her strength. I knew she had led "a double life," caught in the tension between worrying about "bare essentials" and cultivating her dreams of "an American family full of love, courtesy, and charm." But I'd never fully grasped the crushing shame of her poverty or her desperate longing for social respectability. I learned about her divorce when I was twelve. But I never knew that for ten years during her singlehood, she'd hidden from all her friends the fact that she'd been married, and she never told anyone there was a Betty. Above all, what cut me to the quick was my mother's pitiful admission that she lied because "the truth was always too hard to bear." That's why she expended so much effort on "concocting stories," to cover up the unbearable truths of her life, be it her immigrant origins, her impoverished living conditions, her poor choice in husbands, or her terminal cancer.

Mom also left a deathbed note for me, though mine is a half-page long. Betty's is a confession, an accounting of the soul. Mine, an ethical will, its tone elegiac, a mother's prayer for the daughter she knew she would never see grow up. Not one to waste paper, she used to make her shopping lists on the back of used envelopes or gift wrap. Betty's note was written on the insurance company datebook pages. Mine on a New York City Defense Corps letterhead saved from her service as an Air Raid Warden during the blackouts of World War II. I kept her note folded up in my wallet for nearly two decades, but after someone stole a friend's wallet, which contained a precious snapshot of her late husband, I had the note framed in Lucite. It now hangs above my desk like a talisman.

Dearest Letty—

You've given me so much joy and pleasure but that's because you are my baby. And I was older and could appreciate you more. Whereas with Betty unfortunately I had been too busy working although she was an adorable baby and a little girl as cute as can be. The family made a big fuss over her. But when you came along, there were a number of other children, cute too, so your dad and I had to make up for the family's lack of attention.

I feel secure now in the knowledge that you have been imbued with a proper outlook on life and you will travel along life's road with dignity, good sense, and high ideals.

And when the time comes for you to fall in love and decide upon a partner for life, you will use great judgment and evaluate carefully

It ends there. No "Love, Mom" or "Have a great life." Not even a period at the end of the sentence. Why would she stop so abruptly? With only weeks to her death, was she in terrible pain or too exhausted to go on? Or did she purposely put down her pen before she could counsel me further, afraid that she might unleash too many repressed demons, the disappointing relationships, the acrid regrets, and cast a shadow across the future I would have to face without her. I tried to imagine what she might have written next had she summoned the strength to continue. Maybe her hope that I would not make the same mistakes that she did, not choose a man because he has impressive credentials or presents well superficially, not get married because I'm afraid to live on my own or too embarrassed to be a spinster. Above all, that I would not stay with a husband who makes me miserable.

In her note to Betty, Ceil finessed the details of her disappointment in my father: "Then there was marriage, and you know the rest." In mine, she distilled her lived experience into that final declarative sentence which, at fifteen, I took as a command, and now, as prophecy. Since Bert and I married barely six months from the day we met, I can't claim to have used "great judgment" or evaluated him "carefully." But I did find "a partner for life" and we do have "a close and harmonious relationship." And I know that would have made her happy.

CHAPTER 13

OUR KITCHEN WAS KOSHER, OUR STOMACHS CHEATED

I'd be hard-pressed to define "the Jews." Are we a religion, ethnic group, nation, people, or all the above? In 2013, the Pew Survey of American Jews asked a couple of thousand members of our tribe what they consider "essential to being Jewish." Because respondents had the option to check multiple boxes, the results are marvelously multifarious. More than 70 percent checked "Remembering the Holocaust." An equal number replied that the most essential thing about being Jewish is "Leading an ethical/moral life." More than half chose "Working for justice and equality." Forty percent answered, "Caring about Israel," and 40 percent said, "Having a good sense of humor." Only 19 percent checked, "Observing Jewish law." I'm fairly certain that my mother would have chosen the first three options and my father the last three, which tells you a lot about my childhood.

✦

Everyone who knew Jack Cottin perceived him to be religiously knowledgeable and impeccably observant. Knowledgeable he was, having been, in his youth, a Hebrew teacher—he learned the language from his grandmother, Max's mother, before he was old enough to go to school—and a tutor of bar mitzvah boys, and, throughout his life, notably skilled at deconstructing tractates of the Talmud and chanting from the Torah with perfect cantillation. But observant? Not always. At least not according to the dictates of Conservative Judaism, the denomination with which we were affiliated and whose rules he ignored when it suited him.

Sometimes, to justify one of his reinterpretations of halacha, Dad would cite an arcane rabbinic opinion; other times, he would offer no citation or explanation, simply opine in that authoritative way of his that brooked no challenge. It would never have occurred to me or anyone else—with the notable exception of my uncle Al, his sister's hyper-Orthodox husband—to question my father's interpretations since he always presented himself as an unimpeachable expert whose intensive Yeshiva education had long ago earned him the right to his pronouncements. Jack Cottin made his own rules. To wit: thirty-nine categories of labor are prohibited on the Sabbath, including the making of fire. Lighting a cigarette requires the making of fire. Yet, somehow, my father, a two-pack-a-day man, indulged his addiction on Shabbat. From sundown Friday to sundown Saturday, he smoked his Lucky Strikes openly inside the house and surreptitiously on the street, yet evinced no guilt whatsoever.

Dad also disobeyed the prohibition against driving on the Sabbath, claiming it was permissible to drive to synagogue because "God doesn't give a damn how we get to shul as long as we come on time and daven (pray) correctly." In the 1950s, when thousands of upwardly mobile American Jews moved to the suburbs and no longer lived within walking distance of their shuls, the decision-making body of Conservative Judaism issued a teshuvah (rabbinic response) declaring it acceptable to drive on shabbat, *but only from one's home to synagogue.* This, to me, confirmed my father's authority. But he didn't act on his principles by parking in front of the Jamaica Jewish Center and putting his cigarette out on the steps. He parked our smoke-filled Dodge four or five blocks away and extinguished his cigarette in the ashtray before we emerged from the vehicle and walked the rest of the way to shul as if we'd made the whole trip from home on foot. Our idiosyncratic practice of kashrut, Jewish dietary laws, was another secret that I knew had to stay within the family. Mom kept a strictly kosher kitchen—separate sinks, kosher soaps, separate containers for meat or dairy foods and their correspondingly specialized dishes, pots, pans, silver, and cutlery. But while our kitchen was strictly kosher, our digestive systems were not. Most Sunday nights, we ate out and we ate traif—at Topsy's, a restaurant on Queens Boulevard in Forest Hills, famous for its Southern fried chicken, corn fritters, impeccably mannered black waiters, and its logo of a pigtailed picaninny from *Uncle Tom's Cabin*. At the Chinese restaurant on Union Turnpike known for its succulent barbecued spareribs and Lobster Cantonese. Or at Lundy's of Sheepshead Bay, where my dad blithely ordered clam chowder and tucked into a dozen oysters on the half shell. I learned how to eat lobster at Lundy's.

Though not explicitly instructed to keep mum, I knew enough not to tell my dad's brothers-in-law about our desecration of Jewish dietary laws. Had my uncle, Ben Sargon, the barrister husband of Esther, Dad's younger sister, known about those Sunday dinners, he would have been scandalized. Had my uncle, Al Schwartz, the smugly sanctimonious shammes (sexton) of New York's massive Temple Ansche Chesed and the husband of Dotty, Dad's older sister, known we ate traif, Al—the uncle with whom Dad frequently debated the finer points of Torah and Talmud in order to determine who was the more advanced Judaic scholar—would have lorded it over Jack until the coming of the Messiah. My father won most of their one-upmanship contests thanks to what the journal produced by the Jamaica Jewish Center for the testimonial dinner in Dad's honor called his "particularly intensive Orthodox training." Here's the rest of that encomium:

Jack Cottin is qualified to represent the Jewish community because of his truly traditional Jewish background and his Jewish erudition. He can read you any sidra and he has done it on many occasions when our staff reader was not available; and he can interpret a gemorrah to delight the heart of your grandfather. When he was in the service of his country toward the end of the First World War, his tefillin were among his absolutely unexpendable equipment.

A sidra, also spelled sedra, is the weekly Torah portion. The Gemorrah, usually spelled Gemara, is an ancient rabbinic commentary. Tefillin are the phylacteries worn during morning prayers. The fact that those Hebrew terms appeared in a publication of the Jamaica Jewish Center without the translations I just provided tells you that virtually everyone in our congregation understood their meaning. All the more reason why I'm so impressed now that they were impressed then by my father's erudition, which he not only credited to his yeshiva training but to the exacting standard set by his father, Max, for his first-born son.

In 1908, Max and Yetta Cottin moved their young family from New Haven to the Upper West Side of Manhattan, where Jack spent a year in a public school before Max, a tyrannical taskmaster, transferred him to the Rabbi Jacob Joseph Yeshiva on Henry Street, an institution renowned for its rigorous Talmud curriculum. (Dad's younger brother Sidney was banished from the family for a while merely for refusing to attend that yeshiva.) If you were a male child in my grandfather's household, you were expected to become a serious scholar of Judaism with a carapace tough enough to withstand the stern demands, punishment, and shaming that Max reportedly doled out daily. That my father and his brothers survived their childhoods is a minor miracle. And having been raised by Max probably explains why, though a crackerjack student, my father was often insensitive, imperious, and impervious to other people's feelings.

By the time I came along, he had abandoned his father's doctrinaire purism and become his own arbiter of Jewish law, which, when it came to our Sunday night dinners, was fine with me. I loved our forbidden indulgences. Spareribs instead of chopped liver? Are you kidding? Southern fried chicken versus brisket? No contest. What he did or didn't do with respect to Jewish tradition was of little concern to me since the parents of most of my Hebrew school friends practiced their own versions of our cafeteria-style Judaism, observing mitzvot in column A through M, while ignoring or cutting corners on those in column N through Z. What annoyed me was the veneer of piety that hid his, and our, secret violations. Above all, I couldn't forgive him for refusing to cut a halachic corner for me the one time I asked him to do so.

⌒⌒⌒⊱⊰⌒⌒⌒

Mom died a few minutes after midnight, April 20, 1955. More than three hundred people showed up at her funeral, and that night, at the shiva, our living room was packed with family and friends, probably 90 percent of them Jews. But when it came time to convene the evening prayer service which requires a minyan to say the kaddish (memorial prayer), Jack looked around and counted only nine real Jews in the room, meaning nine men. A minyan needs ten.

In 1955, I knew as well as anyone that no branch of Judaism would count a woman to make the quorum for a minyan, or anything else of ceremonial importance. Nevertheless, I asked him to count me in. I felt entitled to be counted. By fifteen, I was a bat mitzvah, a daughter of the Commandments, I'd been confirmed, attended the Yeshiva of Central Queens for two years, graduated from our synagogue's Hebrew school and Hebrew high school. Above all, the woman we were memorializing was my mother.

"I want to say kaddish for my mommy. I need to say it, Daddy. Count me in. Please."

On that night, my father, the man who had always made special rulings for himself, who smoked cigarettes and drove his car on Shabbos, and ate traif on Sunday nights, refused to cross the line. He looked at me, surprised. "You know I can't do that, ketsileh. It's *assur* (forbidden)." With that, he reached for the phone, called the Jamaica Jewish Center, and told them to send us a tenth man. When the stranger arrived, we had to give him a yarmulke; he hadn't thought to bring his own. He couldn't locate the mourner's kaddish in the siddur; Jack had to find it for him. I heard the tenth man recite the Hebrew prayer haltingly and mispronounce several words. None of that mattered. Biology decided the issue: he could pass the physical. I couldn't. After the service, the tenth man stayed for coffee and cake and listened while Ceil's friends told stories about her. He offered me his condolences on his way out. "I'm sorry I never met your mom. Sounds like she was a wonderful woman."

I can't prove it, but I think my father refused to count me in the minyan because, unlike his smoking and driving on the Sabbath, or eating lobster dinners out, he could not have hidden from the eyes of his friends, relatives, and peers, that he, a public paradigm of Jewish observance, allowed a mere girl to count.

CHAPTER 14

NO ONE WOULD TELL SIMMA ABOUT SADYE

The Chester family, 1941: Sadye, Herman, Marvin, Faith ("Sistie)

In June 1945, Mom's younger sister, Sadye, gave birth to her third child and hemorrhaged to death in the recovery room. Stunned by grief, her husband, Herman, who operated a hand laundry in Upper Manhattan, felt it would be impossible for him to work, keep an eye on his two older kids, *and* take care of an infant, so my mother, the iron hub of the Halpern family wheel, took the baby home from the hospital and promised to raise her until Herman found a new wife.

Losing the youngest of my three aunts when I was six years old was a horrible shock and a harsh introduction to mortality. I had yet to experience death in any form, even the passing of a goldfish. That a human being as vibrant as Sadye could be gone forever was inconceivable. I see her, bubbly as a spritz of seltzer, dancing in a knee-length polka-dot dress with a flower tucked in her upswept hair, her gap-toothed smile adding a fillip to her charm. But grafted onto my grim memory of her disappearance from my world was a compensatory gift, the sudden appearance at the foot of my bed of a white wicker bassinet with a baby in it.

My sister Betty and her boyfriend, Bernie, had recently announced their engagement and plans for a wedding the following June, and I'd been dutifully preparing myself for life as an only child. But now, this! A living doll for me to fuss over, dress, bathe, and change several times a day. The baby, a cheery, chirpy, blue-eyed imp named Simma (for Sadye), stayed with us until she was two, at which point her widowed father, Herman, married a woman named Vera, a gregarious, warmhearted war refugee. To be perfectly honest, by the time they retrieved Simma from our family and folded her into theirs, I was ready for my adorable little cousin to ship out. She'd been calling my parents Mama and Dada for some time and demanding more and more of their attention—and getting it.

The youngest of the twelve cousins on the Halpern side, Simma Chester now lives with her husband on a small farm in Northern California where she keeps a goat, makes chevre (goat cheese), and designs magnificent wearable art (alias jewelry) that she creates using precious gems, metals, hand-hewn beads, and natural stones. I've always considered her the most striking-looking member of our family. Well into her seventies, she glows from within like a Woodstock flower child. Her piercing blue eyes and long hennaed hair attract attention the minute she enters a room, as do the dramatic handmade necklaces she wears, the rings on every finger, including between the joints, and the multiple studs along the borders of each ear. To top it off, she has fabulous dimples.

When she comes East to visit her grandkids and show her newest line of jewelry to museum gift shop buyers, the two of us always try to get together. A few years ago, during one such visit, we met for brunch at an outdoor café across from Lincoln Center. I told her I was writing this memoir, and she agreed to talk to me about the secret her father and family hid from her for so long. As I recall, we both ordered poached eggs on avocado toast.

"How would you rate your childhood on a scale of one to ten?" I began, gingerly.

"Ten."

"What! You spend the first two years of your life in another family's home, you barely see your father who's working twelve hours a day six days a week to support three kids, your sister and brother are much older than you, with no inclination or ability to visit you on their own so they're basically strangers, then your dad suddenly shows up married to Vera, a woman you never met before, who has a daughter of her own and no one sees fit to inform you that your mother died the day you were born."

My rapid-fire summation made my cousin laugh. "Right."

"And you call that a ten!?"

Simma nodded. She said kids don't form retrievable memories until they're four or five, so I shouldn't feel insulted that she has only one image of her life with me, Ceil, and Jack, a muscle memory of my father carrying her, "a sleepy little girl," from the car to the house. What she *does* remember clearly is "growing up in a bubble of love." What made her early childhood a ten, she says, was being adored, pampered, attended to, and accepted unconditionally by Herman, Vera, and the rest of her relatives, and reasonably well tolerated by her big sister and brother.

Memories of her tall, handsome, certifiably brilliant brother leapt across my mind stage. A piano prodigy and science brainiac, Marvin Chester became a world-class physicist who was mentored by Richard Feynman and taught quantum mechanics to graduate students at UCLA for more than thirty years. His sister, Faith, was his polar opposite, mentally sluggish and physically awkward (more about her in Chapter 33).

"Didn't you ever wonder who *we* were, the Halperns, I mean? Most kids have two extended families, you had three—Herman's, Vera's, and Sadye's. How did you parse Sadye's side if you didn't know she existed in the first place?"

"I never thought about it one way or another. I just knew I belonged to a big, boisterous clan and all my relatives loved me. I never demanded to see a family tree."

I ask Simma when she first found out about Sadye and who told her.

"Faith did. It was the summer of 1955. I was ten. I came home from summer camp, and Vera was not at the bus station, which was disconcerting. I was taken to Faith and Eddie's apartment in the Bronx. I remember Faith sitting across from me in the kitchen, stone-faced, her arms folded across her chest while I was pounding the table with my little fists, wailing, 'Mommy! No! Mommy! Mommy! Mommy! No!' Faith told me to stop crying because Vera wasn't my real mother anyway. That was it. I couldn't take in what she was saying. It was like the top of my head had blown off. 'Wait! What? Who died? Who's my *real* mother? What are you *talking* about?' I learned later that Vera had died of cancer and was buried by the time I got home from camp."

My cousin's sapphire blue eyes sprang a leak. I reached across the table and handed her a tissue. She gazed across Columbus Avenue to the fountain on Lincoln Center Plaza, where a column of water soared high up in the air before dropping a curtain of water into the pool below.

"I ran out of the kitchen, dashed in the shower, and stood under the spray for a long, long time. I'll never forget that moment. I just cried and cried, letting the hot water pound down on my head and mingle with my tears.

"Vera was a great mom. Learning that she wasn't my biological mother didn't change my love for her or make my grief any less grueling. What did change after her death was my life. My dad felt he couldn't keep me and still run the laundry, so he made me move in with Faith and Eddie. They enrolled me in a new school. Fifth grade. That was the end of my idyllic childhood."

"You mean until then, you had absolutely no inkling that Herman had a previous wife or that you had a previous mother, and you weren't Vera's biological child?"

"None."

That would have been hard to believe had I not been duped by my own parents. "What about Marvin and Faith? They were raised by Sadye; they must have loved her. Are you sure they never even dropped a hint?"

"If they did, it never registered. Since we're talking about secrets, years later Marvin admitted to me that a part of him was relieved when Sadye died because she was overly ambitious for him, more than he was for himself, and he often felt burdened by her expectations."

It crossed my mind that his mother's expectations actually may have fueled (or goaded) Marvin's talents and adult achievements, the substance of which is far beyond my ken. (One of his articles is entitled, "Evidence for a Configurational Emf in a Conducting Medium." And here's a line from his Wikipedia entry: "Among his more substantial contributions to the field, he predicted and demonstrated a Bernoulli Effect in the electron gas.") I wish I could call up my cousin Marvin and fact-check his sister's claim, but he died in 2016.

"What about family photos?" I asked Simma. "You must have seen pictures of Sadye with Herman. I know I've seen dozens of them. Didn't you ask anyone who's that strange woman with Daddy, Marvin, and Faith?"

"Never."

"So, the whole family—including members of your generation and mine who were old enough to remember there was a Sadye—none of us ever said a word? Why aren't you pissed that you were lied to for ten years?"

"Nobody lied to me; they just didn't tell me the truth. (Echoes of my father.) I'm sure they did it out of love, not malice. Everyone probably thought, *She's a happy kid. Vera's the only mom she's ever known. If she finds out her mother died giving birth to her, she might hate herself for being born.* I'm sure they were just being protective."

I was not so sure. My hippie cousin tends to give everyone the benefit of the doubt while I, child of lying parents, handmaiden to the Old Testament God, stand ready to rule in judgment. But both of us agreed on one fact: that the day we learned the truth about our respective family secrets was a turning point in our early lives. I stopped trusting that people were who they seemed to be. Simma went from basking in a "bubble of love" to living with her joyless sister and brother-in-law.

"On the surface, we got along, but Faith and I were never close," Simma said. "Fun wasn't in her repertoire. She was not just a decade older than I but a little slow and different from me in every way and she was always on my case to obey her. I used to chalk it up to me being a rebellious teenager. Now, I know my sister was hard on me because just by being alive, I reminded her of *her* role in Sadye's death."

I hadn't realized Faith *had* a role, but she believed hers was a very crucial role of which she was deeply ashamed. It seems that Faith had been fiercely jealous of four of her cousins, each of whom had a younger sibling: Betty had me, her little Bunny. Aunt Tillie's kids, Danny and Judy, had their newly arrived baby brother, Joel. Aunt Rona had recently given birth to Sue, a baby sister for Pris. Faith wanted a baby sister or brother, *too,* wanted one so desperately that she kept badgering her mother to get pregnant despite

Sadye's having made clear that there was no reason for her and Herman to have a third child and lots of reasons *not* to. First, they already had a girl and a boy, Faith and Marvin, the perfect family. Second, it costs money to raise a child, and Sadye and Herman were financially strapped. Third, at this stage of their lives, neither of them had the energy to start over again with an infant. Fourth, the apartment was too crowded as it was, and they couldn't afford a larger one. Faith, impervious, determined, just kept begging until Sadye finally gave in and got pregnant. And gave birth to Simma. And died.

Faith blamed herself. Had she not been jealous and selfish, had she not hounded her parents so relentlessly about having another baby, Sadye would be alive today.

"She never stopped feeling guilty for what she did. She thought she murdered our mother."

"Wow. Did you ever feel guilty about being born?"

"Nope, it never occurred to me. But I know Faith resented me. That was another of her guilty secrets. Poor thing hated herself for causing Sadye's death and hated me for being alive when her mother wasn't."

After Faith blew the lid off and told Simma there was a Sadye, Simma wanted to know more about her birth mother, how she looked, what she was like, what they might have had in common. My mother was already gone by then, but Simma started asking Tillie and Rona a lot of questions about their sister, Sadye. "You have her vitality," one would say. Or, "You have her laugh." Or, "You look just like her." Simma thought their answers sounded like something a casual acquaintance might say about the deceased. They had no endearing anecdotes to pass along to Simma, no memories from when Sadye was young, no stories about her and Simma's father, Herman or funny things she did with Marvin and Faith before Simma was born.

"That's what I was hoping for," Simma mused. "Instead, I got the feeling that no one wanted to talk about Sadye."

Misrepresentations, misconceptions, lies, omissions, distortions, false claims, fictional identities, missing people, previously unknown children, all these may come to light when a buried secret is revealed. But revelation doesn't necessarily explain motivation, the reason someone thought something had to be hidden in the first place. My cousin and I have different theories about why the Halpern women clammed up about their dead sister. Being positive, forgiving, and laid-back, Simma thought what the aunts did was motivated by compassion, that they hid Sadye's existence and chose not to tell stories about what a wonderful woman she was because it would have made Simma feel even worse about never having known her "real mother." I thought our aunts' silence was motivated by shame. Deep down in their shanda-pocked bones, they may have been embarrassed that their sister died in childbirth. I know my mother used to whisper the answer when someone asked her what happened to Sadye. For a modern woman to bleed to death in a New York City maternity ward in 1945 seemed so Old Europe, like something that happened in 1890 in a shtetl in Hungary, or in 1910 in a tenement on the Lower East Side. What would people think? That Sadye had picked a second-rate obstetrician? That Herman could not afford the best care for his wife? That maybe the reason Sadye was alone and untended in the delivery room was because according to Jewish law, a woman who has given birth is in a temporary state of pollution or impurity and subject to "primitive" taboos against touch, and an enforced period of seclusion?

"My hunch is that your mom's sisters were ashamed and afraid that people they knew would jump to all those humiliating conclusions."

No stimulants for us, I thought, when our server brought Simma's herbal tea in a tall mug, my decaf cappuccino in a cup the size of a cereal bowl. *We're pumped up on the mysteries bequeathed us by our family.* I'd based my hypothesis on the general inclination of the women in our family to convert fear of shame into denial. That's what I'd done, worried what people would think if they knew I had a brain tumor, a fact that, at that point, I had not shared with my relatives, Simma included.

"What's your take on my theory?" I asked my cousin.

She called it provocative but not persuasive. I pressed my case. "Eradicating Sadye from your backstory didn't just cheat you of your biological legacy, it erased her from the family's collective memory bank. I think your aunts felt guilty about their part in that erasure. After all, they were her *sisters*, and the four of them were incredibly close. When you began questioning them about Sadye, they ghosted you and gave you little in the way of personal stories because they would have had to own up to *not* talking about her during those ten years when they never even mentioned her name."

"Whatever," Simma said with a dimpled smile. "Either way, I'm fine with it."

I'm not fine with it. Sadye's past was Simma's prologue. I still hold a tiny grudge against my mother and aunts for hiding Sadye's existence and denying my cousin her genetic history and maternal legacy. I resent them for obliterating the life Sadye lived before she died, which, like the lives of all our mothers, was worth preserving in the minds of the living. I regret that when asked about their sister they hid behind tepid generalizations that obscured who Sadye was as a woman and a person. Apart from remembering her polka-dot dress and gap-toothed smile, I couldn't offer my cousin any fully fleshed memories of her biological mother. Nevertheless, to fill the void that our aunts didn't, or wouldn't, I told Simma I'd made a few deductions based on Faith's guilty secret: if she did, as she claimed, pester her mother to get pregnant, and Sadye did, in fact, bow to her pleas, that alone carries profound implications about the character of Simma's birth mother. It establishes that Sadye made the decision to subvert logic and her own desires so that Faith—a girl with mental and physical deficits and a deep sense of inferiority—could have what she most craved, a baby to love. Instead of hiding Sadye to protect Simma, our family should have immortalized Sadye for her maternal sacrifice and devotion. Instead of burying Sadye twice, once in the ground and then in a secret, they should have regaled her daughter with as many stories as they could remember of the mother she never knew.

Cousin Simma, circa 2018

CHAPTER 15

THE LESS YOU KNOW

A photograph is a secret about a secret.
The more it tells you the less you know.
—Diane Arbus

When I was a kid, I looked at the pictures in our family albums on countless occasions without realizing that I wasn't really *seeing* them, the way I didn't really see my mother's hairbrush or my father's shaving mug, my sister's organdy-skirted dressing table, or the pine paneling in our finished basement. The photographs were just there, as familiar as my feet. Had I been more observant, I might have paid attention to the empty rectangles on so many of the albums' pages and inquired why on those pages the tiny black stickers with slots that secured the corners of other photographs merely defined the dimensions of pictures that weren't there?

Had I inquired about the missing photos, Mom might have retrieved a shoebox from its hiding place and pulled out snapshots of her first family doing what young families do when they're happy or pretending to be, Joe Holtzman carrying baby Betty on his shoulders, perhaps, or Ceil and Joe fussing over her in her crib. Had I been more alert, I might have asked Mom why there were no pictures in the albums or around the house of her and Dad at their wedding. I might have pressed Dad about why there wasn't a single photograph of him with Betty as a babe in arms. Maybe, reluctant to lie to my face, he would have fessed up and admitted it was because, until she was in that Jewish boarding school, they'd never met.

Judy, Rena, Betty in Shrub Oak, c. 1939

I do remember questioning my mother about a picture that showed three little girls in summer sunsuits and brown braids. I knew the one on the right was Betty and the little one was my cousin, Judy, but who was the girl in glasses? Mom said she was a distant cousin who visited us when I was a baby. "You're too young to remember her."

Why would I doubt her word? What child would contradict a mother's identification of a family member? What daughter would be suspicious of a parent's answer to a simple question? I would, now. Now I look at the world differently, distrusting appearances, doubting what I see, disbelieving what I'm told. Back home after the visit to Winthrop, I opened the album to the photo of the three girls and showed it to my father. I asked him if the "distant cousin" standing next to Betty was his daughter. Dad winced and said yes. Mom apologized for having lied about Rena being a distant cousin. Dad volunteered that he took the snapshot at the girls' boarding school, which was where he and Mom first met. Saturdays and Sundays were the school's visiting days, but for some reason, Ceil and Jack never appeared on the same days. Nonetheless, Betty and Rena, who'd become friends, were present during the visits of each other's parent, which was how Betty came to know and adore Jack, and Rena came to feel equally fond of Ceil, to the point where the girls started scheming to get their respective adults to visit on the same day. Fueled by the common fantasy that, once introduced, Ceil and Jack would fall in love, get married, and join households, the girls concocted a compelling reason why each parent had to arrive at 10:00 a.m. the following Sunday and both agreed. The rest, as they say, is history. Rena's dad and Betty's mom appeared in the visitors' lounge at the same time that Sunday, the girls introduced them to each other, the four of them spent the entire day together, hiking and picnicking, the couple got along famously, Jack asked Ceil to have dinner with him in the city, they started dating, fell in love, and got married. And guess who were the flower girls at their wedding.

As for joining households, that plan began auspiciously but ended sadly. At first, Dad, Mom, Betty, and I lived in an apartment on Grand Avenue in the Bronx, and Rena stayed with us as often as Jack's custody arrangement allowed. I assume the two girls also spent weekends or vacations together since the shopping bag brought to light that photo of Rena, Betty, and our cousin Judy, wearing braids and summer rompers at our grandparents' ramshackle farmhouse in Shrub Oak, New York. Over the moon about being stepsisters, Betty and Rena became "real "sisters after Dad legally adopted Betty. Years later, when I finally met my sister Rena and worked up the nerve to ask why she'd suddenly disappeared from our charmed circle, she told me her mother made her quit seeing us because Jack had stopped paying child support. *Whoa! Doesn't sound like something Dad would do*, I thought, and wasted no time before confronting my father with her accusation, which he immediately and vociferously denied.

"If that's true, why didn't Paula take me to court? Why didn't she have my wages garnished? Or send me to jail for nonsupport!? Because it's a lie, that's why. She never forgave me for leaving her. Paula made me stop seeing Rena to punish me."

Since I never knew whom to believe, I blamed the shanda, which allowed me to make sense of what was otherwise unthinkable—my father's abandonment of his first daughter—and imagined a scenario that supported my thesis. Mom was fond of Dad's daughter, but when Rena came to the Bronx for one of her visitations, Ceil must have had to explain who Rena was and where she fit into our family. Had my parents identified her as the child of Jack but not of Ceil, people would know he had a previous wife. And since Betty was two years older than Rena, Betty couldn't be Jack's daughter because, in 1925, when she was born, he was married to that previous wife, which means Ceil was married to a previous husband. To avoid the exposure of what was then considered a shanda, my parents decided to introduce Rena as a cousin, which wasn't an airtight solution since there was always a chance that she would mess up and call Jack Dad in front of other people. And were Paula to relent and let Rena stay with us for longer periods of time, she would have to be enrolled in a local school, which would require the names of her parents, and unless Jack lied outright, the "cousin" ruse would be unsustainable.

As it happened, when Paula barred Rena from ever again visiting with her father and his new family, Ceil realized this was their chance to whitewash the canvas, cover up the disgrace of their divorces, and invent a shanda-free past. All they had to do was move from the Bronx to Queens, start fresh without Rena in the picture, and present themselves as the happily long-married couple that Mom wished they had been from the start.

When it first came out, I saw the film *A Man and a Woman*—a French version of my parents' story, starring Anouk Aimee and Jean-Paul Belmondo—and cried my eyes out. Ceil and Jack weren't elegant French lovers but traditional Jews bent on saving face and determined to be, if not exemplary, at least impeccably respectable. Redacting their earlier marital missteps, they were able to build a new narrative on firm ground with improved optics. Rena's disappearance, whatever its impetus, let them shed the last remnant of their imperfect pasts like a lizard sheds its skin. When asked about themselves by their new friends in Queens, they could perpetrate the fiction that they were now, and had always been, a perfect Jewish American family. The story of my parents' meet-cute romance beguiled me until their betrayal of one of their little matchmakers drained it of its magic. Initially, I couldn't reconcile the parents I knew with the people who sacrificed Rena on the altar of their personal reinvention and social acceptance. My rage at their duplicity was unalloyed; my moral judgments lacked nuance. Yet, once I came to understand the power shame wielded over the lives of twentieth-century Jews, their fixation on "what others think," a trait I used to denigrate, became more comprehensible. And since their letters uncovered the hidden power dimensions in their marriage, and the exacting pressure of the Jewish communal ideal, I have become more forgiving of their secret yearning for respectability and the choices it dictated.

Jack and Ceil on their honeymoon, Atlantic City boardwalk, 1937

Still astonishing to me, however, is the extent of my gullibility. Dozens, maybe hundreds, of snapshots were pasted into our family albums and the framed photographs that stood on display in my childhood home, any one of which could have alerted me to my parents' scam. Their so-called "honeymoon picture," for example. I missed several clues in that one. Taken in Atlantic City, it shows Ceil and Jack seated in one of those grand wicker loveseats that couples got wheeled around in on the boardwalk. Had they been married in 1923 as claimed, Dad would have been twenty-three and Mom twenty-two, but the couple in the wicker pedicab are clearly at least a decade older. What's more, their hats are totally out of sync with styles typical of the early 1920s. In the picture Jack is wearing a fedora straight out of a 1930s Bogart movie, and Ceil has on a jaunty side-tilted number of similar vintage. Had the photo been taken in the early '20s, he would be sporting a bowler, derby, or boater, and she, like every woman in America, would be wearing a cloche. Those discrepancies escaped my notice when I was kid oblivious to fashion, but I also missed them when I was old enough to register anachronisms. Yet not for a moment did I suspect that my parents lied about their wedding date. What child would? And why would a grown-up do such a thing?

Even more obvious was the tip-off staring me in the face in the photo taken at the wedding of my mother's brother, Lou. Lined up with him and his bride were Lou's four sisters—Ceil, Tillie, Sadye, and Rona—and their respective husbands—Jack, Ralph, Herman, and Ben. Years after both of our parents were dead, my sister Betty brought to my attention that our father is facing forward in that picture while our uncles are standing at an angle to their wives. More tellingly, Jack's upper body is framed by feathery brush strokes painted in tones that blend with the background. Photoshop didn't exist in those days, but photography studios employed artists adept at enhancing or altering a scene when necessary, for instance, when a woman wanted visual documentation to support a lie. In 1937, Ceil had the studio substitute her new husband's picture for that of the man who had actually been standing beside her at her brother Lou's wedding. Joe Holtzman had been cut out, and Jack Cottin pasted in. That's how assiduous she was about expunging evidence of her marital mistake.

CHAPTER 16

THE KNIPPEL

L ong story short: Jack controlled the money in my parents' marriage. All of it. (Which was not a lot, though I wasn't aware of it at the time.) Their checking account was in his name; he paid the bills, filed the tax returns, and refused to tell Ceil how much he earned or what was in the bank. Many husbands of his era did the same and some still consider it a man's role to provide for his wife and family and handle all the finances. I don't think he used his control of the money to make her servile or beholden. But by asserting his right to privacy about all things financial and withholding essential information from his nonworking wife that affected her security and well-being, he established, without making it explicit, that he was in charge and Mom wasn't.

To put it baldly, she and I were equally dependent on my father for our food, clothing, and shelter, not to mention special treats. Yet he used to congratulate himself for his magnanimity because she didn't have to *ask* for money. Every Friday morning, he gave her an allowance based on his estimate, not hers, of the weekly budget required to buy what was necessary to run the house and take care of me. She assumed that he was managing their savings and investments, which, as I said, would turn out to be nonexistent. She, too, didn't know that then, but like many women, she found ways to compensate for her involuntary ignorance and disconcerting powerlessness. Much as she did in her young teens when she started working in a garment factory to help cover her parents' expenses, and in her twenties and thirties when she was a single mother working to support herself and pay Betty's boarding school tuition, Ceil was frugal to a fault—bargain-hunting, buying day-old bread, choosing recipes that called for cheaper cuts of meat. She also managed to squirrel away a nut or two from her weekly allowance and hide it from her husband in a secret place.

One day, while playing dress-up, I was rooting around in her lingerie drawer for a frilly nightgown that might transform me into a nymph or diva, when I found under her bras and girdles, a nylon stocking with cash in it. I presented it to her as if it were a specimen requiring an identification tag. Flustered, she said it was her *knippel*, and she was hiding it because she wanted to be sure I have a nest egg when I grow up, money no one can touch. Even Daddy.

It must have been hard for her to break ranks with her husband and confide in me. Then, hesitantly, choosing her words with care, she explained the purpose of a knippel. "If a woman has money of her own, she won't have to ask anyone's permission to spend it. I've been chiseling a few dollars out of my allowance every week and tucking them in here and look!" Mom held up the nylon stocking so I could admire it. "See how much I've saved!" The stocking was about half full. Dollar bills, mostly, some fives, even a couple of tens peeking through.

"Is knippel Yiddish for stocking?"

Mom laughed. "No, sweetie pie, it's Yiddish for mad money."

Belated curiosity sent me to Google where the literal definition of knippel popped up in a newsletter called, *HerMoney*. The word derives from "knop," Yiddish for "a pinch," writes Jean Chatzky, whose research is illuminating. While Jewish women used to pinch a knot of fabric in their aprons and hide money in it that they'd salvaged from their household allotment, keeping a stash of secret money for their own purposes is a cross-cultural female phenomenon. Indian women call their version of the knippel "god's money" and use it to make donations to charities or buy candy for their children. Fifty-five percent of Japanese women admit they keep their *hesokuri,* or "belly button money," hidden from their husbands. An Italian grandmother might use a pillowcase as her savings account or "wear many aprons, one on top of the other, and hide her money in the pocket of the bottom one." These days, says Chatzky, women all over the world hide their money where "a partner wouldn't think to look—in a box of tampons in a bathroom drawer, a jar tucked behind the soup cans, or zipped into the inside pocket of a rarely used purse."

"What's mad money?" I asked my mother. Remember, I was a child.

"When I was a girl and my friends or I went out with a man, we always kept a few dollars in our purses in case we got mad at him and wanted to go home. We hid the money in a secret compartment because we knew he would be insulted if he saw it, as if we thought he might not be able to pay for our dinner. Mad money was like an emergency exit. I knew I could always escape from a bad date." Or a bad marriage, Mom was probably thinking. The possibility of escape, be it from poverty, a sweatshop job, Joe's violence, or Jack's insensitivity, I now realize, was never far from her mind.

CHAPTER 17

DON'T LEAVE ME AND TAKE YOUR SECRETS WITH YOU

My sister had the same mother I did, but you'd never know it. The woman who raised Betty was ashamed of her impoverished, immigrant family and the cramped tenement she shared with her parents and six younger siblings. Betty's mother was a survivor of domestic abuse, a divorcée, a single mother who worked long hours, first as a sewing machine operator, then as a dress designer, and saved enough money to enroll her daughter in an upscale boarding school so she could acquire the knowledge, confidence, and polish that Ceil herself had missed.

Having found it painful to part with my three-year-old twins at a local nursery school where they spent a scant three hours in the morning, I cannot comprehend how Betty's mother could have sent her at that tender age to a school miles from New York City and kept her there until she was twelve. It's the one thing Mom did that baffles me to this day. When I asked Betty what she thought about Ceil sending her away, she was surprised that I was surprised. Boarding school was wonderful, she insisted; it was the making of her, and Mom sent her there for the right reasons.

"The alternative was for her to leave me with her parents all day while she was at work, and she refused to have me grow up speaking Yiddish as my first language and living in the crowded tenement she'd been ashamed of since she was a child. Grandma Jenny still had young kids at home; she was stressed out all the time, and she put up with a lot of crap from Grandpa. That's not the atmosphere Mom wanted for me. She wanted me to become a strong, confident, well-educated woman who spoke English without an accent."

I'm not convinced that our mother's motives were so selfless. At best, they were mixed. Her deathbed note to Betty includes the stunning confession that she had presented herself to the world—for ten years!—not as divorcée with a child, but as a never married single woman. She hid from her friends the fact that Betty even existed. Yet Betty claimed to her dying day that she didn't resent Mom for keeping her a secret or sending her away. On the contrary, she was grateful.

The mother my sister knew was an independent woman who was the sole support of herself and her daughter, and then married my father and let him control the finances. The mother Betty knew watched her daughter graduate from college and become a teacher, wife, and mom. The mother my sister knew lived long enough to become the grandmother of her children.

I had a different mother, a stay-at-home mom who was smart, artistic but stymied by her lack of confidence and lost opportunities. The mother I knew was warm, loving, energetic, and creative, unsparingly devoted to me but fearful and overprotective. The mother I knew died when I was a teenager; never saw me graduate from high school; never met my husband, my three children, or six grandkids; never witnessed my life's work.

By the same token, my sister and I called the same man Daddy yet, given our disparate views of him, you'd think we had different fathers. Betty worshiped Jack. To hear her tell it, he was her savior, liberator, mentor in shining armor. I, on the other hand, focused on our father's tarnished breastplate and feet of clay. I wanted her to acknowledge his shortcomings, especially his callous treatment of our mother, which colored my view of him all my life, and which Betty, having left home before the worst of their conflicts exploded, had not witnessed close-up. I wanted her to know all the ways I felt neglected by him. During my last visit with her shortly before she died, we were sitting across from one another, I on a bridge chair pulled close to her recliner, she nestled under her afghan throw, scratching her bald head where the chemo left itchy patches, when something got us talking about Dad, and Betty began singing his praises. How he fussed over her and worried about her, pinched her cheeks, checked her homework, yelled at her for leaving the lights on or tossing her coat on a chair instead of hanging it up in the closet. "He gave me a normal family and treated me like a *real* daughter. I'll always love him for that."

"You *were* a real daughter," I said. "He adopted you, for God's sake."

"You're right," she replied firmly. No one who knew her, including her husband and kids, would describe my sister as an overly emotional woman, but whenever she reminisced about Dad, she choked up. "He was the father I'd always imagined and never thought I would have. He did so much for me."

"Like what? I asked, not combative, just curious.

"For one thing, he made me think clearly. When I was in my teens, he trained me to argue; he wouldn't let me get away with saying 'always' or 'never.' When someone said, 'You're just like your father,' which people did all the time, we would wink at each other. I was thrilled that they just assumed we were flesh and blood. I was so much like him, and proud of it. No one ever guessed I was adopted."

Allow me to pause here for a short commentary on Betty's adoption. In the years since that day on the beach, I've heard some version of "Dad adopted Betty," a thousand times. It's been central to my understanding of the *real* story of my family. However, the shopping bag turned up yet another joker in my parents' house of cards, namely this letter to my mother from my teenaged sister, who was home with Dad and attending Jamaica High School while Mom and I were wintering in Miami Beach:

March 8, 1941

Dear Mom,

Let me set your mind at rest as to Joe. It has been more than a week, almost two since I heard from him. That is, since you called him. You must have stirred him up a bit as I got another check from him for $10 payable to your name. Since he won't consent to Daddy adopting me, I want to get all I can out of him. Maybe it's spite. But what would you call his withholding his consent? don't worry about my seeing him. I won't.

According to my parents' truth-telling session on the beach, Jack adopted Betty almost immediately after he and Ceil got married. Allowing time for the formalities, I assumed the adoption would have been complete by the end of 1938. Yet, Betty's letter is dated more than three years later, and, by her own account, her biological father was still "withholding his consent." Which means she was still Betty Holtzman. So, how come the stationery on which she'd written that letter is imprinted "Betty Cottin"? (She also signed it, "Your devoted daughter.") If I recall correctly, which I do, the name she wrote on the cover of all her notebooks, the flyleaf of her textbooks, and the top of her test papers, was Betty Cottin, and her report cards were issued to Betty Cottin, therefore she had to have been registered at Jamaica High School as Betty Cottin. Now I'm thinking, if Joe Holtzman had not yet consented to the adoption by 1941, who's to say he ever gave his consent?

Finding no adoption papers in the shopping bag, I emailed my sister's three surviving children. Had they ever seen such a paper among her belongings? None had. Her oldest son, Steven, said he was in high school before he learned that Jack wasn't his mother's biological father, a fact that came to light when Steven was setting the supper table and discovered at the back of the silverware drawer a birth spoon engraved, "Betty Ruth Holtzman." Confronted with the spoon, Betty Ruth Cottin admitted the secret that she had kept all those years from her own kids—that she was Jack's *adopted* daughter. But maybe she wasn't. What if her biological father, Joe, never consented and the adoption was never legalized? Was it possible that Betty simply appropriated my father's name and behaved *as if* he was her father much as our mother avoided the citizenship test and behaved as if she was a citizen?

My sister wanted to be a "real" daughter" and became one the way our mother became a "real" American: by willing her desire into being. If I'm right and she took it upon herself in 1937 to counterfeit her identity and call herself Betty Cottin in life and in school, then she had to have done so with our father's agreement, cooperation, and willingness to lie to school and other authorities. Which they obviously did successfully for the next nine years since both her high school and college diplomas say Betty Cottin, and the printed invitation to her wedding says Betty Cottin will marry Bernard Miller on June 23, 1946. Thus did Betty Cottin become Betty Miller, burying her misdemeanor for life. To my mind, this elaborate subterfuge definitely earns my sister a place in the family pantheon of great pretenders. Also due posthumous recognition is our father, who, though licensed to practice law in New York, conspired with Betty to commit what is now called "school enrollment fraud" and got away with it.

<hr />

The larger point is this: Betty turned cartwheels to enter Jack's magical penumbra while I couldn't stop pricking holes in it. My sister and I had totally different perspectives on the same man. Like her, I appreciated his intellect, and I remain thankful to him for prodding me to achieve and for taking me seriously as a thinker. When he was around, he made me feel smart. He took an interest in my opinions, and, as he did with Betty, he taught me to defend my point of view. Trouble is, he wasn't around much. He would come home from the office, eat dinner with me and Mom, then head out to meetings, endless meetings. I wanted a father who didn't just monitor how I performed but cared about what I thought and felt, a father who was interested in me, eager to spend time with me, made me his priority. I wanted more. For my sister, who had never been fathered at all, whatever he did was enough.

In that last conversation, I told her I understood why she would adore Dad and credit him with changing her life. What I didn't understand was her giving him a pass for abandoning Rena. Betty, ever the loyalist, leapt to our father's defense. "That's not fair. Paula put every obstacle in his path…"

"No," I insisted, "he left our other sister with a crazy woman. All those years, he never tried to rescue her."

"We don't know the truth about what happened. All we know is, when Rena came to the house, broke and upset, he didn't hesitate to take her in. She needed money and legal help, and he came through. Give him credit for that, okay?"

"You were up in Peekskill, Betty. I was home the day she showed up; I saw who took her in without hesitation. Mom, that's who. It was Mom who insisted he step up and help her with her legal problems. Mom who made up the bed in the attic and ran a bath for her and invited her to stay until she could sort out her life."

Betty asked me to crank up the recliner, as if she was gearing up to play defense. "You're right, I wasn't there, but I came home the following weekend and I saw how kind he was to her."

"You saw a guilty man trying to make up for his sins. It's time to take off your rose-colored glasses and see Dad as he was."

"Rena's the one who should feel guilty. She never called us during all those years. Don't you think our 'other sister' could have picked up the phone?" When Betty's fingers put air quotes around those words, I understood for the first time that she'd never really reconciled herself to Rena's status in the family.

"Dad was the responsible adult," I said. "The ball was in his court."

"He had to stay away from her because of her mother's threats. But Rena could have come looking for us any time. She was fourteen when Paula cut off her visitations. We were listed in the phone book. She could have called or hopped the subway from the Bronx to Jamaica. She could have tracked us down, but she never did."

"Let's talk about what you did or didn't do." I should have shut my mouth, but I got riled up on behalf of my other sister and fired off a fusillade I would later regret. "Rena was your friend when you were in that boarding school. Presumably, you cared about her. Did you protest when she suddenly dropped out of your life? Did you fight for her? Did *you* call *her*? Try to find her? I was a baby, but you were fifteen or sixteen when we moved to Jamaica, old enough to do your own search. Maybe you didn't *want* her to come back. Maybe you liked being my one and only big sister. Maybe you signed on to Mom and Dad's faked history because you didn't want me to know Rena existed. And you didn't want to share Dad with her."

Betty's rebuttal came in an explosive stream, as if it were sludge backed up in a pipe and someone finally opened the spigot. "Rena was my friend. We plotted together to get Mom and Dad to meet. We were flower girls at their wedding. I was overjoyed when she came for her visits and stayed with me and you in our bedroom. I loved that the five of us became a family, and I felt awful when she stopped coming and we moved to Queens, and I never saw her again…" Betty gulped for breath. The cords in her neck looked like straps.

"Never mind," I backed off. "It's water under the bridge or over the dam."

"Wait a minute, I need to say this. I hated losing Rena, and I'm not proud of what happened. But Mom and Dad were determined to start fresh with no baggage, and I was so thankful to finally have a home and family, I would have done anything they asked."

Watching her summon the strength to defend herself almost killed me. I got up and, propping my hands on the arms of her recliner, leaned down and kissed my sister's bald head. "It's okay, Bets. It's okay."

I still feel guilty for starting that conversation with my beloved sister. It was a mistake to open old wounds at the end of her life.

But she was the only one in the world who could offer a reckoning and assemble the truth. I interrogated her to find out what she, and only she, knew. All that time, I kept thinking, *I'm losing you; please don't take your secrets with you.*

CHAPTER 18

LIKE ALL CHILDREN REARED AMONG RADICALS, WE HID THINGS THAT COULD GET US IN TROUBLE

Aunt Tillie, who lived next door to us in Jamaica, was a fearless rebel at a time when female conformity was next to godliness. Our family's resident radical and free-thinking troublemaker, Tillie was my girlhood inspiration, an exemplar of principle and gumption in a world of go-along-to-get-alongs. She believed it was more important for women to be well-informed and useful than ornamental, feminine, and domesticated. I knew it was possible for a woman to take herself seriously because Tillie did. She talked about current affairs as if her views were as worthy of consideration as Walter Lippman's. Mailed annotated newspaper articles to family members as if an opinion column could change their minds. Pulled a relevant pamphlet out of her purse in the midst of a heated political argument to prove her point. I watched her live her values every day.

During World War II, she worked the night shift drilling holes in the wings of fighter planes. Twenty years before Rachel Carson wrote about pesticides, Tillie was scrubbing fruits and vegetables. She ate wheat germ and yogurt when the rest of us were still spooning white sugar on our Corn Flakes. She took the subway to Union Square to listen to soapbox orators inveigh against the evils of capitalism and often engaged in some rabble-rousing herself. I fully expected to come home from school one day and see J. Edgar Hoover standing on the shared doorstep of our semi-attached houses with Aunt Tillie in handcuffs. Though she was never called to testify before the House Un-American Activities Committee, a couple of faux-friendly FBI agents did stop by several times to quiz her about her "comrades." My mother, who was as shy as her sister was daring, was a stealth leftie but not the type to march or demonstrate, always came to Tillie's defense at family dinners when my father, a middle-of-the-road Democrat, called her an apparatchik and ridiculed her "communistic ravings." Meanwhile, I listened and being an idealistic kid, found it hard to disagree with the Marxist creed, "From each according to his ability, to each according to his needs."

In 1953, after Stalin imprisoned nine Russian doctors, six of them Jews, and tortured them for allegedly plotting against the Soviet leadership, Tillie left the party and became a militant critic of the Soviet Union. In the 1960s, she marched on Washington for civil rights and demonstrated in support of Russian refuseniks and other victims of anti-Semitism who'd been denied the right to immigrate to the US or Israel. Once, my four-foot-nine-inch aunt was handcuffed in front of the Soviet Consulate and brought before a judge who said he would let her go with a warning if she promised not to do it again. "I can't make that promise, Your Honor," she'd replied. "When someone hurts my people, I have to protest." Tillie lost me when she started sending me articles lauding Rabbi Meir Kahane, the Jewish nationalist rabbi and founder of the Jewish Defense League, a far-right group whose goal is to "protect Jews from anti-Semitism by whatever means necessary." (The JDL has been on the FBI's list of terrorist organizations for years.)

Like all children reared among radicals, I knew if I didn't keep mum about the opinions and affiliations of some of my relatives, I could get them in trouble. During the Red Scare when the mere accusation of being a "fellow traveler" could result in job loss, ostracism, and ruin, hiding one's politics was the only way to stave off exposure and arrest. I understood, without being told, not to mention within earshot of strangers my mother's loathing of Hoover or my aunt's affinity for Lenin. No one had to tell me not to talk about the dictatorship of the proletariat or Marx's theory of surplus value. From an early age, my antennae were finely tuned to recognize reactionaries who might be informers. When my seventh-grade teacher asked me how I came to choose *Spartacus* for my book report, something in her tone set off alarms. I had raved about the novel in my paper, but I didn't admit that Tillie recommended it; I said I'd found it on the new fiction shelf at the library. I had no idea what could be objectionable in a book about a slave revolt in ancient Rome, yet I remember feeling relieved when the teacher moved on to a pupil who'd written her book report on *The Yearling*. Later, Tillie told me that the author of *Spartacus*, Howard Fast, had been blacklisted because he'd raised funds for orphans of the Spanish Civil War and served time in prison for refusing to name names before Congress.

Tillie raised my consciousness about violations of civil liberties by the federal government. Because the FBI was wire-tapping her phone and those of other "housewife communists," I wasn't surprised when, in the 1960s and early '70s, it was revealed that Richard Nixon kept an enemies list and the FBI had spied on antiwar groups and civil rights organizations. J. Edgar Hoover was known to view "women's libbers" as deviants and feminism as a mortal threat to family values. In those years, we suspected some of our more militant groups were under surveillance. Still, I was gobsmacked while researching a cover story for *Ms.* on the FBI's infiltration of the women's movement ("WLM" in the Bureau's parlance) to discover in the 1,200 pages I'd managed to obtain under the Freedom of Information Act the extent and absurdity of their efforts. When ten women attended a feminist meeting in Soho, one was likely to be an FBI plant. While these "moles" were slavishly precise about participants' license plate numbers, the meeting's locale ("3rd fl. apt, rundown building"), the women's eye color (brown, blue, hazel, flecked), hair styles (Afro, straight, pony-tail, bangs) and outfits (bell-bottoms, torn jeans, mini-skirts, tie-dyed T-shirts), they were utterly confused by feminist political theory, misunderstood the wide spectrum of feminist opinion, garbled movement terminology, and misspelled names that somehow had evaded the Bureau's black-out pens. Some women were described as "revolutionaries" if they didn't shave their legs or as a threat to "the American way of life" if they wore work boots and overalls. It was laughable until you realized they were serious about this "evidence" and building a case against us could destroy our lives.

Given my family's antipathy to Hoover and his goons in the '50s, and my rank disdain for the FBI's infiltration of the women's movement in the '70s, you can imagine what an out-of-body experience it was for me to find myself rooting for the intelligence agency and its director in 2019 and '20, when they resisted the executive overreach of Donald Trump. I could not believe I'd lived to see the Bureau on the right side of history.

CHAPTER 19

THE ANTITHESIS OF A SECRET

I met my husband on my twenty-fourth birthday, Sunday, June 9, 1963, at The Pines, a tiny community on Fire Island, where he and six friends from law school had rented a house for the summer without realizing it was a gay community. All heterosexuals, they solved that problem by importing women. I was one of the imports. I came to the beach that Sunday morning as the casual date of one of the seven lawyers, a sweet guy but not a keeper, and ended up falling for another, Bert Pogrebin, who also had driven out for the day. When the group set up a net for beach volleyball, Bert played on the opposing team, and I had ample opportunity to study him and appreciate his good looks, lanky athleticism, and endearingly infectious humor. I flirted with him over lunch. We agreed with each other during the group discussion of Hannah Arendt's book *Eichmann in Jerusalem*, which had just been published and was the object of heated controversy. (Remember "the banality of evil"?) On the ferry back to the mainland, while my day date was busy talking to the other guys, I ambled over to Bert, who was standing at the railing enjoying the sunset over the bay. We had a lively conversation and a lot more laughs, and by the time the boat docked on the mainland, I was sufficiently smitten to take the initiative and slip him my business card, having already written my address and telephone number on the back.

In those days, I was a publishing executive (see Chapter 29) with a staff of two. Bert was a labor and employment lawyer. I did not need a labor and employment lawyer for two staffers, but I told him I might. Four days later, he called to say he was with some friends at the annual San Gennaro Street Festival in Little Italy, which was not that far from my place on West 12th Street in the Village, and he wondered, assuming I was free, if he could come over. By himself. I said sure. That launched a whirlwind relationship during which we discovered the amazing number of things we had in common. Family origin (Hungarian/Russian), Jewish heritage (Ashkenazi/Yiddishkeit), cultural tastes (folk music/protest art/novels by Bernard Malamud), as well as our revulsion for Richard Nixon, Barry Goldwater, George Wallace, and Bull Connor. We also shared something few couples did in those years: both of us grew up in left-wing families and knew how to hide their politics from the world.

I think I really fell in love with Bert the night he picked up his guitar and belted out the labor union classics, "Which Side Are You On?" and "Solidarity Forever." When he launched into "The Internationale," my thoughts marched back to my Aunt Tillie's living room where Paul Robeson's commanding bass voice rumbled out of the speaker of her phonograph singing the Soviet anthem at a volume I could hear through our families' shared wall. As teenagers, Bert read his parents' copy of *The Nation* and I read my parents' copy of *PM*, New York's progressive newspaper. In 1963, we considered ourselves miles more worldly-wise than friends of ours who'd been weaned on their parents' *Time* magazine or *Saturday Evening Post*. We both believed that Julius and Ethel Rosenberg were innocent, the espionage charges against them trumped up, and had they not been Jewish, they would not have been electrocuted. (In 1995, the Russians declassified cables from the 1950s that revealed to our dismay that Julius was a Soviet courier and Ethel an accessory. Our theory about why they received capital punishment still holds.)

From the moment we met, Bert and I also have been in synch on nonpolitical issues that make some couples go for each other's throats: sex, money, childrearing, music, food, what constitutes ethical behavior, which car to buy, where to live, or what to do on vacation. One of us being late to the theater or squeezing the toothpaste tube from the top can start a squall; otherwise we don't find much to argue about. If one snaps at the other, it doesn't set off an avalanche of accusations. ("You always…" "You never…") In the heat of anger, we've never said anything hurtful enough to shake the foundations of a marriage. If we argue in the daytime, we're generally over it within an hour. Either one of us apologizes, we reach a compromise, the conflict gets solved in some practical way (two tubes of toothpaste), or he says something that makes me laugh. If we argue at night, we resist the standard marriage manual advice to "Never go to bed angry; keep talking until you solve it." Both of us prefer to go to bed mad, knowing that whatever caused our disagreement will either be forgotten in the morning or seem too trivial to rehash.

Our daughter, Robin, thinks we should be curious about why we've lived together with so little strife for such a long time. A proponent of the benefits of therapy, she believes her father and I have repressed unexamined issues related to our childhoods. She's probably right. And now that I've examined my parents' behavior through the prism of guilt, shame, and secrecy, I'm sure those issues include the fears and superstitions I inherited from my mother and the rancor I witnessed in my parents' union, which Robin believes I must have unconsciously determined never to reproduce in mine. At this writing, fifty-eight years into our marriage, I say, if it ain't broke, why fix it? This is probably too facile, but I attribute our comity to the fact that my husband is the perfect antidote to the toxic parts of my father. Also, that Bert and I both subscribe to three unbreakable "nevers"—Never betray each other's trust. Never keep secrets from one another. Never doubt each other's fidelity.

Letty and Bert, bike trip in the Loire Valley, France, 1989

When I showed him a draft of this chapter, he laughed at that last sentence. "Aren't you forgetting about HER?"

Oh, right. HER.

One day about five years ago, I needed the phone number of a friend of ours, but my iPhone was out of juice so I asked Bert for his phone and started scrolling through his contacts. My blood froze when the word HER, in capital letters, jumped off the screen along with a number. "Who's HER?" I asked, struggling to keep my voice steady.

He glanced at his phone. "No idea."

For one dizzying moment, my entire marriage hung in the balance. I clicked on HER and pressed the call icon.

A male voice answered. "Hey, Bert. What's up?"

"Who's this?"

"Oh, hi, Letty. It's Herb."

Herb. Husband of Ruth. Friend of both Bert and me. I grinned. "Sorry for the butt call, Herbie." Then, turning to my husband, I said, "HER is Herb Teitelbaum. Shall I add the B?"

<hr />

Bert is the antithesis of a secret. He's guileless. Never pretends to be what he isn't, or to not be who he is. Doesn't posture or preen. If he's worried—about a family member, one of his legal cases, or the future of democracy—I'll hear about it, a lot, and feel it in his wakeful nights. If he has an ache or pain, he tells me, and tells me, then tells me again. If he's happy, he shows it. When something good happens, he savors it, and says, "Let's go out and celebrate!" He doesn't need to prove his masculinity or big-foot others in order to feel like a man. He's a Harvard-educated lawyer with a stellar, decades-long career under his belt, but I've never heard him brag about himself (only about his kids, grandkids, and me). He doesn't create imbroglios or problems; he sorts things out, for his clients, of course, but also for the people he loves. He has never in his entire life made a scene. He has never humiliated any of my relatives or belittled me in front of others, or demanded that I account for every penny, or gotten up from the dinner table and slammed out of the house.

Why am I telling you all this? To balance the many things I've done wrong or experienced sadly with the one thing I did right, which was to create a marriage with my husband completely different from that of my parents, a life entirely unburdened by the sort of shame, regret, and secrecy that fill the letters they wrote to each other eighty years ago.

Letty and Bert (Photo, Morton I. Hamburg from his book,
Couples: A Celebration of Commitment, 2000)

II
PRIVATE SHAME

CHAPTER 20

THEY'LL SAY I'M NOT READY FOR KINDERGARTEN

September 1944. I'm dressed in a starched white blouse and the robin's-egg blue skirt Mommy designed and made for me to wear on this, the most important day of my life. I'm standing on the steps outside P.S. 131 in Jamaica, waiting for her to pick me up after the first session of my first semester in kindergarten. She was supposed to be here at noon and she's already five minutes late. I'm worried about her. And I have to pee.

The other mommies run for their kids the minute they get here, acting as if they've been apart for three weeks, not three hours. It's wartime after all; anything can happen while a child is out of sight. My mommy is an air raid warden in the Civil Defense Corps, so I think maybe a practice drill is what's keeping her. Whenever she takes her white helmet down from the shelf in the hall closet and goes off to protect us from the Nazis, I feel proud. Also scared. Right now, though, all I can think about is the water balloon in my belly.

Miss Lange is keeping me company outside school. She is reassuring me, "Don't worry, Loretta dear, I'm sure your mother will be here any minute."

No one calls me by my real name except my teacher. I've been Bunny all my life. Some of my friends call me Cottintail, which is fine with me since I happen to love Peter Rabbit. Hearing Miss

Lange say Loretta makes me feel like she's talking about someone else, someone more grown up than I feel right now. She says it in her kind kindergarten-teacher voice, but her eyes betray a forced mirth, and her fingers are twirling a lock of her hair the way I chew on strands of mine when I'm scared. She flashes her kind kindergarten-teacher smile at the moms oohing and aahing over their children's splotchy finger paintings and lumpy clay sculptures. Miss Lange calls what we kids produced this morning "works of art." Mine is a pair of pipe-cleaner eyeglasses with lenses I made from a sheet of yellow cellophane and fastened with Scotch tape. I hook one fuzzy stem behind each ear and hope the inserts will hide my eyes while I blink away my tears. Miss Lange says my creation is "quite special."

The last of my classmates head home with their moms on foot or pile into rattling prewar sedans and chug off, windows rolled open to the soft autumn breeze. I'm the only child left. Miss Lange obviously has things to do, easels to wipe, clay to wrap in plastic and put away, so I dare not ask her to take me inside to use the Girls Room, it would only add to her distress. Besides if I'm not in front of the building when Mommy arrives, she won't know where to find me.

I rivet my gaze up the street and try to pray our old Dodge into view. The water balloon in my belly is full to bursting. I'm tightening my tummy muscles with all the might I can muster. The last time I had an accident I was a toddler. "I'd like to sit on the steps if that's okay," I tell Miss Lange.

My teacher wears her shoulder-length hair parted in the middle, each side fastened just above her ears with a small tortoise shell comb. She looks like Hedy Lamarr, neat and ladylike, and the pattern on her dress picks up the blue of her eyes and the pinky-purple of her lipstick, and her purse matches her shoes. I don't want to disappoint Miss Lange. I want to be neat and ladylike too. But this is an emergency. She bends with a straight back like a ballet dancer and brushes off one of the marble steps. "Oh dear. You'll soil your pretty skirt," she says, her eyebrows knitting a tent on her forehead at the sight of the grime on her pink palm. "Are you sure you want to sit here?"

"Yes, I'm sure," I reply, planting my bottom on the marble step before she can object. "I was so excited about starting school today I didn't sleep much last night, so I'm really, really tired." Pressing my thighs together, I smooth the robin's egg blue skirt across my lap and spread it like a fan. Miss Lange steals a furtive glance at her watch. I'm only five years old, but since my big sister, Betty, taught me to tell time over the summer I know what it means when the little hand is on the twelve and the big hand is on the three. It means Mommy is fifteen minutes late on the most important day of my life.

I stare at my patent leather Mary Janes. I have to pee this minute! Can't hold it in anymore! Can't stop it. Can't let it burst out or Miss Lange will hear it whoosh. Oh, God! Here it comes…right now!! I try to imagine myself at Jones Beach or the Rockaways where Mommy usually lets me pee in the ocean or silently into sand. That's what I'm doing now, controlling it with my muscles, letting it out, little by little, slowly and soundlessly, making sure my skirt is hiding it from my teacher's gaze. If she sees I've wet myself, she'll think I'm not toilet-trained and she'll tell Mommy I'm not ready for kindergarten. Checking my lap, I'm relieved to see the half-circle of my skirt has concealed the puddle pooling beneath my panties, the yellow ones that say Monday. I remember putting them on this morning because I knew my first day of school was on a Monday and my sister had also taught me to read.

The big hand is on the five when Mommy finally drives up to the curb. Usually, her wavy brown hair frames her freckled cheeks, and her eyes, as brown as Hershey's kisses, are smiling, and when she goes out, she wears a tiny hat with a little veil, and nylon stockings with straight seams up the back of her legs. What I'm saying is, usually my mother looks as neat as my teacher, but now, rushing toward us, Mommy's hair is matted with sweat and she looks like she's been crying.

"Bunny, darling, I'm so, so, sorry," she blurts out, trying to catch her breath and appear calm. "I hope you weren't scared. And, Miss Lange, please forgive me for inconveniencing you. I was stopped at a red light, and one of Dugan's Bakery vans rammed me hard." Mommy points at our car, whose rear bumper is pressed against its now crumpled fender. "I wasn't hurt, neither was the driver, but we had to stay at the scene of the accident and exchange license numbers and wait for a policeman to come, and it took a lot of time. I knew I was keeping you waiting and I feel awful about it, only there was nothing I could do."

It must look weird that I didn't fly into my mother's arms after waiting for her all this time, but no way was I going to expose my puddle with my teacher standing there. I stay seated on the marble step, encircled by my skirt like a tadpole on a lily pad. Miss Lange's kind kindergarten voice tells me she looks forward to seeing me in class tomorrow. I thank her for keeping me company, and she turns and disappears into the school building. Only then do I burst into tears and tell Mommy I peed. She's not mad, just shrugs off her gray cardigan and ties its sleeves around my waist so when I stand up her sweater covers my shame. At home, she hoists me onto her lap and rocks me until I stop sobbing and doesn't care that my wet skirt is soiling her dress.

"It's not your fault, sweetie. You had an accident just like I did. You couldn't help it." She snuggles her nose in the nook of my neck and whispers, "When something isn't your fault, you have nothing to be ashamed of."

In a few years, I will take a walk with my parents on a cold, windy beach and they will tell me their secrets, and I will get my first inkling of what my mother was ashamed of—facts, events, and accidents beyond her control, circumstances she was powerless to change yet felt obliged to cover up with a fiction of her own invention. When something isn't your fault, you have nothing to be ashamed of. If only she'd believed her own words.

CHAPTER 21

SHE LIED TO ENHANCE HER PAST AND PRESERVE HER DIGNITY

Kids in my neighborhood used to ask each other, "What does your daddy do?" (We knew what our mommies did because they all stayed home and we watched them do it.)

"My daddy's a lawyer," I'd reply. Sometimes, I'd say "attorney-at-law" savoring the stately phrase and its impact.

"Wow! Like Perry Mason?" they asked, meaning the character in Earl Stanley Gardner's bestselling books. (The TV character didn't appear until the late 1950s.)

Class is a touchy issue for Jews. Today the Jewish stereotype would have us all working at Goldman Sachs or founding Facebook. In the 1940s and '50s, most of my friends came from working-class families, their fathers wore overalls or commercial uniforms, held jobs in the garment industry, or ran neighborhood shops. My mother's younger brothers, Herbert and Milton, worked in sales. Her brother Lou owned the coffee and tea store that my Grandpa Nathan started on the Lower East Side. Aunt Tillie's husband, Ralph, was an accountant who had a stationery store. Aunt Sadye's husband, Herman, operated a hand laundry. Aunt Rona's husband, Ben, was a jewelry maker. On my father's side, his brother Lou worked for a manufacturer of American flags. (A proud Communist, he never saw his job as inconsistent with his politics. He said he didn't hate his flag or his country, just wanted America to be true to its ideals.) Dad's brother Sid was a manufacturers' rep. Two younger brothers died at a young age. Outclassing them all, Jack Cottin—City College, Class of 1920, NYU Law School, 1923, attorney-at-law—wore a suit and tie every day and took the subway to "the city" (our name for Manhattan), where he had an office with his name on the door and a private secretary.

Jack and Ralph, the accountant, were the only "professional men" on my mother's side of the family and the only male blood relatives on either side to matriculate beyond the twelfth grade. All my relatives deferred to Jack, which could not have been easy on my seven uncles who had fewer achievements but more than their fair share of male ego. In one of Betty's letters to Dad when he was in Palestine, she appended a flattering anecdote about how Aunt Tillie coaxed good behavior out of her son Danny, then six, not by citing his father, Ralph, as a role model but by promising, "If you're a good boy, you can grow up to be a big man like your Uncle Jack."

The only woman of my parents' generation with a college degree on either side of my family, or Bert's for that matter, was my dad's sister, Esther. Ten years younger than Jack, gutsy and adventurous, Esther Cottin traveled the world on her own and during a trip to Jerusalem met a Jew from Bombay, India—Ben Sargon, a British barrister—and married him three weeks later. That Uncle Ben, surely an intellectual match for my father, was a man of quiet dignity with a degree from Cambridge who had trained in law at one of the Inns of Court in London. Aunt Esther became a Hebrew teacher, first in India then in Winthrop, Massachusetts. Cosmopolitan, educated, sophisticated, both of them, yet they also bowed before Jack, too polite, or intimidated, to challenge his authoritative pronouncements.

The fact that my father was considered the reigning intellect on both sides of our family lent me secondhand luster and my mother a set of sterling credentials in an era when married women derived their status from their husbands. Paradoxically, the prestige that Ceil gained through her marriage to Jack was overridden by her shame about being so undereducated compared to him. And rather than assuage her academic inferiority complex, he occasionally exacerbated it by calling her a "greenhorn" (a wet-behind-the-ears newcomer), though when she bristled, he always claimed he was just joking.

❦

Esther Pogrebin's wedding photo
c. 1932

Ceil's "high school graduation"
photo c. 1915

Once, when Betty was visiting our New York apartment, she stopped before the display of old family photographs mounted on the wall in the entry area and pointed to a two-part picture frame, in one side of which was mounted a studio portrait of our mother, dark hair pulled back and tied at the nape, a scattering of roses on the table beside her, a rolled-up diploma in her hands; on the other side a studio photograph of my mother-in-law Esther dressed in a filmy white wedding gown and holding a beribboned bouquet of flowers.

I'd framed the two pictures in tandem to highlight the similarities between the women, but in that moment, peering at them with my sister Betty, what struck me were their differences. My mother-in-law is smiling into the camera, obviously thrilled to be a bride, while my mother is unsmiling, though one would think she'd be pleased with herself since the picture appears to be her high school graduation portrait. Only she knew that she was a poseur, the pose itself was a pretense.

"Mom treasured that photograph," Betty recalled, her eyes wistful. "She told me she couldn't afford the studio fee, but the photographer let her pay it off in installments. Took her three years to do it." A wad of tissue materialized from my sister's sleeve. "She'd picked the diploma and silk roses out of the photographer's prop trunk and arranged the setting herself. She always kept that picture where every visitor could see it. Most people had no idea she never graduated from high school."

In the somber eyes of the girl clutching the fake diploma, I saw the woman forever humiliated by her lack of formal learning. "I can't believe Mom would lie about her education."

"She didn't have to. People don't go around asking you what degrees you've earned. Unless you're applying for a job. In that case—I mean if someone had grilled her point-blank—she would have admitted she only got as far as eighth grade. But it would have shamed her."

"Like Dad used to shame her when he quizzed her on things he knew she didn't know. Remember the time he asked her the date of the Battle of Hastings?" I lifted the double frame off its peg and dusted its glass with the tail of my shirt.

Betty grinned. "No, but I remember when she couldn't spell hors d'oeuvres."

"He was always putting her down to puff himself up."

"That's not true. He was just teasing her," my sister insisted. As usual, her love for our dad brooked no criticism.

Returning the double frame to its nail, I wondered if Mom's staged "graduation" portrait may have been her first undertaking in what would become her lifelong project of self-creation. Though I'd known her to be a highly ethical person, when it came to enhancing her past and preserving her dignity, she was a fluent dissembler. Cover up, lie, reinvent, or omit were her go-to responses to any fact or reality she believed might be a shanda. No one had to know what it was like to live as a family of nine crammed into three small rooms, or to work in a factory making artificial flowers, or to sleep with Tillie in one cot, face to feet, or in hot weather on the fire escape, two heads on one feather pillow.

I would come to regret not asking her more questions about her early years in this country, but when I was young details of her childhood (and my father's) were of little interest to me. I could not have imagined that she would be gone before I was old enough, or cared enough, to figure out who she was and how she came to be, and I would someday yearn for every tidbit or morsel of her history that anyone might throw my way. Mom rarely talked about the past unless prodded. Maybe that's why a story I coaxed out of her one soft June evening shortly after I turned fifteen seemed as worthy of preservation as the gardenia corsage I would later press between the pages of a book. I was getting dressed to go to my high school boyfriend's senior prom, and Mom was buttoning the back of my lemon-yellow tulle strapless gown, which took some doing since it had many tiny buttons, when she suddenly asked me, "Don't you feel proud when your friends come here and see where you live?"

In 1950, we moved to the second house my parents owned since leaving the Bronx for Queens, and thanks to an uptick in my father's law practice, this one was double the size of the structure we'd shared on 167th Street with Tillie and Ralph, and it was in Jamaica *Estates*, one of the classiest neighborhoods in Queens. Though it wasn't as grand in scale or elaborately furnished as others nearby, it had a spacious back yard and much larger rooms that our previous home, and my mother had decorated it beautifully, yet comfortably. I used to hang out with my friends all over the house, on the half-moon loveseats in our wall-to-wall carpeted living room; in our sun-filled kitchen, having brownies and milk after school; in the TV room, which doubled or tripled as my father's study and "the library," or in our finished basement where my friends and I played Doris Day and Frank Sinatra records or tuned in Martin Bloch's "Make Believe Ballroom" on the radio. Besides Dad's fully-equipped tool room, the basement was outfitted with a full bar that featured all sorts of colorful liqueurs, for instance, mint green Crème de Menthe, a slender, super-tall, triangular flask of golden yellow Galliano, and a deep purple raspberry liqueur called Chambord, that comes in a ball-shaped bottle topped with a gold crown. I assume Dad bought the cordials for the shapes of their containers and the color of each liquid since the bottles were never opened in all the time we lived there. Their purpose was to impress my parents' friends.

I remember that house with sorrow, because it's where my mother sickened and died, but also with fondness thanks to the pajama parties I hosted, two girls tucked into sleeping bags on the floor of my bedroom, another in the twin bed that stood catty-cornered to mine. I remember the festiveness of Mom's Shabbos and holiday dinners, the only occasions when we ate in the dining room, whose wide doorway was flanked by a pair of curlicued wrought iron gates that I used to imagine had once graced the entrance to a Spanish hacienda. I remember sunbathing on the lawn, surrounded by lilacs in the spring, hydrangeas in the summer. For all that, after a few years on Wareham Place, I suppose I took the pleasures of the house for granted. Now, as I reconstruct every room in my mind and marinate in my youthful memories, the image of Mom buttoning me into my prom dress came back to me along with her question. And my reply.

"To be honest, I've never given a moment's thought to what my friends think about where I live."

Mom said I was very lucky to feel that way. When she was my age, she was ashamed of where she lived, so much so that she used to give her suitors the address of her uncle Will's apartment house and have the young men pick her up there as if it was her home. Will and his wife, Mary, owned a dress factory and lived in the northern reaches of the Bronx. Their building wasn't the Waldorf Astoria, but their apartment was far more presentable than Jenny and Nathan's tenement flat on the Lower East Side. Besides, Mom said, Will spoke much better English than my grandfather.

Years later, Tillie filled in the details on her oral history tape. She said Will enjoyed playing Dad in front of his niece's gentlemen callers, which makes me wonder how my grandfather felt about the arrangement. It seemed that Will, his brother-in-law, who had bankrolled the tickets for Jenny and the four children to come to America and pressured Nathan to stay in their marriage, was now masquerading as Ceil's father because Nathan, her real father, was an embarrassment. Assuming he was aware of the masquerade, Nathan must have been humiliated by it. Based on what I now know about his willingness to abandon Jenny and the kids, I can't help feeling he deserved it.

For my mother to arrive at her uncle's apartment before that evening's suitor got there, she had to leave work at the end of a ten-hour day and travel on two subway lines to the last stop in the Bronx, then walk several blocks to the building. And no matter how late it was when her date brought her "home," she would have to wait until he was safely out of sight before dragging herself back to the subway for the long trip downtown. Considering the time, effort, and energy it took for her to pull off her elaborate charade, that story, almost more than any other, proves the stranglehold that shame must have had on my mother.

CHAPTER 22

NAME CHANGERS, GAME CHANGERS

A name can hide history, heritage, family origin, dramas of dislocation, loss, power, exploitation, and domination. Some people's names are like secrets. That thought took hold of me recently in response to the 2021 *Times* obituary of ninety-two-year-old Rajie Cook, the legendary Palestinian-American designer of symbols and pictographs—such as the bicycle in a circle with a line through it or the universal sign for male and female restrooms. When he was in the fourth grade in an elementary school in Newark, New Jersey, his Arabic first name was preemptively changed to Roger by a teacher who said Rajie was too difficult to pronounce. "In a flash my birth name was changed," Cook told *Bucks County Magazine*, "but my parents raised no objections in deference to the educator." Before Rajie was born, his paternal grandfather's last name, Suleiman, also had been altered by others. Turks occupying Palestine changed Suleiman to Kucuk, which means small in Turkish, and when the British took over the country, they changed Kucuk into Cook. Roger reclaimed Rajie years later when his heritage became important to his art. To my mind, it's kind of neat that a man who personally experienced the mutability and impermanence of a name became the creator of dozens of simple, stable, universally recognized symbols whose comprehension is entirely independent of nationality, language, or pronunciation.

Talk about having one's name changed by others: Moishe Margolies, who was born in Jerusalem in 1921, came to America at age eight knowing Hebrew and Yiddish but not a word of English. On his first day of school at the Salanter Yeshiva, his teacher had all the students stand up and say their English names. Moishe didn't quite understand what was going on but did manage to say "Moshe." The teacher, presumably believing he was doing him a favor, "Christianized" his name to "Morris." The name stuck, even though he always hated it. He introduced himself as Murray when he met his wife. His aunts, uncles, nieces, and nephews never stopped calling him "Moish." His obituary listed him as "Morris B. Margolies." But, since he'd been ordained at twenty-one; served the Jewish community all his life, including twenty-five years in the pulpit at Kansas City's Congregation Beth Shalom; and died at ninety, most people just called him "Rabbi."

My real name is Loretta Jo. (I say "real" when referring to the name given to us at birth by our parents.) As a child, I went by "Bunny," a nickname bestowed on me by my dad, who used to say I was as cute as a bunny. Ashkenazi Jews name their children after deceased relatives to perpetuate their memory and Loretta was meant to honor my father's late mother, Yetta, though my mother once confessed that, secretly, she felt she was naming me for her favorite actress, Loretta Young. My middle name, Jo, was for my father's maternal grandfather, Joseph, but again, Mom intended it as a paean to Jo Marsh, her favorite daughter in her favorite novel, *Little Women*. To my mind, Loretta conjured an "old maid" school-marm or a dowdy librarian, whereas Louisa May Alcott's fictional character was a smart, brash, independent, aspiring girl writer, like me. Someday, I'll change my name to Jo, I told myself. Fate had other plans.

I'm in the third grade. Our teacher is calling the roll. When she says, "Loretta Cottin," I raise my hand and shout "Present" in a strong, confident voice, as she'd taught us to do. At that, the new girl with straight bangs and buck teeth, a recent arrival from England, who sits at the wooden desk behind me, declares with haughty British assurance, "Oh my, no! You're not a Loretta! You're a Letty!" The instant she says it, her 't's' tinkling like a hostess's dinner bell in a Victorian play, I feel like a different person. "Leh-ttee!" she says again, in her crisp high-tea accent. This time, the word resounds like the ping of a silver spoon on a crystal goblet. It makes me feel celebratory and buoyant. I claim it with my whole being as if it had been written in ink on my birth certificate: Letty Jo Cottin. That's who I've been all along. That's who I will be from then on—a Letty.

Valence is the term psychologists use to describe a word's intrinsic goodness or badness. Names, especially, carry weight; feelings; memories; expectations; ethnic, religious, and national identity; even physical and emotional associations. When I was single and someone wanted to fix me up with an Irving, I was less inclined to say yes than if his name was Bob. Some of us feel our names fit us perfectly; other names and their owners seem comically or tragically mismatched. I've heard people—a Maud, in one case, a Seymour in another—joke with a wry smile that a hospital nurse must have clipped the wrong name card to their bassinet.

I never felt like a Loretta. It's not that I was ashamed of the name. It wasn't a bad name or an ugly name, but it weighed me down, and when I had to answer to it in school or a doctor's office, I felt like an imposter. But as soon as the little Brit renamed me, "Letty" settled on my thin shoulders like a gossamer summer shawl, its colors light and cheerful, befitting a child who aspired to be light and cheerful. Wasting no time, I asked my teachers and classmates to call me Letty and, when I got home, demanded the same of my parents and, to my surprise, they agreed. (Though, like most speakers of American English, myself included, almost everyone pronounced it "Leddy.")

Years later, Mom told me why she'd been amenable to the change. She had previously run into an old acquaintance who, upon meeting me, had asked her how she came to name me Loretta Jo, the first name favored by Italians, the middle name by "Southern crackers." My guess is, having grown up surrounded by Zeldas, Gittels, and Shaynas, she may have chosen Loretta Jo because, to her ears it sounded *American*. She had no idea that a name could telegraph a child's ethnic origin. At any rate, after her friend's comment, Mom started to call me Bunny, the nickname my father had dubbed me at birth. Better an animal association than the shanda of a name that suggested I was an Italian-Catholic. Unwittingly, by becoming Letty, I relieved my mother of the embarrassment of my given name and reaffirmed her loyalty to The Jewish People.

Actually, what worried me at the time was my *father's* reaction to my precipitous name change. By abandoning Loretta, would I be dishonoring his mother? No, he assured me, Letty was fine with him. Yetta had died in Palestine before I was born, but he was sure she wouldn't mind either; dead people don't look down from some heavenly dominion and judge the living. I should just enjoy being Letty. Which is precisely what I've done since third grade, never imagining there would be more to the story.

⌒⌒⌒⌒⌒

In 2008, my cousin, Wendy, the one who lives on a moshav (farm cooperative) near Jerusalem, sent a group email informing me and the other surviving Cottin cousins that after a long hiatus she had visited Grandma Yetta's grave in Tiberias and found its headstone in serious disrepair. If we all chipped in to have it restored, Wendy assured us, she would get the job done. I contributed to the project and thought no more about it until, several months later, another group email arrived from my Israeli cousin, this one with a photo attached of our grandmother's restored headstone, its formerly indecipherable inscription now sharp as a woodcut. Since I have difficulty reading Hebrew when the words are written without vowels, I was grateful to Wendy for appending an English translation:

Here rests a modest woman
Dear and excellent
With a good heart and soul, gentle
Intelligent in her respect for G-d and belief
Yenta Cottin
Daughter of Reb Yosef Halevi, of blessed memory,
Died in the sixty-first year of her life, passed away
5 Tammuz 5696 [equivalent to June 25, 1936]
May her soul be bound up in the binding of life

I reread the English translation, then stared in disbelief at the Hebrew letters that composed my grandmother's name. Yud. Nun. Tet. Hay. Even without vowels, I recognized that those letters didn't spell Yetta, they spelled Yenta!

Wendy must have anticipated my confusion because she included the derivation of the name and assured me that Yenta comes from the Yiddish word *yente* whose original meaning is gentle, genteel, or noble. Small comfort that. Linguists can probe the vicissitudes of derivation until Tisha B'Av. Every Jew knows what a yenta is. I may as well have been named for the gossipy matchmaker in *Fiddler on the Roof.*

Any lingering guilt I may have felt about abandoning my real name turned to sorrow at the sight of the stone bearing my grandmother's "real name," the name she'd declined to use during her lifetime, the name that may have embarrassed her or, at the very least, ill-suited her, as Loretta had ill-suited me. But now, her grandchildren's well-meaning donations and a good scrubbing had consigned her to sleep beneath that unwanted appellation for eternity or until another century's windstorms scoured the stone to dust and no one was left to take notice or care.

For me, however, the photograph of Yetta's headstone offered concrete proof, more than eighty years after her death, that my paternal grandmother had changed her name when she was alive just as I'd changed mine. I'll never know why she did it, but thanks to that unexpected revelation, I felt a visceral connection to her for the first time. By quitting Yenta and becoming Yetta, she had created a new self and claimed the power to name, no small thing for a woman of her time. Or mine.

Something else troubled me about the stone's inscription. Jewish law dictates that children mourn their deceased parents for eleven months after burial while adults mourn the deaths of their spouses and children for only thirty days. A bereaved husband is permitted to marry after those thirty days. A bereaved wife must wait ninety days before marrying again so that her betrothed can be confident that she's not pregnant by her deceased husband. Halacha also dictates that the timetable for the unveiling of the headstone is flexible so long as it takes place before the one-year anniversary of the person's death. Israeli Jews typically schedule the unveiling at the completion of the first thirty days; Jews in the US usually wait the year. In either case, certain words and phrases tend to recur on Jewish gravestones. In addition to the deceased's name, birth and death dates, the common phrases include, "Devoted wife of...," "Beloved father of...," "Adored grandmother of." It bothered me that Grandma Yetta's stone memorialized her solely as "Daughter of," obliterating the nearly four decades she spent as the devoted (some would say saintly) wife of Max Cottin, as well as the beloved mother of seven and adored grandmother of several. An anonymously written family history dating from the 1940s describes Max as harsh and scholarly, and Yetta as a gentle soul. When I finally met my secret sister Rena, I asked her about our grandparents because she was old enough to have known them before they left for Palestine. "Max was a rigid disciplinarian, a martinet, an autocrat, and a cold fish," Rena said, sneering. "I disliked him so intensely that I refused to name my son after him even though Dad asked me to. When Max was around, Yetta barely said a word. But I had a soft spot for your namesake. In all the time I knew her, she uttered only one sentence to me: 'What is your favorite vegetable?' I said peas. Sure enough, every time we visited her after that, she served me peas."

Yetta and Max Cottin, c. 1930s

Since Max was the only other member of the Cottin family who was in Palestine when Yetta died, it was probably he who decided what her stone would say. He took a second wife immediately after the end of the thirty-day mourning period for Yetta and the unveiling of her gravestone happened a few days later. My guess is that my grandfather made an executive (patriarchal) decision to omit "wife of Max" from her monument in order to please his new wife and, being a cold fish, he likely saw no reason to pay the stonecutter to engrave "mother of..." and list Yetta's seven children. That could be one guess too far, but whatever his reason, he buried our grandmother under a name she never used and probably didn't like. According to my older cousins, Max had bullied and belittled Yetta for years. Did he also have to wipe out the only identities that gave meaning to her life?

From Biblical times until today, our tribe has boasted a long line of noteworthy name changers, starting in Genesis. When Avram and Sarai became the world's first Jews, God changed their names to Abraham and Sarah because their previous names "were insufficient to empower them in fulfilling their new mission, to convince humanity that there was only one God." We've all heard stories of customs officials changing our grandparents' names at Ellis Island. The Folklore Archives at the University of Southern California contain an oral history by a Jewish woman who claims that her three great-uncles, all with the surname Levenbuch, came through Ellis Island separately and "when they started their life in America one received the name Levenbook, one was Levenbrook, and one was Levenburg." A colleague of my husband, Tracy Ferguson, snagged my attention at a law conference when, upon hearing that someone had won the lottery, he exclaimed, "*Halevai af mir gezogt*" (It should happen to me). I wondered how someone with a name like Ferguson could speak such authentic Yiddish. Maybe his dad was Irish-Catholic, but his mother was a Jew from the Old Country? Nope, Tracy replied, both of his parents were Jewish. But when his father passed through immigration and was asked his name, he got nervous and blurted out, "*Sheyn fergessen*" (I've already forgotten). The officer wrote down, "Sean Ferguson." Sounds apocryphal, and it *is*.

In her book *People Love Dead Jews*, Dara Horn explodes the myth that customs officers Americanized Jewish names because the names were too hard to say or spell. In fact, it was our immigrant forebears who invented that cover story rather than admit that they had changed their own names for practical reasons—either because they couldn't find jobs or buy property in certain neighborhoods if they had foreign-sounding names (true today for many Black people with African-sounding or other nontraditional names) or their children were ridiculed or bullied in school. Jews couldn't tell the truth about their motivations, Horn writes, because it would confirm " two enormous fears: first, that this country doesn't really accept you, and second, that the best way to survive and thrive is to dump any outward sign of your Jewish identity, and symbolically cut that cord that goes back to Mount Sinai." So they blamed the intake process at Ellis Island and relabeled themselves to survive.

During the Third Reich, Jews changed their own names when a recognizably Semitic handle could be a death sentence while a false identity offered the possibility of escape. With an alias on their forged passports, thousands of Jewish refugees re-created themselves anew and assimilated into the general population of their adoptive countries. Hollywood moguls changed the names of Jewish movie stars for commercial expediency and marquee appeal. (Betty Joan Perske to Lauren Bacall, Issur Danielovitch Demsky to Kirk Douglas, Bernard Schwartz to Tony Curtis.) The late Peter Bogdanovic, son of Jewish immigrants fleeing from the Nazis, once said, "I wanted to look like Bill Holden because I wanted to be a real American boy and do all those wonderful things. And with a name like Bogdanovich there wasn't much of a chance." He didn't change his name; he *made* his name by becoming a superlative director (*The Last Picture Show, Paper Moon, What's Up, Doc?*).

Israel's founders, who arrived in Palestine earlier in the twentieth century, changed their names for life-affirming reasons. Girded by optimism, they jettisoned their Ashkenazi labels and took Hebrew names that negated the stain of the diaspora; spoke of Jewish strength, pride, and history; and foretold a new breed of Jew. The country's first prime minister, David Gruen, became David Ben Gurion (Hebrew for lion cub: an apt description of the scrappy five-foot-tall hero of independence). Szymon Perski became Shimon Peres; he named himself for Perez, son of the biblical character Judah, and the Hebrew term for "bursts forth." Golda Mabovich, "the girl who made Milwaukee famous," married Morris Meyerson in 1917 and went by his last name until 1956 when she changed it to Meir, "one who shines." The symbolism of Israel's early pioneers renaming themselves had a lasting impact on the young nation's collective psyche, jump-starting the engine of recovery, rejuvenation, and reinvention that's been powering Israeli-Jewish identity ever since.

Resilience and transformation often go hand in hand; the trick is to alter the superficial parts of the self while keeping one's heart, soul, and essence intact. The chameleon-like ability of The Jewish People to adapt to the unexpected has been one of our enduring strengths and effective survival strategies. While I view name changing in that light, other descendants of the immigrant generation see it differently. Postmodern purists, perhaps under the influence of identity politics, believe that by accepting "Americanized" names, our parents or grandparents betrayed family, faith, and heritage; that they were cowards for letting themselves be named-shamed at the gateway to the United States. They say changing from Horowitz to Howard was a shanda. I say our grandparents and great-grandparents weren't passive sheep, waiting for a hot branding iron to sear an American flag on their rumps; they were pragmatic, shape-shifting realists whose willingness to accommodate to their new home country and its culture is what got them from "there" to "here."

My father always said that his father, Max, arrived in New York from Minsk with the surname, Katan, Hebrew for "small," which, as pronounced in his Russian-Yiddish accent, sounded like "Caught-yon," and that the customs man, unsure of how to render Caught-yon into spellable English, simplified it to Cottin with an "i." That may have been Max's cover story but, as Dara Horn noted, customs officials didn't write the name of each incoming refugee on a blank line, they checked off her or his name on an existing list of authorized arrivals. Therefore my grandfather obviously renamed himself for reasons buried in the murk of time.

My mother was no stranger to the alchemy of a name-changing, either. Her given name, Sarah, is corroborated both by the hand-written list of Halpern offspring that surfaced from the shopping bag and by the elephantine recollections of my aunt Tillie who said Sarah came down with a life-threatening case of whooping cough when she was a teenager and their mother changed her name to save her life. Superstitious to a fault, Jenny believed that the Ayin Ha'ra, the Evil Eye, was always on the prowl for a weak, vulnerable, or sick child to steal away into the nether world, but if you spit three times (not literally, just made the thpu-thpu-thpu sound produced by the tongue darting through pursed lips), said "*kinne-hurra*," to ward off the Evil Eye, and gave your child a new name connoting strength and resistance, you could trick the malevolent spirit into leaving empty-handed. Jenny renamed Sarah "Cyral," which means "masterful." It worked; Cyral got better.

Sometime after her divorce, my mother changed her name to Ceil, the French word for "heaven." Maybe she thought Cyral sounded too British or too masculine. Maybe she contracted another grave illness and thought a name change would deflect the Evil Eye a second time. My guess is that she changed her name to fit her own "new life-mission," which was to be sophisticated and worldly-wise. She didn't live long enough for that. Ceil died of cancer at fifty-one. (Later I would discover proof that she'd been lying about her age for years. In fact, she was fifty-three.)

Since the third grade, when I changed my name from Loretta to Letty, I've survived two major illnesses without giving myself a new name. But while I was going through treatments for the breast cancer in 2009 and the brain tumor a few years later, I confess to invoking my mother's thpu-thpu-thpus and kinnehurras about a million times. Thus far, they work.

CHAPTER 23

MY MISSING UNCLES

My father was one of seven siblings, two of whom were entirely absent from our lives and never discussed. All I knew about my father's mysterious brothers were their names: Edward and Meyer. Whenever I asked Dad about them, his answer was always, "They died young."

"How?

"Edward had some sort of glandular disease. Meyer, I'm not sure."

"How could you not know how your own brothers died?"

"I just don't."

"Do you have any pictures of them?"

Dad said there were none. "Period. The end," which is what he always said to cut short a conversation that made him the least bit uncomfortable.

The day my granddaughter came by to rummage through my files, I pulled out my father's college yearbook, class of 1920, so she could see what her great-grandfather looked like at her age. Up front, on a page headed "Yearbook Staff," was a photograph of a young Jack Cottin smiling above the caption, "Business Manager." Absent the mustache that he would acquire in his thirties and wear for the rest of his life, he looked like himself, same pale eyes, same Clark Gable ears. I hadn't cracked Dad's yearbook in ages, and I don't know why, this time, though never before, my eye got snagged by a photo captioned "Assistant Business Manager," and below it, a name that literally made me gasp: Edward Cottin. The only physical trait my father had ever mentioned about that mysterious missing uncle was his glandular disease and there it was writ large on Edward's face. His puffy cheeks looked the way mine do when I'm trying to blow up a resistant rubber balloon. Steroids didn't exist until about twenty years later, but Edward resembled the kids I saw at Memorial Sloan Kettering Cancer Center when I was being treated there. And the boy in the picture looked really young, more like a freshman in high school than a college senior. Dad never said how old Edward was when he died; however, extrapolating from the fact that the baby of the Cottin family was my uncle Sid, and a typical number of years (typical pre–birth control) separated him and the next oldest surviving offspring, it made sense that Edward was born during that span, which would have made him between four and six years younger than my dad. And since Jack graduated from CCNY at twenty, and Edward's photo establishes that he was there at the same time working on the same yearbook, that means he was between fourteen and sixteen years old in his senior year. Sounds to me like a child prodigy. Yet Dad had never mentioned that young Edward was his college classmate. And according to my Cottin cousins, none of the other four surviving siblings ever talked about their precocious brother to *their* children. That, by itself, was baffling.

I'm making a big deal about the ghosting of Edward because it baldly contradicts typical Jewish family behavior and the dictates of Jewish tradition. Most of us consider it a mitzvah, a commandment, an obligation, to memorialize our deceased loved ones. We keep them alive by evoking their memory at every opportunity, by telling and retelling their stories, by lighting a yahrzeit candle and saying kaddish for them every year on the anniversary of their death. Edward was not just a kid with a glandular disease. He must have been off-the-charts brilliant to have blown past the rigid Jewish quotas of the early twentieth century and qualified in his early teens for admission to CCNY. That achievement, in itself, would have brought great *nachas* (pride and pleasure) to the average Jewish family whose members would have honored his memory and savored every detail of his short life. Why didn't the Cottin family do the same? Were they so saddened by his premature passing that they could not bear to mention his name? Or did they feel there was something shameful about his glandular condition or about Edward himself?

Meyer, the other brother who "died young," having left no educational footprint, presents an even murkier mystery. One of my cousins thinks Meyer may have perished in the influenza pandemic of 1918. Another heard rumors of his involvement in "the mob," something about Prohibition, guns, crime, murder, which would explain why, when my cousins and I asked our parents about Uncle Meyer, we got shut down. Contemplating the two missing branches on my father's family tree, I now believe that my mystery uncles may have been erased for failing its patriarch's unforgiving standards of perfection—Edward, for contracting the terrible malady that malformed his body and caused his premature death; Meyer, by getting himself killed under suspicious circumstances. From what I've learned about my Grandpa Max—who had temporarily disowned his then-adolescent son, Sid, for refusing to attend an elite yeshiva—I think it plausible that he felt personally shamed by the fates of Edward and Meyer to the point where he banned even the mention of their names. Trained to obey their exacting, judgmental patriarch, my uncles' surviving siblings seem to have fallen into line and behaved as if Edward and Meyer never existed.

CHAPTER 24

I DIDN'T OWN A CASHMERE SWEATER

I was no child prodigy, but thanks to New York City's "Special Progress" program, I skipped a grade in elementary school and a grade in middle school, which explains why I was only sixteen years old in September 1955 when my father drove me up to Waltham, Massachusetts, and dropped me off at Brandeis University. A few weeks into the semester, I realized that I was both the youngest member of the freshman class and the only motherless child in my dorm—Ceil had died only five months before—and that any sign of grief on my part made several of my fellow students squirm. I learned to skate past the unpleasantness of my loss and hide those aspects of my personal situation that might arouse their judgment or pathos. Most kids that age have yet to master the skill of conveying sympathy without awkwardness. To spare my friends discomfort, I kept my feelings under control and mindfully cultivated the confident façade of a cheerful college coed. I wanted to be liked, not pitied.

Which didn't stop me from feeling sorry for myself when, in an unconscionably short period, without discussing any of it with me, my father sold our house; rented a one-bedroom apartment; assigned me a daybed in his vestibule; parceled out to relatives most of my mother's personal effects, china, and silver; and gave away everything in my childhood room, my bedspread and drapes, both hand-made by Mom, my desk, bureau, night table, even the little white Arvin radio I used to play at top volume to drown out my parents' arguments. I'm not saying Jack was a cruel man, just practical, insensitive, self-involved, and proud. Which is my indelicate way of introducing the embarrassing subject of money.

Dad with his sailboat, the "Heaven" c. 1920s

My father had supported himself through school—Townsend Harris Prep, the city's most selective school for gifted boys; then City College, which he'd entered at sixteen; then NYU Law School—by teaching Hebrew school twenty hours a week and tutoring four bar mitzvah boys per year at $150 each, a princely sum in those years. His earnings bought him a spiffy little canoe with a sail, his one personal indulgence; the rest of the money went to his father to help cover household expenses. (Scrap irony: Mom named herself Ceil, heaven in French, Dad named his sailboat "Heaven." Just sayin'.) Enforced self-sufficiency had been character-building for him, he said, as it would be for me. That's how he told me he would be paying my tuition, room, and board but all my other college expenses over the next four years—books, clothes, activity fees, pizza, beer, aspirin, "feminine stuff," cigarettes, movies—would be my responsibility.

～✺～

We arrive at my dorm, Hamilton C; my father helps me carry my belongings upstairs, then leaves without much ado, no reveries about this landmark transition or how much he's going to miss me. Totally his style. No surprise. Once he's gone, I focus on what's happening around me, girls popping into each other's rooms, putting up posters—Van Gogh's sunflowers, Monet's lily pads—introducing themselves to one another, making conversation as they, with the help of their mothers, empty the contents of their trunks into closets and drawers. Batches of cashmere sweaters—V-necks, turtlenecks, sweater sets in every color—spill from their luggage. At sixteen, I did not own a cashmere sweater, nor had I ever owned a cashmere sweater. The girls admire one another's clothes. I'm in no hurry to open the three white, leatherette valises (high school graduation gifts from Betty and Bernie), in which I've deposited all my worldly possessions. The small one is a boxy cosmetic case worthy of Kim Novak, but my collection of cosmetics amounts to a tube of Pond's "Honey" lipstick, a compact containing Max Factor's pancake makeup, a face sponge, and an eyelash curler, so I'd filled my case with pjs and underwear. I leave the valises unopened on the floor where my father had dropped them. I wait until my roommates and the other girls have gone to the dining hall before I retrieve my wool and Orlon sweaters from the glamorous faux leather suitcases.

Another slide clicks into my mental viewfinder: my freshman friends invite me to go with them to Brighams, the Cambridge sweet shop, to buy ice cream cones. While they're asking each other if they have enough time to get there and back before our late afternoon classes, I'm thinking, *Do I have enough money for an ice cream cone?* I don't. "Gotta stay to write a paper," I tell them, embarrassed to admit that though I may appear to be a middle-class coed like them, they have fathers who would never let them run out of money while my father will pay my tuition and room and board, but not a penny more.

After settling in at school, I wrote to my sister, "Please save all the letters you receive from me while I'm at Brandeis. I'd like to reread them someday and trace whatever growth and maturity takes place." Betty, a natural saver, thankfully did as I asked, deposited all my college letters, about two dozen of them, in that commodious shopping bag, which continues to pump out evidence of my adolescent angst. I don't remember feeling deprived or being stressed out about money, but reading my words now for the first time since the 1950s, it's clear that I kept myself on a tight financial leash.

November 1955, two months into my freshman year: "Dear Betty, Brandeis has done so much for me already, it's fantastic! 1) I am so conscious of being educated. I feel like a magnet attracting all this marvelous new information. 2) I've become extremely discriminating in my choice of courses, friends, movies, ways to spend my time. 3) I've learned the value of time and I use every second of it. 4) I'm so conscious of money and its conservation that I border on the point of parsimony. 5) I've learned to hold my beer."

January 1956: "My date took me to a luxurious delicatessen, Jack & Marion's in Brookline. For $1.25, I ate ten bigger than jumbo shrimp, French fries, coleslaw, and tomatoes. Delish!"

May 1956: "Never mind sending my high school prom dress. I won't be needing it 'cause I decided not to go to the spring dance. I don't want to spend all that money on one night."

My sister had money troubles of her own, four kids to feed on the modest salary her husband, Bernie, earned as principal of Peekskill High School. Still, her packages kept coming—a throw pillow, a wrap, home-baked brownies, an occasional check. Judging from my ardent thank-you notes, Betty also made occasional deposits in my hope chest, a large metal foot locker, kept in her attic, to which she was the only contributor. One of my thank-you notes refers to a copper-bottom Revere Ware saucepan, about which I was "thrilled to pieces. It would have taken me years to afford it." The gifts she sent me on my seventeenth birthday elicited an extravagant gush of gratitude:

> *I have to drop everything to write and tell you of my amazement and excitement. The dress is absolutely gorgeous and thanks for buying it in the shade of green that's my best and very favorite color. The bag is stunning, perfect for the dress and the beads add that extra touch and match beautifully. My dorm mates are drooling—they wish they had such a thoughtful, generous and unselfish sister.*

Meanwhile, my dorm mates didn't think twice about buying an ice cream cone. They owned circle pins, Ferragamo shoes, and silk neckerchiefs. They had moms who took them shopping at Bergdorf's and Bonwit's, and dads who sent them flowers on their birthdays. I was too embarrassed to admit that my dad—who they knew was a lawyer, drove a nice car, and wore snazzy sports jackets the few times he visited me—wouldn't contribute a dime to my expenses.

In one report to Betty, I described taking two jobs on campus, twelve hours a week at ninety cents an hour—six hours at the university's Office of Public Affairs doing typing and publicity and six hours as secretary to the Hillel director, Rabbi Irving "Yitz" Greenberg, a brilliant theologian who, with his wife, Blu, would later become dear personal friends. On the side, I tutored athletes in English and biology. "You're probably thinking I've assumed too much responsibility," I wrote, "but I feel I should start saving for my marriage and my future."

Three months later: "I've put away $125 from my campus jobs! I opened my own savings account in a Waltham bank and I am not going to touch that money!"

On June 9, 1957, Dad came up to Brandeis to take me out to dinner for my eighteenth birthday. When we met in the lobby of my dorm, he presented me with an odd-shaped gift. "Before your mom died, I promised her I'd give you this when you turn eighteen—and I always keep my word, right ketsileh?"

I tore off the wrapping and burst into tears at the sight of my mother's knippel. Years before, when I'd happened upon it in her lingerie drawer, the nylon stocking was half full of crumpled bills and half empty and limp. Now, stuffed thigh to toe, it was as stiff as the leg of a mannequin. At the end of the evening, after my father dropped me back at my dorm, I shook the knippel out on my bed and counted the money. Somehow, between the day I found it and the day she died, Mom had squirreled away from her paltry household allowance almost $2,000, the equivalent of $18,000 today. It was more cash than I'd ever seen and, doubtless, more than my poor mom had ever in her life accumulated in her own name. I used some of the money to buy myself a French compact car, a nifty powder-blue Simca (a brand discontinued in the '70s), which transformed me overnight into the most privileged girl in my group, the one who could drive other girls into Cambridge or Boston. The rest I deposited in my Waltham bank account and vowed not to touch until after graduation.

I must have kept that promise because Betty kept sending me cash infusions.

> *Your $50 check was like a deus ex machina. I shall treat it prudently and I'm sure it will carry me comfortably until June. Will pay you back as soon as possible. Hope it wasn't a strain on you, but I was really at rock bottom—like down to 48 cents. Being a senior*

has been expensive. My books for the semester ran more than I'd expected but don't tell Daddy because I don't want to spend even five minutes justifying my expenditures and listening to him lecture me on how to live within my budget.

Then, a week before graduation:

I've been selected to receive an English award at an Honors Convocation next week. I sure hope the prize is money. It would solve so many problems. I'm terribly sorry I haven't been able to afford to give your children any presents recently. Believe me, I want to, and I look forward to years when I can make up in some measure all that you and Bernie have done for me and all that your four little darlings have meant to me. I don't want to ask Daddy for help. Maybe you could tell people in the family who ask what I might like for a graduation present that they should give me money.

For four years, I struggled to live on my meager earnings from a patchwork of jobs that took me away from my studies, yet I never questioned the cognitive dissonance of my situation—or why my father, a seemingly successful middle-class lawyer who supposedly earned a good living would demand that I support myself through my teen years with not a lot of help from him. Now, the revelations in my parents' letters have raised the distinct possibility that his success was a posture and his "good living" a mirage. Rather than stoking my resentments, the letters have moved me toward a more sympathetic interpretation of what had always struck me as my father's callous indifference. I used to view the shanda as Ceil's signature fixation, a product of her shtetl origins and childhood humiliations. But I've come to believe that Jack, too, was weighed down by the threat of shame, only his was a product of his gender, his patriarchal family, and social milieu. In the Jewish world of the 1950s, a man who couldn't support his family was not a man.

Was it possible that my father's unilateral decision to sell our house and relegate me to a daybed in his new apartment's entry hall was not born of selfishness and insensitivity to my feelings of loss and abandonment, but of shame and his refusal to admit that he was unable to afford an apartment with a second bedroom? Could it be that the reason he didn't give me any spending money in college was not to teach me financial independence but because he didn't have a dollar to spare? What a great relief it would be, even these many years later, were I able to believe that his actions sprang from a paucity of resources, not of love. Was he *performing* prosperity to save face? If so, I would sympathize with him retroactively and forgive him posthumously. Few things could shame a husband or father more than being unmasked as an inadequate provider. I knew that. But I never imagined my self-assured dad would wear any kind of mask in the first place. Looking back, I recognize now that compelling social forces in his upwardly mobile Jewish community—namely masculine pride and the loom of the shanda— were enough to make my father, or any man of his generation, lie about his finances. If that's what her did and why he did it, I would move the knob on my icebox to defrost. I would understand.

These meanderings were furthered by a piece in the *Times* about "the power of middle-class shame," the phrase social scientists use to describe the stigma of "financial floundering," and the quandary of men weighed down by an "obsession with privacy" who "don't always acknowledge what is troubling them." That succinct profile fit my father to a T. It explained why he agonized over the price of each souvenir and reprimanded his wife for wasting a few extra pennies on postage stamps. And why, to our family's amazement, after practicing law in New York City for more than fifty years, he left no estate. Zero, bubkis, zilch. "Obsession with privacy" explained why he would not tell my mother how much money he made (or didn't) and why he kept her, a grown woman, on an allowance. Better to control her total budget than have her rack up bills he couldn't afford. And where I was concerned, better to shut off the tap completely than have to say no each time I called from Brandeis and asked for a little money.

⤳⟐⟐⤵

Mom's knippel bought me my independence. After graduation, I moved to an apartment at 344 West 12th Street in Greenwich Village. "I'm paying $68.42 per month for a 15'x 14' living room with a small working fireplace, built-in bookcases, a mini kitchen recessed in the wall, and a 13'x 14' bedroom with a closet," I wrote to Betty (who lived with Bernie and their four kids in a rambling Victorian pile in Peekskill). "I also negotiated with the previous tenant to buy his nearly new sofa and double bed and two lamps for only $230!" Perky, proud of myself, and just turned twenty, I had a roof over my head, a secretarial job in the editorial department at Simon & Schuster, and a mutt I named Morpheus (for the god of dreams, of which I had plenty). And I bought my first cashmere sweater.

When the knippel account ran dry, I made ends meet on my fifty-five dollars a week paycheck until, now and then, it fell short and my cupboard was as bare as Mother Hubbard's. Hunger was new to me. My hippie friends were even worse off than I, so there was no hope of my popping in on them at supper time and being asked to pull up a chair. My friends didn't have supper; they had martini olives or granola bars. Shame prevented me from telling my sister that, after being so proud of myself, I'd run out of cash and food. She wasn't sending me brownies anymore, and I couldn't pay for the gas to drive up to her new house in Larchmont every time my stomach growled. As for my father, I wouldn't give Mr. Self-Sufficient the satisfaction of knowing I'd botched my budget.

All that is my vaguely self-pitying preamble to the money-related secret I'm most ashamed of: during my first few years living and working in New York City, I occasionally accepted a date with a man who was of no interest to me, even someone I didn't like, solely because he asked me to dinner on a day when all I had in the house was a banana. Unlike one of my girlfriends, I never was hungry enough to trade sex for supper. But there were times when I consciously and deliberately took advantage of traditional male and female sex roles. I knew I could count on some guy to treat me to a three-course meal because, in 1959, that's what men did. So long as I had suitors who would buy me dinner and expect no more in return than a goodnight kiss, I would never starve.

CHAPTER 25

RATHER THAN LIVE IN DISGRACE, I DECIDED TO KILL MYSELF

Back to Brandeis for this memory: at eighteen, I was young to be a college senior but old enough to get pregnant. I seemed to have missed the memo on contraception, an ignorance partly attributable to my not having a mother to explain ovulation, partly to the textbook in my hygiene course that showed a fetus curled up in a woman's uterus but no mention of how it got there, and partly to the fact that I trusted street myths like, "You can get pregnant from sperm on a toilet seat, but you can't get pregnant if you do it standing up." Boys in my crowd kept a packet of Trojan condoms in their wallets, now and then flashing it at a girl like me who would rather be hung by her hair over a pit of vipers than show the slightest interest in contraception because it might suggest that she was interested in sex. Which, however true, would be unseemly for a Nice Jewish Girl.

Had Ceil lived, I doubt she'd have ventured beyond Birds and Bees 101. I probably wouldn't have confided in her anyway; talking about sex would have embarrassed us both. Like many Jewish mothers, her medical specialty was constipation, and her all-purpose cure was a warm-water enema. Everything else in the physical realm fell beyond her purview. When I started showing signs of puberty, she transferred me from my pediatrician to our family doctor, who happened to be the father of my diehard crush since second grade and the last person I would have asked about birth control. Nor would he be inclined to ask a fourteen-year-old girl if she wanted to be measured for a diaphragm. Family doctors, most of them male in the 1950s, were not inclined to discuss pregnancy prevention with adolescent girls or unmarried women. The pill had not been invented yet. A virgin's body was thought to be nobody's business but that of her future husband. All of which explains why I was dumb enough to have sex without a condom and get pregnant in the fall of my senior year.

At that point, I knew only two things about abortion: it was illegal and it cost hundreds of dollars, which I did not have. The only person I knew who had a lot of money (or who I *thought* had a lot of money) was my father, so I violated his dictum that I cover all my expenses on my own and, despite my fear of incurring his deep and lasting disappointment in me, I told him I needed an abortion. He didn't try to talk me out of it or ask who the father was. He didn't lecture or scold me (neither did he comfort me). He told me to leave all the arrangements to him. I have no idea how, but he found a gynecologist not far from his apartment who was willing to perform the procedure. A few weeks later, I described the experience in my diary:

> *I went to a darkened doctor's office accompanied by Daddy and his wife. I hated having her along, but he insisted we might need a woman in case there were complications. His wife acted as if we were asking her to rob a bank... There were no complications. The abortion cost my father $350. I promised I would pay him back.*

It took me more than a year, but I repaid every cent.

In June 1991, the *New York Times Magazine* published a piece in which I admitted I had an illegal abortion in the fall of my senior year in college. My objective, beside normalizing the procedure undergone each year by about a million American women, was to inspire pro-choice activism, and rebut the "pro-lifers" who, without regard for a woman's body, health, feelings, or circumstances, insist that she carry her unwanted pregnancy to term, like a breed mare, then give the baby up for adoption. I did not admit in that column or any other piece I've written in the last fifty years that in the spring of my senior year, I had another abortion.

Discovering I was pregnant a second time threw me into a full-blown panic attack. The idea of going back to my father and stepmother, or the gynecologist in Jamaica, was a nonstarter. I was supposed to be a smart girl. I was supposed to have my life under control. How could I make the same mistake twice within six months? And a month before graduation. In my world, Nice Jewish Girl was not a cliché; it was an edict. A NJG was expected to pick up her college diploma with an engagement ring on the fourth finger of her left hand and an intact hymen in her vagina. A pregnant NJG was an oxymoron, the mother, so to speak, of all shandas. I'd heard stories about NJGs being spirited out of town before they could "show" and kept there until after they delivered. Parents invented elaborate stories to cover for their daughters' six-month absences. ("Arlene is taking a semester abroad." "Laurel won a scholarship to art school out West." "Rebecca got a weird bug; she's being treated at an infectious disease clinic in Brazil.") That way, the unwanted child could be born in secret, the family lawyer could discreetly arrange for its adoption, the girl could return home with her reputation intact and her appearance unchanged, and none would be the wiser.

The alternative was irrevocable shame. The girl would be disgraced; her child would be a "bastard," which, in those days, wasn't just a swear word but the term for a child "born out of wedlock," while the father seldom was even identified by name.

Women who gave their babies up for adoption often searched for their children years later and found them. Or their children found them. My friend Jane O'Reilly successfully hid her pregnancy when she was a senior at Radcliffe, knowing she would be expelled were it exposed. Jane moved off campus with her secret. She took her final exams in a raincoat. She gave birth a few days later, put the newborn up for adoption, never breathed a word about it, and graduated with her class in 1958.

"It was like the Scarlet Letter era," she recalled, fifty years later in an interview with the *Harvard Crimson*. "It was the worst thing that could happen to you…my feelings ran up and down a scale of rage, grief and shame," she said of the thirty-three years before her grown daughter found her, years sacrificed to the unforgiving idol of female purity.

My unwanted pregnancies were far and away the most shameful secrets I'd ever hidden from my family. I didn't confide in my sister, Betty, a mother of four, or my other sister, Rena, who'd turned up in my life a few years prior, or my married aunts, or female cousins, most of whom had multiple children and presumably knew a thing or two about sex. I couldn't confide in them because, in my eyes, they were moral exemplars and I was a scarlet woman. The idea that any of my upstanding female relatives might excuse my transgression, much less know where to find an abortion doctor, was beyond my imagination. Rather than face their judgment, I decided I would kill myself. With no access to a weapon or a lethal drug and being too squeamish to slash my wrists or swallow poison, I narrowed my options to leaping off the Bronx-Whitestone Bridge or jumping in front of a subway train. Soon my hysteria was too extreme to pass off as PMS, and when my roommate, Selma Shapiro, a Nice Jewish Girl from North Adams, Massachusetts, wouldn't stop badgering me to tell her what was wrong, I blurted out that I was planning to commit suicide because I was pregnant. After she wrapped her arms around me and let me cry my eyes out, the two of us went downstairs and knocked on the door of our dorm counselor, Lisel Judge, whose day job was coaching the Brandeis women's fencing team but who also served as everyone's strong but warm, unshakable, and unflappable surrogate mom. Once a highly ranked fencer in Germany, Lisel was barred by the

Nazis from competing in the 1936 Olympics because her father was Jewish. My fear of being shamed must have seemed absurd in comparison, but upon hearing my secret, she assured me that getting pregnant didn't mean I was a bad girl; it just meant I needed a diaphragm. She comforted me and took charge without making a big deal about it, and the next morning, she plugged me into an underground network of abortion whisperers who pointed me toward the saintly Dr. Robert Spencer, a licensed physician.

I called for an appointment, trembling with anxiety. His plainspoken nurse told me what to expect of the procedure and what to pack for my overnight stay at his clinic, where I would be observed post-op. Oh, and one more thing, she said: should I have a car accident or get stopped for any reason on the New Jersey or Pennsylvania Turnpikes, I was to tell the trooper I was a patient of Dr. Spencer's, and he, the officer, would let me go with a warning or arrange for my car to be towed and alert the clinic that someone needed to come to pick me up. That sounded bizarre, but the nurse was so matter of fact, I just took down her instructions. Fortunately, my roommate and I never had occasion to test those magic words; Selma drove me to Ashland without encountering law enforcement. For years afterward, I heard parallel accounts from other women who'd been patients of Dr. Spencer, several of whom claimed to know why his name worked as a Get Out of Jail Free card. Apocryphal or not, the story was that the good doctor had once saved the life of a trooper's daughter who was near death after a botched kitchen table abortion, and since that time, the officer's colleagues up and down the highways in both states had been protecting Dr. Spencer and his patients. (And, when necessary, sending their own wives and daughters to his clinic.) By the time he died in 1969, Dr. Spencer had performed more than 100,000 safe abortions in his spotless clinic in Ashland, Pennsylvania.

Five years later, I met Bert, and within three months of our first date, he asked me to marry him. I said yes but after a couple of sleepless nights and a running battle between my commitment to truth and my fear of abandonment, I decided I had to admit my illegal abortions. Nothing required me to fess up. Selma would never have blown my cover. But I wouldn't be able to live with myself if I weren't completely honest about my past. Given how abortion was reviled back then, it would be unconscionable for me to begin our life together without confessing my secret.

We were lounging against a cascade of pillows on the bed in my Greenwich Village single-girl apartment, when I told my newly minted fiancé that I had something to confess that might make him change his mind about marrying me. The thought of losing him released torrents of sobbing so convulsive I could barely continue. Bert waited, heard me out, took me in his arms. "None of that matters," he said. "All that matters is us and our future." We were married three months later.

I will be forever grateful to Selma, a lifelong friend; to Lisel Judge, the dorm counselor/fencing coach, who died in 2017 at the age of 101; and, above all, to the kind, caring, nonjudgmental doctor who safely terminated my inadvertent, unwanted pregnancy and allowed me to graduate with my class and move on with my life. Thanks to Robert Spencer, I didn't jump off a bridge or in front of a train. I wasn't forced to carry to term a child I was not emotionally prepared to be responsible for or financially able to support. I could wait until I was ready to settle down with a permanent mate and establish a stable home in which a child—or in our case three children—could be welcomed, cherished, and nurtured to adulthood.

The procedure was medically safe, sanitary, and uneventful, and I was treated with the utmost sensitivity and respect. Yet, I have never forgotten the indignity of the clandestine, the terror and loneliness, the abject shame. Had abortion been legal then, I could have been spared all that. Were sexually active young women not branded as trollops who disgraced their families and brought shame on The Jewish People, I would not have come so close to killing myself. In those years, thousands of women lost their lives to bungled illegal procedures, self-induced abortions (knitting needles, lye, throwing themselves down a flight of stairs), or suicide.

And because their parents, husbands, boyfriends, and confidants were too ashamed to admit how and why they died, and to advocate for reform, it took the feminist movement and a decision by the Supreme Court (constantly challenged, ever eroding, presently disappearing) to give women the right to control their own bodies.

One night while I was writing this chapter, I couldn't fall asleep for wondering how my college boyfriend had experienced my crisis pregnancy. Was he scared? Did he ever tell anyone? Had the memory stayed with him? Parachuting into my consciousness is a tall, reserved young man with dark good looks and sorrowful eyes. The night I told him I was pregnant, he punched a hole in the cinder block wall in his dorm room and broke several bones in his hand. Ashamed of himself for not using protection, he was as devastated as I was by the pregnancy and ready to do whatever I wanted. I said I wanted an abortion. He accepted my choice. Unfailingly kind and solicitous, he said he would come with me, stand by me, pay for the procedure, do whatever he could to make things right. I declined his help. I told him I had to do this alone. And I needed to end our relationship. It was an enormous relief to me when he backed off. I was then, and will forever be, grateful to him for honoring my wishes.

After that sleepless night, I decided to search for the boy/man who'd shared my secret. The internet and the Brandeis Alumni office helped me find him—retired, living out West, second marriage, children, grandchildren. One day in the summer of 2019, I sent him an email. He replied almost immediately, saying he was stunned to see my name in his in-box after all this time, but he was willing to talk. I called. His voice was older, deeper, tentative. Would he give me his perspective on what happened between us, I asked, and is it okay if I take notes and include excerpts from our conversation in my memoir? He said yes.

Together we turned back the clock, but he was the one who recalled all the details, things I'd forgotten eons ago, things I'd needed to forget. As he talked about our relationship and how much it had meant to him, sweet recollections poured out, memories of where we used to make out, "your favorite clearing in the woods, the little pond with the rope swing, that grassy spot on the hill; there's a huge building there now." He remembered the night we "went all the way," a strange evening, a party in some goofy farmhouse, a bunch of hippies smoking dope and drinking heavily. "We had a few shots and slept together in one of the bedrooms."

I asked how he felt about my choosing to terminate the pregnancy.

"We were kids," he said. "We weren't going to get married and start a family at that age. But abortion was so foreign to me; it was illegal, and it was such a big thing then, such a huge secret. The truth is, it wasn't the abortion that affected me most; it was you having dumped me. That broke my heart. You said we couldn't see each other anymore. The relationship I thought we had, and the one you thought we had, turned out to be very different. I was nineteen, and my feelings for you were"—he paused, his voice caught in his throat—"a lot of love. When you said you wanted to stop seeing me, I was distraught. I couldn't go to my classes, couldn't study, think, eat. All I could do was sleep. I knew I'd hurt you because I was the reason you had to have the abortion. At the same time, I was devastated when I saw that our relationship was not going to be what I thought it was. It messed me up real good. I like something awful had happened that left a big hole in my stomach and my heart. Keeping the abortion secret wasn't hard for me because I never tell people things they don't have to know. I've always been pretty quiet: I find if you don't say things, you don't say stupid things. I didn't have that many friends anyway, so on my end no one knew."

A cough, then silence. For a minute, I thought the line had gone dead. Finally, he resumed. "It was you who revealed the secret…"

"I did??"

"Yeah, in that column you wrote in the *Times Magazine* in the 1990s."

"That piece wasn't about us! It was about what women had to go through. It was about the secrecy and shame around abortion, even though it's legal now, and why adoption isn't the solution to unwanted pregnancy. It wasn't about you. I didn't name you."

"You didn't have to. You said the boy was on the basketball team. He had a broken hand. Anyone who knew us when we were dating knew that was me. The weekend your piece came out in the paper, I was at one of my class reunions." (He and I graduated from Brandeis in different years.) "Everyone at the reunion was talking about it and asking each other if they knew who the guy was. 'It wasn't me,' a few of them said. 'Was it you?' Others asked, 'What the hell are they talking about?' I said, 'I have no idea.' I was being protective of you. A couple of people put two and two together because they remembered my hand being in a plaster cast. My brother knew I'd dated you, so he figured I was the boy. When I came home from the reunion, my wife was sitting there reading the column, and she asked me if I was the boy. I shook my head, told her I didn't want to talk about it, but she kept pressing and eventually, I had to admit it. Otherwise, I never said a word about it—even though it wasn't a secret from then on because of your article."

Chastened, flooded with regret for having hurt this man, first by shutting him out of my life after the abortion, then by writing about it with no thought to its impact on him, I told him how much I appreciated his willingness to open up about what was obviously, in its way, as harrowing a memory for him as it had been for me. I thanked him for his honesty now and his kindness then, for trying to protect my honor and my privacy, for taking my call. I apologized for being insensitive to what he was going through at the time and breaking his heart, and causing him discomfort and embarrassment when my *Times* column appeared. I reiterated that my intention was not to implicate him, but to describe an ordeal that I and so many women had to endure when abortion was illegal.

As our conversation wound down, we exchanged details about the lives we'd lived, the families we'd created, our careers, health, the places we'd put down roots. He told me he's been following my writing, "so I know you're a liberal." I asked about his politics. He said he leans left on social issues but conservative on most everything else.

It was 2019 so I ventured my political litmus test, while making it sound like small talk. "Are you saying you *like* Trump?"

"I hate his racism and crudeness, but I like a lot of the things he's doing. I don't want open borders—"

I interrupted him before he could say more, loath to let his next line spoil the moment.

"It's a good thing I broke up with you," I joked. "If we'd stayed together, we never would have lasted."

～✦☙✦～

I kept that ~~traumatic episode~~ chapter of my life hidden from those closest to me, not because abortion was illegal, or because I thought it wrong to refuse to bear a child I'd be responsible for before I knew how to be responsible for myself. I hid it because abortion was scandalous, and I'd rather be dead than see my private shame become a family shanda.

One Sunday morning in 1962, sitting in my sister's kitchen of her house in Larchmont, where I'd gone to spend the weekend with her and her family, I suddenly heard myself speak my secret. Bernie had taken the kids out for pancakes so Betty and I could have a leisurely breakfast together with no distractions. We sat across from each other at her kitchen counter. She'd put out paper placemats but cloth napkins, a noteworthy concession to elegance for a harried mother of four who did two wash loads a day. I lit up a Marlboro and felt a stab of nostalgia as my sister, mimicking our mother's garnish, sectioned two grapefruit halves with the exactly right implement, a curved serrated knife, then hulled two perfect red strawberries and placed them, point up, at the center of each half. She scooped Maxwell House coffee into the basket of her percolator and plugged it in.

"I'll get the milk," I said, and went to the refrigerator, which abutted the screen door that opened onto her backyard. Noticing the Sunday paper rolled up on the doorstep, I opened the door, picked up the paper, and brought it to Betty along with a gallon of milk. (Everything in her fridge was family size.) She put it on the counter, front page up. It was the local paper, and the lead story was local: I read the headline aloud: "Woman Bleeds to Death in Motel Room After Illegal Abortion."

Betty frowned. "That reminds me of Aunt Sadye, hemorrhaging to death in the delivery room."

To me, this was even worse. Not only was the woman dead, but now everyone in Westchester County knew *how* she died. I skimmed the story. "It says she left a husband and five children. I bet she never even told him she was pregnant. When she walked out of the house that day, she probably said she was going to visit a sick friend."

"Right." Betty nodded, speculating further, as women do when we start thinking the worst. "She probably got a babysitter and told her she'd be back in a couple of hours. Imagine how desperate she must have been to have an abortion in a motel room. She had to be terrified when some guy showed up with dirt under his fingernails and said he was the doctor. God knows what instruments he used. It must have been a nightmare experience. And the whole time she was probably scared that the cops would burst in and arrest her."

The coffee bubbling and burbling inside the glass knob at the top of the percolator mesmerized me, each rise and fall turning the coffee a darker shade of brown, its rhythm synchronized with the thump of my beating heart. My sister was describing my nightmare, the ordeal I'd been imagining, the fate I'd feared would be mine before I found my way to Dr. Spencer. I blurted out my story, finishing in a pool of tears.

"Oh, honey! I'm so sorry you had to go through that alone. I should have been there. Why didn't you call *me*?"

"I didn't want you to think badly of me." I grabbed the strawberry to blunt the taste of shame.

"How could I think badly of you, honey? I had one too. I know what it's like."

"*You!?!*" I almost spit out the berry.

"I thought you knew. Almost *all* of us had abortions—cousins, aunts, Mom."

"*Our* Mom?"

"Our mom was just my mom then. She had an abortion a few months after she left my father." (I flashed on Dad's barbell diagram, the circle marked "Joe," the man who went for his belt when little Betty knocked over a lamp.) "He kept begging her to go away with him for a weekend and try to salvage their marriage. Tillie and Grandma convinced Mom to give him another chance. She and my father went to some resort in the Poconos. The reconciliation failed—obviously—but she got pregnant."

I was utterly flabbergasted. "How did Mom figure out where to get an abortion in the 1920s?"

"Grandma found someone."

"*My* Grandma?!" Echoes were all I seemed to be contributing to the conversation.

"Jenny had already had a couple of abortions herself. After seven kids, can you blame her? Nothing was easy then. Birth control was nonexistent, primitive, or unreliable. Everyone was struggling financially. And after Sadye died in childbirth, why would a woman want to get pregnant?"

The percolator emitted a short beep and quit burbling. Betty unplugged the pot and filled our mugs. I can't remember what we had for breakfast that morning other than coffee and a half grapefruit with a strawberry on top. Maybe she made scrambled eggs or oatmeal, or maybe we just kept talking. The details are lost to time; but I still have the letter I received from her a few days later.

Dearest Letty,

I came away from our conversation saddened that you never felt you could confide in me. How had I given you the impression that I was so highly moral minded, so innocent of the world and its human ways, so removed from reality, that I would be shocked by your revelations? How have I failed to show you that I am normal, quite human, and even understanding. I'm very grateful that you finally felt you could talk to me. And, of course, I fervently hope that now that our dialogue has begun, it will continue. I don't know if I succeeded in getting across to you my one main and deepest feeling—that no matter what you have done, or will do, or why—I will never think less of you or love you less than before you told me. You are both sister and daughter to me—as dear to me as my husband and children.

Yesterday I simply listened—it has taken so long for you to talk to me that I just wanted to be a good listener. Do you want me to do more? Ask me. The past is fruitful if we learn from it, and don't make the same mistakes again. More than anything, I wish happiness for you, and contentment. There is so much more I want to say—and cannot find the words. I'm amazed that so much could have happened to you of which I had absolutely no inkling. I hope we can keep on talking, will always be close.

As ever, with so much love,

Your sister, B.

After that, there were no more secrets between Betty and me. We stayed close and kept talking until she died on August 2, 2013, at eighty-eight.

CHAPTER 26

FAMILY ENVY

My father remarried in August 1956. Back then, no one I knew had a stepmother; all my friends, cousins, and classmates came from intact nuclear families. In college, besides envying girls who had spending money, I envied girls who had normal, happy families. "Envy attracts bad luck to the person being envied," was another of my mother's axioms. When I was a child, and someone called me cute or clever, Mom saw a dark thread of jealousy running through the heddle of their praise, the Evil Eye hovering, waiting to zap our family with adversity to counter God's gift of me being cute or clever. Ceil, a congenital people pleaser, would express her gratitude for the compliment but, as soon as she could manage it discreetly, she'd perform her usual ritual: make the "thpu-thpu-thpu" sound and send a kinnehurra into the cosmos to ward off malicious spirits. At night, after tucking me into bed, she would press her lips to my forehead and say a final thpu-thpu-thpu as if to suction out whatever atoms of envy may have besmirched me that day.

Kinnehurra, being Yiddish, has different English transliterations (*kinehora*, is equally common), and Jews say it for many reasons, foremost among them the belief that you should hide your good fortune or it might be subverted, and if anyone finds out about it and envies you, a kinnehurra can preempt the Evil Eye from noticing. JewishAnswers.org explains further that "hiddenness acts as a type of protection against the evil eye, in accordance with the Talmudic idea that 'blessing only rests upon something that is concealed from the eye.' For this reason, when people relate their, or others, gains, assets, or blessings, they say 'kein ayin hora.' Wealth, physical and spiritual, is not distributed evenly in the world. G-d gives to one person something that He does not give to another. This can naturally cause envy, which essentially is an emotion that corresponds to a sense of injustice. The Torah tells us that the resulting spiritual energy can actually trigger a process of judgment against the one who is envied and lead to very destructive consequences for them!"

In 1956, with a deceased mother, a neglectful father, an icy stepmother, and no place to call home, I sometimes found it impossible *not* to envy other people's families. And while I had two much-older sisters, one a domestic goddess with a wonderful husband and four great kids, one a world-class intellect with an independent life and a PhD, both of whom I idolized, my roommate, Amy Medine, with whom I shared a dorm room during my first three years at Brandeis, had two seemingly perfect parents who visited her as often as she would let them and a younger sister who idolized *her*. When Amy became engaged in our junior year, her mother helped her choose her silver and china patterns, composed her engagement announcement, and planned every detail of her wedding. Could the contrast be any starker? I asked in a letter to my sister.

> *It's impossible to live with 30 girls, day in and day out, and not assimilate some of their family joys and happy anecdotes without it all piling up until one day, depression hits hard. Today was that day. While Amy's mother was calling and caring, it reminded me of Mommy doing all those things with you before your wedding and how perfect everything was and I fell into a funk. I can't help comparing my life with other people's and I always come out on the short end of the stick. I want things to be perfect for me too.*

What strikes me about the overwrought verse I churned out in college is the endurance of my loneliness, the freshness of my pain:

> *The Sabbath queen forgets this house*
> *But I remember—it is the seventh day.*
> *Who will say Amen if I don't chant the hollow song,*
> *And sweep the weekday shadows out*
> *And keep the Sabbath neat.*
> *Dance by white queen, there is no mother here*
> *To welcome you with cooking smells and gentle prayer*
> *The child must kindle Sabbath lights and bless them.*
> *The slaughtered ram has come to lick his blood away*
> *To wash the crimson stain that marks this house*
> *with emptiness, for the Angel of Death.*
> *Claim the child now—tear the trembling lips away*
> *I cannot find the breast in the cold depths of the grave.*

After Amy got married and left school, I acquired a new roommate, the aforementioned Selma, whose bustling Jewish family became my new paradigm of domestic harmony, rapport, and love. The first weekend I spent at Selma's home in North Adams, Massachusetts, observing how effortlessly she interacted with her delightfully chatty, supremely confident mother, big bear of a father, and three lively brothers, I could not help feeling, Mom's warning to the contrary, a twinge of you-know-what. My envy wasn't noxious; I didn't want to take anything away from Amy or Selma. I just wanted my own version of what they had. Later, I would learn that neither of those families was as ideal as it looked. (Selma admitted only after she read this book in manuscript, that she had envied *me*. Why? Because my dad was a lawyer in New York City while her dad was a junk dealer in the boonies.) But at the time, compared to my detached father, his self-centered wife, and my admirable but mostly unavailable sisters, I romanticized my roommates' kin and felt embarrassed by my so-called life.

Besides inheriting my mother's superstitions, I seem to have replicated her eternal pursuit of perfection, as if such a state were possible. John Wesley, the eighteenth-century theologian, said, "Absolute perfection belongs not to [humans], not to angels, but to God alone." Preaching otherwise to housewives of the '50s (and their impressionable daughters), magazines like *Good Housekeeping* and *Ladies Home Journal*, propagandized perfection, goading women to aspire to virtuosity in homemaking, child-rearing, floor-waxing, flower-arranging, and sex. Enslaved to an unachievable ideal, Mom suffered when she thought she'd fallen short. Despite her proscription against envy, she clearly coveted the homes and marriages of native-born American women, whose lives she perceived to be perfect. Put together, the media models of American womanhood that I absorbed by osmosis, plus the strivings of my mother and nearly every Jewish woman I knew, trained me to pursue perfection in domestic matters. I've often felt a compulsion to fulfill my mother's unrealized goals and live the life she couldn't. Which, to a large extent, I have. Long gone is the private shame I carried as a girl about my shattered home life. Gone, too, my youthful envy of other people's families. If anything, these days, I secretly worry that other people might envy mine. And I say a lot of kinnehurras.

CHAPTER 27

"OF COURSE NOT, HE'S JUST ARTISTIC"

In Jewish families, at least those I knew, the bachelor uncle, with all its attendant innuendos, was never quite as whisper worthy as the maiden aunt. A man who was single until he was thirty might be the subject of occasional gossip, but there was always the possibility that he had not yet found the right girl. A woman who was single at thirty was a reject, unclaimed, unwanted, unmarriageable; a spinster, and a shanda.

To avoid or postpone their aging daughter's humiliation, and that of her family, many Jewish parents had an inviolate rule that none of the younger siblings could marry until the older daughter(s) found a match. In the 1920s, that rule kept my Aunt Tillie and Uncle Ralph in limbo for years, unable to tie the knot while Ralph's older sister had no suitors in sight. Finally, hope extinguished and patience exhausted, they drove to New Jersey with two friends and got married by a justice of the peace (nearly unheard of among Jews back then). However, being dutiful kids, they kept their marriage a secret and continued living with their respective parents for two more years, at which point they revealed the truth and had a belated proper Jewish wedding. Had they waited until Ralph's older sister married, they might still be waiting. She died a spinster in her eighties.

I had two bachelor uncles. My mother's youngest brother, Milton, who carried a brass money clip shaped like a dollar sign and wore a thin mustache and Hawaiian shirts, died in his mid-fifties, unmarried, yet never aroused a whisper. (Maybe because he lived out West where none of us could see what he was up to.) The other bachelor uncle, my stepmother's brother, was movie-star handsome and buff. Perpetually tan, he wore tight pants and fitted shirts unbuttoned to his navel, and quoted Tennessee Williams with dramatic flair. I didn't know homosexuality existed until I was in college, and one of my fellow actors in a Brandeis theater production made a point of telling everyone he preferred men. ("Coming out" had no sexual meaning then; it was a high class term for a debutante's introduction to society.) With my college friend in mind, I asked my stepmother if her brother was a homosexual (gay wasn't a gendered word yet either). "Of course not," she replied, huffily. "He's just artistic."

Oddly enough, several years before homosexuality registered on my radar screen, I learned about "gender reassignment surgery" having learned that phrase from my mother in my own house when I was about thirteen. I vividly remember coming home early from junior high school, and overhearing her on the phone talking about Christine Jorgenson's "sex change operation." Naturally, I pressed my ear to the kitchen door to eavesdrop. Jorgenson had recently made news as the first American to physically transition from male to female via surgery, and I had devoured every story about her with rapt fascination. (I still remember the front-page headline in the *Daily News*: "Ex-GI Becomes Blonde Beauty.") Mom was repeatedly reassuring the person on the other end of the phone, someone named Carl, that he would make a very attractive woman, much prettier than Jorgenson, and promising this Carl person that she would help him "practice how to sit like a lady, choose perfume, things like that…" She went quiet for several moments, listening, then, "You don't have to decide that now, Carl. You can live anywhere, Chicago, San Francisco, New York. See how you feel after the operation. For now, just think about how much you've wanted this. And now it's actually going to happen."

The instant she hung up, I barged into the kitchen and plunked myself down in the alcove we called our dinette. "What was that about?"

"Nothing," Mom said, turning her attention from the pot of chicken soup simmering on the stove to the bowl of batter on the counter. "That was *not* nothing, Mother!" I folded my arms in defiance. "I am not leaving this room until you tell me what's going on."

"I can't." She moistened her hands under the water faucet, scooped up a lump of batter, shaped it into a ball, and dropped it into the fragrant soup. Steam wafted up from the pot, slicking her face. She raised the skirt of her flowered apron and mopped her forehead. "It's private."

"Not anymore. I heard you tell him he'll be prettier than Christine Jorgenson after the surgery. You also said he could be happy in a bunch of different cities. You may as well tell me who he is and why you're involved."

Mom released a long sigh and turned off the flame under the soup. Without looking in my direction, she went to the sink, scrubbed the matzah meal batter off her hands, and dried them on a striped dishcloth, joined me at the kitchen table and told me this man's well-guarded secret.

About a year before, one of our Cleveland cousins had called her to ask if Ceil would help a good friend of theirs, a nice man who was planning to have an operation like Jorgenson's at a New York hospital. His name was Carl and he would soon be coming to town for pre-op consultations and needed someone to be his advocate and moral support. The Cleveland cousin thought that, of all her East Coast relatives, Ceil would be the right person to do that, and she had accepted the assignment.

Since then, Carl had called Mom several times, and they'd had long conversations during which he had confided in her what it was like to grow up feeling he was meant to be a girl, that he might look like a man on the outside but he always knew he was a woman. He'd asked Mom's advice about how to respond to all the women in his close-knit Midwestern Jewish community who kept teasing him about being a bachelor and trying to fix him up with their sisters, daughters, or nieces. Should he tell them the truth or finesse it? Should he take girls out on dates to avoid suspicion until he has the operation? How should he prepare his friends for his transition?

Mom said Carl had called today to let her know that his operation was scheduled for the following week and he was scared, not of going under the knife, but of being a failure as a woman. He dreaded going back to Cleveland, looking ridiculous, walking wrong, getting stared at by his friends, and rejected by his family. That's why Mom suggested he consider moving to New York or another big city where no one had ever known him as Carl and he could simply start fresh and be accepted as Carol, the name he'd chosen for when he becomes she, the person he was meant to be. Ceil, as should be clear by now, was a robust proponent of fresh starts.

Profound disbelief battled adolescent confusion while I listened to Carl's story. As I've said, Mom and I had never discussed sex, let alone sexuality, sexual orientation, or gender dysphoria. Yet, somehow, behind my back, my mother had become head cheerleader for a transwoman six decades before the LGBTQ revolution. Of all the Halpern relatives in New York City, why would our Midwestern cousin choose Mom to be Carl's sounding board and secret-keeper? Did the cousin know my mother better than I did? How else had she intuited that Ceil's own feelings of self-shame would insure her empathy and compassion for Carl's struggle? Whatever the reason, Mom turned out to be the right person for the job. She knew how it felt to be trapped in a reality that contradicts the person one knows oneself to be. She'd gone to great lengths to change the parts of her life that didn't fit her dreams—passed as a high school graduate, pretended to live in her rich uncle's apartment, buried her embarrassment at having been an abused wife and disgraced divorcée, and reinvented herself as a respectable Jewish matron. Like Carl, Ceil had changed her outside to match her inside. For both of them, reinvention wasn't a matter of performance or pretense, it was about authenticity, repair, and transformation.

CHAPTER 28

"CONCEALMENT MAKES THE SOUL A SWAMP; CONFESSION IS HOW YOU DRAIN IT"

My nephew Jeffrey was the youngest of Betty and Bernie's three sons and the most mischievous. Blond and handsome but ill at ease around people, Jeffrey lowered his eyes when addressed directly, and often left the dinner table while everyone else was chatting over coffee and cake. My sister used to attribute his "different" behavior to the fact that his birth had been medically complicated and, as a child, he'd suffered a couple of mini seizures. None of us guessed the secret he'd been hiding since he was a boy. Nor that I would be the one he would choose to expose it.

Jeffrey graduated from Boston University with a masters in social work. He lived on a kibbutz in Israel for a year, worked as a resident counselor at New York's 92nd Street Y, spent some time in Texas, then moved to San Francisco, where he went back to school, trained in electronics, and found a good job. From then on, he came east only for Passover and Thanksgiving. I seldom gave him a moment's thought between visits until sometime in the late '80s, I received his letter—the first he'd ever written to me. Enclosed was a newspaper clipping about a lesbian mother who, based solely on her sexual orientation, had lost custody of her child. Attached to the article was a one-sentence note: "Hi Letty, since you're a feminist, I thought you'd be interested in this awful injustice."

I handed my husband the note and the clipping. "Call me crazy, but I think my nephew is trying to tell me he's gay."

Bert read them. "You're crazy."

"I'm pretty sure it's a coded signal. He's saying he's sick and tired of hiding his sexuality, but he doesn't have the nerve to tell his parents."

"Betty and Bernie could handle it. They're grown-ups."

"They're old-school grown-ups. I bet Jeffrey's afraid they'll be horrified, judgmental, love him less. He wants me to help him kick himself out of the closet."

"Why you?" Bert cross-examined.

"Because I'm fourteen years younger than his mother. And a lot hipper."

"You're also fourteen years older than he is. You're almost forty, hon. You're square."

"My niece and nephews don't consider me square. They see me as Auntie Mame," I insisted, referring to the free-spirited character in Patrick Dennis's novel of the same name. "When I lived in the Village, I used to ride them around on the back of my motor scooter. Jeffrey knows I smoke weed. I demonstrate. I march. I'm not homophobic. He's counting on me to make the connection between the lesbian mother's case and discrimination against gay men."

"And?"

"And he wants me to prepare my sister and brother-in-law for what he's going to tell them next month when he comes home for Thanksgiving."

Bert said something lawyerly about the danger of drawing inferences unsupported by evidence.

"Here's the evidence." I waved the clipping in the air. "It makes no sense except as a coded signal. I'm calling my sister."

I read Betty her son's note, summarized the newspaper story, and gently proposed my theory. She cleared her throat a few times and asked me some questions but didn't call me crazy. Then she got Bernie on the extension and had me repeat everything to him. My brother-in-law, a former captain in World War II, a historian, a PhD in education, who, at that point, was principal of New York's Hunter College High School, asked what books I thought he and my sister should read to learn about gay life. I rattled off a few titles and suggested they contact PFLAG—Parents and Friends of Lesbians and Gays—an organization known for counseling people unfamiliar with homosexuality, especially parents of kids who'd just come out.

"It can't hurt to be ready when he tells you," I ventured.

"*If*," said my sister.

"Okay, if. But if he does admit he's gay, promise me you won't ask him, 'Are you sure?'"

"Promise," they said.

Taking my hunch to heart, my sister and brother-in-law sought advice from PFLAG and read Merle Miller's *On Being Different: What It Means to Be a Homosexual*, and James Baldwin's *Giovanni's Room* in time for Jeffrey's arrival for Thanksgiving. He came out to his parents within an hour of crossing their threshold. Not only did they absorb his news with equanimity, but they also encircled him in a double hug and assured him that they loved him and would always love him, no matter what. That weekend, my nephew was a changed man—confident, relaxed, even serene. Recently, I asked his oldest brother, Steve, how he'd reacted when Jeffrey came out to the family. "It really freaked me out. Not because I condemned homosexuality—I didn't and don't—but because it made me doubt my whole sense of reality and my fundamental understanding of who my family was and had been all my life. I think that's why he stayed closeted for such a long time, because he was afraid to crack the image of our perfect suburban Jewish family."

I used to think of Janus, the mythical Roman deity who is visually represented by one human head with two faces, each looking in the opposite direction, as an avatar for my nephew Jeffrey. One side of him always seeking perfection and guarding against shame, the other side yearning for authenticity and truth; one Jeffrey pretending to be the perfect Jewish son, the other Jeffrey shielding his parents from the shanda of having spawned a homosexual. Only after he'd rejected the tyranny of perfection and overcome his fear of shame could he unite his two sides, wear one face and start moving forward.

Secrets flutter through the chambers of the heart like ghosts who won't give up the haunt. Yet when we speak something once thought unspeakable, when we admit a devastating humiliation, or a violation of societal norms, we shrink the immensity of our shame to human scale and the truth told finds its reflection in the eyes of the one who hears it and makes the choice to accept us as we are. Or to forgive what we'd imagined to be forever unforgivable. In that moment, the burden lifts, the window opens, and we're free. A recent book review written by the journalist Brooks Barnes about a biography of a closeted Hollywood society figure of the 1920s reminded me of my nephew's coming out experience. Barnes opens with this personal admission: "I grew up in Montana at a time when it was most definitely not OK to be gay, much less have a gay father. I know how secrets can corrode your insides, resulting in a toxic, bubbling shame. And I know how healing it can be to expose secrets to daylight. The opposite of what you worry is going to happen happens. The people you care about run toward your vulnerability and respond with theirs."

When I visited Jeffrey in San Francisco at the end of the '80s, he told me how joyfully he had been "remade" by coming out to his parents and everyone else. At ease at last in his own skin, he became more engaged with the world. He volunteered with the Sierra Club and various gay rights organizations, was an active member of Congregation Sha-ar Zahav, a gay-friendly synagogue, devoting his formidable mechanical skills to keeping its building shipshape. He took pleasure in working to restore San Francisco's tracks and trolleys, participating in the Market Street Trolley Festival, making art from leaded glass, making things grow in the soil. During that visit, he took me to his favorite Vietnamese restaurant. Over a feast of spring rolls, chicken with peanut sauce, sticky rice, and Chinese beer, he talked about how homosexuality was still being pathologized and AIDS had heightened its stigma. He said his friends were succumbing to the epidemic, one by one, and he knew he could be next.

I produced a breathy "Thpu! Thpu! Thpu!" to exorcize the Evil Eye before it could target my nephew.

Jeffrey flashed me a grin, then turned serious. "Auntie Letty," he said, a throwback to my youthful honorific, "I'm a happy man now. If AIDS gets me, it won't be a tragedy because I have no regrets. I've led a fulfilling life. I just want you to know that."

Jeffrey died in 1991, four years before protease inhibitors were approved by the FDA. He was thirty-eight years old. At the funeral, his rabbi, Yoel Kahn, said, "Jeffrey's devotion to our synagogue was seen not in plaques on the wall but in the screws that held them to the walls, in the wiring and door handles and fixtures and hundreds of other details which Jeffrey systematically repaired and struck off his list of things that needed doing." Our family sat in the sanctuary of Congregation Sha-ar Zahav listening proudly as we wept over our loss. After their son's passing, Betty and Bernie established a speakers' program at the synagogue in his name. They became substitute parents for young gay men and listened, with a compassion born of empathy, to desolate kids talk about their loneliness and fear. They comforted people who'd lost lovers, family members, and friends to AIDS; men who'd stopped planning their future because they didn't think they had one; and those who'd been disowned by their homophobic relatives.

Richard Akuson, a Nigerian lawyer and gay activist, received a scathing text after he posted online a photo of himself hugging a male friend. The text was from his brother; it said, "Please refrain from all these shameful acts. Everyone is tired of you. Mommy is crying, Daddy is crying. If you don't value relationships, we do!"

Akuson texted back: "Block me if you are tired of my shameful acts. I won't be the first or last person to be rejected by his family."

Gay kids all over the world have been disowned by their parents and reviled by their relatives, the same people who used to love and protect them. Disdain for their sexuality or nontraditional lifestyles, fear of disgrace and embarrassment (especially in religious families) have turned mothers and fathers into avenging moralists. My appreciation for Jeffrey's parents' response to his coming out was renewed in March 2021, when I happened upon this heartbreaking letter to the *Times'* advice columnist, Philip Galanes:

> *I am a queer high school senior and the daughter of evangelical Christians. I have kept my sexuality secret from them. During the pandemic, I got lonely, so I started chatting on LGBTQ message boards. Unfortunately, I was careless with my browser history. My mother saw it and freaked out. She made me swear I'm not a lesbian. I did. My parents are also making me talk to their minister every week. If I don't, they say I will have to leave home. They also threatened not to help with college costs next year. (They're not kidding.) So, now I'm lying to their minister too. I hate this! I like to think of myself as a good person. Should I come clean?*

To my relief and his credit, Galanes recognized this girl's situation as one that justified constructive closeting, or what I call survival secrecy. He advised her to "keep lying! You are not a bad person." Focusing on the power differential between the girl and her punitive parents and the harm they could inflict on her present and future life, he declared honesty to be "a luxury you can't afford.... For now, focus on safety; keeping a roof over your head and staying in school.... Remember: you didn't choose any of this. And self-preservation is nothing to be ashamed of."

I also gave thanks for Betty and Bernie's kindness when I read excerpts from *I.M: A Memoir* by Isaac Mizrahi, the fashion designer, who grew up in an observant Syrian-Jewish family and attended Brooklyn's Yeshiva of Flatbush. Born eight years after my nephew, Mizrahi had no name for his gay identity when he was a child. He just knew he loved art, theater, design, Judy Garland, and Barbra Streisand. And that such passions were unacceptable for a Jewish boy. "Even before I knew exactly what it was I was ashamed of, I felt shame. I had no real understanding of myself, just a constant vibration, a faint register of dread that followed me around and sometimes erupted into mysterious depression." He remembers being five years old, on a carnival ride, waving to his parents "like a homecoming queen I'd seen on TV," and watching his father turn his back on him.

In *Fire Shut Up in My Bones*, Charles Blow's memoir about coming to terms with his bisexuality, the author, an African American, writes, "Concealment makes the soul a swamp; confession is how you drain it." My nephew's note to me was his first step toward confession; his conversation with his parents drained the swamp. No one should have to say this, we should be able to take it for granted that a gay child's mom and dad will be open, accepting, and kind, but not every parent is, so I'll say it anyway: I was proud of everything my sister and brother-in-law did from the night I called them about Jeffrey's letter and newspaper clipping, to the years after his death when they found ways to honor his memory. Betty and Bernie didn't turn their backs on their kid. They didn't feel ashamed of him. They simply loved him.

CHAPTER 29

I NEVER REPORTED THE MEN WHO MOLESTED ME

The Brett Kavanaugh hearings throttled me back to the night an aggressive, hot-headed writer assaulted me in his hotel room.

When I worked as a publicist at Bernard Geis Associates, a small publishing company in Manhattan, Brendan Behan, the bad boy Irish poet and playwright who was famous for his bestselling book, *Borstal Boy*, and infamous for drinking everyone under the table, was one of my authors. Actually, "author" was a misnomer, since three years prior, he had signed a contract to write three books for the firm but had yet to turn in a single page. This story begins one morning in 1962 when Behan, having left his house in Dublin the night before to buy a pack of cigarettes and decided on the spur of the moment to catch a flight to New York, called Geis, my boss, from a bar at Idlewild Airport (now JFK), and said he'd be arriving at our premises within the hour ready to buckle down on the first book he owed us, and would we kindly commandeer a spare typewriter, a bottle of Jameson Gold Reserve Irish Whiskey, and an empty office so he could start writing immediately? Geis, excited by the prospect, sent me out for the whiskey and a potted palm for the empty office and asked me to set up the typewriter with a few reams of paper and an ashtray.

A week later, Behan had yet to show up. However, we knew he was still in town because one of the gossip columnists reported that he'd been thrown out of P.J. Clarke's pub for starting a brawl. That's when Geis gave me an assignment well beyond my pay grade: "Find Brendan and get him writing."

I began my search, handing out notes to the vagrants and ladies of the night who hung around the Chelsea Hotel, where I'd learned Brendan was registered, and leaving messages for him with bartenders and drinking cronies at his favorite haunts on West 23rd Street. "If you run into Brendan, tell him to meet me tonight," I wrote, and provided the address of an all-night party I was planning to attend in Greenwich Village. I was counting on the promise of free booze to lure him downtown, and sure enough, around two in the morning, he bellied up to the punch table (along with several of the emissaries I'd deputized to corral him). Brendan was a sad sight—whiskey-soaked, his brogues relieved of their shoelaces, his shirt smudged with what appeared to be that morning's egg yolk, his trousers cinched around his rotund gut with a length of clothesline—but he was there. Drunk. Wasted. Reeking. But there. I linked his arm with mine and tried to steer him toward the door, but he refused to leave the party until he'd finished belting out every verse of "Roll Me Over in the Clover." Finally, I enlisted the assistance of a couple of strapping revelers who helped me get him into a taxicab. The doorman at the Chelsea helped me shovel him out of the taxi. The bellman helped me wedge his teetering humpty-dumpty frame through the revolving door and into the lobby, where I reminded my renegade author of his contractual obligation and secured his blubbering promise to appear the following morning ready to start work in the office I had made ready for him. Exhausted, I said goodnight to my unsavory charge, and turned to the street with the intention of revolving myself out.

"Where d'ya think yer goin', Missy?" I glanced back. Brendan had picked up one of those bottom-heavy, free-standing bronze ashtrays and, wielding it like a baseball bat, fixed his bloodshot eyes on the lobby's huge plate glass window. "Go now," he snarled, "and I'll send this fucker out with ya. But it's leaving through that winda!" The desk clerk gasped. The bellman froze. "Berney Geis sent you to take care of me, so take care of me. You accompany me to me room or I'll smash that winda to smithereens and tear the place apart. Y'hear?"

I heard. Immobilized, I quickly calculated the risks and benefits of doing what he asked. Nobody was waiting up for me; no one even knew where I was. I was twenty-two, single, living alone. Brenan was thirty-eight, overweight, and too plastered to do me any harm. On the other hand, were he to shatter the window and wreck the lobby, the desk clerk would call the cops, the management would sue for damages, Bernard Geis would have to cover the costs, and the media would have a field day. Not the sort of publicity I was paid to achieve for our big-name authors.

I decided to accompany him to his room. The bellman relieved him of the brass ashtray. Brendan stared at me as we rode the elevator to his floor. He took my arm when we walked down the hall, as if he needed support, but the instant we entered his room he grabbed me, slammed the door behind us, and threw me on the bed. It happened so fast; suddenly I was on my back, and he was on top of me, thrusting, groping, stinking, sickening me with his sharp soured breath. I resisted with all the force I could muster. I cried, kicked, squirmed, beat his chest with my fists, stunned by the brute strength he'd summoned up from his leaden stupor. I could have been drumming on a sack of wet sand. Crazy as it sounds, while he was pawing at my inert body, my well-trained PR brain was mindful of the consequences of attracting the cops, which, inevitably, would have drawn the press. So, I swallowed my screams and just kept keening *Stop! Stop! Stop!* until the last of my strength petered out. But an unfamiliar voice rose from some primal place in my core when he shoved his hand between his belly and mine in search of his zipper, and without logic or forethought, I heard myself say, "*Brendan! You can't do this to me! I'm a nice Jewish girl!*"

He raised his head from my neck with a start and stared at my face with piercing eyes, as if seeing me for the first time. "For Jesus's sake, lass, why din't ya say *that* in the first place?? Feck it!" Bolting upright, he swung his legs to the floor, smoothed his disheveled shirt, and tucked it into his pants, as if in response to a nun's reproof. "Don't be worrying yerself, girlie," he smiled crookedly. "Y'know I love the Jews."

I watched in utter disbelief as he perched his broad butt on the edge of the bed and gently patted the mattress to indicate he wanted me to sit beside him. I shook my head vigorously, scootching backwards on my buttocks until my spine rammed the headboard, and I sat there, trembling, as he jauntily delivered himself of a lecture on how much the Irish and the Jews had in common. For openers, our shared hatred of the English, who'd persecuted Jews in Palestine during the British Mandate, and have been hounding the Irish Catholics since the Reformation. Both peoples suffered calamities, he said; the Irish, the "Troubles," the Jews, the Holocaust, which, he allowed, "was quite a bit worse." He reminded me that the Irish and the Jews both fought wars of independence. Both were known for their grit and wit. Both produced more literary geniuses, songwriters, and storytellers than the Brits and the Krauts put together. He compared the shiva to the wake, the Last Supper to the seder, Catholic confession to Yom Kippur. He ended his discourse not with the old brag bomb, "Some of my best friends are Jews," but rather, "Some of the best Jews are my friends." At the top of the heap, Behan ranked Bobbie Briscoe, the first Jewish Lord Mayor of Dublin, whose parents migrated to Ireland from a shtetl in Lithuania but chose to name their son after Robert Emmet Briscoe, an eighteenth-century Irish patriot and revolutionary rather than for Moses or some Lithuanian rabbi or Torah scholar. My now-sober tutor assumed I was aware of what Bobbie did for the IRA and Sinn Fein, but did I realize that he also accompanied Eamon de Valera to America and took time from the Irish cause to raise money for the Irgun? "Think of it, Missy! Bobbie Briscoe and Menachem Begin were blood brothers! Ain't that savage." (Meaning "brilliant.")

Half my brain was listening to Brendan's fiery harangue, while the other half was planning how to get me out of that room alive. If my assailant could interrupt himself en route to an act of rape in order to show off his knowledge of Jews and Judaism; he could just as unpredictably pick up the assault where he left off. His hulking body was still too close for comfort. I wanted to go home. Dawn was filtering through the window shade, and I'd regained enough strength and composure to stand up and walk to the door. So I did, and he let me. What's more, he suddenly became polite as a priest, and insisted on accompanying me to the street and helping me into a taxi. A few hours later, as promised, he showed up at my office, showered, shaved, and seemingly sober. But he couldn't start writing, he said, until he'd sat on every secretary's lap and serenaded her with "Whiskey in the Jar." Then he stretched out on the couch in my office and took a two-hour nap.

That afternoon, I arranged for a typewriter to be sent to his hotel room, and he started writing the book that became the ribald, rambunctious *Brendan Behan's New York*, in which he regaled readers with tales of his peripatetic bar crawls and a host of other adventures in Godless Gotham. He never mentioned his attempted rape.

The Brett Kavanaugh hearings revived these memories and not in a good way. Being blind drunk still passes as a legitimate excuse for all manner of male misconduct. I can't know if Brendan Behan had an alcohol-induced blackout that night and had no memory of what he'd done, or if he believed he'd done nothing wrong. All I know is, he never apologized to me, and I never told anyone what he did. Nor did I press charges against him or complain to my boss. Why would I let him get away with it? Because no working girl wanted to be known as a troublemaker, especially if she was lucky enough, as I was, to be one of the few female executives in a glamorous field like book publishing. Whether my case were to be tried in the press or the courtroom, I knew, based on every other woman's experience with sexual assault, that I would be blamed for bringing it on myself. Why did I go up to his room in the first place? Why was I out so late at night? What was I wearing? Something provocative no doubt. Brendan was a red-blooded male; he must have thought I was asking for it, wanted it; maybe I was seducing him for his celebrity, or his power, or his money. (Of which there was never much, his royalties having been squandered on drink as soon as he cashed the check and found a pub that was open.) Had I complained about the assault, I would have accomplished nothing beyond embarrassing my company and humiliating our star author, and, pugnacious as he was, Brendan would have retaliated with some scurrilous accusation that undoubtedly would have sullied my reputation more than his. The upshot: Bernard Geis Associates would have lost the next three books by the universally adored Brendan Behan, and I would have lost my job.

Our violent encounter remained my secret until 1970, nearly a decade after it happened, when I described it, far too offhandedly I now believe, in my first book, *How to Make It in a Man's World*. I told my female readers not to expect a line like, "I'm a nice Jewish girl!" to save them from rape unless their attacker happened to be an Irishman with an appreciation of Jewish history and tradition. Instead, I advised them to stockpile their own "perfect sentence to extricate [themselves] from sticky sexual encounters." In 1970, my consciousness had yet to be raised. I was unaware of the nascent women's liberation movement, or of the frequency of rape. It would be five years before Susan Brownmiller published her landmark book, *Against Our Will: Men, Women, and Rape*. Five years before rape shield laws would deny defense lawyers the ability to use the sexual history of a rape victim to shame and silence her. Six years before sexual harassment was legally defined as sex discrimination. Twenty-one years before Anita Hill testified against Clarence Thomas for sexual harassment on the job. Twenty-four years before passage of the Violence Against Women Act. And fifty-eight years before the #MeToo movement provided the sisterhood and solidarity that made survivors of abuse and rape feel safe enough to tell their stories. Now, in 2022, I'm ashamed of having sugarcoated my ordeal in Brendan Behan's hotel room, reducing it to a breezy anecdote, and I'm embarrassed by how blithely I transformed an aggravated assault by a powerful man into a "sticky sexual encounter."

Brendan wasn't the only man who made it hard to be a woman in a man's world. During the thirteen years I worked in book publishing, other men—offhand I remember an editor, a journalist, a book salesman, an agent—made moves on me that were offensive or infuriating. I reported none of them. Too well-behaved to rock the boat, too eager to be liked, and afraid, were I to complain, that my exciting career would be irreparably damaged by the blowback, I laughed off every incident no matter how frightening or discomforting, and thus became a complicit enabler of the continuing predation of my so-called gentleman colleagues. My silence, and the silence of my girlfriends and every working woman I knew, spared sexually aggressive men like Brendan Behan, if not from criminal charges, from the public humiliation they deserved, and gave them a free pass to assault the next woman with impunity. Thus did the hidden pandemic of workplace sexual abuse renew itself, unseen and unchallenged until a few brave women blew the lid off and said, "Me too."

CHAPTER 30

WERE YOU EVER ASHAMED OF YOUR MOM?

Growing up one wall away from my Aunt Tillie almost, but not quite, prepared me for my mother-in-law, the most unfiltered, uninhibited person I've ever known. A card-carrying member of the Communist Party, she, like Tillie, knew when to keep her mouth shut. And though her mannerisms, humor, cooking repertoire, and fluency in Yiddish unmistakably identified her as a Jew, to her it was merely an ethnic label. Esther Pogrebin was, as she put it, an avowed Jewish atheist.

When my husband was five, he hung up one of his father's socks near the dumbwaiter in their apartment building in Brooklyn, hoping it would pass as a Christmas stocking when Santa came down the chute. There was nothing in the sock the next morning and not because Esther wanted to teach him that they were Jewish; because she believed religion was the opiate of the masses, and a Christmas stocking could be its gateway drug.

Whether she was reacting to a painting on your wall or your opinion of FDR, my mother-in-law could have given a master class in bluntness. She told it like she saw it, lived her politics out loud, and demanded similar behavior from her children. When the family moved to Roosevelt, New Jersey, Esther made Bert hand-deliver the *Daily Worker* to every house in town, secretly tucking the

Communist party newspaper inside the *Daily News* or whatever "reactionary" rag the regular newsboy had tossed on their neighbors' lawns.

Esther Pogrebin, center, and her Communist Party comrades collecting tin cans for the U.S. war effort and campaigning for the Allies to open a Second Front in Western Europe, c. early 1940s

"Mom never hid her Communist affiliation," her daughter, Marcia, told me. "She proclaimed it at town meetings." She also collected funds for the Communist party on the streets. It took guts to do that at the height of the Red Scare when the FBI was ordering surveillance of "Negro agitators" and socialist union bosses and bugging the phones of leftist Jewish housewives. Movie theaters in Southern New Jersey were still segregated in Bert's youth, but Esther insisted that he sit with her in the "Negro Section," the least desirable part of the movie house, usually the rows closest to the screen where, no matter what you did—chin high, neck stretched, head back—you missed the wide-angle vistas.

"Don't make a scene, Ma," he would plead as she dragged him down the aisle. "They don't want us here!" But his mother, who'd marched with oppressed workers against capitalist bosses, was damn well going to sit in solidarity with Black people to protest segregation. And take her son with her.

"Were you ever ashamed of your mom?" I asked my husband.

"Never."

"Were you ever embarrassed by her?"

"All the time."

"For instance?"

"When she sang 'The Star-Spangled Banner' at town meetings."

My mother-in-law's fearlessness impressed me. I often told her how much I admired her courage and how grateful I was that her strong views and bold advocacy had prepared her son to accept similar actions and commitments from me, albeit on gender issues. I thought my feminism would, if not align, at least cohabit with her Marxism, but I was wrong: to her, the only struggle worthy of attention was that of workers against bosses. Women's mistreatment at the hands of men—whether sexual violence or economic injustice—didn't qualify, in her terms, as oppression.

When I talked about Esther to my friends, I always described her as a brave iconoclast and a feisty spirit. I made her prickly personality, ornery moods, and contrarian habits sound quirky, nervy, charming. When I wrote about her, I credited her political ferocity. I never admitted the pain inflicted by her constant criticism of me or the frustration of not being able to please her. Only now, revisiting our relationship, do I feel a rush of anger and hurt, the resurrection of decades of humiliation, and the secret shanda of my failure to win her love.

At first, I was determined to be the daughter-in-law of her dreams. On Mother's Day, six months after Bert and I were married, I invited Esther, her daughter, Marcia, and younger son, Mark; and her sisters, Molly, Pearl, Helen, Belle, and their husbands and children—about thirty people in total—to our New York apartment for a lox and bagel brunch. On Hanukkah, I invited them to our latke party and gave everyone a bottle of wine as a take-home favor. For her seventieth birthday, I organized a dinner at The National, the fabled Russian restaurant in Brighton Beach, Brooklyn, where Esther and her sisters and brothers-in-law, all immigrants, tanked up on vodka and feasted on foods they remembered from the Old Country. When she turned eighty, I hired a Klezmer band with a soloist who knew all the Yiddish songs Esther loved and asked them to bring an extra microphone so she could sing along with the group. I praised her stuffed cabbage, blintzes, and rugelach and asked for her recipes. I called her "Mom," hoping, eight years after my loss, that she might fill the hole mine left behind. She refused to be maternal toward me. She already had three kids whose lives she monitored closely; she didn't need another child. Marcia, a clinical social worker, hypothesized that her mother resented me for displacing her in her son's affections. From 1958, when his father died, until I came into his life five years later, Bert, the eldest, had called Esther regularly, talked politics with her, told her about his legal cases, drove out to New Jersey once a month and sat in her kitchen while she served him her home-cooked dinners. No wonder it took so long for her to accept that his wife, and then his three kids, had become his priority.

Time never softened her tough stance toward me. Her audacity was breathtaking. As soon as we moved into our first apartment, she asked for a key so she could come and go unannounced; it was Bert who told her that was a nonstarter. When our twins were born in 1965, she criticized my childrearing style, how I'd decorated their room, how I dressed them. She nitpicked my taste in food and furnishings and bad-mouthed me to my own kids. In 1968, a few days after I finished writing my first book, I went into the hospital by appointment to deliver our son, David, by Caesarian section, and Esther drove in from New Jersey to help Bert take care of Robin and Abigail while I was gone. A week later, I came home to find that my mother-in-law had edited my three-hundred-and-fifty-page manuscript and inserted sentences or crossed out sentences on almost every page. In ink. In 1968. Pre-computers. On the one and only copy of the manuscript. Before I could submit it to my publisher, I would have to retype the whole thing. I wanted to banish her from our lives, but how could I excommunicate my children's sole surviving grandmother? The answer is, I couldn't.

Her ultimate act of unadulterated chutzpah happened in 1972 at a conference hosted by the governor of New Jersey and his State Commission on Women. I'd been invited to be the keynote speaker at the conference and, since Esther was a thirty-year resident of New Jersey, and a member of the Roosevelt, New Jersey, Borough Council, I invited her to come as my guest and sit with me at the governor's table. I expected her to use the opportunity to buttonhole the state's chief executive and discuss local issues—taxes, traffic, education, pollution. Instead, she lobbied him on behalf of workers, praised the labor movement, and ridiculed the women's movement. Mind you, she did this at a conference on women at which I was the headliner.

The event organizers had seated her on one side of the governor and me on the other so I couldn't kick her under the table when she started telling him what I was really like. "My daughter-in-law talks like a feminist, she's an editor of *Ms.*, but behind the scenes, she makes dinner for her husband and costumes for her children."

I couldn't believe my ears. "Mom! What are you doing?"

"Just telling the truth." She smirked. Mercifully, a staff member interrupted to say it was time for me and the governor to take our seats on the stage so the program could begin.

Driving back to Roosevelt, I lit into Esther, told her how much I resented her undermining me in front of the governor and everyone else at our table.

"What do you mean 'undermine you?' All I did was tell them you were a good wife and mother, and you make dinner and Halloween costumes, which is true. When I last checked, those were compliments."

"Don't be coy, Mom. You were implying that I'm a fraud, a housewife in feminist clothing. You were trying to delegitimate my politics."

"I just wanted him to know you're not one of those radical libbers."

"Mom! I *am* one of those radical libbers. I have no problem answering to that label. And it pisses me off when you misrepresent me and distort what the women's movement stands for. I didn't invite you there to tell the governor that I cook and sew."

"I'm an American citizen." Esther rolled down her window, lit a cigarette, and exhaled noisily. "I can tell the governor of New Jersey whatever I want."

I gave up and turned on the car radio.

From then on, when she pushed my buttons, I always gave up. Rather than hostility and confrontation, I chose sympathy and empathy as the preferable route to amity. I tried to put myself in Esther's place. I thought about the many hardships and disappointments that hobbled her dreams: The Communist Party never recognized her years of devotion to the cause and her role as a Marxist educator and labor organizer. The Soviet Union imploded along with her hopes for a proletariat revolution. Bert's father, Abe, a hat blocker, was seasonally unemployed and she had to scrimp to pay the bills. After Abe died of bone cancer in his mid-fifties (probably from prolonged exposure to the chemicals used to block felt hats), Esther had to support three kids on his $10,000 ILGWU life insurance. When that money ran out, she worked part-time in a nursery school, or a real estate agency. And, in her later years, she battled two cancers, lung and colon. When it became difficult for her to manage on her own, she left behind her home of forty years in the town she loved and helped build, and forty years' worth of friends, and moved to a senior citizens residence in Manhattan to be near Bert's family and Marcia's. Focusing on her story made it easier to excuse her behavior. Loneliness, financial insecurity, an empty nest, a failed revolution, poor health, advanced age, and being taken for granted could embitter her and make her resent me or any other woman who had been spared such burdens. I decided not to pile on. I gave up the fight.

Here's the irony: I admired Esther; she interested me as a person. I know people who are totally incompatible with their mothers-in-law; they have different backgrounds and beliefs and merely tolerate one another for the sake of the husband/son and kids/grandkids they both love. Jokes about mothers-in-law abound because so many people don't like theirs. I, on the other hand, started out feeling wildly enthusiastic about mine and eager for the two of us to be close. Passionate about the issues she cared about, sure-footed in her analysis of people and power relations, Esther's values and interests were as familiar to me as those of my own family and her similarity to my Aunt Tillie was uncanny. I loved Esther's Yiddishkeit (a homey, folksy brand of Jewishness). I expected her to feel something similar about me and my passions. More than that, I thought she would treat me as a second daughter, and I intended to be the perfect daughter-in-law. To my sorrow, the relationship I'd imagined never materialized. For thirty years, her disapproval remained an irreparable dent in the gleaming surface of the family I'd created to heal the cracks and fissures in my childhood. My failure to win her approbation became my secret shanda. I was ashamed of my inability to make her love me. When my every effort to please her met with rejection or criticism, I became, in my own eyes, unlovable. I hated that my children were witness to my pathetic pandering and my perennial failure. To neutralize the pain, I transformed Esther's quirks into entertaining anecdotes that amused my friends, but I never told them how impotent I felt against her provocations or how hurt I was by my inability to crack her shell. I hid the truth because I didn't want my friends to think I'd done something to cause her rejection. I was afraid they would say, "She sounds like such a terrific woman; why do you think she's not nice to you? What did you do wrong?"

Bert and I were at his mother's bedside the night she died. To my everlasting amazement, about an hour before she drew her last breath, my mother-in-law, eighty-two years old and weak as a wraith, gripped my arm hard, pulled me toward her, and whispered, "I treated you badly. I'm sorry. You deserved better."

At her funeral, Rabbi Mychal Springer, the family friend who officiated, noted the symbolism of Esther the atheist dying on Purim, the holiday on which Jews read the only sacred book in our canon that never mentions God. In Hebrew, the scroll is called the "Megillah," in English, "The Book of Esther."

More than a quarter century after her death, my mother-in-law appears to me, now and then, sharply etched, opinionated, incensed about something or other, her image conjured by some politically relevant event: the death of activist-folk singer Pete Seeger. A fundraiser for the Veterans of the Abraham Lincoln Brigade (soldiers who fought against the fascist tyrant, Franco, in the Spanish Civil War). The bizarre phenomenon of the word *red*, once a pejorative term for Communists, having become the color code for Republican states. All these years, I've been harboring a secret wish that embarrasses me because it's so self-referential: I wish Esther had lived a few more years so she could make good on her apology.

III
GUILTY SECRETS

CHAPTER 31

TWO-TIMING JUDAH MACCABEE

I'm walking up New York's Lexington Avenue when the Salvation Army Santa ringing his bell in front of Bloomingdale's suddenly morphs into another jolly fat man in a red suit. I remember how he looked sitting on his golden throne on a stage in the toy department at Gertz's department store in Jamaica. I see him surrounded by strands of multicolored lights snaking around the toy displays, Christmas presents piled high beneath a tree sparkling with ornaments and the sound of "Jingle Bells" on the speaker system. I see Mom and me, age four or five, waiting in a long line for a long time before we finally climb the stairs to Santa's workshop and she plunks me on the fat man's lap.

"Ho, ho, ho, little girl! How are you, and what would you like Santa to bring you for Christmas?"

His beard looks like a nest of white mop cords that got stuck to his face by mistake. Looped to his ears by elastic bands, it tickles my cheek as I lean closer and whisper, "We celebrate Hanukkah, but could you still bring me a two-wheeler? A Schwinn, please. Blue, if you have it."

The vision that glides through my brain in front of Bloomingdale's ends with that wish.

What did the man in the red suit say to the little Jewish girl? No recollection. Why did my very *Jewish* Jewish mother take me to visit *Saint* Nicholas in the first place, and how did she explain who he was? Memory dims. But I bet she'd convinced herself that he was a seasonal symbol not a Christian icon, and Christmas was about cookies and presents, not the baby Jesus. Always eager to adapt to American ways, she probably rationalized our visit this way: "If the goyim think it's worth waiting in line for an hour so their kid can whisper in Santa's ear, why shouldn't my little Bunny have her turn on his lap? What harm can it do? Besides, Gertz was giving every child a free candy apple as they left the workshop, and they didn't have a separate tray of apples for Jewish kids who don't believe in Santa.

I can't recall whether she bought me a toy while we were there or not. But what she said on our way home stayed with me. She said this was "our special adventure" and not to tell Daddy about it when he comes home for supper. Like any kid, I relished the guilty pleasure of hiding something from my father. Now, as I head up Lexington Avenue on a cold winter afternoon, I'm wondering what required this adventure to be kept secret? What made Mom feel guilty in retrospect about sneaking off with me to see St. Nick? Was it because she'd done it behind her husband's back, without his permission, and presumably against his wishes? If so, did she consider her transgression a betrayal of Jack, Judah Maccabee, or of Judaism itself? Was she embarrassed about falling for the Santa sell and the commercialization of Christmas? Had we been seen by someone, a friend of hers from Sisterhood or Hadassah, who might tell tales about this travesty—Ceil Cottin, Jewish mother! Wife of the president of the synagogue! Standing in line at Santa's Workshop so her little girl could sit on the lap of a surrogate saint? Like many puzzles in my mother's life, I can't solve this one. But she must have believed she'd done something wrong because she never again took me to see the jolly fat man in the red suit. I did get the blue bike. But not for Hanukkah. In June, for my birthday.

CHAPTER 32

THE MENORAH

My father could talk your ear off about the First Amendment or the Fourth Commandment, but when it came to emotions, his were as opaque as the frosted glass in his office door. That he was not in the least bit sentimental would have been obvious to anyone who observed the cavalier way he disposed of my mother's belongings after she died.

If I had to guess what he was thinking when he gave away the blue-rimmed china she used for our Shabbos dinners, it was probably something like, *Why would a college girl need service for twelve?* Apparently, it never crossed his mind to put the dishes in storage until I had a home of my own. And when he gave away Mom's Persian lamb topper, he probably thought, *A fifteen-year-old would never wear a fur coat.* He was right: I wouldn't. But had he asked, I would have loved to use it as an everyday comforter, snuggling under it when my dorm room got chilly, breathing in the fragrance that lingered in its satin lining. Lost on my father was the power of attachments, the way an object can evoke a life, a moment, one's mother, as if she were not gone forever, just down the hall in the next room.

The shanda wasn't his downsizing; it was his insensitivity, haste, and disregard for the objects his wife had so carefully chosen to decorate, animate, and enrich their daily lives. To the best of my knowledge, my father did not hold a tag sale, yet when I came "home" from college to his new apartment I knew it would never feel like home to me. Too much was missing. Gone were my mother's cooking utensils and baking supplies: her tin pie plates, manual eggbeater, flour sifter, pastry cutter, pastry brush, the rolling pin she'd kept sheathed in a cotton covering that looked like an infant's onesie. All gone, along with the promise of pie. To this day, I wish he had saved the yellowware mixing bowls that, for me, conjured chocolate layer cakes, the batter she let me lick off the wooden spoon. More than mere objects, her kitchen supplies embodied the woman who used them, who gave them purpose.

Dad wasn't ashamed of what he did; I was ashamed for him. Embarrassed by how quickly he'd eradicated her presence. Injured by how thoughtlessly he'd shrunk my world. He sold our seven-room house, rented a three-room apartment, put a daybed in the hall for me, and assigned me two shelves and six hangers in the hall closet for my belongings. ("You won't need much space from now on, since you'll only be coming home on school vacations, and after graduation, you'll get married.") But he was the one who got married—the summer between my freshman and sophomore year in college, barely sixteen months after my mother's death—and didn't tell me until he returned from his honeymoon and presented me with a stepmother.

I have nothing against stepmothers, per se. Some of my best friends are stepmothers. And I wouldn't go so far as to call mine evil; simply snide, duplicitous, egocentric, and narcissistic. In my 1991 memoir, I described my father's new wife as,

> ...a Southern belle with an exaggerated drawl, Jewish but unschooled in Judaism and unobservant, fifty-four years old but relentlessly girlish and charming—and self-centered to a fault. She is given to dramatic color-coordinated outfits and dyed black hair styled sleek as patent leather into a chignon at the top of her head. I am in my peasant-blouse-and-black-tights Bohemian phase. His wife and I have nothing in common but our mutual distrust.... She is to my mother as polyester is to silk. She's a phony. I hate my father's wife. It does not occur to me to hate my father for choosing her.

None of my friends knew about Dad's precipitous actions, his wife, his apartment, or anything else about my family situation. That was my secret and divulging it would only have added shame to the pain. Sleeping in his vestibule wasn't all that bad, I told myself; the square footage probably added up to my share of my three-person dorm room. Kids all over the world make do in far less space. Having my own room had been a luxury, and yearning for Mom's hand-made curtains would not bring them back. Besides, the vestibule in my father's apartment had no windows.

If not for my sister's generosity and foresight, I would own almost nothing to remind me of our mother. When Mom died, Betty was thirty and well enough situated to claim and store some of the things our father was so eager to give away. Ensconced with a husband and four children in a Victorian house in Peekskill, New York, she had an attic and took me up there eight years later, when Bert and I were married and furnishing a new apartment in the city, so I could collect the contents of the "hope chest" she'd been filling for me since I was fifteen. That's when I saw all the paintings, a dozen or more of them, painted by Mom when she was in her mid-forties and early fifties. Bored with housewifery, she'd taken an art class at Queens College, bought an easel, an old fashioned wooden palette, tubes of oil paint of every hue, and a stack of clean white canvases, and she'd began making landscapes, mostly scenes of my grandparents' farmhouse in Shrub Oak, and still lifes of objects on display in our home in Jamaica.

The most evocative of them is her Shabbat table still life. She must have known she was dying because she painted two of the same composition, one for Betty, one for me. I remember when she set up her easel in our small dining room on 167th Street, arranged a display of Jewish ceremonial objects on the table, and started working on one of those paintings, which became mine, her thumb protruding through the hole in her wooden palette as she squeezed paint from different tubes, and blended them to match the color and texture of each item in the tableau—the silvery sheen on Dad's kiddush cup, the plush velvet of his crimson tallit pouch, the brass candelabra with two Lions of Judah carved into its crest, the orange glow of the Shabbos candles reflected on the surface of the crystal decanter. I watched her create a shade somewhere on the spectrum between purple and maroon that precisely captured the color of the burgundy within the decanter without the wine muddying the gloss of the crystal. Dad's oversized prayer shawl, creamy-white, slashed with black stripes and fringed with hand-tied tassels, is loosely draped against the background of the scene, and resting on the table is his leather-bound siddur, its pages tipped in a muted red. When I look at this painting, I see the Sabbaths of my childhood, a woman's paean to a man's Judaism.

My husband jokes that I'm so sentimental I get nostalgic about the present. Point taken; I've been known to get weepy at the sight of a grandchild's baby picture or the smell of an old book. In one dictionary, nostalgia is defined as "wishful desire," in another, it's "a longing for home or familiar surroundings; homesickness. A bitter-sweet yearning for the things of the past." Both accurately describe how I feel when I think about a ceremonial object that does *not* appear in any of my mother's paintings: our Hanukkah menorah. I haven't laid eyes on it since Dad died, but I see it as clearly as the cup in my hand right now. Its silver backplate etched with the tablets of the decalogue. The eight tiny oil vessels lined up along its base, the diminutive oil pitcher and shammash hooked to loops on either side of the menorah. When Dad downsized, he didn't give away any of our Judaica, the ritual objects that were Jewishly meaningful to me; he kept them. And when he and his Southern wife picked up stakes and moved to a condo in Florida, the meno-rah went with them.

Every Hanukkah, I miss it. I remember it. I want it back.

I want my menorah back because sixty years later, its memory won't fade along with the memories of everything else I've had to let go. Believe me, I don't need another piece of Judaica. Brass can-dlesticks line our dining room windowsill. Kiddush cups crowd the shelves, one for every member of the family, plus one each for the prophets, Elijah and Miriam. We have a dedicated dish for

Rosh Hashana apples and honey; a spice box, a seder plate, a box full of whimsical but workable dreidels that I hang from ribbons tied to the chandelier during the eight days of Hanukkah. And we certainly don't need another menorah. We collect them (Duh! Overcompensation, right?). Old ones from Yemen, Persia, Turkey, Poland, Russia, Morocco; new ones crafted here and in Israel; and, best of show, a commanding brass and steel menorah designed and forged by our grandson, Zev, when he was a senior in high school. I love them all, especially Zev's, but none cannot replace the one preserved in the aspic of childhood nostalgia. What I wouldn't give, even now, for that menorah. A final tether.

<hr />

After my father died, his wife and I never saw each other again. Since she was about his age, she, too, must be long gone, so in all probability, my childhood menorah is now in the possession of one of her children or grandchildren, maybe even a great-grandchild. Whoever they are, I can't help resenting them, people I've never met, for owning this piece of my history. I feel guilty for begrudging the innocent members of my stepmother's family when they can't possibly know what the menorah means to me, or even that I exist. I feel guilty about fetishizing my mother's menorah because people matter, things don't. But when people aren't around anymore, all we have left to remember them, besides endearing stories and enduring love, are the things they held in their hands, used in their lives, and cherished.

CHAPTER 33

THANK GOD NOTHING LIKE THAT IS HAPPENING IN MY FAMILY

W hen conversation flags at a dinner party, all I have to do is ask people to define the difference between shame and guilt and we're off to the races.

"Shame is Christian, guilt is Jewish," someone is bound to say and do a credible job of supporting that thesis. Mordecai Finley, a Los Angeles psychologist, historian, philosopher (and the world's only rabbi with a black belt in jiu-jitsu), maintains that Jewish guilt is about "insufficiency," not living up to the "standards and expectations of our people." He explicates with a composite quote from a common stereotype—the nagging Jewish Mother. "Why don't you see me more often? Why aren't you a better son? Why aren't you as good as your brother Sheldon? Look at your cousin, look how great he is."

The late Jonathan Sacks, for twenty-two years the esteemed chief rabbi of the British Commonwealth, told a BBC radio audience, "In shame cultures, what matters is what other people think of you: the embarrassment, the ignominy, the loss of face. Whereas in guilt cultures, it's what the inner voice of conscience tells you. In shame cultures, we're actors playing our part on the public stage. In guilt cultures, we're engaged in inner conversation with the better angels of our nature…. In shame cultures, if you've done wrong, the first rule is, don't be found out. If you are, then bluff your way through. Only admit it when every other alternative has failed, because you'll be disgraced for a very long time indeed."

In short, the antidote people prescribe for disgrace is secrecy. Dump your shame into a box and bury it.

I derive the distinction between guilt and shame by parsing the linguistics. For instance, why do we say, "I *feel* guilty" but "I *am* ashamed?" To me, the reason is obvious; it's the difference between feelings and actions. "I *am* ashamed" conveys a negative self-assessment. "I am guilty" admits an act of wrongdoing. Guilt is the by-product of our actions toward others; shame is the by-product of our judgment of ourselves. Guilt says, "I did a bad thing"; shame says, "I am a bad person." Of course, there are exceptions: a man who steals a loaf of bread because he's hungry may feel guilty about it without being ashamed. And a woman who's been raped may be ashamed because she feels violated without being guilty of anything.

It bears repeating that neither guilt nor shame is exclusive to Jews. My cousin Debbie's husband, Steve, a fire fighter whom she met on 9/11 while volunteering at the World Trade Center disaster site, is a strapping 6'2", blond, ruddy, unfailingly jovial Christian. To me, he looks invincible but when I asked him about guilt vs. shame, his expression changed; suddenly, he looked like a little boy who's been told to wear a dunce cap and stand in the corner. Steve told me his mother used to shame him a lot. When he did something wrong, even if it was just letting his hair grow long, she used to rub one index finger against the other and say, "Shame on you." It made him feel she was disappointed in *him*, not just in what he'd had done, but in him as a person, and as her son.

A friend of mine who was raised Catholic in an interfaith household but considers herself ethnically Jewish, said her Jewish side is always telling her, "You can do better," while her Catholic side says, "You're a lost cause." The actor Ben Affleck, raised by a

Catholic mother and a Protestant father, told an interviewer that he felt guilty about his alcoholism (which helped end his marriage to Jennifer Garner, the mother of his three children), but guilt isn't as bad as shame because shame is "really toxic." Silvan Tomkins, the psychologist who coined the term "toxic shame" in the 1960s, defined it as a chronic sense of unworthiness. I think of it as a festering stew of self-loathing that corrodes, debilitates, and yields zero positive by-products. Guilt, however, can lead to improved behavior and the development of a moral and ethical baseline, which, as I look back on my life, is what Jewish guilt has done for me. (Though, in some cases, my correctives have been too little or too late.)

One of the relatives about whom I feel terminally guilty is my cousin, Faith, the one who shocked her sister, Simma, with the news that her real mother was Sadye, not Vera. Cousin Faith, nick-named Sistie at an early age, was born with mental and physical deficits that the adults in our family did not name or explain and we children intuited but never understood. In the birth order of the Halpern cousins, Sistie, the daughter of Sadye and Herman, was number five. Prissy (née Priscilla), the daughter of Rona and Ben, came a year and a half after Sistie, and I, daughter of Ceil and Jack, was born eighteen months after Prissy, who became my best friend even before I could talk. Whenever our families got together, which was often, Prissy and I were inseparable. Our moms had to remind us to play with our older cousin, and we tried, but those coerced threesomes were awkward and more often than not, Sistie was the odd girl out. When Prissy and I played let's pretend, Sistie just watched, confused by our improvised dialogue. When we invited her to a tea party with miniature china, she knocked over her cup. Most of the games we loved were beyond her. She had trouble playing checkers and Go Fish, and she was hopeless at Pick-Up Sticks.

I'm cataloging her inadequacies not to dishonor her memory but to emphasize how obvious those deficits were and how painful it must have been for her to constantly be thrust into situations in which she couldn't measure up. I know our mothers meant well. Yet their understandable desire for Faith to have someone to play with, and their habitual inclination toward smoothing over differences and papering over conflict, made things worse, not better. Tensions mounted whenever Sistie showed up and Prissy and I could never measure up to our mothers expectations that we find a way to integrate her in our activities.

Prissy, left, and Bunny (Letty) in Shrub Oak with
Elsie as a bovine backdrop, c. 1942

For several weeks every summer, our moms, Rona and Ceil, took Prissy and me, and later Prissy's baby sister, Sue, upstate to stay with our maternal grandparents at their farmhouse in Shrub Oak, New York. Those were halcyon days filled with storybook activities. Prissy and I planted seeds, picked flowers, flew kites, played catch, harvested berries, jumped rope, milked our neighbor's cow, had picnics in the meadow, raced to the chicken coop to gather eggs in our baskets and brought them home, still warm. During the dog days of summer, we would put on our bathing suits and dash through the sprinkler or splash in the wading pool or beg one of the adults to take us to the beach at Lake Peekskill or Lake Mohegan. When Sadye brought Sistie and her brother, Marvin, up to Shrub Oak to spend a few days with our moms and us, we were, as usual, instructed to include our older cousin in our play, and, despite her being ungainly, we tried. At least, I think we did, though I've probably been deluding myself all these years because the truth is too distressing.

One day, she must have done something that really got on our nerves because, mortified as I am to resuscitate this acrid, guilt-ridden memory, Prissy and I lured Sistie into the chicken coop and locked her in with the hens. I'm not sure how much time passed before we opened the latch, but I'll never forget her cries, her tear-stained face and rumpled sundress, the feathers stuck in her hair when we let her out, and I've never gotten over my shame. There's simply no way to absolve us of our cruelty. We were mean girls, selfish, pitiless, and what we did was inexcusable. I can't remember our punishment, but I hope it was severe. Yet I also fault our mothers for not explaining our cousin's limitations to us in child-level terms that might have made us more accommodating and empathic. Rather than simply ordering us to play with her, they could have suggested games that were more suited to her abilities and helped us figure out how to compensate for her deficiencies without hurting her feelings. Of course, in order to do those things, they would have had to admit that she *had* deficiencies. But no one spoke about differentness. Her struggles were glossed over as if they didn't exist.

Various combinations of Halpern cousins spent summer holidays together at our grandparents' farm house in Shrub Oak, NY. The six kids in this snapshot are, top row: Marvin Chester, Letty (Bunny) Cottin in the arms of Betty Cottin; middle row: Faith (Sistie) Chester, Danny Kahn; front, center: Priscilla (Prissy) Darvie. June, 1940

I would like to believe that our mothers were trying to "mainstream" Sistie with the two cousins closest to her age. But neither the word nor the concept of mainstreaming existed when we were kids. More likely, it was hard for a Halpern to acknowledge that a child in our family was cognitively "slow" and physically challenged. The fact that Sadye and Herman had spawned a boy as brilliant as Marvin yet also produced an "imperfect" child like Sistie could best be accommodated by being ignored.

Public attitudes toward people with special needs, hardly enlightened in the 1940s and '50s, were further complicated by the teachings of our tradition, which, to my mind at least, are maddeningly contradictory. At the same time as Leviticus commands us, "You shall not insult the deaf or place a stumbling block before the blind," the list of those ineligible to act as witnesses in a beit din, a Jewish court of law, includes thieves, slaves, gamblers, usurers, men who are deaf or mentally incompetent, and *women*, regardless of their intellectual or physical condition. In theory, Jewish law holds that each of us is created in the image of God; therefore, every human being is of equal value. In practice, most Jews considered women to be inferior to men and a disabled child to be a tragedy, if not a curse; a punishment, perhaps, for a parent's sins. Should one child's deficiencies become known in the community, it could destroy the marriage prospects of all the other children in that family, all of whom would be suspected of carrying similarly defective genes. The only solution to such a Class A shanda was secrecy.

It wouldn't surprise me if Sistie's impairments were kept under wraps to protect the rest of us from being considered unmarriageable. She did get married, at twenty, to a man named Eddie, a Holocaust survivor, who appeared dour but, I've been told, was a kind, dutiful, and solicitous husband. Apparently, wifehood increased Sistie's status in the family since everyone started calling her by her real name, Faith. In time, Faith gave birth to a daughter, Sharon, who was "normal," and a son, Steven, who was born with cerebral palsy and "used a wheelchair." That term, as opposed to "confined to a wheelchair," is the preferred locution these days; however, in Steven's case "used" was a misnomer since he could hardly move a muscle on his own and had to be pushed from place to place and dressed and fed by others. The task of fulfilling his needs must have been daunting to a young mother with deficits of her own. But during the rare times when they attended family gatherings, I observed Faith caring for him with inexhaustible patience and love.

At one such event, when Steven was in his late teens, I watched Faith spoon soft food into his open mouth, intermittently mopping his chin with her napkin. When he finished eating and she had untied his bib from around his neck, I decided to initiate a conversation. I wasn't sure how to begin or how he might respond because, like Sadye had done with Faith, Faith never talked about her son's impairment or suggested ways the family might best relate to him. At this point, still consumed by shame for the way Pris and I had treated her as a child, I wasn't comfortable asking Faith for advice. I picked up a small bench and carried it toward them—by then, at least I knew enough to speak to people in wheelchairs at *their* eye level, so they didn't have to crane their necks and look up. I thought I might open our conversation by commenting on Steven's shirt, which, I believe, was a navy blue plaid. I placed the bench at one side of his wheelchair but didn't sit down because of what I saw happening. His lips had turned white, his eyes were as round as saucers, his hands were twitching. Did he think I was going to attack him? Had I come too close too quickly? Was he afraid I might ask him a question? Did he even know who I was? Rather than add to his distress, I turned to Faith and asked what I'd done to upset him.

"It will pass," she said, kindly. "You can sit down." I sat down and complimented her on her son's shirt. I complimented her on her hair. I talked about the weather.

Faith has been gone for years. So has Steven. But writing about them has reawakened my guilt. I didn't do right by either of them.

⁓⁓⁓

Not too long after that incident, I read a story about the alarming rate of opioid addiction among the children of Russian Jews in

Brooklyn and how their parents were too ashamed to reach out to the rest of the Jewish community for help. *Thank God nothing like that is happening in my family*, I thought, grateful that we'd been spared the sorrow, and the shanda, of substance abuse. Commenting on the story to one of my daughters a day or so later, I remarked, "Isn't it unusual for there to be no alcoholics or drug addicts in a family as large as ours?"

"Really, Mom? *Really?*" Rolling her eyes, my daughter named two close relatives—a young woman struggling with heroin addiction who, at that very moment, was serving her fifth prison sentence for dealing; and a twentysomething man whose drinking problem had been painfully obvious to his father and everyone else during our previous Thanksgiving dinner when he'd left the table inebriated and disappeared upstairs before the turkey showed up. I found him flaked out in a darkened bedroom, sobbing, and asked if he wanted to talk. "If you want to listen," he replied and poured out all the repressed feelings and fears he'd been trying to drown in beer.

I know drug and alcohol abuse is a disease that has ravaged every group and category of person, rich or poor, but I could have sworn our family was immune to that particular problem because I grew up believing Jews don't drink, we eat. In a scholarly article entitled "A Jewish Drunk Is Hard to Find," the historian Glenn Dynner describes the "sobriety stereotype" of Eastern European Jews. To me, that wasn't a stereotype; it was a fact. Before we moved to the house in Jamaica Estates, which had a finished basement with a real bar, my parents used to keep a fifth of Canadian Club and a fifth of slivovitz on a shelf in our linen closet. The bottles grew dusty with disuse. None of us knew anyone who was hooked on drugs or alcohol. Dad said he had a doctor in the 1930s, a Jewish doctor, who tried morphine because he wanted to know how it felt. It felt euphoric, so he kept writing prescriptions for himself, got hooked, and died of an overdose. I've never forgotten how shocked everyone was when my father told that story. "Such a shanda!" they said. "How could a smart Jewish doctor be so stupid."

That young relatives of mine had been struggling with alcoholism and heroin addiction troubled me more than I could admit. It also awakened my inherited fear of the shanda. How could two smart Jewish kids get hooked on booze and heroin? They must be so ashamed. How could I help them quit? I couldn't. Confronted by this up close and personal proof that Jewish exceptionalism can't protect our children, and feeling impotent in the face of something I couldn't fix, I followed my mother's template and buried what I couldn't bear.

SuEllen Fried, a friend who volunteers in the Lansing Correctional Facility in Leavenworth County, Kansas, told me about a session on shame that she'd recently facilitated with a group of male inmates. "What's the elephant in the room in your family?" was their topic. The first prisoner to speak said, "The elephant is my alcoholism. Everyone knew I had a serious drinking problem, but when our family got together no one confronted me because they didn't want to cause a scene at a happy event." Another volunteered, "The elephant is that I keep getting out of prison, and then I do the same dumb stuff and get sent back." A third, sighed, "I've brought so much shame to my family. The elephant in the room is me."

In case it's not obvious by now, the elephant in my family of origin is a crippling fear of the shanda.

CHAPTER 34

PITY IS BETTER

Left to right, Betty, Grandma Jenny, and Aunt Joan, c. 1943

The biblical commandment, "Be fruitful and multiply," was more than fulfilled by the women on both sides of my family. My two grandmothers each had seven children. The four Halpern sisters and two Cottin sisters each had two or three. My sister Betty had four, Rena had two, and I had a twofer and a singleton. Only Joan, the wife of my mother's brother, Herbert, was childless; "barren," as she'd put it years before when she confessed the problem to Herb's mother, Jenny, who told all the Halpern women of childbearing age—Herb's sisters, Ceil, Tillie, Rona, and Sadye, and his oldest nieces, Betty and Judy—all of whom pitied her. When Joan was around, the family tried to keep their kids out of sight so as not to rub her nose in the nachas (prideful pleasure) a barren woman could never hope to enjoy.

Infertility is a sorrowful state for anyone of any religion or ethnic background, but after the Holocaust, Jewish women who could not conceive or carry a child often bore the added misery of shame. "When a Jew can't reproduce, the source of the problem is immaterial, the outcome is the same," a friend with fertility problems once told me. "It's like genocide." After the Second World War, our job was to replenish our people's decimated numbers. To that end, every Jewish women was expected to give birth to at least one living, breathing, squalling symbol of our survival.

Herbert and Joan had settled in Florida early in their marriage and only came north for weddings, funerals, and major Jewish holidays. I always looked forward to their visits, especially to my conversations with Joan, whose soulful sophistication was a nice change from the chattering verbosity of my other aunts. I liked that Joan kept her hair in sleek upswept rolls on either side of her head long after that wartime style had gone out of vogue and that her smile could barely contain all her teeth, and she often said things I'd never thought of before, which most people didn't.

In 1968, she and Uncle Herbert came to New York for the Passover seder at Betty and Bernie's place in Larchmont. That year tables filled the living room end to end, extended across the entry hall and into the dining room. Joan and I were seated about ten yards apart but could see each other across the room so as soon as my father ransomed the afikomen from the children, and everyone finished singing "Had Gadya," I sent my aunt a let's-get-outta-here signal and gestured toward the glassed-in porch. It took a while for me to wriggle my way behind the long line of chairs, and harvest hugs from relatives I'd missed when we'd first arrived. En route through the kitchen, I grabbed a chocolate-covered matzah, split it in two, set each piece on a paper napkin and gave one to my aunt who had already brought out two cups and a small pot of tea.

"Hey, Letty! Mazel tov!" she beamed, flashing her toothy smile as I sat beside her on the rattan couch.

"Thanks," I said quickly, deflecting her attention to the matzah. "I like Streit's best, don't you? Their dark chocolate makes all the difference." I had recently given birth to my son and felt embarrassed by my fecundity.

"Tell me about your little David," she said, brightly. "And the twins, how are those two little angels? It must be a great shock for them to suddenly have to share their parents with an adorable baby brother."

"Everyone's doing pretty well, thanks." I flicked a matzah crumb off my black pants. "How are you and Herbie enjoying Florida? Do you miss the snow?"

"Not a bit."

The message imprinted on my napkin caught my eye, another opportunity for deflection. "Look! It says, 'Matzah: The feast without the yeast.' Clever, right? Each napkin has a different wisecrack about Passover. What's on yours?"

Joan obviously sensed my awkwardness. I felt her hand on my arm.

"Letty, relax! It's okay to talk about your children. I could have had kids if I wanted."

"What did you just say?" The matzah slid off my napkin onto the rug, thankfully chocolate side up. "Are you *kidding* me? Say that again?"

"I've never been barren. I've been pregnant twice. I've had two abortions. The reason why I told everyone I couldn't have kids was because I couldn't tell them I didn't *want* kids. From the day Herbie brought me into this family, everyone *hocked mir a tchainik* (hassled me) about getting pregnant. They wouldn't quit. 'You're so thin, Joan.' 'How long 'til we see a belly, Joan.' 'What are you waiting for, Joan?' 'Better start soon or you won't live to see your grandchildren.' Your mom and aunts were driving me nuts. You know Herb's great with kids. You and Prissy used to love his ventriloquist act, remember?" (I remembered. We thought our uncle and his wooden sidekick were as good as Edgar Bergen and Charlie McCarthy or better.) "The truth is Herb never wanted children and neither did I but we couldn't admit that, not in *this* family, not after what Hitler did to us. It would have been a shanda. So I gave myself a problem they couldn't fix: I told them I was barren."

I was speechless. I'd known women who were ashamed to admit they were infertile, women who hid their miscarriages, women who wouldn't admit they'd had abortions. But I'd never known a woman who hid the fact that she was *fertile*. "Are you telling me we've been pitying you all these years for nothing?"

Joan gave me an archetypal Jewish shrug—shoulders raised, arms turned out, palms up. "Sorry. What else can I say?"

Still shocked, I persisted. "Don't you think my mom and aunts would have backed off if you gave them a romantic reason?"

"Such as?"

"Such as, 'Herb and I are so in love we can't imagine sharing each other with a child.'"

Joan shot me a look over the rim of her teacup. "You're speaking a foreign language, Letty. Your uncle and I were married in 1946. Have you ever heard a Jewish woman of my generation admit that rather than devote her life to her children, she preferred to concentrate on her life with her husband? Have you ever heard a Jewish woman say, 'Rather than spend thousands of dollars on educating a kid, we'd rather travel the world together?'"

She was right. According to Jewish tradition, the central purpose of marriage is lifelong companionship *and* the creation of a family. The Hebrew Bible recounts the agonies of women who can't conceive, their longing, their shame, their abject despair, how incomplete they were until God blessed them with a child (a son of course), or two at a time if she was lucky. Once God deigned to intervene, Sarah gave birth to Isaac (at ninety and nursed him). Rebecca bore Isaac twins, Esau and Jacob. Rachel had Joseph, then Benjamin. Tamar also had twins, Peretz and Zerach. Hannah prayed and wept and prayed some more until she became pregnant with Samuel. Manoah's (unnamed) wife gave birth to the mighty Samson.

Recalling those foundational stories, I realized what a brilliant move it was for Joan to cut off the nagging by claiming she was barren. In the 1940s—and still today in some communities—a Jewish woman who admitted that she preferred to live "child-free" would have been called every name in the book: deviant, selfish, egomaniacal, egocentric, narcissistic, solipsistic. My mother and aunts would have launched a full-court press. First line of attack: "It's unnatural, Joan. What's wrong with you? Motherhood is a woman's highest purpose." Next round: "How can you do this to your husband? Refusing to bear his child is an insult. Every man wants a son to carry on his name." Finally, the guilt offensive: "America just fought a war to save us from the ovens. Don't you care about the continuity of The Jewish People? You have to have children. You owe it to the Six Million."

Joan was right. Pity was better.

CHAPTER 35

AT LAST, RENA

I was fourteen when my father's daughter showed up on our doorstep. Since learning of her existence two years before on the beach in Winthrop, I'd been wildly curious to meet her, but having no idea how to begin the search, I had relinquished the fantasy of our reunion. Then, one brittle cold day in 1954, she found us. My mother and I were upstairs in our house on Wareham Place in Jamaica Estates. Mom was sick in bed, I was in my room doing homework. When the bell rang, I ran down, opened the door, and there, on our welcome mat, facing the street as if she thought she was being followed, stood a female figure with a long brown braid that ran down her back halfway to her waist.

"May I help you?"

The young woman swiveled around and stuck out her hand like a wooden soldier. "Hi, Bunny, I'm Rena. Your sister."

Dad's diagram flashed before my eyes, the Rena circle dangling from the Jack-Paula crossbar, the snapshot of the little girls in braids and cute cotton sunsuits, and here, in the flesh, all grown-up but still round-faced, was the girl in rimless glasses, the "distant cousin," wearing steel-frames now and one braid, instead of two. Before I could run upstairs to announce the arrival of this incredible apparition, it slid past me into the living room, sat itself on one of our half-moon loveseats, and took its time looking me up and down.

I stared back at her, warbling, "Rena...Rena!...Rena??" like a stuck cuckoo clock.

"That's my name," she replied coolly, and gestured for me to sit on the opposite loveseat, and, dispensing with preliminaries, she addressed me as if I were a peer. "I've come to ask your father—our father—for help. If you knew me, you'd know how humiliating it is for me to find myself in the role of supplicant. I wouldn't be here had Paula not gone completely off the rails. Her paranoid schizophrenia has been my cross to bear since I was a child, but she's completely deranged now; her outbursts have increased in frequency and severity to the point where I fear for my life. It's imperative that I move out of our apartment, she's given me no choice, but I don't feel safe returning for my things without a marshal. I'll need your father to obtain an order of protection; that's the only reason I'm here. Although I must confess what great pleasure it gives me to see you, Bunny." A smile lit up her face. "If I recall correctly, the last time we were together, you were in a playpen."

"I'm Letty now," I said, as if that were the most important thing she'd missed.

Having heard our voices, Mom appeared at the top of the open stairway in her nightgown and, gripping the railing, slowly made her way down. When she saw who our visitor was, she cried out Rena's name and descended the last few stairs with more vigor than I'd seen her expend in weeks. Rena hurried toward her and taking her arm, helped her cross the living room to the loveseat, where they sat thigh to thigh while Rena explained her plight.

My fixation on the day my phantom sister showed up is second only to my preoccupation with the day my parents told me their secret. Both events have made multiple appearances in my work, for instance, this excerpt from *Deborah, Golda, and Me* (which I've revised for clarity and edited for concision):

> *After a reunion with our father that can only be described as sedate, and a dinner during which my mother seems to be trying extra hard to make her feel*

welcome, Rena spends the next few weeks in our attic bedroom. I rush home from school every day to spend time with her, as if she's a visiting mermaid who might disappear with the next wave. This new sister of mine is a true nonconformist, even a tad eccentric. Absent a trace of self-consciousness, she talks about cybernetics and physiometry, and enjoys correcting everyone's grammar, vocabulary, and pronunciation. Her arcane comments send me rushing to the dictionary to look up words like tautology and anima, which she sprinkles through her speech like glitter (and which I will define correctly when I encounter them months later in the College Boards exam).

"She has a 180 I.Q. and a PhD. from Columbia," says my father one evening. "She's an anthropologist specializing in Gypsy cultures and speaks twenty Romani dialects." He seems proprietary, as if Rena's intelligence was entirely of his making. As she brings me into her world, I realize I'm the sister of an intellectual prodigy who is also a Romani princess. She takes me with her when she visits the Gypsies in Upper Manhattan among whom she did her doctoral fieldwork. I meet the king of the tribe who treats her like his daughter. Meanwhile, Rena doesn't treat my father as her father, which mystifies me.

"I came here because I had no place else to go for help," she says, when I ask why she's so frosty to him. "He could do without me when I was a child. I can do without him now."

"But he wanted to keep seeing you," I insist, parroting Dad's side of the story. "He stopped trying when your mother threatened to harm you if he ever got in touch with you."

"My mother harmed me anyway," Rena says, bitterly. "And he knew she would. The truth is, his visitation rights were contingent on his paying child support and when you were born, he stopped paying. So, she stopped my visits. He never fought for me."

I refuse to believe Jack could do such a thing. Therefore, I cannot believe Rena.

It's been three decades since I wrote that, and I still don't know who was telling the truth. In the 1950s, I didn't want to know. A firm answer would have required me to give up one of them—the sister I'd just found, or the only parent I had left. Now, as I struggle to make sense of the discrepancy between my father's story and Rena's, I'm ready for the truth but the shopping bag disgorged no letters that might settle the matter, only a tantalizing, ultimately opaque, agonizingly vague divorce decree. Filed in 1932, in Rockland County, New York, in favor of the plaintiff, Pauline M. Cottin, against the defendant, Jacob Cottin, on account of his adultery, the decree orders said defendant "to pay $15 per week for the plaintiff and $15 per week for the child, then age four years, eleven months, and a lump sum of $180 as further alimony." No mention of when child support was to terminate or what enforcement measures or penalties would be imposed should the defendant fail to fulfill his obligations. With that yellowed document, my search for the truth—whether Jack was a deadbeat dad or Rena was a liar—hit a wall.

But from the moment my secret sister appeared on our doorstep in 1954, I recognized in her an entirely unfamiliar brand of female: strong, assured, acerbic, confrontational, cocky. In no time at all, I was besotted, captivated by her erudition, enchanted by all the ways she was different from the women in our family and every other woman I'd ever known. Adjectives cram the pages of my diary, descriptions of Dr. Rena Cottin that placed her in a category of one. Twenty-seven at the time we met, she was running an organization that helped immigrants who were physicians in their countries of origin to bone up on American medical practices so they could pass their boards and get a license. She was so whip smart, edgy, articulate, and accomplished that she numbered among her friends and mentors Dr. Ruth Benedict, the world-renowned anthropologist and folklorist (who, by the way, did pioneering work on the distinction between shame cultures and guilt cultures) the founder of cultural relativism, and lesbian partner of Margaret Mead. Most memorably, Rena maintained a close, ongoing relationship with the Matchwaya Romani tribe whose culture she'd studied for her doctorate. These urban gypsies lived along Upper Broadway in ordinary apartment buildings whose storefronts advertised the Matchwayan women's arcane specialties—Fortune Teller, Psychic, Crystal Ball Gazing, Mystical Prognostications, Palm Reading. Tarot Cards, Oils, Charms, Brews. Outside, inside, or on a platform in their streetfront windows, beribboned women, their eyes edged with kohl, sat at tables covered by fringed velvet cloths and predicted each client's future. In the apartments above, Matchwaya people lived their busy lives and enjoyed frequent feasts, to which, when Rena was invited, she brought me. What could be more thrilling for a cloistered Jewish girl from Queens than to break bread with a Gypsy king, his big-hearted family, and his lively subjects? I'd never seen anything like a Romani tribal feast, the gusto of their appetites as they scooped up garlicky stews with fresh-baked pita and passed around platters laden with slabs of grilled beef or succulent lamb and everyone partook of the same hunk of meat by pulling off as much as they wanted. The men wore black mustaches and gold rings; the women, colorful garments, thick gold necklaces and bracelets. ("You're looking at their life savings," whispered Rena, who sat beside me on the floor, both of us lounging on enormous cushions. "Gypsies don't trust banks; they turn their earnings into gold and wear it.") I noticed that women and men were equally attentive to the children of the tribe, and adults treated kids like miniature human beings, soliciting their opinions on whatever topics were under discussion, rather than speaking baby talk or relegating them to the children's table the way my family did at our holiday gatherings. ("That's how they prepare the next generation for autonomy and leadership," Rena whispered. "The kids learn to think and speak for themselves.")

With the passing weeks, I became more and more attached to my newfound sister—an intellectual polymath, Gypsy princess, trainer of foreign doctors—unaware that my original sister, the suburban housewife and harried mother of four, whose life was cooking, cleaning, and carpooling, was feeling eclipsed and jealous. This I hadn't known until the shopping bag yielded this note that Aunt Rona, Mom's youngest sister, wrote to Betty on January 27, 1955.

> *Dear Betty,*
>
> *This letter has been pending since the conversation we had at your mother's house in December. Our subject was Rena and the fact that you felt she threatened your relationship with Letty. The fear in your heart touched me profoundly. My reply to you at the time was that nobody could ever replace you in Letty's heart. You were brought up together and your ties are solidly cemented. However, I did say that encouraging the friendship with Rena would be advantageous to all of you. I'm sure Rena would welcome your acceptance of her.*
>
> *We are not a demonstrative family, but a clannish one and have a great deal of pride and love for each other, not easily detected. But in the course of our conversation my affection for you was overwhelming and you were once again my little sister and I wanted to protect you.*
>
> *Betty dear, should you ever feel that your security is threatened for any reason, always remember, your family is behind you, especially your "big sister"— Aunt Rona.*

Rona was only fourteen years older than Betty (the same spread that existed between Betty and me), which, to my mind, explains their unique closeness and Rona's "big sister" reference. I hope my big sister felt fully reassured by our aunt's letter. Had I known Betty's feelings at the time I would have doubled down with my own firm assertions. She was not only my first and most beloved sister but my second mother and for the next fifty-eight years, until she died, my most loyal champion. No one could ever replace Betty in my heart.

As for my second sister, Rena, once I entered Brandeis, I became disenchanted with her smug superiority after I discovered that she wasn't the only genius in the world. Until then, I'd worshiped her intellect and mimicked her eccentricities; now I had access to dozens of brilliant professors, scholars, writers, philosophers, guest lecturers, and classmates. No longer was she the smartest person in my life. I realized that she adored me as long as I was her acolyte. When I began to chart my own course and form new relationships, she turned sour, condescending, and judgmental. When I dared to contradict her opinion, she bristled and lashed out, and I talked back. "I had a real fracas with Rena," I wrote to Betty in my senior year. "It's over now but the scars on both sides are irreparable." By the time I graduated and moved to New York, my interaction with my second sister had dwindled to a semiannual lunch and an exchange of greeting cards on Rosh Hashana.

I know relatively little about the family Rena created with her husband, Murray Gropper, a pale, slight man who always looked as if he was afraid someone might ask him a question he couldn't answer. Unlike Bernie, Betty's husband, whom the family respected without reservation, my father never thought much of Rena's husband and told her point-blank that she was "nuts" to marry someone so far beneath her level of intelligence. I found it impossible to assess Murray's intellect or anything else about him since he hardly spoke and when he did he mumbled.

I later learned that Murray had been a jazz pianist with a trio called The Three Bars, who once appeared on *The Ed Sullivan*

Show, and played The Copa and The Sands. I can't imagine anyone as introverted as my brother-in-law doing gigs in bars and supper clubs where performers are expected to engage in charming repartee between numbers and socialize with the audience between sets. I also found out recently that when he was a kid, Murray was accepted to Julliard, but his father, a mean drunk who played the cornet in vaudeville, insisted his son quit school to busk with him and pass the hat in the subway. Eventually, Murray became a music arranger and session musician, one of those versatile piano players whom recording studios kept on tap to back up their star performers (Count Basie, for instance), and was known for his ability to make any singer or solo musician sound good. Nevertheless, his career went down the tubes for reasons that remain murky. Either he wouldn't bribe corrupt cops to let him keep his cabaret card (required for a musician to play in venues where liquor is served), or he wouldn't shoot smack with other musicians, which pissed off heroin dealers and club owners who found it easier to cheat players out of their pay if they were stoned.

When Bert and I became engaged in October 1963, I suggested, and he agreed, that we ask Gershon Levi, my childhood rabbi at the Jamaica Jewish Center, to officiate at our wedding. Rabbi Levi said yes, even though we decided not to get married at the JJC but at Temple Ansche Chesed on West End Avenue in Manhattan, a synagogue I chose because eighteen years before, my sister had walked down the aisle in that sanctuary flanked by both Mom and Dad (with me, just turned seven, as her flower girl). On December 8, 1963, only Dad would escort me to the altar. But if I returned to the same aisle in the same synagogue, I thought my mother's astral presence might join us.

With a scant three months to prepare for the wedding—and me doing PR for six different authors in the shank of the fall publishing season—I barely had time to shop for a bridal gown, much less deal with caterers, musicians, cake makers, and florists. I asked my father to take charge. Not a smart move. He had never shown the slightest interest in menu-planning, much less noticed what constituted a beautifully set table; that was Mom's bailiwick. Still, he was all I had, therefore I left everything up to him.

Murray was out of work at the time, so Dad hired him to play the piano, which he probably did very well, though his music was no match for the din of animated Jewish conversation. Other head-liners at our wedding included the shammes of Temple Ansche Chesed, my gruff, goateed uncle Al Schwartz, the husband of Dad's older sister, Dottie, and my father's erstwhile opponent for the title of top Torah scholar in the Cottin family. Without consulting me or Bert, Dad subcontracted control of the proceedings to Al, who empowered himself to chant Hebrew prayers from the choir bal-cony during the ceremony and hired his son-in-law, rather than a professional photographer, to take our wedding pictures which accounts for their mugshot lighting. (But I digress.)

Rena and Murray had two kids, Karen and Avram, nicknamed Avi. On the rare occasions when we saw the four of them, they seemed oddly detached from one another as well as from the rest of us. The one time I asked Rena if we'd done something to alienate her family, she responded with an arch, "Not at all. We simply pre-fer not to socialize." So, it surprised me when they accepted Betty's invitation to the eightieth birthday party she had organized for our dad in a Westchester catering hall. There, too, the Groppers were aloof, uninterested in getting to know their relatives or having us get to know them.

Rena and I didn't see each other beyond those twice-a-year lunches, usually at a coffee shop near Hunter College, where she taught. But I kept track of her achievements. I read and praised her book, *A Gypsy in the City*, which was based on her doctoral work, and I felt genuinely proud of her distinguished career at Hunter, from which she retired in 1991 as professor of anthropology emer-ita. I also kept in touch with my niece, Karen, so I knew that Murray died of Parkinson's in 1995, at which point Karen decided to cut herself off from Rena and Avi—because they wouldn't let her move back home with her six cats—and she never saw or spoke to them again.

My niece, an earnest, intense young woman with an almost avian fragility worked for years as a word processor in the law firm of Weil, Gotshal & Manges. Witty and well-read, with markedly liberal politics, a passion for social justice, and a kind heart, she was prone to take in strays, human and feline. I found her to be a fluid writer—at least based on her annual holiday letters—though the urbanity of her text was compromised by the kitschy photograph that always accompanied it, a different picture every year of Karen posed against a colorful swatch of shiny fabric, snuggling cheek to whiskers with a furball named Kreplach, Strudel, Sasha, or Sheba. Though my niece always wore a sweet smile, she never looked happy.

With each passing year, Rena seemed less interested in scheduling our already sporadic lunch dates. Cryptic emails would arrive from her, mostly to update me on her increasingly troubled son. In the early 2000s, she wrote, "Avram is living with me." "Avram is working in a flower shop." "Avram is taking courses." Avram "has serious mental health issues," "lost his job," "is angry and hostile." In 2009, it was "Avram has gone off his meds and become really impossible to live with, and his psychiatrist has instructed the social worker to talk to him about making other arrangements." Rena wrapped up that bulletin with, "Letty, please remember that being of good cheer is conducive to good health." Given its context, the pathos in her postscript saddens me to this day. Every fall, a store-bought Rosh Hashana card arrived from her, along with a folded sheet containing two or three typed paragraphs updating me about her health, Avi's health, and whatever progress she'd made on her current academic project.

After another long hiatus, this popped up in my email: "Avram has been diagnosed with manic-depressive syndrome and I have asked his psychiatrist to get him out of my house because I am scared to death of him now." Alarmed, I phoned her immediately. No answer. No answering machine. No response to repeated emails. A few days later, apropos of nothing at all and entirely out of character, she sent me a crude sex joke. A few months later, a chain letter. Six months after that, a request to connect on LinkedIn. I tried to reach her after each message. On September 25, 2011, her annual High Holy Day card arrived by snail mail without the usual year-end update. I emailed her to say I missed it. She wrote back, "The less said about last year the better." I called her to see how she was doing. No answer. No voicemail. No reply.

As each of my books was published, I used to mail a personally autographed copy to each of my sisters. In 2013, the book was, *How to Be a Friend to a Friend Who's Sick.* Rena's one-sentence thank-you note arrived the following week. That was the last time I heard from her. Every subsequent effort to connect was fruitless. Similarly iced out were our Cottin cousins, among them Babette, who in 2018 told me it had been five years since she'd last seen my sister "in a nursing home in Flushing. Avram was there, trying to be appropriately social. His devotion to her was obvious. I brought some fruit and pastry which she enjoyed. Avi refused to eat any, saying he wanted to save it for Rena. For some reason, she'd never allowed us to visit her at home."

After that, she simply vanished. Now and then, I would Google obituaries for Rena M. Cottin, Rena C. Gropper, Rena Cottin Gropper. Finding none, I gave up. For the first twelve years of my life, I didn't know I had a second sister. Now I didn't know if she was alive or dead. We had come full circle.

One day in March 2019, a former student of Rena's called asking for her email or phone number. I gave the woman the last contact information I had for my sister but explained that she had dropped out of time and space and everyone in our family had finally stopped trying to reach her. The woman said she remembered Professor Gropper had a son named Avram; she would try to track him down. *Good luck with that,* I thought, remembering the email in which Rena reported that Avi had gone off the deep end.

Two days later, my phone rang. "Hi, Aunt Letty. This is Avram Gropper."

Avi sounded like a stranger because he was. We had not seen each other since 1980 when he and his family came to Dad's eightieth—yet we talked easily, and he sounded calm and coherent. He told me that Rena had been suffering from dementia for years and died in her sleep on November 9, 2018, a month before her ninety-first birthday. Chilled by the news, and nonplussed by his matter-of-factness, I asked Avi if his sister was aware of their mother's passing. He said Karen had stopped speaking to him twenty-five years ago because of the cat business, which I'd forgotten, but her lawyer had called him one day to inform him that she had died of cancer the previous August (which explained that year's missing holiday letter and kitten portrait), leaving an estate of about $100,000 and her will would be probated on such-and-such date. Apparently, she had been dead for several days before her neighbors reported a foul odor coming from her apartment. When the police forced open her door, they found her body and sixteen cats.

Avi is well past sixty now. He told me he's bipolar. His last job ended in 2002, and since then he's been living on disability. During that first conversation, he said he was "getting into Judaism," going to a shul near his house to say kaddish and participate in a bereavement group. I asked how he was managing without his mother. His answer was poetry.

"Mom was a huge tree who protected me, a little sapling, from wind and storms. But also from the sun. Now I have to learn to live on my own."

"Why didn't you reach out to any of us when she died?"

"I never knew where she kept her address book."

"Couldn't you ask her friends to help you find us?"

"Mom didn't have any friends."

Months after that phone conversation, I discovered my father's divorce decree and noticed that it identified his first wife as Pauline, not Paula, which made me doubt my memory of my father's barbell in the sand. A stickler for facts, I called a couple of my cousins and asked if they remembered whether my dad's first wife was Pauline or Paula, but they'd been born long after Dad's divorce, none had met the women, and none recalled Rena mentioning her mother's name. I realized who would know the answer.

"Avi, what was your grandmother's name?"

"Paula."

"Did you know her?"

My nephew said he'd never met her but he remembered Rena's stories about her. That she'd been diagnosed with schizophrenia, so it evidently runs in his maternal line. That she used to see snakes slithering out of the sink drain. That she'd once held Rena out the window five flights up and threatened to drop her. I, too, had heard those stories from Rena. Then Avi told me something Rena never had. "Mom always believed both her parents hated her and that's why they sent her to boarding school and sleepaway camp. Mentioning the camp reminded Avi of another story she told him. One summer she was in her bunk jumping up and down on her cot when she fell off and hurt her leg quite badly, and, thinking cold water would dull the pain, she limped down to the river to soak her injury. She made friends with some Native Americans kids who were playing with a turtle at the water's edge and they told her about their tribal customs and beliefs, among which was the legend that the American continent exists because a huge tortoise carried it on his back, Rena named the snapping turtle Hercules. Avi said he thought his mother's interactions with the Native American children had sparked her interest in anthropology.

"Did she tell you anything about your grandpa Jack?"

"You mean Grandpa Mustache?"

Last I knew, Dad and Rena were estranged; she resented him, maybe rightly hated him for abandoning her, and he resented her for making him feel guilty. Yet "Grandpa Mustache" sounded like a term of affection and suggested a degree of familiarity that I found baffling. "Did you spend any time with your grandpa?"

"Nearly every Sunday during the 1970s. He and your step-mother came over for Mom's homemade pizza. She used to get up early on Sundays and clean every crack and crevice before they arrived. Of course, that didn't stop Grandpa from saying our house was dirty. Which it wasn't."

Time out for cognitive dissonance: in the 1950s when I slept over at her apartment on Gay Street in the Village, Rena never made so much as a piece of toast or picked up a dust cloth. How was I supposed to jibe Avram's domestic tableau with my image of the woman who was too cerebral to notice a cobweb? Why would she be kneading pizza dough and scrubbing the floor on her hands and knees to please the father who stopped paying child support, left her with a crazy mother, and never tried to rescue her? I wondered if Avi was delusional and those pizza Sundays were his wishful fantasy; hadn't Rena once told me her son was schizophrenic?

I probed gently. "That's amazing, Avi. But it's hard to believe. When I last saw your mother and my father together, the temperature in the room was one degree below zero."

"I know. Mom always felt unloved by her father, by *both* parents, by everyone, really." The way Avi said *unloved* made it even more devastating than abandonment, which it is, when you really think about it. Being abandoned is a one-time cataclysm, feeling unloved an ongoing drip-by-drip rejection, an erosion of a person's worth and value. Unloved transmutes into an identity: you become The One Who is Unlovable. Avi seemed to be saying that Rena's revenge was "love-bombing," a slyly manipulative technique used by an aggrieved person to win another person's trust and affection in order to gain control of the relationship. Homemade pizza was Rena's love bomb; Jack's Sunday visits, his penance.

"Mom couldn't control all the horrible things that happened to her when she was a kid. That's why she tried to control every person and every relationship in her adult life."

"I bet she couldn't control Grandpa Mustache."

"Right," Avi chuckled. "He was king, and we were his subjects. I remember when Mom was looking for a house, she saw one in Jamaica Estates that she liked a lot, but she wouldn't buy it because it was too close to her father's. Family was never a happy subject for her. She called it 'an experiment that failed.' Ours failed, for sure. My mother reenacted her mother's cruelty toward her by treating my sister, Karen, like her scapegoat. My father was deeply depressed. He worshipped the ground Mom walked on but she had no respect for him. I once heard her say, 'Murray broke his word: he told me he would take care of me and he didn't.' My sister never got over her first love, a motorcycle guy named Walter, who was found dead under a tree in Central Park surrounded by drug paraphernalia. Karen became a cat lady. I was drunk and stoned all the time, a real *trombenik* (ne'er-do-well). I had a vasectomy at twenty-three so I'd never pass my misery to another generation."

~~~

The suffering my sister Rena endured in her ninety-one years is unfathomable, starting with her father's disappearance and her mother's abuse and ending with her daughter estranged, her son part caregiver, part menace, and her once brilliant mind hollowed out by dementia. She was an anthropologist. Anthropology is the study of what makes humans human, how people get along with each other, how they build community. Yet she died with no friends. Rather than think about her degraded final years, I catapult myself back to my youthful infatuation with the secret sister who appeared on our doorstep in 1954, the Gypsy princess with the long braid who talked like a thesaurus. That's how I choose to remember her. I'm not sure what I could have done to make things better. But the guilt and shame that engulf me as I recount her story tell me I didn't do enough.

CHAPTER 36

GIRLHOOD PAIN, GROWN-UP GUILT

On July 25, 1982, shortly after 7:00 a.m., my stepmother called from Florida, a phenomenon in itself. She sounded distraught.

"Your dad is failing. I think you should come down here today. As fast as you can."

My family and I were vacationing on Fire Island, a finger of sand off Long Island separated from the mainland by a six-mile body of water. To reach my father's bedside, I used every mode of transportation except a hot air balloon—pedaled a bicycle to the dock, took a ferry to the mainland, a car service to LaGuardia, a plane to Miami, a cab to their condo—rushing from one vehicle to the next, but still didn't make it. When I got there, his wife said his body had already been picked up by the mortuary.

I screamed at her. "How dare you wait until this morning to let me know my father was dying? Couldn't you see how sick he was? Why didn't you alert me days ago so I could get there in time to say goodbye?!"

She screamed back: "Don't blame me! Blame your father. He wouldn't let me call his family. He made me swear that if you called, I wouldn't tell you how bad it was. He didn't want you to see him in that condition." I hated my stepmother, but I believed her. Everything she said sounded like my father. What was hard to believe was that an eighty-two-year-old man who knows he's about to die wouldn't let his children and grandchildren see him because he didn't look his best. That was ludicrous, even for someone as controlling and vain as my father. I had a lot more to scream about, but I was too exhausted; besides why bother? Yelling at his widow would accomplish nothing, and if I never said another word to her as long as I lived, that would be too soon. As I sat there on her living room couch surrounded by my stepmother's relatives, whom I barely knew, and friends of my father, whom I'd never met, and watched them eat pastries and listened to them murmur platitudes, the thought of spending the seven days of shiva with these people made me sick to my stomach. I knew I had to get out, no matter what anyone thought of me or how it might look. I needed to return to my family. I told my stepmother I felt sick and I didn't want to inconvenience her; I'd be better off home. When I asked her if I might have my father's tallit, his Bezalel edition of Shir Ha'shirim, "Song of Songs," and his Jewish War Veterans "Queens County Commander" garrison cap, she said okay and took the trouble to locate them among his belongings. On the flight home, I sat in a window seat and wedged one of the airline's crib-sized pillows between my cheek and the side of the plane so I could see the sky, and willed my memories of my father to float by, like soap bubbles, snagging one at a time before it burst, considering what each meant to me and where it fell short, then letting it drop technicolor rain on the carpet of clouds below. When Bert met me at LaGuardia, I asked him to drive me out to New Montefiore Cemetery to visit my mother's grave.

Rena had more than enough reasons of her own for not attending our father's funeral. Betty would have gone in a trice, but she and Bernie had contracted to spend two years running the American School in Belgrade and couldn't afford the price of a round-trip flight to Miami from the former Yugoslavia. Shocked that I'd chosen to leave the same day I arrived at Dad's condo, Betty wrote to ask how I came to my decision. I would not have remembered my thought process of forty years ago had this response not turned up among the letters in the plastic bag. "I wasn't going stick around for the father who rarely stuck around for me. Besides, the funeral would have been the height of hypocrisy squared. First of all, he had himself cremated, which is a violation of Jewish law. Second, his wife chose someone to deliver the eulogy whom she likes but Dad didn't, so that was a sham. Third, why would I attend a funeral for a man who hated funerals?"

Anger hardened my heart because of the way he chose to die, and a residue of it clings to me now nearly four decades later. But his letters have pierced that carapace with pinpricks of compassion, an emotion I'd never before experienced in relation to my father. By giving me my first glimpse of the insecure man behind the strutting bantam cock, the poseur beneath the plumage, his performance anxiety and concern for appearances, and the toll it took on him to maintain the façade he'd cultivated of a successful lawyer and prosperous provider, I came to understand that what he maniacally sought when he went to endless meetings and made commitments to endless Jewish organizations, was the adulation, approval, and praise that his demanding father had withheld. Given the man Max Cottin was, and the man he'd raised his son to be, Jack probably did the best he could. Still, my newfound compassion isn't enough to stop me from lamenting the loss of the father I never had, or from letting this childhood pain overrule my grown-up guilt. As a daughter, I claim the right to feel short-changed; as a Jew I'm ashamed of dishonoring my father with a shanda of the first order: my refusal to mourn him with the rituals I've performed religiously for my mom for the last sixty-seven years. I only say kaddish for my dad on Yom Kippur, at Yizkor, the solemn synagogue memorial service, and I don't light a yahrzeit candle for him on the anniversary of his death. Since he didn't let me say kaddish for her, I wouldn't say kaddish for him. Since he'd deprived me of his attention when I was a child, I would deprive him of my attention in perpetuity, as a mourner. Never flagrantly cruel or physically abusive, he was "merely" self-centered, insensitive, and unavailable. I have friends whose fathers were brutal and incestuous, so my inability to forgive mine for being absent makes me feel mean-spirited and small. Shouldn't I be grateful that when he was there, I was his Bunny, his substitute son, his ketsileh? Why was that never enough? Because a child doesn't live comparatively; she only knows what she knows and how it feels.

The Fifth Commandment says, "Honor thy father and thy mother." Though not obligated to say kaddish for her father, a Jewish daughter is supposed to attend his funeral and light a memorial candle that burns for twenty-four hours on the date of the Hebrew calendar's anniversary of his death. But since my father didn't do for me what a father is supposed to do for his daughter, I've chosen to memorialize him differently. I exalt him for doing good works in the world. I credit him with taking me seriously as a thinking person and for encouraging, if not forcing, me to be independent at a young age. I praise him for giving me an extensive Jewish education (for a girl) and for modeling a strong bond to The Jewish People and the State of Israel. But he wasn't sentimental about me, and he didn't raise me to be sentimental about him. I'm still trying to be what he wanted.

CHAPTER 37

JUST SKIP SUPPER

I have no experience with eating disorders as currently understood. All I know is, until I was in my twenties, I basically hated food.

As an infant, I rejected nearly everything edible or potable, a fact well-documented in Mom's letters to Dad from Florida, where she and I, then eighteen months old, spent the winter of 1940–41. Even before our ship docked in Miami, she complained, "Bunny hasn't eaten one teaspoonful of solid food since we boarded this boat, she won't even drink orange juice." A few days later, "I feed her but she spits everything out." And just before he was due to come to visit us: "I'm trying so hard to fatten up that little tomboy of ours before you get here, but it's no use."

Photos of me at a year-and-a-half show a toddler who looks a tad chubby, yet Mom was sure I was wasting away. Besides worrying about my health, she worried about how my eating habits would look to other people, what they might think and say about us, about her. Was she a bad cook? Did she not understand nutrition? Was her baby malnourished? During the war years, my food boycott embarrassed her. Children were starving in Europe; America was the land of plenty—even with rationing—how dare I refuse to eat? It was humiliating. Naturally, Ceil being Ceil, she blamed herself. Why couldn't she entice me; what was she doing wrong?

"Bunny" in Miami Beach winter, 1940-41

She tried every stratagem. Hid spinach in my mashed potatoes. Sprinkled sugar on my shredded wheat. Sliced the crusts off a PB&J sandwich and stamped it out with a gingerbread man cookie cutter. She made food art. Turned radishes into roses. Skewered tiny meatballs on colored toothpicks. Begged, bribed, and punished me. Nothing worked. I resisted every blandishment and perfected stratagems of my own, rearranging the items on my plate to make it appear as if I'd had a bites of each so I could claim to have tasted it, shoveling half of my stuffed cabbage onto Dad's plate when he left the table to answer the phone, spitting my rejects in a napkin and then tossing the little bundle in the space between the refrigerator and the wall when neither of them was looking. Until one day our old Frigidaire went on the fritz, and the repair man pulled it away from the wall to inspect its motor, exposing two or three years' worth of wadded napkins, to my shame.

Now and then, she got so frustrated she sent me to bed without dessert, a perverse penalty that only served to exile me from the kitchen and prevent any chance encounter with a dish I might deem palatable. When banishment backfired, she defied the recommended food pyramid—proteins, vegetables, grains, fruits—and offered me a blatantly unbalanced menu consisting only of the foods I actually liked, 90 percent of them white or yellow: cheese blintzes with sour cream, bagels with butter and cream cheese, Saltine crackers (matzah during Passover) slathered with sweet butter, potatoes with butter and sour cream, spaghetti with butter and parmesan (with maybe a dollop of ketchup), and noodles with cottage cheese.

Brown was the color of the other 10 percent of the foods I would deign to eat as a child. That category included My-T-Fine chocolate pudding, Milky Way bars, chocolate milk, brownies, potato latkes (pancakes), and *gribenes*, the crunchy brown morsels left in the pan after you've rendered small globs of chicken fat in a hot fry pan. (Some call gribenes "Jewish pork rinds.") But my all-time favorite meat treat was lamb-chops-on-paper—three or four strips of crispy meat that seemed to require special rituals: Mom always opened the kitchen windows, turned the exhaust fan to "High," cooked them in a skillet she kept in a brown paper bag under the sink behind the box of Rinso, fried the strips until they got crisp enough to stand on their own, and served them to me on a paper plate. If nothing else, that rigmarole should have set off alarm bells. Same with the paper plate. Like most kosher households, ours contained enough crockery to serve a regiment: one set of dishes for everyday dairy meals, one set for everyday meat meals, and two sets, dairy and meat, for company meals (plus four parallel sets solely for use during the eight days of Passover). Then again, why would I be suspicious? What an adult observer might find peculiar, children, not yet conversant with social norms, regard as natural. My unquestioning acceptance of the habits of the mother I relied on for succor and safety, plus her exclusive control over the kitchen and everything in it, gave Ceil the freedom to cook bacon, which she considered a health food, and keep it a secret from those who would judge her for it.

Until I was ten—when we moved from Jamaica to Jamaica Estates—my best friend was a little Irish Catholic girl named Sue Bohn. Sue lived across the street from us with her big brother and very sweet parents who always invited me to join them for Christmas tree trimming or Easter egg decorating. One summer morning, Sue and I were playing trading cards at her kitchen table, and I was quite pleased with myself for having negotiated several excellent single card trades—Sue's Old Ironsides card for my Eiffel Tower card, my Ginger Rogers for her Esther Williams, my Montana cowgirl for her grass-skirted Hawaiian dancer. Around noon, Mrs. Bohn said we had five minutes to clear all our cards off the table so she could give us our lunch. I watched her slather mayonnaise on white toast and pile on a slice of tomato, a lettuce leaf, and three strips of my favorite meat treat.

"What a great idea!" I commented. "I've never had lamb-chops-on-paper in a sandwich."

Sue's mother, looking puzzled, replied, "It's a BLT." Then, "Oops, sorry, Bunny. I forgot Jews don't eat bacon. How about a tuna melt?"

I demurred, claiming I'd promised to be home for lunch, quickly gathered up my card collection, wrapped a rubber band around it, and ran across the street in tears. I found Mom in the kitchen rolling out dough for a pie crust.

"Lamb-chops-on-paper is *bacon*, Mother!" I slammed the stack of cards on the counter and planted my fists on my nonexistent hips. "*It's bacon!!* How could you lie to me?"

Mom wiped her floury palms on her apron and tried to put her arms around me. "I had to, for your own good. You have to eat, sweetheart."

I wriggled out of her embrace. "All this time, you've been feeding me traif! Why?"

She sank into a kitchen chair. I couldn't tell if she was sad or scared. "I've been feeding you traif because I love you and I can't let you stay skinny forever. Our goyishe neighbors and their children are forever eating bacon and their kids are much stronger and sturdier than you and I thought it might make you strong and healthy too, so I gave it to you and I was so happy when you liked it, but I couldn't tell you what it was because I didn't want *you* to have to lie to Grandma Jenny. You know how glatt kosher my mother is. If she knew there was bacon in this house, she would never eat here again." Mom's hand flew to her forehead as if the very idea of her mother finding out what she'd been making for my after-school treat was unthinkable. Her palm left a smudge of white flour, as if she'd been hit with a snowball. "I didn't tell Daddy so he wouldn't have to lie about it either. But you've seen how I cook it; I'm so careful about never letting it touch anything but that one pan, never using that pan for anything else, and serving it to you on a paper plate so it never comes in contact with our dishes. I know I'm cheating on kashrut. But I'm sure God understands."

<hr>

My food repertoire expanded exponentially when I started dating boys who ordered cheeseburgers and pepperoni pizza. In my twenties, I finally acquired an appetite and began making up for all those years when I hated food. In my thirties I became a *fresser* (Yiddish for "glutton"), one of those really annoying women who can consume a huge bowl of spaghetti and meatballs and a hefty piece of key lime pie without gaining an ounce. This was lucky for me but unpleasant for my girlfriends whose relationship with food was as extreme as mine used to be, but in the opposite direction.

They practically had to wire their jaws shut to shed a few pounds and feel good in a bathing suit while I was mindlessly wolfing down as much as I wanted of whatever I wanted, whenever I wanted it. Many years ago, my dear sister-in-law Marcia complained that she'd put on too much weight over the holidays, so I bought her a beautiful dress one size too small. I thought it would inspire her to lose five pounds in order to fit into it. Oblivious to her frustration, and having never experienced how stubbornly an extra five pounds can cling to a woman's hips, I expected the dress would hang in her closet as a friendly reminder of her goal. It had the reverse effect; it made her miserable. Another time, when she declined a piece of birthday cake because she was on a diet, I accused her of being a killjoy, suggesting brightly, "Why don't you just eat the cake now and skip dinner tomorrow?" She stared at me as if I were a space cadet. I didn't realize normal people got hungry three times a day. I'm not sure I even understood that food could make you fat. My issue was never fear of gaining weight; it was fear of being force-fed. Menopause put an end to the high-octane metabolic rate I'd taken for granted all my life. In three months, from out of nowhere, twenty pounds materialized on my five-foot-four-inch frame and wouldn't leave. At the age of fifty-three, I bought my first bathroom scale. Suddenly, I had to count calories and avoid carbs. (Until then, I didn't know what a carb was.) I gave up butter, blintzes, and Milky Way bars and upbraided myself for all those years when I was insensitive to what other women were going through. I asked Marcia to forgive me for the too-small dress. Laughing, she assured me that she'd absolved me of that sin decades ago, though the speed with which she recalled the incident told me it had left an indelible mark.

My naivete in those years was only exceeded by my thoughtlessness. I still feel guilty about being so dismissive of my friends' weight problems. Guilty for chiding them when they ordered yogurt and berries for breakfast instead of pancakes and maple syrup, or a green salad for lunch instead of fettuccini Alfredo. Guilty for all the times I blithely suggested just skip dinner. This is a long overdue mea culpa. Suffice it to say, I've paid dearly for the oblivion of my youth. Right now, a gorgeous, slinky, Emilio Pucci dress, a birthday gift from one of my daughters, hangs in my closet unworn and unwearable. Last year it skimmed my body. This year it's skintight.

I don't remember anybody in my family ever fat-shaming or being fat-shamed. The implications of that statement didn't hit me until I read my friend Alice Shalvi's memoir, *Never a Native*, in which she describes her "first experience of adult perfidy." She was a young adolescent when she asked if she could be a bridesmaid at the wedding of her aunt and uncle. They told her they'd decided not to have any attendants. Months later, Alice saw, standing under the chuppah at the bride's side, "a slender, very pretty little girl of my own age, wearing a floor-length dress and a wreath in her hair.... Feeling the blood rush to my cheeks and the tears to my eyes, I angrily blurted out, 'But you said you weren't having any bridesmaids!' There was an embarrassed silence. Nobody knew how to respond to my accusation. The reason for her deception was all too clear...[the other girl] was slim and pretty, I was fat and plain. She would grace the wedding cortege and increase the number of compliments received, while I would have aroused nothing but disdainful ridicule.... Hurt and envious, I sobbed throughout the ceremony."

Not being overweight didn't stop me from feeling ashamed of being underweight. In ninth grade, I wore thick athletic socks to bulk up my bony ankles. Compared to my curvy post-puberty girlfriends, my arms and legs were twigs, my breasts could pass for mosquito bites, my shoulder blades stuck out like wings. None of the women in my family were as scrawny as I, but none were fat either. Grandma Jenny was basically shapeless. My uncles used to call my aunts "zaftig." My cousin Faith, when she was still called Sistie, was a bit chunky, but I have no recollection of my mother, aunts, or cousins ever hassling her to diet or of weight being one of the topics discussed at our family dinner tables. So when the women's movement added "sizeism" (bias against fat people) to its agenda of social ills worth fighting, I had trouble figuring out if I should count myself among the culprits.

One day, I was trying on clothes alongside several other women in one of those large communal changing rooms with mirrored walls and hooks to denote each shopper's space. A couple of teen-aged girls came in and hung a batch of size 2 jeans on the hooks directly across from a sixty-ish woman with doughy thighs and a belt of midriff fat as thick as a life preserver. Swathed in matronly underwear—cotton bra, stretch girdle, control-top panty hose— she was trying on plus-size muumuus, frowning at herself in the mirror as each commodious garment strained against her ample breasts and protruding belly until, inevitably, she yanked it off and dropped it on the changing room floor. The teenagers, who'd been watching her mounting agitation, began giggling and made no effort to hide their sneers. A repressed memory blindsided me before I could remonstrate against their casual cruelty.

<hr />

A cousin of mine, whom I'll call Faye, always had a credible reason for declining invitations to family events. Once, it was a strep throat, then a work deadline, another time a sick boyfriend, a broken carburetor. As the excuses became more and more lame, some of us speculated about why she might be avoiding us. Was she embarrassed about being single and childless in her forties while the rest of us had mates and kids? Was she afraid we'd interrogate her about her love life or insist on fixing her up with our neighbor's friend's brother-in-law's nephew? Could she be a lesbian, and if so, did she anticipate our heterosexist disapproval? Maybe she was ashamed of how she made a living. (This possibility wasn't so far-fetched as you might thing: one of our cousins had earned extra money doing phone sex, another once worked at a massage parlor.) Faye's older sister shot down our theories. "She's doing fine. She likes her job. She has a nice boyfriend. She's just busy."

That ended our guessing game until our perennially elusive, formerly petite cousin made a surprise appearance in the body of an exceedingly large person in a flowered muumuu. As she pushed through the gate to the backyard where we were all attending another cousin's pool party, two women recognized her—which wasn't easy since her formerly delicate features were lost in her full moon face. The women were sitting under an awning twenty yards from the gate but near enough for me to hear their derogatory comments.

"Omigod! It's Faye! I can't believe it"

"How could she let herself go like that!?"

"She's humongous!"

"It's a shanda!"

Overweight people get dissed every day; that's not news. But until my cousin showed up in her muumuu, I had denied such scorn in myself. After all, I'm a feminist; I believe in body positivity and pride. I've written articles bemoaning Western culture's absurd beauty standard. I decry the fact that the average fashion model weighs 117 pounds and wears a size 2 or 4 while the average American woman weighs 170 pounds and wears a size 16 or 18. I've called out manufacturers whose clothing lines start at 0 (the vanished woman) and stop at size 12. I thought I had my consciousness raised and my "sizeism" under control, yet there was no denying my head-snapping reaction to Faye. I felt sorry for her, and deeply ashamed that a woman, especially a woman in our family, could allow herself to get that fat. My politics and values were clearly contradicted by those feelings. Yet the feelings were familiar. Back in Chapter 2, I blithely remarked upon my grandmother's rotund unibosom and thick waist. What I didn't admit was how often a sheepish voice in my head whispered, "Please God don't let me age like that." I remember laughing at a greeting card that said, "Inside every fat girl is a skinny girl who got eaten by the fat girl." One of my thinnest friends believes the minute she lets down her guard, she'll become her 300-pound sister.

Years ago, when I spent time with one of the women's move-ment's most remarkable intellectual heavyweights [*sic*], all I could think about was her body, her physical image. I kept wishing she'd lose 100 pounds before hitting the road for her next lecture tour. I worried that her looks might turn college kids off feminism. *She'll confirm the fat feminist stereotype*, I thought to myself. *She'll be rid-iculed, caricatured, her message eclipsed by her size, her audience dis-tracted by her effort to fit in one of those chairs with a desk pad arm.* I wasn't supposed to think that way, but I did.

Most people believe the abhorrence of fat is a biological instinct, a "natural," inborn response to an aesthetically disagree-able form. Accordingly, our culture regards it as "normal" that fat repels, while thin attracts. We're oblivious to the halo effect that accrues to thin women and enhances the ways in which they are perceived and received. My friend Gloria Steinem is a prime illus-tration of this phenomenon. Since she first rose to prominence more than fifty years ago, Gloria has been an astonishingly effective organizer, leader, and feminist role model because she's brilliant, eloquent, persuasive, and witty, but also, let's face it, because she's beautiful and thin. This reality contradicts the movement's ethos (and Gloria's, for that matter), which holds that everyone has equal value regardless of race, gender, faith, class, sexual orientation, or *weight*. In a perfect world, all of us would be judged by who we are and what we do, not how we look. But in the real word, it's still a lot easier to mobilize people for feminist causes if you're not fat.

I'm being purposely plain spoken about this because we won't be able to defeat rampant anti-fat bias until we admit we have it and kick down the barriers to unlearning it. One barrier is belief that aesthetic preferences are instinctual and therefore immutable. Another is the tendency to conflate being fat with being out of control—not just of one's body and appetite(s), but, implicitly, of one's workload, moral standards, and time schedules. Fat people are often equated, consciously or not, with self-indulgence, sloth, ineptitude, weakness, and surrender to one's primitive inclina-tions. My cousin Faye literally *embodied* this out-of-controlness.

The sight of her aroused our secret fear of our own vulnerability to surrender. We disdained what she had *let happen* to her body because it meant we, too, could let it happen to ours. Anticipating our reaction, she'd stayed away from us for years rather than face us and feel shamed. Faye was brave to show up that day, but she's never come to another family gathering. Who could blame her? The shame is ours; mine.

⁓⁓⁓

On the other side of the sizeism coin is a young relative I'm calling "Angela" because I promised her mother, "Helen," that I would give them both pseudonyms. I used to think Angela was skinny because she's a dancer and dancers are constantly in motion, burning calories, practicing or performing. In fact, she's been bulimic for nearly half her life, starting long before she became a dancer, and at this point, her mother says, Angela's health is seriously at risk.

In high school, she hid her symptoms amazingly well. Her parents, having no experience with eating disorders, didn't know what behavior to watch for. She finally told them the truth when she was having a tough time in college and needed money for psychotherapy. "It's scary," Helen told me. Years of compulsive binging and purging have taken their toll on Angela's heart, gums, throat, esophagus, psyche, and self-image. "Controlling their bodies is what dancers do, but Angela can't control what goes into her mouth and believe me she tries. She'll have dinner with us, then go to the bathroom and throw it all up. Or, she'll say she can't eat with us because she's going out with her friends, then she'll come home, sneak up to her room and gorge on the snacks she hides under her bed. The hardest part of managing bulimia is letting go of the hiding." I asked Helen if she'd requested anonymity because she, too, is hiding something: her guilt about feeling embarrassed by her daughter's emaciated appearance.

"Not embarrassed, protective. Because she's so terribly ashamed of herself."

CHAPTER 38

JEWS GO TO COLLEGE. END OF STORY.

I feel guilty that my husband and I let our son go to the Culinary Institute of America. Esteemed as it was in the 1980s, and continues to be today, "the other CIA," as it's known, was a two-year program that conferred an associate degree; it was not a college or university. Though David had been accepted by several liberal arts schools, he was determined to attend the Cadillac of cooking schools and build a career in the restaurant or hospitality industry. Recently revitalized by a new generation of innovative celebrity chefs and an explosion of genre-defying new cuisines, the food world was experiencing a sea change and sparking a radical transformation of American tastes. To our son's bedazzled eyes, nothing compared to the CIA, whose graduates were being hired in the country's finest restaurants and corporate kitchens. We were not happy with his choice.

"Jews go to college" was one of the undisputed maxims that Bert and I grew up with. Neither of us could imagine another path for David, a smart kid who loved books and music; played guitar, hockey, softball; cared about politics and a million other things. We said the CIA curriculum would limit the scope of his learning and exclude all the other subjects that interested him. Why cheat himself of a liberal arts education? We nudged him to choose one of the colleges that had accepted him, but we didn't nudge very hard. Nor did we admit to one another that our resistance to the CIA came from a place of ignorance about fields that differed from those we knew well. We were raised in families whose definition of important work spanned from law to medicine with journalism in third place. Bert graduated from Rutgers then Harvard Law School. I earned a BA with distinction in English and American literature. Our twin daughters never even considered an alternative route— they went to Yale. Everyone we knew attended college. College, we told our son is where you'll read the Great Books, Greek drama, Milton, Freud, existential philosophy, de Beauvoir, Arendt. You'll hone the tools of critical thinking. You'll learn to understand the double helix and appreciate twelve-tone music. When you go out into the world, a college degree will signal your competence and achievement. Our prism was, in its own way, distorted, circumscribed, prejudiced, and arguably retrograde. David must have known by then—though I'm not proud to say this—that we were educational snobs.

But it was the 1980s, and we were New Age parents. We believed in respecting our children's individuality, and our son's love of cooking had been evident since he was a small boy standing on a stool at the kitchen counter helping me wash lettuce or dredge chicken breasts in breadcrumbs. When he was six, I overheard him ask a couple of friends who were over for a play date, "What's your favorite treat?" One boy said Mallomars. The other said Pringles. David said, steamed artichokes with Hollandaise sauce. At eight, he could transform a few slices of leftover roast beef into a savory stir-fry. At ten, he and a couple of other kids in our Manhattan apartment building took a cooking class from a high school neighbor who taught them the recipes she'd learned from her mother, who'd learned them at the Cordon Bleu. (I still have the loose-leaf notebook containing those handwritten, chocolate-smeared pages.) At fifteen, David was one of twenty youngsters featured, along with their favorite recipes, in *The Fun of Cooking*, Jill Krementz's book of photos and profiles of kids whose favorite room in the house was the kitchen. At sixteen, he got himself a summer job as a line cook at Tavern on the Green, the iconic restaurant in Central Park. How could his father and I stand in the way of our son's dream? We couldn't. He went to the CIA.

Two years later, his graduation put to shame every other school ceremony we'd ever attended. Spiffy in their starched white chef coats and toques, members of the CIA's 1989 graduating class prepared and served a five-course dinner to their parents, relatives, and friends. It was a hoot and a happening, and David was in his element. From there, he launched himself on a career path that has proven both rewarding and frustrating. Working long hours for modest, never munificent, wages, he apprenticed in the kitchen of Le Cirque under Daniel Boulud, one of the French master chefs, then moved to the front of the house—meaning out of the kitchen and into management. Over the years, he has been a manager at such esteemed New York establishments as Jean-Georges and the late, lamented, Picholine, and as general manager at Dune Restaurant in the toney Ocean Club in Nassau. He spent five years as GM of the legendary Brasserie in the Seagram's Building before it closed for good, then became GM of the Manhattan branch of Tommy Bahama, a vibrant restaurant that's part of the lifestyle brand of the same name. He's done well in a tough industry while supporting his two sons (and an ex-wife). Still, I can never get out of my mind a conversation his father and I had with David when he was in his mid-thirties and he let drop that he wished he had become a lawyer.

"You can still be a lawyer!" we said. In unison.

"Yes, but I would have to go back to school, and who knows how much credit they would give me for two years of culinary school. I'd need two more years of college for a BA. Then, assuming I did okay on the LSATs, I'd go to law school for three years and rack up more student loans. I have two kids. I can't drop out of the workforce for five years and pile up all that debt."

"We'll help."

"Thanks, but in five years I'll be forty, pretty old for a fledgling lawyer."

"In five years, you'll be forty whatever you do," his father observed. "Why not be forty *and* a lawyer? If that's what you want, go for it!" It wasn't that Bert needed his son to pick up his mantle or inherit his law practice. And it wasn't that either of us was ashamed of what David did for a living; on the contrary, his career had added perks and privileges to our lives, preferred entry into top restaurants, reservations at the last minute, and extra courses brought to our table compliments of the chef. But once David shared his regret about not pursuing a law career, we thought that he might decide to change course.

He didn't. At that point in his life, five more years of school was daunting. Too much of a climb. Too late. Too hard to catch up. That was when guilt overwhelmed me; his surrender to the status quo was on us. In 1986, he was eighteen. We were the adults in the house. Had we been old-fashioned parents, we could have overruled him by fiat and enforced our decision with the power of the purse. When he graduated from high school, he could have attended two four-year-schools, Boston University and Johnson & Wales University, that offered culinary arts and sciences as well as courses in business and criminal justice, and earned a college degree, which would have allowed him in his mid-thirties to change careers to a host of other fields. Instead, we'd let him go to a school that awarded a two-year associates degree in culinary arts, and now that he wanted to do something else with his life, he was hobbled by it.

David has always been our most easygoing child. He's kind, witty, generous, and optimistic. His personality is magnetic. He has the inner serenity of an old soul. He's wise and forgiving, a devoted dad and a loyal friend. I hope he thinks we've been there for him at every juncture of his life. But I will always hold us responsible for failing him when it mattered. We gave him freedom at a time when we should have given him boundaries and stuck by them.

Close friends of mine have tried to assuage my guilt. They said, had we issued a fiat—"no college, no money"—he might have obeyed us but felt frustrated, infantilized, and angry enough to sabotage his own education. Bullying him into submission could have eroded his confidence in his own judgment and tarnished our relationship with him for years to come. That unhappy outcome was plausible, to be sure. Still, I can't help wondering if we could have said more than we did or said it better.

CHAPTER 39

MOTHERGUILT

Left to right, Robin, David (in his monogrammed chef's jacket),
and Abigail at the Culinary Institute of America, late 1980s

For good and ill, I seem to have replicated some of my father's patterns. Organizing events, mobilizing people, and taking action gave me satisfaction and pleasure. I've always enjoyed founding new groups to advance a cause and get things done. What I didn't see when our children were young was the price they paid for those commitments. Whether the focus of my work outside the family was on women, Jews, or Israel, it sometimes led me to shortchange my role as a mother.

My adult daughters have made that point over the years, done so gently and without rancor, and though it was hard to hear and too late to fix my mistakes, I'm now able to look at their childhood through their eyes, see what they saw, and deal honestly with the guilt that seems endemic to women like myself who feel split at the root between the demands of family and work. When I get weepy about my missteps, Robin and Abigail stress that they're proud of who I am and what I contributed to the social justice movements I supported. But their awareness of my triage process—daily attempts to balance family time with work, meetings, phone calls, and writing assignments—made them feel that the hours we spent together were precious. I felt that way too. It's what made me do more than just hang out with them; it's why I planned adventures and outings and created elaborate art projects. I tried to give them proverbial "quality" time to compensate for the unprogrammed, open-ended hours I did not, or could not, supply.

When the girls first confessed their feelings, I actually dug up twenty years of old datebooks (I'm a pack rat) and reviewed every page of every calendar from the day they were born to the day their brother, David, who was almost three years younger, moved out of the house into his own apartment. If that makes me sound defensive and desperate, it's because I was—defensive because I knew that I had prioritized my family, and desperate because it was too awful for me to imagine that my kids ever felt otherwise. The datebooks proved that, at most, I was out one night a week and not for a meeting or professional commitment, but for an occasional dinner with their father or our friends (though I was amazed at how minimal our social lives were when the kids were young). Except for my consciousness-raising group's sessions in the 1970s, most of the meetings I attended were held in the daytime when the children were in school. I worked at *Ms.* magazine three days a week but was home by six. The other four days I was physically there, though admittedly, while writing I was not always available. When deeply absorbed by a project, I would tape a note to the door of my study: "Mom Writing. Do Not Disturb." Three times during my children's childhoods, I spent six weeks at writers' colonies in Upstate New York, Massachusetts, or New Hampshire. During those interludes, my meals were either delivered in a basket to the doorstep of my secluded studio in the woods or served in a dining room to all the artists, musicians, and writers-in-residence, and I could hunker down and write in blissful isolation. Taking those chunks of uninterrupted time for my work—as so many male writers, artists, and composers have guiltlessly done for centuries—was the only way I could make meaningful progress or meet a tight deadline on a book.

I knew my absence was felt at home (and would have been distraught had I not been missed), but Bert was there and because all the family logistics fell to him and he managed them well, I never worried about the children's welfare. In fact, I felt as if those absences were a gift to him in that he learned more in those few weeks about our children's habits, needs, fears, and friendships than most dads learn about their offspring in the course of a lifetime. Without me around, the relationship between the kids and their father had solidified and deepened, and Bert agreed it was a good thing for them to experience life solely under his tutelage. We were lucky that, barring an appearance in court, he could usually control his schedule and therefore be present when I wasn't. But we couldn't label something felicitous that our daughters experienced as destabilizing. So what if I called them from the writers' retreats every evening at dinnertime and spoke to them at length, one by one? So what if I was absent for six weeks three times over the course of their childhoods as long as I was there all the other weeks of their lives, trying my best to be as good a mom as possible? And I had twenty years' worth of datebooks to prove it. Doesn't matter, is the point. The point is that Robin and Abigail (David, less so, apparently) came away feeling that they had to compete for my attention with my activism, articles, and books. My putting a good spin on the situation made them feel spun. They didn't welcome my pronouncing the arrangement beneficial when they simply missed me. No one can substitute completely for someone else, and though Bert did everything that needed doing and gave them buckets of love and attention, my physical absence left an emotional toll that I'd never reckoned with. What's worse, without meaning to, I'd made them feel guilty about their hurt feelings. Being smart, sensitive kids, they understood how invested I was in balancing motherhood and my movement work, and they were afraid to undermine my belief that I'd succeeded.

As for my involvement in the women's movement, highfalu-tin as it sounds, I felt privileged to be part of that long-overdue, life-changing revolution. I believed in feminism's goals and principles with every fiber of my being—still do—and worked hard for social changes that would better the lives of all women. I felt similarly driven to work for intergroup harmony between Jews and other groups, be they African Americans, Palestinians, Christians, or Muslims—and impelled to do whatever I could, through my writing and advocacy, to help bring an end to the Israeli-Palestinian conflict. My passions kept pulling me in different directions: I loved being a mom, I needed to write, and I wanted to feel useful in the larger world. All at the same time. I also believed that my husband and I were modeling a new paradigm: a vibrant, loving home presided over by two equal parents, both with interesting adult lives that we shared with our kids at the dinner table.

As a woman who came of age in the middle of the twentieth century, I felt grateful to be free of the resentments and frustrations that were common to older women like my mom—wives and mothers who sacrificed their own dreams to serve everyone else in their family. When I thought about it, which wasn't often unless I was writing about it, I concluded that my children had benefited from seeing up close and personal an in-house template for how a woman can fulfill Freud's stated ideal of human existence, which is the ability to combine love and work in the same lifetime. But in the bustle of those years, I missed some vital signals, from my daughters especially, that they wanted and needed more of me.

And, without meaning to, I'd given them the impression that any criticism of my mothering would have been devastating to me. Recognizing that I was trying my best, they did not have the heart to name the problem. In hindsight, I should have opened a clear path for them to express their feelings without fearing that their candor would invalidate not just my motherhood but the entire feminist project.

Though all three of us are journalists, my daughters and I have different orientations to our work. They always had jobs they loved, but once babies materialized, Robin and Abigail found it wrenching to leave for an out-of-town assignment. I don't recall ever agonizing that way. In fact, I remember welcoming the segues back and forth from my work life to my home life. Each day spent in one of those worlds recharged my batteries and made me appreciate the other even more. And when involved in movement activities, I felt I was fighting for the freedom of their generation as well as mine to choose both, rather than be pressured into making an either/or choice between the two worlds.

For a few brief periods during her short life, my mother also had jobs she loved. I've always known that she was promoted from sewing machine operator to junior designer at Hattie Carnegie (her era's Donna Karan), and that she deeply regretted having to leave that job to work for her uncle Will, Jenny's brother, who had financed their voyage to America when Nathan wouldn't. But before I found the cache of old letters, I had no idea that she'd also worked as an assistant at a literary agency, handling correspondence with authors, a job uncannily similar to those I had early in my publishing career. When she was young (and still today, in many instances), a stay-at-home wife was a badge of a husband's financial success. So, after she married my dad, Mom quit the agency, abandoned her dress designing aspirations, and became Mrs. Jack Cottin, the derivative identity that defined her for the rest of her life.

A yellowed 1945 clipping from the now-extinct *Long Island Daily Press* shows "Mrs. Jack Cottin, president of the Women's

Auxiliary of the Jewish War Veterans," in a belted suit jacket and flowered hat, "packing 500 Passover boxes for convalescing Jewish soldiers." *The Jamaica Jewish Center Bulletin* lists Mrs. Jack Cottin as the "Good Will Chairman responsible for sending greetings to synagogue members who've had simchas and occasions of sorrow." Vice President of JJC's temple's Sisterhood, Mrs. Jack Cottin, presided over meetings at our synagogue. And in our Jamaica living room or backyard, Mrs. Jack Cottin hosted teas or brunches for Hadassah, "strawberry lunches" for the Women's International Zionist Organization, canasta parties for Pioneer Women, and mah-jongg games to benefit the National Council of Jewish Women. However satisfying those volunteer projects may have been, there were other things that would have added new meaning and new challenges to *Ceil* Cottin's daily life, namely designing clothes or devoting more time to her painting, the pastime she discovered in midlife but never had a chance to seriously pursue. I saw bound up in the contours of my mother's life the emotional cost of being confined to chores like housekeeping and childrearing that, worthy as they were, failed to provide an outlet for her interests or make full use of her creativity.

That I was determined not to replicate her sacrifices undoubtedly explained why I felt no ambivalence about moving back and forth between my publishing job and my family life. For my daughters and many other women, the issue is complicated; for me, not. I wasn't wired to agonize. I suppose I inherited my father's ability to be absent without guilt because I felt, as he had about his commitments, that the work I was doing was important. I also believed I was giving my children everything my dad failed to give me. Though I can't alter the person I was, or deny my lack of angst about the choices I made, I wish I had stopped to explain to my kids, in the moment, why, at times, I needed to be unavailable. It wouldn't have invalidated our closeness, or the achievements of the women's movement, had I acknowledged every parent's aching truth: much as we try our best to strike a balance between our kids' needs and our own, the scale isn't always level; sometimes it tilts to one side, and we tilt with it.

Ceil dressed in her own creations, c.1920s

While I'm issuing mea culpas, I should probably apologize for some of the articles I've written in the past. Because they reflected my unconflicted feelings, I may have made the maternal balancing act sound easy and therefore caused women who experienced more ambivalence to feel guilty, inept, or inadequate. I didn't always acknowledge that, in addition to the personal trade-offs for whatever decision she makes, it's impossible for a woman to achieve anything close to "having it all" unless she has a partner willing and able to share the load—or failing such a partner, then a full-time housekeeper and a nanny. Without my husband's active co-parenting, financial contribution, and respect and enthusiasm for my work, I could not have juggled my writing and civic commitments along with the kids' play dates, doctors' appointments, birthday parties, dance lessons, piano recitals, sporting events, and theatrical performances.

Legacy matters to me, especially now. I want to leave my children something tangible and true, a story they can draw upon to create their own stories, a mix of groundedness and buoyancy, those cliched "roots and wings." My parents' combined legacy was part inspiration, part cautionary tale. Though short in the making, Mom's example was my template for dedication to family, love of beauty, and hunger for meaningful creative expression. Dad's eagerness to initiate, take responsibility, and assume leadership in the Jewish community was my first model of what activism looks like. But as a couple, their volatile relationship was the prototype for everything I did not want and would not tolerate in a marriage,

A line in Isaiah predicts that a child shall lead us to a more perfect world. It took my daughters to give me insight into my choices and help me see how linked they were to the lives of my parents, how I both resented my father and became him, why I both revered my mother and broke her mold. In my zeal to avoid their mistakes, I made new ones, which I've been ashamed to admit until now.

CHAPTER 40

I COULDN'T GIVE HER MY BLESSING

In 1991, one of my daughters almost married a Catholic, and I panicked. Despite being involved in interfaith dialogue groups and committed to religious freedom and harmony, when it came to intermarriage, I turned into Tevye. Close-minded. Immovable. Unreachable. Somewhere along the way, I'd come to believe, as did Tevye, that when a child "marries out" it's tantamount to a death in the family. Traditionally, Jews have rent their clothing, sat shiva, and recited the kaddish. But there's a big difference between the two grief states: death carried no shame; intermarriage was a shanda.

In the 1964 Broadway version of *Fiddler on the Roof*, Tevye, the father of five daughters, struggles to find the sweet spot between Jewish tradition and this newfangled thing called marrying for love. After much cajoling by his first and second daughters who've proclaimed their love, respectively, for a poor tailor and a political agitator, both Jews, Tevye gives them his blessing. But he draws the line at his third daughter's choice, a Russian gentile. That marriage he will not bless. Were he to bend that far, he would break.

Unmitigated by songs and sweetness, Maurice Schwartz's film *Tevye*, released in 1939 as German tanks were rolling into Warsaw, has Tevye bluntly informing a Russian priest, "If any of my daughters married one of your boys, I should rather see her dead, or me dead. And if I had ten daughters, I should rather see all of them dead than to marry one of yours."

Unlike Tevye and Ceil, I wasn't born in a shtetl, nor was I an immigrant for whom the democratic ethos of interreligious respect was a new concept. American pluralism and Jewish particularism coexisted in me without conflict. I've never had a problem being both a committed Jew and a universalist, and I pride myself on valuing people for who they are and how they behave, not for their religious or ethnic identity. But when my daughter fell in love with an Irish-Catholic who took his faith seriously, and she talked as if she might marry him, I couldn't bring myself to give her my blessing. Wait, that's too tepid; I had a meltdown.

The judgment of others played no part in my distress. Most of our Jewish friends are secular or minimally observant; several have kids with non-Jewish spouses and "half Jewish" grandchildren. What consumed me was the thought that were Abigail to marry this Catholic, whom I'll call Kevin, and raise Catholic, or even half-Catholic, children, she would break the chain that bound our family to its ancient forebears going back 3500 years and dishonor the memory of our relatives murdered in the Shoah. How would I explain to their ghosts why a child of mine—not forced at the point of a sword to convert, not threatened, whipped, or flayed—could turn her back on her people, disregard millennia of Jewish martyrdom at the hands of Catholics, including a long line of popes, and allow her presumptive husband to insist, even by half measure, that she raise her children in his faith? I know this sounds melodramatic, but I saw a hoard of angry ancestors clawing out of their graves to reproach me: "See what your universalist hogwash has wrought! We didn't endure centuries of horrific persecution so your branch of our family tree could be sawed off by your daughter. Is this what we died for?" If I sound over the top, it's because I've never rid myself of the bogeyman of my childhood: Hitler, plain and simple. Until the Allies won the war, I lived in terror that the führer would be on the next plane to New York, round us up, build a death camp on Jamaica Avenue, and turn my synagogue into a crematorium.

Still, my overheated reaction to Abigail's beau took me by surprise. I beat my chest and harangued my husband, who shared none of my despair but kept asserting that Kevin's Catholicism was the least of it; he was the wrong man for our daughter for a dozen worrisome reasons and my objections to his faith were making her defensive and distracting her from reaching a clear-eyed assessment of him on her own. The truth is, I couldn't help myself. What's worse, I came down so hard on her that I drove her away. Literally. When Kevin left for his first year at Stanford Law School, Abigail went with him. She said she wanted to explore a new landscape, but I'm sure she also wanted to escape my guilt-tripping her about her obligations to The Jewish People.

Abigail found a job at the public TV station in San Francisco, bought a used Honda, made her way on unfamiliar turf. Our relationship, which had always been effortlessly warm and close, entered a deep freeze. Email didn't exist then; we rarely spoke on the phone, seldom exchanged letters. After months of being agonizingly shut out of her daily life, it finally dawned on me that she might actually marry this man and put down roots three thousand miles away, and if I didn't find a way to accept Kevin, the rift between my daughter and me would be unbridgeable, unbearable, and entirely of my own making. I had two options: accept her choice or lose her.

I flew out to California and begged her to forgive me for having interfered so heavy-handedly in her personal life. Were Kevin to become her husband, I promised I would learn to love him, and I would love their children from day one, no matter how she chose to raise them. To my everlasting relief, we reconciled, resumed talking on the phone and writing to each other. Time passed; I stayed mum and eventually felt prepared for the inevitable. One night the following summer, Abigail called to say she had broken up with Kevin and would be moving back to New York. The realization that he wasn't the right man for her was strictly hers. But had I not taken myself out of the equation, I'm not sure she could have made the decision to leave him without feeling she was doing my bidding. It embarrasses me now to admit the extent of my meddlesome intrusion into her private affairs. I'm ashamed that I made her relationship with Kevin my problem. I recognize that my behavior left scars, flickering fears she'd never felt before, of rejection, isolation, and the terrible possibility that something she did might actually make me love her less.

Six months later, the right man came along, a blind date set up by a mutual friend. He happens to be a Jewish boy from Skokie, Illinois, and she's been married to him for almost thirty years.

IV

PUBLIC SHAME

CHAPTER 41

TWENTY MILLION PEOPLE KNEW OUR SECRET

"Shame is now both global and permanent to a degree unprecedented in human history. No more moving to the next town to escape your bad name. However far you go and however long you wait, your disgrace is only ever a Google search away."

That's how Helen Andrews, author of *Shame Storm*, describes the tectonic shift in the dynamics of public humiliation. In today's world, it takes multiple forms—online shaming, cancel culture, calling-out, user-generated negative reviews (of books, articles, actors, restaurants), doxing (publicizing someone's home address and other personal information), and revenge porn (posting sexually explicit images and videos)—which have exponentially increased the breadth, reach, and power of anyone bent on assassinating the character and destroying the personal and professional reputation of anyone else.

In her September 2021 piece in *The Atlantic*, Anne Applebaum labels people who attempt to shame and ruin others "The New Puritans." Their target can be a public figure, coworker, neighbor, competitor, or former friend and their accusation—which often uses a principled political attack to disguise a petty power struggle—charges its target with having broken "social codes having to do with race, sex, personal behavior or even acceptable humor, which may not have existed five years ago or maybe five months ago." The New Puritan's objective is to get the targeted people ostracized, defamed, ridiculed, boycotted, fired, rendered unemployable, unmarriageable, or otherwise defined out of the community with which they are most closely identified, or whose respect they need most in order to maintain their self-esteem, success, or status. Reread that last sentence and you'll have an accurate description of what Jews of my parents' generation did—without the benefit of social media—when they wanted to destroy the reputation of a fellow Jew whose behavior they deemed a shanda.

In the secular world of the twenty-first century, prominent victims of cancel culture have included J. K. Rowling, author of the *Harry Potter* series, who was pilloried as "transphobic" for supporting a researcher who maintained that transwomen aren't women; TV host Ellen DeGeneres, whose show lost advertisers, A-list celebrity bookings, and audience ratings after she was called out for tolerating a toxic work environment and sexual misconduct by three of her producers; *New York Times* editorial page editor James Bennet, who had to resign after being mercilessly criticized by his colleagues for publishing an op-ed by a GOP senator who argued for federal troops to be called in to put down Black Lives Matter protests. Also canceled was a previously anonymous high school senior from Leesburg, Virginia, a white girl named Mimi Grove, who was forced to withdraw from her "dream college"— the University of Tennessee, where she'd had been accepted—after a three-second video in which she'd said the N-word was posted on social media. Viral went the video, whereupon thousands of outraged students, alumni, donors, and others, deluged the U of T with tweets and emails that succeeded in pressuring school officials to demand that Grove withdraw from the freshman class. What put the brouhaha on the front pages and, at least to my mind, demonstrates the hazards of cancel culture, no matter how egregious the behavior it seeks to punish, is the backstory that has since come to light.

Grove was fifteen when she posted the video on Instagram four years ago. It caused no ruckus. But it was never forgotten by Jimmy Galligan, a biracial African American classmate of hers, who, in the past, had frequently complained to school authorities about widespread use of the N-word by his fellow students (to no avail). Jimmy purposely delayed re-releasing Mimi's video until he knew it could do the most damage. His goal, he admitted, was to shame her and thus teach all his White classmates a lesson—that there would be consequences for their racist acts. Turns out, however, that Mimi had made the video not to promulgate White supremacy but to announce to her social media friends that she had just received her learner's permit. Her way of expressing her excitement was to look into the camera, exclaim "I can drive!" and mimic a rapper's ebullient use of the N-word. Moreover, a couple of months before Jimmy reposted her four-year-old video, Mimi had responded to the killing of George Floyd by urging her Instagram friends to "protest, donate, sign a petition, rally, do something" in support of the Black Lives Matter movement. So, here's my quadruple takeaway: Life is complicated. Jimmy was right to call out racism in his high school. Mimi was wrong to use the N-word, but she isn't as racist as you'd think. And not all wrongs make shaming right.

Before Instagram, Snapchat, TikTok, and Twitter, people who had been disgraced could outrun their shame and disappear into a new, self-created biography, which is what my parents did with notable success. Mom's brother, Lou, did the opposite: he showcased a family conflict, creating a scandal that followed him like his own shadow. The problem began when Lou's wife became pregnant with their first child, and Lou, deciding he needed a steady income to support his growing family, asked his father, Nathan, to sign over to him the tea and coffee store on the Lower East Side. Nathan, ready to retire anyway, said yes to Lou with no thought to the repercussions. Whereupon Herbert, the middle son, flew into a rage on behalf of himself and his younger brother, Milton, and demanded that all three of the Halpern boys receive equal shares in the store. Given the rigid gender role stereotypes of that era, I wasn't surprised that Herbert's hunger for justice didn't extend to his sisters—my mother and three aunts. What stunned me was what happened next. Rather than press his case privately, Lou got himself booked on *The Good Will Hour*, a wildly popular weekly radio program whose host, John J. Anthony, a high school dropout and former taxi driver with zero social science credentials, promised to solve the personal problems of his guests. Heard on seven hundred stations by twenty million listeners, the show's opening line—"Mr. Anthony, I have a problem!"—was as familiar in the 1930s and '40s as "Live from New York, it's Saturday Night!" is today. Lou went on the program and told Mr. Anthony—and Mr. and Mrs. America from sea to shining sea—his problem was that his brothers, neither of whom were married, were trying to cheat him out of the store their father gave to him. As the eldest son, and with his wife pregnant, shouldn't he be entitled to take over the family business?

Lou and Nathan in the family store (date unknown)

I was not yet born when this fracas shattered the unity of the Halpern siblings, so I called up Judy, my eldest living cousin (daughter of Tillie and Ralph), whom I adore but see infrequently since she lives in Palo Alto, California. Twelve years my senior, Judy was a teenager during that ignominious episode, and she told me what happened: Mr. Anthony decided in favor of Uncle Lou, though his victory came at great cost. Today, you might say, he was canceled. His brothers declared him a dead man, and his parents and sisters maintained their distance from him for the rest of their lives. No doubt Herbert and Milton would have carried a fierce grudge against Lou for cheating them of their share of the store. But it would have been a private family matter. What elevated the incident to the realm of calamity was Lou's public exposure of the problem. At that time, for a Jewish son to broadcast a sensitive family quarrel to the ears of twenty million strangers was a disgrace beyond repair.

(Mentioning *The Good Will Hour* reminds me of a scene from my childhood, the time I ran downstairs during one of my parents' screaming fights and intoned in my let's-pretend adult voice, "Mr. Anthony! I have a problem: my mommy and daddy are always arguing." That stopped my father cold; he burst out laughing and hugged me to pieces, and the two of them called a truce. The next time they started going at each other, I interceded again, shouting above my father's harangue, "Mr. Anthony! I have a problem." That time, Dad sent me to my room and just kept yelling.)

I had two Uncle Lous, one Cottin, one Halpern, but can't recall ever visiting the home of Lou Halpern, my mother's brother, the family's Benedict Arnold. Yet, based on the photo reproduced below and on the cover of this book, Lou and his family could not have been excommunicated from our midst since his three remaining sisters (Sadye had died) and their husbands are among the fifteen honored guests shown on the dais at the bar mitzvah in 1948 of Lou's eldest son, Teddy. Back row: my aunts and uncles, Ralph and Tillie Kahn; Ben and Rona Darvie; cousin Danny, older son of Tillie and Ralph; Bertha Halpern, Lou's wife; cousin Teddy, looking like he'd rather be someplace else; Uncle Lou Halpern; and Ceil and Jack Cottin. Ceil, the perpetual peacemaker, must have convinced her sisters that occasions of consequence required them to suspend Lou's ostracism and show up with their families so the younger generation would not suffer from the breach. Seven Halpern cousins are pictured. In addition to the upright teens, Danny and Teddy, seated from left are Letty in tulle; Sue, younger daughter of Rona and Ben; Joel, younger son of Tillie and Ralph; and Pris, my favorite, older daughter of Rona and Ben, luminous in satin; and Eddy, the bar mitzvah boy's younger brother who, I distinctly recall, was bullied by his father into dancing with me. Herbert and Milton, neither of whom had spawned a younger generation, were immune to Mom's pleadings. Having sworn they would never attend any event where Lou was present, they're conspicuously absent from the photograph, and, as far as I can tell, neither of them ever saw or spoke to their brother again.

CHAPTER 42

PERIOD. END OF SENTENCE.

When I was in the sixth grade, Bertha, not my Uncle Lou's wife but a young war refugee new to our school, took the wooden hall pass, went to the bathroom, and came back to class with her sanitary pad dangling outside her skirt. As she walked up the aisle to her desk, the Kotex slapped against her rear end like a tail. Worse yet, it was smeared with blood.

One boy laughed out loud, pointing to her back, unleashing a hail of taunts and jeers. Another stood up and flapped his fingers at butt level, imitating the bouncing pad. This new form of American insolence puzzled Bertha. "Look behind you," a girl called out. "Look behind you!" I have never forgotten the horrified expression on Bertha's face when she glanced over her shoulder and saw the object of her classmates' mockery, how her body stiffened at the sight, how frantically she twisted her thin torso, reached behind her back, tore off the pad, and stuffed it in her school bag, the naked humiliation in her eyes as she slunk to the front of the room and ran out the door. Had our teacher been a woman, I'd like to think she'd have known what to say. But that year it was Mr. Heffner, a nice man with kind eyes and hair as wavy as Liberace's, and he had no clue how to respond to his mortified pupil's predicament beyond restoring order and excusing Bertha to go home early.

She never returned to our school. Her public shaming was my introduction to menstruation as catastrophe, my first inkling that a woman's natural bodily functions could elicit ridicule and disgust.

No doubt witnessing any child's abject humiliation would have left an indelible memory. What burned Bertha's disgrace into my brain, was the femaleness of her shame. Born that day was my life-long terror of "staining," soiling the back of my dress, my pants, the upholstery, my host's bedsheets, running out of tampons, showing a tell-tale hormonal distemper, or otherwise revealing to the world that it was "my time of the month." Despite my promulgation of feminism's body-pride messages, I was never able to rid myself of the conviction that a bloodstain on the back of my skirt would be more shameful than the scarlet letter on Hester Prynne's chest. Once, while touring a women's health clinic, I squirmed at the slogan superimposed on a poster of Rosie the Riveter: "Anything a man can do, I can do bleeding." My first thought was, why would you want to remind people that we bleed? And when I saw a muscle man in a tee shirt that said, "Never trust anything that bleeds for a week and doesn't die," the sheer misogyny of its message reminded me of why, whenever I had my period, I wanted to hide. Dehumanizing a woman as a thing, implying that menstruation is an illness rather than a bodily function that's as normal for a woman as seminal emissions are for a man, and suggesting that women's hormones make us fundamentally inferior and untrust-worthy summed up the most sexist views of the most sexist men I'd ever encountered or heard about.

Exhibit A: Dr. Edgar Berman, personal physician to Vice President Hubert Humphrey, proclaimed in 1970 that women were unfit for leadership because of "the raging hormonal imbalance of the periodic lunar cycle." For a physician to believe that half the human race is emotionally unbalanced and not to be trusted with serious responsibility is patently ludicrous, yet Berman was far from the only man who held that view and treated women accordingly.

Orthodox Judaism's laws of Taharat Ha'mishpacha posit that a menstruating woman is *tamei*, ritually impure, and a man who touches any part of her body, or any object she has touched, will be defiled. My father explained this to me when I saw an Orthodox friend of his refuse to shake my mother's hand, and again, when I asked my parents why they slept in a double bed but some married couples, for instance, Aunt Dottie and Uncle Al, had twin beds. Dad said taharat hamishpacha was the reason. An Orthodox man won't have any physical contact with his wife when she's tamei and won't touch any woman who isn't a member of his immediate family. One night at the Shabbos table, Dad and Uncle Al, the shammes, who, you'll recall, took over my wedding, had an argument about whether women are allowed to touch a Torah scroll. Al said no, she might be tamei. Dad said yes, and proved Al wrong by citing a quote from Maimonides, the towering scholar of the Middle Ages, and another from Joseph Caro, who codified Jewish law in the Shulchan Aruch, both of whom ruled that the Torah cannot be desecrated by human touch, male or female.

My Israeli friend Alice Shalvi, who was raised Orthodox in London in the 1950s, recalled that menstruation was never spoken of in public and "even between women was referred to as though it were a disgusting but unavoidable disease." During those same years, my girlfriends and I called our periods "the curse," "the red tide," being "unwell," or "falling off a roof." If a girl needed a pad or tampon, she asked another girl in a whisper so the boys couldn't hear and when she got it, quickly hid it in her purse or pocket. And when a girl seemed easily irritated, boys accused her of being "on the rag."

I assumed those days of pubertal shame went the way of the 45 RPM record, but a recent op-ed in the *New York Times* suggests otherwise. About her daughter, who started menstruating in the fifth grade, Samantha Hunt wrote, "the same girl who at six paraded her first bloody, lost tooth around a restaurant was now expected to become an expert at keeping secrets—tampons stashed in her lunch box, knowing winks with other girls and the old tried and true method of tying a sweatshirt around her waist. Do we keep girls' bodies secret to protect boys? And if so, protect boys from what? The truth that female bodies are complicated and full of wonder?"

I was the last of my friends to menstruate. Older girls kept saying I wouldn't feel like a woman until I got my period, so I prayed for it and prayed for it, and at age fourteen years and four months, it finally came. Be careful what you wish for has been my advice to late-blooming girls ever since. When I proudly brought my stained panties to my mother, she muttered something in Yiddish and slapped me across the face. Having never before been struck by either parent, I was more stunned than stung. I demanded an explanation.

Mom said Grandma slapped her and her sisters the day they got their periods, and she slapped Betty when she got hers. So now she was slapping me. What harm could it do, a little smack to get God's attention? All she did was pray that her slap be the worst pain I would ever know as a woman. (Suffice it to say, it didn't work. I had brutal menstrual cramps, a full day of labor with my twins, and two C-sections, after which I couldn't laugh or cough without pain for weeks.) Mom took the occasion of my first period to forbid me to use tampons because the cardboard tube could tear my hymen and nullify my virginity. She showed me how to attach a sanitary pad to the hooks on an elastic belt that I was to wear underneath my panties. When I got to college, I threw out all my pads and paraphernalia after my roommate taught me to insert a Tampax. I would not become Bertha.

Like a bad dream, the image of my disgraced classmate came back to me the night I saw *Period. End of Sentence*, a film about women and girls in an Indian village who had no access to sanitary products. According to "The Logical Indian," a digital media platform for Indian Millennials, girls in many rural areas are banished to faraway huts when they're menstruating and, despite a Supreme Court ruling prohibiting the practice, women of all ages are banned from temples. The girls portrayed in the documentary were too ashamed to attend class during their menstrual periods, so they missed a week or more of classes every month or dropped out of school entirely. When a sanitary pad machine was installed in their village, thanks to start-up funds from kids halfway around the world at a school in Los Angeles, the women's lives were changed. The LA kids joined with feminist activists in India to help launch "The Pad Project," which taught the women of the village how to manufacture and market their own pads, helping them to become entrepreneurs while freeing their sisters from blood and stigma. The night the film won the 2019 Oscar for Best Documentary Short, I remembered Bertha and wrote her this letter in my head:

I have never forgotten the humiliation you suffered years ago in our class. I'm sorry the boys taunted you, sorrier still that some of the girls were complicit in your shaming. I was horrified by what happened. But I did nothing to stop it. None of us girls did. I understand now that what caused our silent passivity was our own embarrassment and physical self-loathing. Though only eleven or twelve years old, we had already absorbed our culture's disdain for the natural functions of the female body, as well as the conviction that menstrual blood is dirty. I was permanently scarred by what you experienced that day in our classroom, so I can only imagine its impact on you. If this letter has made its way into your hands, I beg your forgiveness.

CHAPTER 43

LOSS, SHAME, AND WHAT I WORE

Until my bat mitzvah, my mother, once a fashion designer, made most of my wardrobe decisions. The outfits I wore for special occasions, many of which she sewed herself, always had panache. Two stand out in my memory: a blue suit she paired with a crisp white blouse and plaid tam o'shanter, the classic Scottish cap topped by a red pom-pom; and a pale-aqua taffeta dress with a shirred bodice and puffed sleeves. Mom dressed me to look like the little girls in Best & Company's ads from the '50s, though she never shopped there—or at Saks, Lord & Taylor, or Bloomingdale's— because their clothes were too expensive.

Ceil's ideas about propriety were as dictatorial as her sense of style. Wrinkles were not tolerated so an ironing board stood at the ready in her sewing room, a narrow, windowed porch just off the kitchen. For the tail of a blouse to pull out of a girl's skirt or slacks was an embarrassment. Underarm pads were attached inside the sleeves of my dress-up clothes though I don't remember breaking a sweat until I was a cheerleader in college. Pre-breasts, I persuaded Mom to buy me a see-through blouse, the hot fashion statement of my junior high school set. She made me wear a cotton under-shirt under the blouse rather than a lacy slip, which subverted the whole effect. Levi's 501 button-fly jeans, alias "boys' dungarees," were off limits because of some Freudian gibberish about a fly front arousing a girl's penis envy by reminding her of the organ requiring that exit route. Instead, I wore "girls' dungarees," which had side zippers and were stupefyingly uncool. When my girlfriends started to "develop," Mom suggested I stuff rolled up socks in the conical cups of a 32-AAA bra, and when I filled out, she steered me away from every top that showed cleavage. Breasts were feminine, cleavage a curve too far.

My wardrobe reached a major turning point when my mother and I went shopping for my bat mitzvah dress at Ohrbach's on West 34th Street. We were in the store fewer than five minutes when I fell madly in love with a black velvet number whose scooped neckline was bordered by a band of crocheted white lace spangled with tiny sequins. Besotted, I hugged the dress to my body and declared it perfect.

Mom gave it a glance and a deep frown. "Bat mitzvah means daughter of the commandments; it does not mean you're all of a sudden a woman." She returned the dress to the rack and kept rifling through the hangers until a lime chiffon confection appeared. She held it up, beaming. I retrieved the black velvet number. Mom yanked it back. "A girl your age can't wear black to a happy occasion. You'll attract the Evil Eye, chas v'chalila! Black is for funerals."

Crestfallen, I worked myself into lather in the middle of Ohrbach's girls department. "Never in my entire life have I seen such a beautiful dress. If I can't wear this dress at my bat mitzvah, it won't be a happy occasion. I'll be thinking about this beautiful dress the whole time." Then I lobbed a few spitballs at my mother's superstitions. "Rabbis wear black at happy occasions, and they don't attract the Evil Eye. Cantors wear black. Choir singers wear black. You don't see the devil circling over their heads. Black is a color, not a curse." I grabbed the dress off the rack again and pressed it to my body. "It has white lace and sequins at the neckline. No one's going to mistake it for a shiva dress. *Please, Mommy!* It would make me feel like Queen Esther. I don't want to feel like a little girl in a party dress when I'm up there on the bimah chanting my haftarah. I want to feel like a young woman. It would give me confidence."

I think that last line was what won Mom over. Maybe it reminded her of times when she herself wore something special to buttress her confidence or transform herself into the person she wished she was but wasn't. Or maybe saying yes to the dress was the only way to put a stop to my tantrum, which was embarrassing her in front of the saleswoman and the other shoppers. Whatever did the trick, she eventually folded, and I came home with the black velvet dress plus a white lace hair ornament to go with it. No one in the family had a run of bad luck because I wore black at my bat mitzvah. But it did cross my mind, when she died three years later, that my dress may have had something to do with it.

Letty in black velvet bat mitzvah dress, February 1952

With Mom gone, Dad was clueless about fashion, so it fell to me to figure out the dress code for every occasion, which look was acceptable for a woman but not a teenager, which neckline was too girlish, which too racy, and how much cleavage was too much. Figure it out I did, if not by extrapolating from her example, then by observing other girls and women in synagogue or around the neighborhood. From them, I deduced such sartorial principles as, Nice Jewish Girls should be sexy enough to attract boys but not so sexy to be called CTs (cock-teasers). Just by looking at me, the (gentile) world will know the sort of family I come from and the values I learned at home. My reputation can be won or lost by the fit of my blouse, the length of my skirt, the shade of my nail polish. A poor fashion choice can tell the wrong story. What I put on each morning or before I go out on a date had the power either to bring honor to The Jewish People or to publicly shame us. I know that sounds grandiloquent, but I still find myself operating under the influence of those principles despite having lived through punk, grunge, tattoos, piercing, street styles, dress-for-success, and all the liberation movements of the last half century. These days, my everyday wardrobe largely consists of jeans or tights, tee shirts or tunics, sneakers or boots. But every now and then, to forestall the threat of a shanda, I have to squelch my inner hippie or suppress my secret attraction to clothes and shoes that sparkle.

These fashion reveries were exhumed when I attended a bat mitzvah on Long Island that sent my bile level off the charts. Seated in the synagogue's sanctuary behind four preteen girls, I noticed that their outfits were so similar they could have dressed off the same checklist. Micro-mini skirts. Belly button–baring tops. Check. Chandelier earrings. Hair blow-dried straight. Check. Stacked high heels. Black nail polish. Check. They all looked ridiculous. No, worse than ridiculous; disturbing, the way toddler beauty pageants are disturbing, because they eroticize little girls. That these four preteeners, heirs to the feminist revolution, had the chutzpah to enter this sanctuary dressed like sex objects-in-training filled me with disgust. Presumably they were here to witness the bat mitzvah of a friend of theirs, a girl who was standing on the bimah on a Saturday morning (not a Friday night, to which girls of my era were relegated, if allowed a bat mitzvah at all), a girl who was wearing a yarmulke, and a tallit, and chanting from the Torah scroll (exactly as a boy would on his bar mitzvah day)—and those phenomena would not exist if not for the indefatigable efforts of thousands of Jewish women (and some good men) who fought like tiger mothers for gender parity in Judaism. Weren't these girly girls aware of that history? Didn't they realize how long it took to make this day possible? Why didn't they show, by their appearance, the slightest bit of respect for this space, that struggle, this day, and their friend's achievement?

As the service progressed, I noticed with unexpected pleasure that all four girls were following the prayers in the siddur and reciting the Hebrew beautifully. They knew the chants and melodies, stood up and sat down in response to the appropriate passages, faced east during the Amidah, answered the call and response during each aliyah, bent their knees at the phrase, "*V'anachnu korim*," in the prayer, *Aleinu*, and straightened up at the words, "*Lifnei melech.*" Based on my observation of them engaged in prayer, I would not be surprised if each of the four girls could stand up and, with no written text, deliver a *dvar Torah* (mini sermon) on this week's *parasha*. Discovering them to be well-grounded in our tradition had a mitigating effect on my outrage. By the same token, girls with that grounding had no business leaving home dressed like a cross between Lolita and Lady Gaga. What were they thinking? What were their mothers and fathers thinking?

I'm not saying twelve-year-olds should dress like dowdy matrons; I'm saying they should not dress for synagogue (or church or the mosque) the way they would for a mosh pit. Young girls have every right to be proud of their bodies, including their belly buttons, and girls should feel free to experiment with their personal style (which, in point of fact, these girls did not, since they all dressed the same). However, rights unmediated by judgment and context add up to arrogance. Their freedom to expose their belly buttons in public stops at the door to the sanctuary.

Something else was on my mind that morning besides the girls' disregard for the sanctity of the setting and disrespect for what prior generations went through to achieve the right to a bat mitzvah. Put plainly, I was afraid the goyim would think badly of us. Channeling my mother, I worried that the non-Jews who were there that day—friends of the bat mitzvah girl and her parents—might draw the wrong conclusion about the sanctity of our religious occasions based on the appearance of the four girls in front of me and others seated elsewhere in the sanctuary who were wearing similar outfits and showing similar amounts of skin. That the gentiles would leave today's service with a distorted view of Jewish values, Jewish parents, or the dignity of our worship. That they would completely misperceive the essence of Judaism or Jewishness, which happens when a few individuals do something embarrassing and the whole group suffers opprobrium. That my people had been publicly shamed, and I was powerless to do anything about it.

What I took home with me that day were two contradictory visions, on the one hand the disquieting image of four exposed belly buttons within spitting distance of the Holy Ark; on the other, the uplifting image of four knowledgeable young women enacting the rituals of their tradition. For me, their fidelity to the Sabbath prayers took some of the onus off their appearance. But would gentiles know enough about Judaism to recognize how much the girls knew, or would they only remember how ridiculous the girls looked? I wish I didn't care what "other people" think about Jewish girls. But I can't help it. I do.

CHAPTER 44

WE LIVED IN THE TENSION BETWEEN PRIDE AND PARANOIA

Cherry-picking intimate disclosures is human. We do it to evade public shame and protect the narrative we've told ourselves and others about our lives. But along with fear of the shanda, I learned its polar opposite, pride in Jewish exceptionalism—the notion that Jews are special. Some conflate exceptionalism with "chosenness," a mistake with serious consequences since divinely sanctioned favoritism tends not to go down well with the non-chosen, any more than a child's claim of being a parent's favorite would be welcomed by its siblings. When asked what it means for us to be God's Chosen People, the standard reply of a Jewish comedian is, "It means chosen to suffer." I was taught that it meant chosen to meet a high standard of morality, model the pursuit of justice, chosen to complete the parts of creation that God didn't finish, the parts that still need to be refined and perfected.

I'm not sure my parents' definition was the same. They deplored negative stereotypes about our tribe (greedy, miserly, nerdy, pushy) while inculcating in me a raft of positive stereotypes as if they were scientific facts: Jews are devoted to family; fiercely loyal; philanthropic; preternaturally successful in medicine, law, and business;

and gifted at the violin. Jewish men make the best husbands. Jewish husbands don't hit their wives. Jewish mothers sacrifice everything for their kids. There are no Jewish alcoholics. I never questioned the accuracy of those bromides, especially the "fact" that Jews are smart. All the children in Lake Wobegon may have been "above average," but every Jewish kid was a budding genius, which might sound superior and self-serving but not entirely far-fetched. Why else would an infinitesimal 0.2 percent of the world's population, account for 20 percent of the world's Nobel laureates?

I wasn't the only one raised on such chest-puffing statistics. When my daughter Abigail was doing interviews for her book, *Stars of David: Prominent American Jews Talk about Being Jewish*, the late composer-lyricist Stephen Sondheim challenged her to name a great gentile musical theater composer other than Cole Porter. Hal Prince, the Jewish producer-director (*West Side Story, Fiddler on the Roof, Cabaret, Sweeney Todd, Phantom of the Opera*) who won an unprecedented twenty-one Tony Awards, said, "I'm so reluctant to go where Steve (Sondheim) went, which is to say, 'We're the best.' Somebody else better say it. Somebody who isn't Jewish. Every once in a while, you find yourself in a room full of accomplished Jewish people and they feel too superior. I don't think anyone should feel superior."

Reflecting the familiar push-pull of Jewish exceptionalism (self-satisfaction followed by self-abnegation), Hal Prince added, "I could say something very arrogant—though I don't approve of it: it's a hell of an elite club...the facts are there. And all I can think is so much of this has to do with how a race of people—or a religious group—dealt with deprivation. [Jews] actually took an isolation that was thrust on them and turned it into an advantage... and that's huge.... There are other races and religions out there and they don't always turn adversity into creativity. And we'll let it go at that."

I can't let it go unless we assume equal responsibility for our scoundrels as for our superstars. As Rabbi Irwin Kula, president of the National Jewish Center for Learning and Leadership, observed after the Bernie Madoff disgrace, "...if we are going to take pride in Nobel Prize winners who are Jewish in name only, and are going to attribute their brilliance to some essentialized Jewish quality—and send around lists to evoke that pride—then we will wind up having to be ashamed of a fixer-bully-crook who is Jewish in name only and attribute his nastiness to some essentialized Jewish quality... we can't have it both ways."

Even worse than an inside-the-Borscht Belt shanda (humiliation within our own community) was a shanda far di goyim, something a Jew does that makes all Jews look bad in front of gentiles. Roy Cohn was a shanda far di goyim. Ditto mobsters Meyer Lanksy and Bugsy Siegel. Double-ditto the miscreants of our era, big shots whose names are unmistakably Jewish—Madoff, Weinstein, Epstein, Weiner, Michael Cohen. Triple ditto, the artistic and nonprofit elites. When #MeToo allegations surfaced about the sexual misconduct of Jewish writers, editors, philanthropists, musicians, actors, rabbis, and scholars, the news shook the collective Jewish psyche to its core, and dozens of soul-searching analyses appeared in Jewish periodicals and elsewhere. Was it because these men had Jewish mothers who spoiled them? Were they "performative," that is, acting out in the manner of Portnoy, as Mark Oppenheimer postulated in his infamous piece in *Tablet* (for which he later apologized) entitled "The Specifically Jewy Perviness of Harvey Weinstein"? As one Jewish publication reported in 2018, the issue of sexual misconduct "has been so dominant that as the High Holy Days approached, a group of rabbis and scholars were inspired to come up with an addendum to the traditional Yom Kippur prayer."

For the sin we committed through inappropriate use of power.

For the sin we committed by inappropriate sexual advances.

For the sin we committed by putting people in power without oversight.

For the sin we committed by not taking seriously the complaints of a colleague.

For the sin we committed by not believing victims when they spoke up.

For the sin we committed by not being aware of our own power or privilege when making an advance...

Growing up, I could never have imagined a time when an acclaimed Jewish opera conductor, movie producer, journalist, professor, or philanthropist would, by his behavior, words, or actions, bring shame to the Jewish community. These men were supposedly the best of our breed, the cream of our crops; they made us proud; they were the men we wanted our sons to grow up to be and our daughters to marry. Not anymore. Now, we're tallying up the victims and calling to account those who tolerated the abusers and covered up their execrable behavior.

Probably because the Hollywood casting couch was a long-familiar trope, I wasn't totally shocked by the revelations about Harvey Weinstein. But I could scarcely believe it when accusations were leveled against conductor James Levine, star architect Richard Meier, artist Chuck Close, Judge Alex Kozinski, journalists Mark Halperin, Michael Oreskes, and Ari Shavit. Even more shocking than the bold-faced names was the parade of ordinary Jews whose misconduct took place inside Jewish institutions. It used to be that every time an article appeared identifying Christian clergy who violated children—more than three thousand Catholic priests in more than a hundred US dioceses, and thousands more ministers and pastors in Southern Baptist, Evangelical, and other Christian denominations—I used to think, *No Jew would ever do that.* Today, of course, I know better; our men, too, are no strangers to moral disgrace. Not just rabbis but cantors, scholars, Hebrew school principals, Jewish camp directors, philanthropists, and CEOs of Jewish organizations, have been accused of sexual harassment and worse. What's more, our community leaders, standard-bearers, and trustees have been as protective of our miscreants as Catholic cardinals and bishops were of their predator priests. Our power brokers have overlooked, concealed, even facilitated the heinous acts of Jewish offenders by opting to shield the men's reputations, preserve their institutions' prestige, and ensure their ability to keep raising money from donors who would otherwise be scared away from any cause besmirched by a shanda.

When publicly shamed by the private acts of prominent Jews, the least we should be able to expect from the offender is contrition and an unequivocal apology. That, thank the goddess, is what we got from journalists Mike Oreskes and Leon Wieseltier. "My behavior was wrong and inexcusable, and I accept full responsibility," said Oreskes, former news director of NPR. Wieseltier, writer and former editor at the *New Republic*, promptly declared, "For my offenses against some of my colleagues in the past I offer a shaken apology and ask for their forgiveness." In stark contrast, after being credibly accused by seven women of sexually harassing, propositioning, or making "inappropriate sexual comments" while interacting with them in professional contexts, billionaire Michael Steinhardt responded drily that his "well-known sense of humor can be insensitive." Compounding the shame, almost a dozen Jewish organizations to whom Steinhardt has donated many millions of dollars, declined to condemn his behavior. In contrast, Hillel International, another recipient of his largesse, launched an internal investigation and, after corroborating the women's accusations, removed him from its board of governors. Jewish Women International, not a Steinhardt grantee, released a statement about him that every honorable Jewish organization should have felt compelled to replicate—"To brush off his words as jokes…is to demean the personal and professional value of all women working in the Jewish community." No doubt JWI will not be among Steinhardt's future grantees.

Now that #MeToo has become #GamAni (MeToo in Hebrew), many of us have been grappling with a number of complicated questions: how should the men who did harm be punished, and what remedy should be imposed upon those who protected the men's reputations rather than their victims' safety and dignity? What remedy is appropriate? What action will both salve the pain of the accuser and respect the rights of the accused? The issue, complex to begin with, really gets thorny when the accused is someone we know, which often is the case since the so-called "organized Jewish community"—those of us actively involved in Jewish issues, groups, and synagogues—is small enough for any of us to have interacted with these men in our personal and professional lives.

I'm thinking of a well-known social scientist with special expertise in Jewish demographics, religious practices, and family life. I've cited his research multiple times in my books and articles. Met him over the years at meetings and conferences and always enjoyed his company. So, I can't overstate my astonishment when several of his former students and current colleagues publicly accused him of sexual harassment and abuse. Others in the community, apparently, were not at all surprised. Those who'd worked with him and for him had witnessed his offensive behavior for years but felt powerless to complain or gain redress, largely because his superiors dismissed his creepy habits with a "boys will be boys" wink and an eye on how dependent their institution was on his sterling reputation adding luster to their public profile and lucre to their fundraising.

When his accusers went public, he admitted they were telling the truth and reportedly apologized to everyone he'd mistreated, humiliated, and hurt. "I take very seriously what women have said about the pattern of my inappropriate behavior. I am deeply committed to changing that behavior, to be someone who acts totally in accord with the great respect I have for women. Over the past year, with the help of my therapist, conversations with several rabbis and my wife, I've engaged in introspection and reflection, seeking to understand the roots of my behavior and how I hurt people, with the goal of ensuring that I never repeat such actions again. That is the essence of genuine teshuvah (repentance), a process that takes time."

Buttressing his words with actions, he resigned as director of a prestigious policy organization and announced publicly that he was doing specific acts of repentance. His close friends made it known that he was working assiduously to repair himself. All well and good. Not every #MeToo miscreant takes full responsibility for his offenses, but he tried too soon to make a comeback and was instantly pilloried for it. So what's next for him and other offenders? Is it enough for an offender to be disgraced and remorseful, or must he endure some concrete form of punishment before his victims can feel justice has been done? If so, who decides what penalty is appropriate for what level of misconduct? Should he be put in cherem (an extreme form of shunning tantamount to excommunication) and permanently excluded from the community? Or should there be an end point after which an offender is assumed to have completed his penance and be allowed to return to the fold? How should the institutions that employed him be held accountable? And who, exactly, should suffer the penalty for what many knew but did nothing about? His superiors who looked the other way? Everyone who covered up the women's complaints? The institution that employed him? The policy organization? Their board members? All of the above?

Finally, how should the rest of us respond? Have we stopped watching the films of Harvey Weinstein or listening to the music of Hitler's favorite composer, Wagner, who himself held rabidly anti-Semitic views? Do we no longer enjoy T. S. Eliot's poetry, or read our kids *Charlie and the Chocolate Factory* or *James and the Giant Peach*, both written by Roald Dahl, a confessed anti-Semite? Should I stop citing the social scientist's data? Never interview him again on issues about which he has expertise? Reevaluate his research in the light of his inappropriate advances to women? Should he lose his teaching job, his tenure, his ability to publish? Be formally rebuked or ostracized and, if so, by whom, for how long, and with what motivation, deterrence or vengeance? Will the Jewish community be intellectually poorer if his work is excised from public discourse, or morally richer if we exact a steep cost for his behavior? In the parlance of today, should he be canceled? Moving further into the weeds, should he be required to add specific commitments of social action to his personal project of repentance and rebirth? Make amends by volunteering in a women's shelter? Take steps to advance the careers of the women he harmed? Give tzedakah (charity) to women's groups fighting sexual abuse? Issue a public apology in an academic forum? How much teshuvah is enough? What's the right route to justice and redemption? Men like Weinstein who've been accused of rape and sexual violence should be tried and if found guilty serve time in prison. But at what point should someone like the social scientist, whose behavior, arguably, was disgusting but not criminal, be considered to have earned a second chance?

Those are some of the questions that many Jews have been wrestling with for years. The answers will be long in coming and carefully crafted. The accused should not be summarily condemned to punishment and lasting shame without due process. But neither should concern for "ruining a man's life" soften the censure or delay the prosecution of a perpetrator who may have ruined the life, career, sex life, and self-esteem of women who have waited years for justice to be done.

Days after the scandal broke, I saw the social scientist at Shabbat services. He and his wife were sitting a few pews away from mine. Our eyes met. He smiled at me. I gave him a tiny wave. He nodded, waved back. His wife, who does much good in the world, turned and smiled. I've known her for years—she's a lovely human being. I raised my arm to give her a slighter broader wave. I don't want her husband put in cherem because she shouldn't have to live forever with the weight of his shanda, and I don't want him to be unemployable because I don't want his family to starve. Then, I remembered the women he violated. Had I been one of them, he would not have smiled and I would not have waved. Seeing him in the pew, my cheeks would have flushed and my body would remember how it felt like to be treated like an object to be toyed with for his pleasure. My mind would be burrowing back to the time of my humiliation, when he had the power to hire me, advance my work, determine my earnings and my future, when he gave no thought to my career or my dignity. That gave me pause, mid-wave. Had I passed him and his wife on my way out of shul that night, I would not have known what to say.

You needn't be an accused rapist or a dirty-old billionaire to shame your fellow Jews; you need only embarrass us on the front page of the *New York Times*. That's where "the paper of record" placed an article about author and law professor Alan Dershowitz in the summer of 2018. The precipitating event was his "social shaming" by his Democratic neighbors on Martha's Vineyard who'd stopped inviting him to their parties because they "found his aggressive questioning of the legitimacy of the special counsel investigation into President Trump was indefensible and unforgivable." Adding injury to insult, Dershowitz went on to represent the pedophile Jeffrey Epstein. Then one of Epstein's accusers named Dershowitz as among the men who abused her on Epstein's property, and when the lawyer defended Trump in his Senate impeachment trial, the trifecta caused the editor-in-chief of the Jewish News Syndicate to pronounce in the *New York Jewish Week*, "Alan Dershowitz has finally worn out his welcome in polite liberal society."

Because we give Jewish wrongdoers the power to shame our entire people, Jews seem more likely than other ethnic groups to suffer from guilt by association. So does our God. I base that *chutz-pahdik* claim on the prohibition against Chillul Hashem, which literally means, desecrating or profaning God's name. Chabad.com amplifies the definition as "an act that brings discredit or reflects badly on the Torah, Torah scholars, the Jewish religion, or the Jewish people." The *Jewish-Englilsh Lexicon* calls Chillul Hashem "an action that might make Jews look bad." Reprehensible in the presence of anyone, such behavior constitutes a more serious offense if a Jew "acts in a shameful manner" in front of gentiles, alias goyim. For those of us old enough to be afflicted with post-Holocaust paranoia, the smallest shanda far di goyim looms as large as an existential threat.

The badge of Jewish exceptionalism gleaming on my chest never stopped the ghost of Jewish paranoia from breathing down my neck. Things were either "good for the Jews" or "bad for the Jews." Kermit the Frog famously sang, "It's not easy being green." Transpose the concept to the Jews and the lyric might read, "It's not simple being special." Or theologically "chosen." Special comes with burdens and responsibilities, skewed perceptions, and weird reactions. My friend Gena Raps told me her mother used to count the Jews killed in a plane crash "as if they were the only ones who died." And if the judges eliminated Miss Israel before Miss Germany in a beauty pageant, Gena had to turn off the TV. To me, that's not in the least bit odd; I grew up with similar nareshkeit (nonsense, foolishness). In my house, and the homes of my relatives, objects, products, and brands possessed ethnic identities. The Dodgers were Jewish; the Yankees weren't. Coke was Jewish, Pepsi not. Rowboats yes, sailboats no. Plymouths, Oldsmobiles, and Dodges were Jewish; Fords most definitely not. Thousands of Jews boycotted Henry Ford's cars to protest his anti-Semitic ravings. Until I got to college, I never knew a Jew who owned a Ford and, though France hasn't been as dutiful as Germany in terms of educating their youth about the Nazi period, I once owned a French car but still can't imagine buying a German car. No matter how much I love the looks of the updated Beetle or Mercedes, my inner eye keeps seeing their military siblings in the newsreels Mom and I watched in Times Square during World War II.

My mother was convinced that most Christians (though not our lovely Irish American and Italian American neighbors) were secret anti-Semites who ridiculed Jewish noses and customs while begrudging our prosperity and competence; that the "goyim" envied our tribal loyalty, strong community organizations, and financial resources, while despising us for rejecting Jesus; that they savored every Jewish scandal as if we deserved shaming for daring to demand the right to both live differently and be treated equally. Mom imagined secret cabals of "anti-Semiten" relishing each story of a disgraced Jew as if it were a reason to exterminate us.

For our family to live in the tension between Jewish pride and paranoia required a finely calibrated balancing act. We had to be morally upright, socially useful, and professionally exemplary but not so upright as to appear arrogant, and not so useful that we become a threat to the majority's status and preeminence, not so laudable that we arouse envy and ignite the embers of anti-Semitism. I believe all my immigrant relatives eventually became American citizens, yet some continued to behave like guests in this country, as if their acceptance and security were granted at the sufferance of "real" Americans. If 3500 years of history had taught them anything, it was that Jews could appear to be safe and successful, then suddenly get rounded up and driven out of any place at any time for any reason or no reason at all. Some Jews kept a bag packed and a batch of gold coins in its hidden compartment should they have to bribe their way over the George Washington Bridge or across the Canadian border. Really.

Besides feeling judged by gentiles, we felt monitored by our fellow Jews—family members, teachers, clergy, and communal leaders—who scrutinized us for flaws and pressured us to lead showcase lives. Mordecai Finley, the LA rabbi with the black belt jiu-jitsu, described these as the main precepts Jews are taught in Hebrew school: do not bring embarrassment to our people, don't marry outside the faith, do support Israel, and do know your history. "If you did those four things, and were a good person, you kind of met the spiritual requirement." If you didn't, you were in deep drek (rubbish).

A friend who was raised with six siblings in an ultra-Orthodox home experienced a different set of pressures: "As soon as anyone finds out you have mental illness, sexual abuse, someone in the family going off the derech (correct path), they put black marks against your name. And when you're not from a very wealthy family, those marks mean a lot…. My parents drilled into us that we had to be perfect students, because if we weren't, no other Jewish family would want their children to marry us. Regardless of what was going on in our lives, we knew that unless we got As in everything, we would face severe punishment."

My cousins and I grew up in environments ranging from ultra-Orthodox to fervently secular, yet I sensed that we all felt duty-bound to fulfill the Jewish ideal of excellence and the American ideal of assimilation. When I fell short on either scale, I knew enough to edit the failure out of my story, and when I slammed into the high bar without clearing it, I hid my dents and bruises from public view.

CHAPTER 45

PORTNOY AND ME

Current debates in the literary world about who has the right to depict the feelings and experiences of a particular racial or ethnic group brought me back to Philip Roth and the trauma he caused The Jewish People, myself included, by exposing us to massive shaming before the eyes of the world. In other words, committing a shanda far di goyim.

I remember arguing with friends about Roth's first book, *Goodbye, Columbus*, a collection of stories in which Jewish materialism, vulgarity, and boorishness were writ large. I was trying to persuade my friends of the egregious unfairness of those stereotypes. They were trying to persuade me that this was literature, not character assassination. When *Goodbye, Columbus* won the National Book Award, it was denounced in 1962 by critics at a Yeshiva University symposium at which Roth insisted that American Jews ought to be socioeconomically secure and psychologically confident enough by now to accept stories about our foibles and flaws. But the defamation hurled at him at that event must have hurt because he said he would never again write about Jews. Something changed his mind, obviously, since he subsequently declared, "My humiliation before the Yeshiva belligerents—indeed, the angry Jewish resistance that I aroused virtually from the start—was the luckiest break I could have had…. I was branded." Being marked by the community as a self-hating Jew was liberating for Roth. After surviving the onslaught at Yeshiva, he gave himself permission to produce many more books featuring members of the tribe, most notoriously, a frank, frequently obscene work of fiction that dealt the collective Jewish psyche an even more punishing blow.

Portnoy's Complaint, published in 1969, is written in the form of a series of psychiatric sessions in which young Alexander Portnoy reveals himself to be a total mess—impotent, neurotic, self-absorbed, abusive, a sex-obsessed Jew with a masturbation compulsion. As if all that mishegas weren't sufficiently humiliating to "the Jews," Roth gave his protagonist a dominant, overprotective mother and a constipated, emasculated father of whom Portnoy is deeply ashamed. Portnoy's complaint was that he was "living in the middle of a Jewish joke." But serious Jews didn't find it funny. At all. In the Jewish world, often called, "the mainstream Jewish community," Roth became persona non grata. Portnoy displaced Shylock as the most despised Jewish antihero of all time. Gershom Scholem, the distinguished Israeli philosopher and Kabbala scholar, called the novel "worse than the notorious *Protocols of the Learned Elders of Zion*." Irving Howe, editor of *Dissent* magazine, trashed Roth's writing. "The cruelest thing anyone can do with *Portnoy's Complaint*," Howe quipped, "is to read it twice." The *New Yorker* declared it "one of the dirtiest books ever published."

Oy-oy-oy was all I could say when I read the reviews. Talk about one Jew representing all of us! The brouhaha stirred up by the book registered on me, my family, and friends, as if Roth's public humiliation of the Portnoy family was our personal shanda. Of course, I bought a copy immediately and took it with me to Vermont for a ski weekend. When I was too exhausted to go out on the slopes after lunch, I hunkered down by the fireplace in the lodge to read it, but only after I had removed the book jacket so no one would see what I was holding. I wasn't afraid people would look askance at me for reading a dirty book; by then Americans were openly toting around titles by Anaïs Nin, Henry Miller, Terry Southern, Jean Genet, even the Marquis de Sade, for God's sake. I was afraid of being seen reading *that* dirty book because it was a salacious novel by an acclaimed, highly visible *Jewish*-identified author, about a

Jewish character who could have been my brother, an unmistakably Jewish boy who got his rocks off by masturbating into a slab of raw liver taken from his mother's refrigerator! (Portnoy to his therapist: "So. Now you know the worst thing I have ever done. I fucked my own family's dinner.") I was ashamed to be seen sitting by the fire stewing in my own people's shame.

Other ethnic groups have been embarrassed by their literary standard bearers, to be sure, but there's a difference. Though Italians were not thrilled with *The Godfather* or *The Sopranos*, they were embarrassed as *Italians*, not as Catholics; they worried about sociopathic gangsters and Mafia hit men becoming representative of Italians, not synonymous with Catholics. By the same token, the Irish may have felt publicly embarrassed by Molly Bloom's thirty-six page masturbatory monologue in *Ulysses*, but they felt embarrassed on behalf of Irish prudes and prudishness; they weren't worried about the book unleashing anti-Catholic bigotry or stereotyping all Catholic women as oversexed. Ditto with the Brits and D. H. Lawrence. If the homoeroticism and nonmarital sex in *Women in Love* or the graphic description of the female orgasm in *Lady Chatterley's Lover* upset refined English readers, they were appalled on behalf of rectitudinous British sensibilities; they were not offended as Anglicans, Presbyterians, or Methodists.

Portnoy eventually became an international bestseller, exponentially compounding our shame and offending Jews, both on the level of our peoplehood and religious identification. Though we're a multiracial, multiethnic people descended from Ashkenazi, Mizrachi, Sephardi, Indian, Bukharan, and other cultural backgrounds; though we hold different nationalities; and make our homes in cities as diverse as Paris, Buenos Aires, Johannesburg, Melbourne, and LA, Jews all over the world were nearly unanimous in judging *Portnoy* to be the greatest literary shanda of the twentieth century.

When I gave the manuscript of *Shanda* to my friend Steve Shepard, the author of *A Literary Journey to Jewish Identity*, a book about Jewish American writers in postwar America, he acknowledged my accurate assessment of the Jewish world's negative reaction to *Portnoy* but he countered, with considerable fervor, that "Roth had the last laugh. Not only did *Portnoy* become a huge international best-seller and make Roth independently wealthy, but the book was eventually deemed to be a masterwork of fiction. In 1998, the Modern Library ranked *Portnoy's Complaint* 52nd on its list of the 100 best English-language novels of the 20th century. And in 2005, *Time* magazine named *Portnoy's Complaint* to its top 100 list of English language novels published since 1923. Not exactly a shanda by a self-hating Jew." Steve added that I was entitled to hate the book, but in fairness I should acknowledge how its "reputation evolved to lofty praise in most literary circles." And so I have, by quoting his eloquent defense of it.

Another of Roth's many literary champions, the late Christopher Lehmann-Haupt, then daily book critic at the *New York Times*, called *Portnoy* "brilliantly vivid," and "shockingly recognizable." Thirty years later, when Chris became a friend, I told him that I and my Jewish American family most emphatically did not recognize ourselves in *Portnoy's Complaint*. To this day, I'll read anything by anyone about people or groups I don't know much about. But when a book is about Jews—no matter how well-written, amusing, ironic, postmodern, hyperbolic, or metaphoric, or how deftly the author and his publishers explain his intention or defend his right to invent or opine—I reserve the right to resist the hype. The plethora of Jewish caricatures in Western painting, poetry, novels, essays, or plays is quite enough to sate any cultural appetite. Why would I applaud a work (by a fellow Jew, yet) whose claim to fame is its virtuosic variations on our capacity to debase ourselves?

CHAPTER 46

MY COUSIN, ISRAEL

My sense of safety and belonging as a Jew in America was shattered in 2017 by the White supremacist riot in Charlottesville and Donald Trump's claim that there were "nice people on both sides." Then came a barrage of anti-Semitic hate crimes: The massacre at Pittsburgh's Tree of Life synagogue. The killings in the kosher market in Jersey City. The home invasion on Hanukkah of a rabbi's residence in Monsey. The assaults on Hasidic Jews in Brooklyn. The signs and symbols brandished by the Trump insurrectionists who stormed the Capitol: "Camp Auschwitz." Swastikas. Crusader Crosses. The Proud Boys slogan, "6MWE"—Six Million Wasn't Enough." Not to mention the avalanche of malicious memes and neo-Nazi dog whistles on the internet. And just the other day, the terrifying eleven-hour siege by a hostage taker at a synagogue in Colleyville, Texas.

When it gets really scary, little Bunny takes cover in the cellar of my psyche shouldering the same dread she felt when she was waiting for Hitler to invade Queens. Then I trusted my parents and their fellow air raid wardens to protect us from a shock attack. Now I worry because, before the pandemic my synagogue on the Upper West Side, a neighborhood synonymous with Jewish New York, posted at our front door a small gray-haired gentleman who checked everyone's backpacks with a flashlight while shuls all over the country were conducting active-shooter drills and hiring armed guards to buttress police security patrols. On the High Holy Days, with a thousand Jewish worshippers inside and only two NYPD cops assigned to us, I felt exposed and vulnerable. Before COVID, when we were still attending shabbat services in person, I found myself gravitating to a seat close to an exit. And after news broke that the feds had foiled a terrorist plot against a Jewish Federation in the Midwest, I thought twice about attending an event at the Manhattan JCC, where concrete barricades already sprout like mushrooms from the sidewalk to protect the building against a car bomb. Suddenly, grim questions that would have been unthinkable five years ago pushed to the front of my paranoid reveries: Where will they hit next—a Jewish wedding, conference, senior center, day camp, kosher restaurant? How bad does it have to get before we pack up and leave? Where would we go? How would we persuade our kids and grandkids to go with us?

As if those concerns weren't chilling enough, I became increasingly troubled by a newly energized, if ancient, phenomenon that, in its way, was as alarming as the spike in anti-Semitic violence. I'm referring to attacks *on* Jews *by* Jews, or, in the words of Jeffrey Goldberg, editor of *The Atlantic*, "the intimate-enemy problem."

The problem crystalized for me when a number of Jewish intellectuals and pundits vilified Peter Beinart, a gifted writer, political analyst, and all-around "credit to our people"—Yale graduate, Rhodes scholar, former editor of the *New Republic*, professor at CUNY, contributor to prestigious periodicals, observant Jew who attends an Orthodox synagogue and sends his children to a Jewish day school—for the article he published in 2010 in the *New York Review of Books* and expanded in his book *The Crisis of Zionism*. His crime was to critique Israeli policies in the West Bank and condemn the American Jewish Establishment for its knee-jerk support of Israel's government regardless of the morality of its actions. At that point Beinart identified as a liberal Zionist, and in the interest of the Jewish State, he warned the American Jewish community that our youth were feeling increasingly alienated from Israel because they could not reconcile their progressive liberalism with the increasingly hardline Zionism of their elders.

A barrage of acid-barbed arrows came at Beinart from all directions: "Why does he hate Israel so?" asked Daniel Gordis, a conservative, in the *Jerusalem Post*, before offering his own answer, that "Beinart's problem isn't really with Israel. It's with Judaism." Bret Stephens, then a columnist for the *Wall Street Journal*, called the book "an act of moral solipsism." Jonathan Rosen, an editor and novelist, writing in the *New York Times Book* Review, accused Beinart of employing "formulations favored by antisemites." Jeffrey Goldberg, of *The Atlantic*, said, rather than "devise ways to get Israel to do what he wants," Beinart chose instead to "make himself feel good about his moral superiority." Summing up the ad hominem onslaught, *New Yorker* editor, David Remnick correctly observed, "There is a big difference between critiquing Peter Beinart's book on the basis of what you might think of his argument and attacking Peter Beinart personally."

In 2014, I was the target of a mini version of the personal assault on Peter. It happened at a political meeting in Midtown Manhattan. I'd just finished signing the attendance sheet when the woman at the registration table, noticing my name, suddenly shouted, "Letty Cottin Pogrebin!" in a voice loud enough to summon a taxi. Then, wagging her finger in my face, she snarled, "Why are you trying to destroy The Jewish People?"

"Excuse me?" I'd never met the woman before and the meeting was about pro-choice Democratic candidates not about Jews, yet she kept yelling that I was an "enemy of Israel," a "traitor to The Jewish People," and a "self-hating Jew." Kids in my old Queens neighborhood responded to name-calling with, "Sticks and stones can break my bones, but words can never hurt me!" The woman didn't hurt me; she scared me. No Jew had ever looked at me with that much hate.

It took me a while to deduce the source of her wrath: an open letter to Mayor Bill de Blasio published in the *New York Times* in which I and fifty other progressive Jewish activists had objected to the mayor having met with leaders of AIPAC, the Israel lobby, and promised them that "City Hall will always be open to you because that's my job." Our letter stated that pandering to lobbyists for a foreign country appears nowhere in the mayor's job description. I assured my hot-headed adversary that I would be equally critical of de Blasio had he promised an Arab American group privileged access to lobby him on behalf of the Palestinians. That neither satisfied nor stopped her. She continued her harangue as if shaming me in front of everyone within earshot would inoculate me against ever again expressing an opinion about AIPAC, Israel, The Jewish People, or anything else. Her strategy—to silence by vilification—has become distressingly familiar.

I survived more than my share of scabrous sexist vilification in the early days of the women's movement, so I'm pretty impervious to personal attacks. As I did in response to antifeminist smears, I try to meet hostility about my views on the Middle East, whether from the left or right, with as much reason and dignity as I can muster. If a fellow Jew accuses me of condemning Israel's treatment of the Palestinians while ignoring other nations' egregious human rights records, I explain that, though I follow world news, Israel is the only country besides my own whose actions affect me viscerally and since I'm a citizen of the US and a soul mate of the State of Israel, I choose to make those two countries my priority. If a fellow Jew asks me how come there are no Palestinians as critical of their people's misconduct as I am of Israel's misconduct, I say, many Palestinians have called out corruption in the Palestinian Authority or bad acts by Arab extremists, but the media only pay attention to Palestinians when they ramp up the violence. My question is, why should Palestinians have to act morally before I can pass judgment on Jews who don't?

If a fellow Jew accuses me of focusing disproportionately on Israel's political missteps rather than taking pride in the miracle of the nation's technological and scientific achievements, I tell them I'm immensely proud of Israeli innovation and many other things about the Jewish State. To name a few, the fact that per capita it leads the world in university degrees, PhDs, physicians, engineers, museums, orchestras, books read and published; and it's the only country in the Middle East where Christians, Muslims, and Jews are all free to vote, and women and homosexuals enjoy full political rights. However, what a country does right, however impressive, must not be used to whitewash what it does wrong.

I feel entitled to criticize Israel not just on the grounds of free speech but because I think of Israelis "as family." That phrase used to sound corny coming out of my mouth until I learned from a national survey that more than 70 percent of Jews in the US employ the same metaphor. The poll conducted in 2019 by the American Jewish Committee found that 13 percent of US Jews consider Israeli Jews as siblings, 15 percent see them as first cousins, and 43 percent as extended family. When I was small and my dad was always rushing off to meetings, I thought he loved Zionism more than he loved me. You might say Israel was my sibling rival. But on May 14, 1948, a month before my ninth birthday, when the UN declared Israel a state, and my parents and I literally danced in the street outside the Jamaica Jewish Center, the new nation and its hardy pioneers acquired a utopian glow and a familial connection. Israel and I grew up together. I witnessed its wonders and worried through its wars. And, over time, as its flaws and misdeeds became widely known and could no longer be explained away, I felt about Israel as I would about a cousin I love but whose behavior troubles me deeply, a cousin I believe can do better.

These fulminations came to a boil in 2018 when the Israeli Knesset passed the "Nation-State Law," which, with the stroke of a pen, diminished the civil rights of the country's non-Jewish *citizens* and demoted Arabic from its formerly equal status with Hebrew as an official language of the state. When the law was first proposed, Mordechai Kremnitzer, former dean of Hebrew University Law School and a senior fellow at The Israel Democracy Institute, expressed the opinion of many Jews around the world when he said, "This is not a deed worthy of being called legislation, this is an aberrant use of the arbitrary force of the majority to deliberately harm the minority. If this is allowed to pass, we won't have anywhere to hide our shame."

Once the bill became law, Kremnitzer went on the radio, broke down in tears, and said he was "ashamed as a Zionist patriot." Passage of the Nation-State Law also became a breaking point for Avrum Burg, an Israeli with impeccable Zionist credentials. The son of the Orthodox rabbi who founded the National Religious Party and represented the NRP in the Israeli Cabinet, Burg himself was a former leader of the Labor Party, speaker of the Israeli Knesset, and chair of The Jewish Agency. Referring to the new law, Burg declared that non-Jews "will suffer from having an inferior status, similar to what the Jews suffered for untold generations. *What is abhorrent to us, we are now doing to our non-Jewish citizens.*" (Emphasis added.) His abject shame at this erosion of fundamental democratic rights drove Burg in 2020 to petition the Israeli Supreme Court to do something unthinkable just a few years before: he asked them to rescind his national status as a Jew. Like Kremnitzer and Burg, many Jews around the world feel personally shamed by the Knesset's brazen contradiction of the bedrock principles contained in the nation's Declaration of Independence, its foundational document, which explicitly guarantees that the State of Israel "will ensure complete equality of social and political rights to all its inhabitants irrespective of religion, race, or sex." *Complete equality.*

The Nation-State Law also violates sacred Jewish texts. It flies in the face of "You shall not oppress the stranger for you were strangers in the land of Egypt," the only commandment in the Torah that is repeated thirty-six times. It flouts one of the most powerful edicts in the Book of Deuteronomy, "*Tzedek tzedek tirdof*" (Justice justice shalt thou pursue). If, as believing Jews maintain, nothing in the Torah is superfluous and every word is there for a reason, then neither the doubling of the powerful noun "justice" nor the choice of the action verb "pursue" is accidental. As one young social activist put it, "The Torah is jumping up and down and waving its arms at us" to underscore something basic to the ethos of Judaism: that it is not enough for Jews to pray for, long for, commit to, or espouse justice. We must *pursue* it until every injustice is obliterated. With these texts and this heritage, I cannot understand how any Jew could *not* be ashamed of Israel's Nation-State Law, which blatantly reifies unconscionable acts committed by our people against another people whose powerlessness and yearning for self-determination should remind us of our own.

Painful as it is to criticize a beloved family member, I find it harder to stand on the sidelines while the state that began as a gleam in the eyes of its founders, and the people whom God intended to become a "light unto the nations" continue to stumble into the dark night of a xenophobic theocracy. Just as a cousin's misdeeds are more disquieting to us than the misdeeds of a stranger, it's inevitable for a Jew like me to experience greater distress when Israel violates its democratic ideals than when, say, Poland or Venezuela does something patently autocratic. And just as I never mistook the Trump administration for "the American people," I refused to conflate Israel's right-wing governments with "the Israelis" or "The Jewish People." I'm with Mark Twain who said, "The only rational patriotism is loyalty to the Nation all the time, loyalty to the Government when it deserves it."

<hr />

The late David Hartman, a revered American Israeli rabbi, writer, philosopher, and founder of the Hartman Institute, once advised Jews who live in the diaspora, "When you criticize Israel, do it like a mother, not a mother-in-law." I take his point. Most mothers criticize out of love with the goal of improving their children. I don't mean to stereotype mothers-in-law since I *am* one, but it stands to reason that, compared to one's mother, a mother-in-law's motives may be less pure. When I criticize Israel's shandas—be it the IDF's dehumanizing treatment of Palestinians, the racist or undemocratic laws passed by the Knesset, or the unchecked power of ultra-Orthodox rabbis to decide who may marry whom or pray at the Western Wall—I do it from a place of love. My shame is an expression of the values I learned from my faith and my family.

And those values do not permit me to stand idly by when proponents of Israel-right-or-wrong attack their ideological opponents as enemies of the state or self-hating Jews, or employ other shaming epithets to stifle the free exchange of ideas.

In 2021, Israel's military chief of staff, Lt. Gen. Aviv Kochavi, recalled the disastrous results of Jews' lack of solidarity in the distant past. Referring to the armies of the future Roman emperor, he said: "While Titus's troops gathered outside Jerusalem, the Jewish fighters refused to unite within, and when factionalism prevailed over patriotism, the Romans prevailed over the Jews." Faced with contemporary White supremacists such as David Duke and Richard Spencer, or Jew-hating acolytes of Louis Farrakhan, now is not the time for us to be setting each other on fire. If factional rifts continue to divide our ranks, we will soon find ourselves incapable of unity and solidarity against today's equivalents of the Romans and the very real threat they pose to our rights, safety, and someday, God forbid, our lives.

CHAPTER 47

BUSHA V'CHARPA

The first thing you notice when you land at Ben Gurion Airport is that Israelis have no use for rudimentary etiquette. I'm generalizing, obviously, but after more than two dozen trips to the region, I can attest that the average Israeli thinks nothing of pushing ahead of you in line, jostling you at the baggage carousel, and growling, "*Yalla! Yalla!*" (Arabic for "Get going!" yet omnipresent in colloquial Hebrew) should you not be moving fast enough to suit them. No wonder international tourists routinely describe Israelis as "smug," "judgmental," "brash," "rude," "brusque," and "arrogant."

I'm not making this up. Take a minute to google "Impolite Israelis" and you'll get more than two million results. "Israelis are blunt and rude. You got a problem with that?" is the tagline on a Jewish Telegraph Agency article by Sam Sokol, who writes, "It is not unheard of to be boarding a bus and watch ticketed passengers duck under the arms of a rider who had the temerity to slow them down by paying the driver cash. Or to be approached by a random stranger who, after talking with you for five minutes, asks why you immigrated, how many children you have, and how much you earn. On Israeli roads, a turn signal is not a sign of intent but of weakness. The Israelis' reputation as a rude, abrasive or merely boundary-less people has made its way around the world…. Famously, in 2015, the tech firm Intel presented its employees with a guide to working with Israelis that warned them to 'expect to be cut off regularly' and that 'visitors are often taken aback by the tone or loudness of the discussion.'"

Israeli behavior is often defended on the grounds of "cultural difference," in this case the difference that comes from living in a hostile neighborhood and having been attacked so often. It also explains why the name for a native-born Israeli, "sabra," is taken from the Hebrew for the prickly pear cactus, a fruit with a tough, thorny outside and a soft, sweet inside. Having known several Israeli sabras, I can attest to the sweetness beneath their barbs. Recently, I asked one of them if he considered the rudeness of Israelis to be a shanda far di goyim?

"What's a shanda?" he replied. That threw me since it's one of many Yiddish words—like schlep, schmuck, or chutzpah—that show up in print and conversation all the time. "A 'Shanda' on America" was the headline on a *Huffington Post* story about hunger. An editorial note in the *Washington Post* posited that "International Monetary Fund chief Dominique Strauss-Kahn might be a 'Shanda for the Goyim.'" [sic] When Peggy Noonan, a columnist for the *Wall Street Journal* and an Irish-Catholic, learned that the stained-glass windows picturing Stonewall Jackson and Robert E. Lee would be removed from the Washington National Cathedral, she tweeted, "A Shonda!" Writer Fiona Adorno tweeted back at Noonan, "The only Shonda is your usage of a Yiddish word to defend idolatry of #WhiteSupremacists. Stick with English. They prefer it." John Stoehr, a contributing editor at *U.S. News & World Report*, tweeted that the removal of the windows is "not a shonda. 'Jews will not replace us' that's a shonda."

At Brett Kavanaugh's Supreme Court nomination hearings, a rabbi who teaches at Fordham University shouted from the visitors' gallery, "It's a shanda!" A December 2019 editorial in the *Daily News* blared, "A Shanda: Shame on some Midwood Jews raising racially insensitive alarms about a charter school in the neighborhood." A few days after the 2020 election, Michigan Congresswoman Elissa Slotkin, discussing the split between moderates and progressives in the Democratic party, told *Politico*, "While I disagree with a lot of people in my party, I still have a lot in common with them. And it would be what we call in Yiddish, a shanda, a shame, a deep shame, if internal politics led to a strategic opening for these completely anti-democratic forces." And in January 2022, nighttime TV host Stephen Colbert used *shanda* twice in his opening monologue.

Since the media use the word with the expectation of it being understood by most people, including non-Jews, I had assumed that a Jew from New York could say shanda to a sabra in Tel Aviv and be understood. I was wrong. Turns out that Israel is the one place on earth where shanda is seldom heard except among elderly Ashkenazi Jews or the *haredim* (ultra-Orthodox), for whom Yiddish is their first language. (It's rare for a Sephardic Jew to speak Yiddish.) When Israelis describe shame, disgrace, dishonor, ignominy, or reproach, they use the Hebrew word for shame, *busha* (pronounced *boo*-sha), often coupled with the word charpa, which means disgrace, to give it more oomph. Spoken together, *busha v'charpa*, means "Shame, shame!" or "What a disgrace!" wrote Shoshana Kordova, in her "Word for the Day" column in the English language edition of the Israeli newspaper, *Haaretz*. Israelis use two words that mean the same thing in order to "intensify the effect," and it works in all contexts; witness these examples taken from Israeli media: a politician declared the paltry amount of the government's old-age benefits to be a busha v'charpa. A blogger wrote that it was a busha v'charpa for the government to give priority funding to settlements in the West Bank rather than to poor villages in the Negev. And the season finale of Israel's version of *American Idol* was called a busha y'charpa because the reviewer thought the wrong singer won. "Whether something is a crying shame or a singing one," Kordova wrote, "it's not truly disgraceful unless you double the dose."

Intrigued by her reporting, I called and asked why she thought native Hebrew speakers use busha to mean shame in a Jewish context, whereas Jews all over the world, regardless of their native language, use shanda?

"It's because Israeli Jews equate the shanda with the power-lessness of their parents and grandparents. Israelis aren't in exile; they're in power, and they've shed that old Yiddish/exilic mentality in favor of a new Hebrew/Israeli mentality."

I'm a big fan of the Hebrew/Israeli mentality when it comes to their grit, gumption, enterprise, humor, and self-confidence. But not when that mentality gives rise to arrogance and boorishness. Think about it: the average Israeli is perceived as rude and insolent. Recent Israeli governments have been known for their disdain for international law and their oppression of Palestinians. Israel's former and longest-serving prime minister, Benjamin Netanyahu, welcomed an overtly racist party into his governing coalition. At this writing, he stands indicted for bribery, fraud, and breach of trust. He was, and remains, unapologetic about cozying up to tyrannical dictators like Victor Orbán in Hungary, Jair Bolsonaro in Brazil, and Rodrigo Duterte in the Philippines. To me and most American Jews, that's a shanda. Most Israeli Jews tolerated it. Which makes me wonder if the absence from daily Hebrew parlance of the judgmental word *shanda* might signify that the "new Israeli mentality" includes the inability to be ashamed.

The late Amos Oz, Israeli's premier novelist, wrote in his final essay collection, *Dear Zealots*, "I am afraid of the fanaticism and the violence which are becoming increasingly prevalent in Israel, and I am also ashamed of them." Despite that harsh condemnation, Oz added, "I like being a citizen of a country where there are eight and a half million prime ministers, eight and a half million prophets, eight and a half million messiahs. Each of us has our own personal formula for redemption.... Everyone shouts, and few listen. It's never boring here."

That's my experience of Israel. It's never boring. Israeli Jews have the freedom to be loud, surly, arrogant, and pushy, which clearly is a great relief from the bad old days when their ancestors had to mind their manners, defer, even step off the sidewalk to let a gentile pass. I'm not saying all Israelis are boors. I'm just agreeing with Jules Michelet, the nineteenth-century historian, who observed, "The most intimate temper of a people, its deepest soul, is above all in its language." Further, I'm suggesting that the widespread incivility experienced by visitors to the country and attested to in millions of Google comments should be viewed as symptomatic of the coarsening of Israel's fundamental character. The fact that the word *shanda* has fallen into disuse might explain why Israelis feel the need to use two words when they want to make clear that they're *really* ashamed.

I'm proud of many Jews for many things—especially our active participation (in far greater numbers than our proportion of the population) in the early civil rights movement, our current resistance to Islamophobia, and our noteworthy generosity to philanthropic causes beyond those that redound to our self-interest. But I'm ashamed of Jews who suppress free expression and punish people for what they believe. It's as simple as that. Fear of shame has served The Jewish People for three millennia as a preemptive censor of bad behavior. I can't help seeing its disappearance from Israeli discourse as a red flag. Maybe Hebrew speakers need to drop busha and bring back shanda if only to keep their lesser angels in check.

CHAPTER 48

SOME SECRETS SAVE LIVES

I still have Holocaust nightmares. Correction: I have one Holocaust nightmare that invades my sleep every three or four years and nearly does me in. Though born and raised in the United States, I come by my hauntings honestly. Hitler murdered 65 percent of the Jews of Europe, among them one-third of my parents' European relatives.

I knew nothing about those people until 1992 when my sister Betty organized a Halpern family reunion at a hotel in Alexandria, Virginia, where, as a result of her research, we all learned the names of our close kin who were killed between the late-1930s through the end of the Second World War. Long before Ancestry.com was invented, Betty pieced together our genealogy and posted across two walls of the hotel's meeting room large sheets of poster paper on which she had drawn a family tree far more complex than the one my father scratched in the sand. Thanks to her efforts, I learned that Grandpa Nathan—who was born Nechemiah in 1877 in Skole, Poland, and who seemed to me to embody the quintessential Ashkenazi—was actually a direct descendant of a Sephardic Jew exiled from Spain in 1492. But the most stunning takeaway from Betty's chart was the graphic proof, visible from across the room, that most of our relatives who immigrated to the US or Palestine in the early twentieth century survived and had branches on their family trees with lots of twigs, while almost everyone who stayed in Europe perished, their branches dead-ending in tragedy:

Beile and Godel—killed with their two children by peasants in Rozanka

Chana and Misha—killed with two children in ghetto of Lvov

Meier, Iser & Chaker—lost in Holocaust

Jonah—died of starvation while hiding in a bunker in mountains near Skole

Samuel—murdered by peasants in Rozanka

Zlata—died of starvation with mother and infant child

Pinchas and Reizel and two children—taken from ghetto by Ukrainian police and shot

Basia, daughter Frida, son Lieb taken from ghetto in Stryj and killed summer of 1943

Milo—beaten to death

Nehemiah—perished with wife, two sons, one daughter in the liquidation of Stryj ghetto

Yisrael—came out of hiding in the forest to buy food and was strangled to death by neighbor

Gittle, Yosel, Moishe, Aaron & entire families—murdered by Nazis

Joseph, Wolf, Jennie, Shalom, Tzudic & entire families—killed in the Holocaust

Brief as they were, Betty's notations tore a hole in my heart. Had my grandparents not immigrated to New York in the first decade of the twentieth century, I might have been born in Poland in 1939, three months before Hitler invaded the country. I might have been among the babies hidden in the forest. My mother might have run out of breast milk. I could have cried incessantly. My parents could have been forced to strangle me as many did to keep their children's cries from revealing the hiding place of the group with whom they'd found refuge. Or I could have died of starvation. Again, I digress, but this time to give a shout-out to the secrecy that enables survival.

In ordinary circumstances, we resort to secrecy to conceal something we consider shameful, to avoid disgrace, or to protect people from information we believe would be hurtful to them. Or we hide our weaknesses to appear more likable, lovable, or employable. However, in extraordinary circumstances—such as war, deportation, or occupation—secrets, concealment, and cover-ups saved lives. I need not elaborate here beyond stating the obvious: during the Third Reich, Jews hid or were hidden, obtained false papers, buried their belongings, and kept secrets, their own and other people's. And "righteous gentiles," at great risk to their own and their families' lives, secretly harbored Jews or helped them escape SS roundups. (I've always been grateful to people like Varian Fry, the affluent Protestant who, as a volunteer for the Emergency Rescue Committee, secretly rescued more than two thousand Jews from Nazi-occupied France, among them, Hannah Arendt, Arthur Koestler, Jacques Lipschitz, Max Ernst, Marc Chagall, Marcel Duchamp, Alma Mahler, Claude Levi-Strauss, and Max Ophüls.)

When the Nazis invaded France in 1940, Marcel Mangel, a sixteen-year-old Jew, Christianized his name, joined the French Resistance, and helped evacuate hundreds of children from a Jewish orphanage in Eastern France by masquerading as a Boy Scout and guiding them to safety in Switzerland. He told the kids he was taking them on vacation in the Alps and kept them quiet during their clandestine journeys by entertaining them with stories he mimed silently. That "Boy Scout" became the world-famous pantomime artist Marcel Marceau, whose father, also a member of the Resistance, was captured by the Gestapo and deported to Auschwitz, where he was murdered. After the war, Marceau said, "The people who came back from the camps were never able to talk about it. My name is Mangel. I am Jewish. Perhaps that, unconsciously, contributed toward my choice of silence."

Secrecy, as a strategy, didn't end when the war ended; it took different forms. Survivor guilt led many to conceal themselves, not behind a false name or a false cabinet, but behind a thick wall of silence, convinced that they could not rejoin the civilized world and lead near-normal lives unless they blotted out the past and reinvented themselves anew. "We were coming to a new country and starting a new life and they thought they were being protective," is how Madeleine Albright explained her parents' decision to hide their Jewish identity and hers. As noted earlier, only when she was being vetted for the post of secretary of state did she learn her parents' secret and the fact that many of her relatives had perished in the Holocaust.

Some survivors felt so mortified by what happened to them, so ashamed of what they'd been forced by their captors to do to others, or so traumatized by the brutality they'd witnessed, that they willed themselves into a self-protective amnesia. They papered over the past or took liberties with the truth. Some could not, or would not, speak at all about the horrors they'd endured in ghettos, work camps, and death camps. Memories were repressed. Murdered children sealed in the aspic of love. New families created. Suffering and humiliation tamped down and repurposed as resilience and strength. Women "forgot" rape and sexual slavery. Men "forgot" having been *kapos*. Children "forgot" a hunger fierce enough to make them steal a crust of bread from a dying parent. American-born offspring grew up in the midst of these hard-won silences, the firewall their parents erected against those blistering memories. While the survivors remained mute, the aftereffects of their suffering reverberated by night, escaping as wordless screams that terrified spouses and children alike. But screams don't translate into stories, and without stories, imagination and nightmares fill in the blanks.

Jews all over America, including my parents and their friends, felt helpless as the CARE packages they sent to their European relatives were returned, stamped "Recipient unknown." When the truth about the Final Solution became known in all its grisly detail, many could not bear to know what they did not know. Riddled with guilt for not having done more to save their kin, some maintained that Roosevelt's unwillingness to bomb the train tracks to Auschwitz, and his concern that the war against Hitler not become seen as a "Jewish war," made it impossible for Jewish Americans do anything more than they did. Assistant Secretary of State Breckenridge Long obstructed efforts to rescue Jewish refugees, drastically curtailed immigration, and stirred up Americans' fear of foreigners by inflating the number of refugees already admitted. (Sound familiar?) Father Coughlin, the rabidly anti-Semitic Catholic priest who had a radio audience of thirty million until 1939 when his program was forced off the air, continued publishing Jew-hating screeds throughout the war years. Some Jews cited those stumbling blocks to buttress their claim that the American Jewish community had done everything humanly possible to save their European sisters and brothers. Those who, in the 1930s and '40s, were afraid to make demands on their political leaders, carried their guilt into the '50s and '60s. Some converted their shame into blame and began asking questions aloud that used to be forbidden: How could Jews go like lambs to the slaughter? Why didn't more of them fight back? Is there something innate in us that makes us weak—a passivity gene, an unhealthy fatalism that smothers the will to resist?

In his book *The Informed Heart*, Viennese psychoanalyst Bruno Bettelheim, a Jew, asserted that instead of hiding in the secret annex for two years, Anne Frank and her compatriots could have "provided themselves with a gun or two had they wished. They could have shot down at least one or two of the 'green police' who came for them...they could have sold their lives dearly instead of walking to their death." Historian Raul Hilberg, author of *The Destruction of the European Jews*, wrote, "During the catastrophe of 1933-45, the instances of [Jewish] opposition were small and few [and] they were actions of last (never first) resort." In *Eichmann in Jerusalem*, Hannah Arendt famously accused Jews of collaborating in their own destruction, calling their response to the Nazis "pathetic and sordid." An emaciated survivor summed up the reaction of his cohort to the American army's liberation of Dachau: When a G.I entered the camp and, with great excitement, shouted in Yiddish,

"You're free! I'm a Jew and you're free!" the prisoner spat in his face and said, "You're too late."

Jews didn't talk much about the Holocaust after the war. Grateful simply for the accident of their antecedents having left Europe for the New World before the conflagration, American Jews concentrated on becoming "real" Americans. Or they identified with the pioneering spirit and military triumphs of the European Jews who created Israel rather than those who perished under Hitler's boot. Six million! Six *million!* For some, the sheer enormity of the victim headcount was—dare I say it—embarrassing, as if the number itself amounted to a humiliating shanda far di goyim. They asked each other how could millions of Jewish men be so emasculated that they didn't even *try* to fight back? How could so many Jews dig their own graves or walk meekly into the gas chambers? To me, those are unspeakable questions. Yet people speak them. Or pose them in a more tepid form: Why didn't more of them resist?— accent on "more," focus on "them." *Them* as opposed to *us.* It must have been *their* ghetto mentality that made our European cousins docile and compliant, whereas *we,* the assertive, indomitable Jews of the New World, would have fought back. Oh, really? Welcome to my quadrennial Holocaust nightmare.

I'm in a sweltering cattle car with fifty other prisoners and my three children. We're packed together like stalks of asparagus, the fetid breath of my neighbors is the air I breathe. So tightly have their bodies pinned my arms to my sides that I can't reach down to pick up my toddler son, who is wedged between my knees, clutching my tattered skirt, wailing. My twin daughters are moaning, crammed against my thighs as I frantically twist my shoulders and hips trying to make space around their tiny bodies so they won't be crushed. But the prisoners push back. Sometime during the night, my son and daughters stop crying. I feel each of them, one by one, go limp against my legs. Daylight stabs through the slats of the car. The train lurches to a stop. Its massive doors slide open. A squad of stone-faced SS men advances across the platform toward their human freight, rifles poised, bayonets mounted, blades gleaming in the sun. I stumble out with the rest of the living corpses, leaving behind, like three heaps of rags, my children.

That's when I wake up drenched in sweat.

"Why didn't more of them resist?" is just another way of saying, "The next time my people are threatened, I won't cower and cave like a ghetto Jew. I'll fight like an American. Better yet, like an Israeli, one of those suntanned IDF officers in crew cuts or ponytails who know their way around an Uzi." Sounds great. If it wasn't a dream. The Holocaust didn't happen because so many Jews lost their courage but because so many Christians lost their humanity. Only a fool would replace a nightmare with a delusion.

I've always been in awe of those who emerged alive from the real-life cauldron of my nightmare and re-created themselves anew. Here's my question for those American Jews who remonstrate against their forebears' perceived passivity: Exactly how would *you* have fought back? Tell me how you would have saved yourself and your children? Would you have run off and joined the partisans, leaving three kids under five to fend for themselves? If not, then how, with three children in tow, would you have evaded the SS roundup and escaped your captors? Where would you get a weapon? Without one, how would you overpower an armed guard? Rather than feel ashamed of Jews who did not fight back, put yourself in that cattle car and tell me a story with a happy ending. Otherwise, quit blaming the victims.

CHAPTER 49

THE MOUSE THAT ROARED

My speaking voice has embarrassed me since puberty. It's one thing to talk like Minnie Mouse when you're four or five, something else entirely when you're thirty, fifty, or seventy. To this day, upon hearing my chirpy "Hello" on the phone, callers who don't know me say, "May I speak to your mommy?"

For as long as I can remember, the sound coming out of my mouth has contradicted the person I am or imagine myself to be. Metaphorically, if the eyes are windows to the soul, the voice must be its window treatment. To push the parallel, if baritones or bass tones are heavy damask drapes, a contralto is a lace panel, and a mezzo soprano is a swag of organdy, my voice is a ruffled café curtain imprinted with Pooh bears.

Friends old enough to remember the golden age of radio have likened my tonal quality to that of Fanny Brice playing Baby Snooks. "You sound so cute," they tell me, as if that were a compliment. When I'm intent on being taken seriously, the last thing I want to sound is cute. I've tried hard to modulate my pitch, but after lassoing a few sentences into the lower register, I inevitably regress and before long, my reedy tones have broken free and galloped back up the scale.

As problems go, a high-pitched voice does not rank anywhere near hunger or poverty, but having such a voice can be, and has been, humiliating for someone like me who earns a portion of her living as a public speaker. I'm thinking of a long-ago political meeting where I delivered a passionate address about women's issues. When I finished, Flo Kennedy, the clever, sharp-tongued, black feminist lawyer, yelled from the back of the room: "Who *was* that? The mouse that roared?"

At one High Holy Day service, the actress Tovah Feldshuh, who happened to be sitting in the pew in front of me, must have gotten an earful of my high-pitched prayers, because at the end of the prayers, she smiled and remarked that my voice was "unique."

"That's one way of putting it," I replied.

She said I might have a future in voice-overs. Had I ever done commercials? I said I had not. She generously offered to refer me to her agent. *Why not monetize Minnie?* I thought, and called up the agent, who had me make a demo tape and dispatched me to several auditions. I found it demeaning to sit in a waiting room with a dozen other women, all with high-pitched voices, all memorizing the same scripts, but I was soon cast in a commercial, a radio ad for a bank, which required me to scream for several seconds at the top of my lungs. My next callback was for a voice-over that made good use of my "unique" sound; that time, I was cast as an animated sock who explains to its owner why it would prefer to be laundered with XYZ fabric softener. After those two experiences, I retired from "the business," and my voice hasn't earned me a penny since.

Voice is both a noun and a verb, a thing and an act, a sound and a symbol. How we speak, and how we use our voice, is as revealing of our thoughts and feelings as any other form of body language. The voice doesn't just give acoustic reality to words, it's a physicalized expression of who we are. Self-help gurus and writing teachers tell their students to "find your voice." Activists and journalists promise "to give voice to the voiceless." Politicians say things like, "We must speak in one voice." Or, "I'll be your voice in Congress." References abound to the passive voice, the dissenting voice, the people's voice, the Voice of America. What fascinates me, and what few seem to recognize, is how voice and shame self-reflect. People who feel shamed don't shout; they whisper. Or they lose their voice altogether.

Ten years after she was drugged and raped at the University of Michigan, Lucy Dhegrae, a professional vocalist, was performing a postmodern composition of sharp sibilant sounds that revived the trauma of her college assault, and from that moment on, she couldn't sing. Her voice teacher advised her not to let anyone know about her affliction, a partial paralysis of her vocal cords. If she didn't keep it secret, the truth could end her career.

"It was like going through the rape again," Dhegrae recalled in an interview. "'Hide this thing that happened to you; don't talk to anyone about it.' You are dealing with this huge personal crisis but feeling shamed about it and completely alone." The singer undertook multiple therapies, psychological, physiological, and meditative, but what most influenced her recovery were scientific articles about sexual assault victims who also had vocal disorders but were able to regain their singing voices after they literally "gave voice" to their violent experiences. She also found a teacher who understood that trauma can be "embedded in the body," namely the vocal cords. Dhegrae regained her voice through a conscientious process of empowerment. She took krav maga, an Israeli self-defense method in which she shouted "No!" repeatedly, an exercise that inspired Caleb Burhans' musical work, "no," performed on video by Dhegrae and featuring six minutes of her newly resonant voice intoning that powerful one-syllable word over and over and over again.

I'm often called upon to give public talks, which I enjoy doing, though acutely aware of the gulf between what I say and how I sound. When my subject is feminism, Judaism, family politics, American politics, or the Israeli-Palestinian conflict, some listeners experience the sort of cognitive dissonance one might expect were Angela Merkel to deliver a foreign policy speech in the voice of a Teletubby. Audiences don't expect gravitas from a voice like mine.; the sonic shock demands that I work twice as hard to gain my listeners' full attention and respect. When I was young and worried about other people's reactions, I used to wear a blazer and high heels to convey the seriousness my voice lacks. Now I depend on my advanced age to command attention and my words themselves to earn respect. Finally heeding the advice Mom gave me in kindergarten, I refuse to be ashamed of something that's not my fault.

CHAPTER 50

OF ALL HER WISHES, ONLY THIS ONE CAME TRUE

Speech and language can be a locus of shame or pride, an engine of unity, or a reason for self-imposed isolation. While I was embarrassed by the tenor and pitch of my voice, my grandparents were ashamed because their heavy Yiddish accents marked them as greenhorns. Rather than hazard being ridiculed or misunderstood, they stopped trying to communicate in English except when it was necessary to relate their most rudimentary needs. Otherwise, they turned off, dropped out, and let their assimilated children and grandchildren speak for them. Without English, they became almost invisible to most unilingual Americans and unknowable to me and my cousins.

These days, the sound of Yiddish, so richly expressive and thick on the tongue, evokes my early family life and gives me pleasure, but as a child I experienced it as the language of loss and fear, dirty jokes and family secrets. My parents, aunts, and uncles spoke the *mamaloshen* (mother tongue) to each other when they wanted to hide from us kids a humiliating experience, an illness, a death, or during wartime a battleground defeat of Allied forces or news about the death camps. When I asked Mom to translate something I'd heard, she would wave me off: "You're American, you don't need Yiddish; this isn't the Old Country"—meaning the place where bad things happened to good Jews. Her response to my request that we take a family vacation in Europe: "Why would I go back? I'm lucky we escaped with our lives."

Immigrant Jews didn't need non-Jews to ridicule their accented speech; they ridiculed each other. Decades after they landed on Ellis Island, relatives of mine were still criticizing family members or friends for "sounding Jewish." How does "Jewish sound?" Like Jackie Mason. A Jew who spoke good English was considered a rung above, a great catch for one's daughter, a worthy spokesperson for the collective. How did "good English" sound? Like Abba Eban.

(Similar in-group bias operated among Blacks, except they judged their own kind not on the metrics of speech but of skin color. Well into the twentieth century, upper-class African American social clubs, professional societies, and economic elites used a visual test to determine whether a person was light enough to be admitted to membership. Some of the nation's most prestigious Black institutions, among them Howard University, sororities like Alpha Kappa Alpha and Delta Sigma Theta, fraternities, even Black churches practiced this blatantly colorist form of discrimination. They literally tacked a brown paper bag to the door and unless your skin was that tone or lighter, you couldn't get in.)

In my parents' social milieu, a Yiddish accent was a distinct social impediment. When my aunt Sadye first brought her boyfriend Herman home to meet the family, her siblings disapproved of him, partly because they didn't like his looks but also, according to Tillie's oral history, "because he couldn't talk well." In English; I'm sure his Yiddish was fine. Jenny and Nathan didn't exactly sound like Sarah Bernhardt and John Gielgud, but they, too, faulted Herman's speech. "Sadye married him anyway," Tillie says on the tape, "because he was crazy about her, and he turned out to be a good husband. But she wasn't happy with him. She became ashamed of him."

I recently read about a survivor of the Auschwitz concentration camp whose entire family perished in the Warsaw ghetto. He arrived in the US when he was nineteen, an age at which most linguists think it impossible to lose one's accent, but this man lost his, he said, because he "didn't want anything to do with anything European." He wanted to be "110 percent American." So successful was he at shedding his accent that until he told his teenage son the truth, the boy had no idea that his father was an immigrant.

My mother, who was at least as determined as that man to speak 110 percent American English, felt severely handicapped in that effort by her surroundings. Yiddish speakers were everywhere—in her immediate family, their tenement building, her heavily Jewish neighborhood on the Lower East Side, her friendship circle, and her fellow employees (and bosses) in the garment factory where she worked twelve hours a day. To compensate for her lack of exposure to native English speakers, and because she was so intent on mastering the standard American dialect, she took night school classes in elocution and perfected her pronunciation and enunciation by mimicking the voices she heard on the radio.

My mother has been dead for more than sixty years, and the passage of time has made it increasingly difficult for me to hear her voice in my head. But I will never forget how proud she was that, rather than sound like "a greenhorn straight off the boat," she spoke like a radio announcer. Of all her dreams of perfection, this was the only one that came true in full. She didn't have to hide or pretend. She didn't have to feel ashamed. Her English was flawless.

CHAPTER 51

"YOU THINK THAT'S BAD?!!"

Doubtless, you've had this experience: as soon as you learn a new word or read about a place you never heard of before, the word or location turns up everywhere. Something like that happened once I began writing this memoir. Suddenly, I noticed how often words like ashamed, humiliated, guilty, scandal, and disgrace come up in conversation. I became attuned to—and frankly amazed by— the many friends, acquaintances, and perfect strangers who were willing to confide their secrets: airplane seatmates (before COVID grounded us), a partygoer I met at the punchbowl, a woman getting a manicure in the chair next to mine, and any number of people who stood in line to have their books autographed after one of my speaking events and lingered afterwards to share an intimate memory stirred up by something I'd said in my talk.

I remember hearing from, or about, a man who'd lost his eighteen-year-old son and was ashamed to tell anyone that the boy committed suicide because they might think he, the father, had done something to cause it. A young woman who was raped by her older brother and never told their parents. A macho guy who claimed he'd seen combat in Vietnam though he spent the war in Canada. A lawyer who supported a secret second family, a woman and two kids, in addition to his legal wife and three kids who lived only a few miles away, and found ways to spend about a third of his time with them. A woman who learned that her uncle hadn't died from hepatitis as she'd been told but from syphilis. A professor who had a stutter since he was a boy and was still trying to hide it. An adoptee who discovered at thirty-five that not only was her real father a Catholic priest, but the woman she thought was her sister actually was her mother, and the woman she called Mother was her grandmother.

My late friend Barbara Seaman—esteemed women's health activist, author of the bestseller, *A Doctor's Case against the Pill*, outspoken advocate for laws against domestic violence—was too ashamed to admit she had endured many years in an abusive marriage because her passivity so starkly contradicted her image as a champion of women's dignity and well-being. In her youth, my friend and fellow *Ms.* editor, Joanne Edgar—a white woman born in Louisiana to strict segregationists and raised in Jackson, Mississippi—was afraid to tell her family she was active in the civil rights movement. While taking courses at a historically Black college, she attended a Joan Baez concert on campus and some gossipy snitch made a list of all the White people there and told Joanne's grandmother, who told her mother, both of whom flipped out. When she took the job at *Ms.*, Joanne didn't tell anyone where she worked, just said she was "in publishing."

More often than not, after I describe one of these secrets, my listeners say something like, "You think that's bad?!!" and then tell me a story they consider "worse." If you responded that way to any of the previous chapters, it's probably because you, like most of us, subscribe to a hierarchy of shamefulness. While I was researching other people's secrets, I heard stories I considered so much worse than mine that I began to question my right to feel wounded by my own experiences. And when a woman confessed to having had a nose job, or boob job, or faked her orgasms, or a man confessed to having weird masturbatory fantasies or faking his resumes, I had to restrain myself from saying, "You think *that's* bad?!!" But no visible bullet hole doesn't mean a person isn't wounded. Some secrets cause internal bleeding, as I learned from four Jewish women who grew up in families like mine where the shanda rules and some secrets leave scars.

Lacey Schwartz thought she was White because her White Jewish parents told her she was White, and none of her White Jewish relatives contradicted them. For the first sixteen years of her life, this young Jew was gaslighted, made to believe black was white so her parents could maintain their charade—the mother could hide her affair with an African American, and the father could live in denial that he'd been cuckolded. For her mom's secret to be safe and her dad to be free to embrace his delusion, Lacey had to be fooled into misperceiving her own racial identity, even though the mirrors in her childhood home reflected a little girl with a caramel complexion and wooly hair. And even though home movies of her bat mitzvah show her as a brown-skinned child amid a sea of Caucasian cousins. And even though a member of her synagogue once told her, "It's so nice to have an Ethiopian Jew in our presence." Watching Lacey's searing documentary *Little White Lie*, I wanted to give her a free membership in Dupes Anonymous.

Same for Elizabeth Wurtzel, another little Jewish girl who grew up unaware of her mother's secret and her father's ignorance. The author of *Prozac Nation*, she posted this tweet in 2018: "At age 50 I discovered my father is a famous civil rights photographer—and not the man I believed was my father." Elizabeth's difficulties with the man she called Father made no sense until she realized why, as she wrote in *The Cut*, "[He and I] never really connected. We tried, and eventually we stopped doing even that. When he died in 2014, I had not seen him since 2001…. I have been working out that relationship all my life, in writing and therapy and conversation, with cocaine and heroin, with recovery and perseverance, and with my thoughts. I think so much… You can't surprise me. But this surprised me." *This* meaning her mother's secret. "My mother was ashamed that she had an affair, so she hid it and made her husband think he was my father…. She was brought up to believe that only bad girls have premarital sex and extramarital sex. She was scared of what people would think. She was afraid of the judgment of her family."

Like me, Elizabeth Wurtzel was raised in an observant Jewish family with a mother who feared the long shadow of the shanda. The difference is, my premarital sex ended in abortion, while her mother's extramarital sex ended in the birth of Elizabeth, and the burden of lifelong shame and guilt. I came around to admitting my secret; Elizabeth's mother kept *her* secret hidden. As a result, Elizabeth grew up with an inchoate sense of dislocation and disconnection from her supposed father, and became a (self-described) exhibitionist, addict, and single childless woman who was promiscuous, frequently drugged, and depressed. "Shame is a terrible thing," she wrote in the reissue of the book that made her famous. "You are only as sick as your secrets." She died in January 2020 of metastatic breast cancer.

In her fifties, Dani Shapiro, novelist, memoirist, writing teacher, and strongly Jewish-identified Jew, sent her DNA to one of those gene-tracing services and they sent back news that she was 100 percent Ashkenazi Jewish on her mother's side, but her father was not her blood relative. According to her genetic profile, Dani, the yeshiva-educated daughter of an Orthodox man descended from Jewish aristocracy, was actually the biological daughter of a Christian student who used to donate his sperm to a Philadelphia fertility clinic to pay his way through medical school. People whose genes revealed unexpected information about their ethnicity, nationality, race, or parentage are nothing new in the age of biotechnology. Yet for me, Dani's discovery of her family's secret was uniquely memorable, partly because she wrote about it with grace and power in *Inheritance: A Memoir of Genealogy, Paternity, and Love,* and partly because she's a close friend of my daughters and whenever I saw her it crossed my mind that she might be one of those kids whose parents never told her she was adopted.

Platinum-blonde, blue-eyed, pug-nosed, and as pink-skinned as a Gerber's baby, Dani is the polar opposite of the stereotypical dark-haired, brown-eyed Jew. When she first mentioned her yeshiva education, I envisioned June Allyson in a classroom full of Barbra Streisands. I'm glad I never said that out loud, since I subsequently learned of Dani's disdain for people who had trouble reconciling her American Beauty face with her Orthodox Jewish credentials. Fed up with hearing things like, "Wow, you don't look Jewish," or, "You could have gotten us bread from the Nazis," she took to dropping Hebrew words to demonstrate her religious bona fides. All the more reason why her stunning DNA results drove her to a dogged pursuit of the truth about her origins. After months of false leads and dead-end streets, she was able to unravel her late parents' most closely guarded secret: Her father was sterile. Her mother had been impregnated at a Philadelphia fertility clinic with a mixture of the medical student's motile young sperm and her father's dispirited swimmers, a process that allowed Mr. Shapiro to maintain the pride-saving delusion that one of his sperm may have made the trip successfully. Dani's quest culminated in a meeting with her biological father and his grown children. She was stuck dumb by how much she resembled them physically, not just in looks but mannerisms, and as they learned more about each other, she marveled at their parallel tastes, talents, and interests. Her similarities to these people, along with an ineffable, almost primal feeling of connection, allowed her to understand the visceral power of biology. Finding them made her whole.

This may sound strange, but as I see it, the secret sterility of Dani's father and the secret fertility of my aunt Joan are products of the same pronatalist coercion. Since most Jews prize fecundity and pity the childless, my aunt's unwillingness to bear a child and Dani's father's inability to spawn one, would have been equally shanda worthy had they been outed. No wonder the truth, in both cases, had to be buried.

I consider the secrets kept from Lacey, Elizabeth, and Dani to be far "worse" than those hidden from me. Why? Because I was hoodwinked about who my *parents* were while those women were kept in the dark about who *they* were. It's a crucial distinction, one that should have made me feel better. But schadenfreude—the pleasure derived from another person's misfortune—couldn't mitigate the sense of betrayal I experienced as a result of my parents' lies any more than my discovery, decades later, that my roommates' families were far from perfect mitigated the family envy that bedeviled me in college. Ranking categories of dupedom is a challenge for social scientists but scant comfort to children weaned on lies.

The worst of the worst is the secrecy around sexual abuse. My first exposure to the scourge of incest was when I sampled the overflowing bags of reader mail received every day at *Ms.* magazine and discovered a large percentage of the letters to the editor were written by women who had been sexually abused by a father, stepfather, or other family member. Since everyone in my parents' generation is dead I can't claim to know for certain, but I found no evidence in the shopping bag or anywhere else that would suggest such outrageous acts occurred on either side of my family. My friend "Ruby," the pseudonym she requested, wasn't so fortunate. Her father, a wealthy Jewish philanthropist and supposed paragon of rectitude, violated her body from the time she was three years old until she ran away from home at sixteen. The aftermath of his horrific abuse messed with Ruby's mind for decades afterward. Equally appalling was the behavior of her mother, a doyenne of Upper East Side Jewish society, who knew exactly what was happening and did nothing to stop it. Ruby used to send me long handwritten letters describing in excruciating detail her father's sexual assaults and the bloodless passivity of her mother. Rather than report the offender and sully her elevated social status, the woman, when confronted by Ruby, denied her daughter's claims and protected the monster.

After Ruby left home, she buried her memories under layers of wanton sex, drugs, and self-soothing; then she pulled it together, excelled in college, ultimately built a successful career as a consultant, and married a loving man with a warm, welcoming family. Until a shoulder injury suddenly triggered a muscle memory of all that she'd repressed. In addition to entering intensive therapy, Ruby also confided in a few close friends, me among them. It was the first time I'd witnessed the enduring agony of an incest survivor at close range. Horrified by what her father did to her, I encouraged Ruby to file charges against the man and blow the lid off her mother's complicity. Ruby wouldn't do it. She did, however, consult her rabbi, and ask if, under the circumstances, she was still obligated to obey the fifth commandment, which required her to honor her father and mother. The rabbi's response was halachic and complex. (What else is new?) He said respect for one's parents is greatly valued in Judaism, but if a parent is abusive, the child is permitted to "terminate" the relationship so long as it's done "with respect." Translation: Ruby was justified in leaving home and separating herself from her abuser but were she to expose her father's shame, she would cause a shanda, which would be "disrespectful." My answer was a lot simpler: Your father forfeited his right to be honored when you were three years old and he climbed on top of you in your bed. Your mother forfeited her right when she came into your room afterward with a washcloth and an aspirin and refused to know what she knew.

One night, I happened to be at the annual dinner of one of the Jewish organizations that benefited from the generosity of Ruby's father. When I caught sight of him and her mother, dressed to the nines and receiving acolytes in the manner of Mafia royalty, you would have thought from my reaction that I was watching Jews genuflect before Adolph Hitler and Eva Braun. I became nauseated. I broke out in a sweat. It was all I could do to stop myself from rushing the podium and broadcasting their crimes. I did manage to stay in my seat, aware that it wasn't my place to do what their daughter had not done and, as it turned out, would never do, which was to expose them before their peers. When Ruby finally found the courage to confront them in private and request the apology that might help her heal, they refused. They also accused her of suffering from "false memory syndrome," called her a liar and a "crazy woman," and persuaded her brother that Ruby was delusional. For years, she kept begging her parents to admit the truth; that's all she wanted. They wouldn't budge. I couldn't have forgiven them. I'm not sure that Ruby forgave them, but she remained the dutiful daughter, took care of them when they got old, nursed them when they were ill, and mourned them in the correct Jewish way when they died.

To this day, she continues to cover up her father's crime. She told me she wants to protect his good name and to spare her relatives from suffering shame by association. She's also convinced that, belated as it may be, exposing him would harm her own professional reputation and the success of her business. I believe that exposing the man would bring cosmic justice to the world and bring Ruby peace. She believes if she shames her father posthumously, the filth will splash back on too many innocent people including all the children in her family. There in a nutshell is the double-barreled power of the shanda: disgrace besmirches, fear of disgrace silences. While there's no equivalence between her father's sexual crimes and my father's emotional inadequacy, she and I have this in common: both of us were "hope-aholics," Gloria Steinem's term for the optimists among us who still believe people capable of change. Ruby's hope that her father would confess and ask her forgiveness was as stubborn and futile as my hope that my father would suddenly become Atticus Finch.

CHAPTER 52

A SECRET-FREE LIFE

I've reconciled myself to a fundamental paradox: I want to be free of all secrecy but not of all shame—only the kind that deflates, denigrates, or dehumanizes particular people or groups. Race-shaming, slut-shaming, poor-shaming, fat-shaming, immigrant-shaming, and all the other put-downs visited on those who don't fit someone's notion of the "norm," that's what I want to see come to an end. I don't wish to be shame-free or shameless. I want the specter of shame to influence human behavior for good, not ill. "Good shame" is prophylactic, preventative, and preemptive. It stops us from hurting other people, stealing their stuff, or fouling the environment. Good shame can be as trivial as whatever it was that made me pick up the crumpled Kleenex that fell from my pocket when I pulled out my phone. Rather than step over it and keep walking, I stooped down and retrieved it because I would have been ashamed of myself if I didn't. Besides the fact that littering is ugly, illegal, and antisocial, I refuse to see myself as a person who leaves her garbage for others to clean up. Good shame buttresses the rule of law and goes by the name of conscience.

In his BBC radio talk, Chief Rabbi Jonathan Sacks said, "Shame has a place in any moral system, but when it dominates all else, when all we have is trial by public exposure, then the more reluctant people will be to be honest, and the more suspicious we'll become of people in public life."

It is onerous and exhausting to conceal something, especially when it's unworthy of secrecy, which so many somethings are. And the effort it takes to keep that something hidden only intensifies the sense that it's shameful. During the years when I hid my brain tumor, I practiced selective secrecy, telling some people and not others, then I couldn't keep straight who knew and who didn't. Now that it's out in the open, the secret no longer owns me.

My friend Eugenia Zukerman, the renowned flutist and author, feels the same way about her medical condition. In a remarkably revealing 2021 article in Health.com, she writes:

> I've learned that it is important to be very open about my diagnosis. When I meet new people, I say, "Before I forget, I want to tell you that I do forget. I have Alzheimer's." After some seconds of silence, the conversation usually continues in a normal way. I know some people who have chosen to cut ties with friends rather than share the news, too ashamed to open up about their diagnosis. I want to avoid that.

Olivia Clement, the woman who threw into the River Seine the envelope containing her French grandfather's worst secret without opening it, describes in the same essay the physical and emotional price her husband paid for his secret:

> Not too long ago I came out of a relationship destroyed by the weight of too many secrets; my husband was having an affair. The web of lies he was spinning became more complicated every day. I watched, as he physically changed before my eyes, burdened by the immense task of keeping part of his life hidden from me. He began to look completely different: always exhausted; he lost the color in his face and he was increasingly hunched over. His moods were more and more erratic. His transformation wasn't unique—research has found that carrying a secret can feel like literally carrying a heavy weight.

I know the freedom that comes of being unburdened by that heavy weight because I've enjoyed a secret-free marriage for more than half a century. Which doesn't mean I'm naïve about the thrill of furtiveness or risk. During the five years when I was single after college, I had my share of transgressive and clandestine adventures. Since then, I've been a sounding board for other people's secrets—women conducting extramarital affairs, gay men who, like my nephew Jeffrey, were concealing their true sexuality; women who, like my friend Ruby, survived sexual abuse; men like my father who pretend to be wealthier or more successful than they are; and women like my mother who are ashamed of their origins. I've known others who, like me, were ashamed of a disease or disability. Having witnessed at close range the corrosion that results from deception and cover-ups, I'm convinced that happiness lies in a secret-free life.

Many of my peers seem to agree. Their children or grandchildren embrace a variety of lifestyles or find themselves in circumstances that in my youth would have been regarded as a shanda worthy of shame and secrecy. Off the top of my head, I can think of a friend's forty-something son who has schizophrenia (recently married, he just became the father of twins). Several people who, despite having postgraduate degrees and raising their kids to go to college, have children who chose not to. One couple whose grandson prefers to wear dresses. Another friend whose grandson is in prison serving a life sentence for murder. Any number of friends whose children or grandchildren are gay, trans, or gender fluid; suffer from physical or mental illness; live with their partners and have multiple babies without benefit of marriage. I'm not saying there's anything comparable about those individuals or their circumstances, only that the reason I know these facts about those people is because my friends talk openly about their children and grandchildren and accept them without judgment. Rather than feel ashamed of those they love, rather than lie or paper over their situations, they and their families are living secret-free lives.

Despite my parents' shame-fueled lies, they weren't entirely off-track. Ceil had it right when she salvaged optimism from the jaws of adversity and met disappointment with reinvention. Jack was on target when he harnessed his aspirations to collective action regardless of whether the goal was to establish a Jewish State or add lox to the Men's Club's bagel breakfasts. Writing about their indenture to the shanda, I've become more compassionate about my family and more forgiving of the painful chapters of my past. I see my parents more vividly. I understand them better. I cherish what I learned from them. I just want mine to be the last generation of Jews who have anything to hide.

ACKNOWLEDGMENTS

This book would not exist without my daughter Abigail's gentle goading, editorial guidance, and constant encouragement, and my husband Bert's loving forbearance during the five years it took me to write it. I am also deeply grateful to my daughter Robin, whose comments on the manuscript were trenchant and invaluable; my granddaughter, Molly Golda Shapiro, for choosing to write about me for her college biography course, incidentally leading me to the long-forgotten shopping bag full of old letters; Andrew Blauner, my indefatigable literary agent, who believed in this book and found the perfect home for it at Post Hill Press; Debra Englander, PHP editor, Heather King, managing editor, and Devon Brown, publicist, all supremely skilled at their jobs and uniquely adept at accommodating authorial idiosyncrasies; Shira Dicker and Malka Margolies, PR mavens extraordinaire, and Susie Cohen, who handles my speaking dates with grace, all of whose commitment to *Shanda*'s success rivals mine; David Kraemer, professor of Rabbinics and Talmud at the Jewish Theological Seminary, who vetted the manuscript for Judaic accuracy; Anita Norich, Yiddish scholar and professor emerita, English and Judaic Studies, University of Michigan, who vetted the Glossary; my dear friend Kathleen Peratis, who compiled the provocative discussion questions for book groups and others; Claire Wachtel, literary consultant, whose early editorial suggestions helped me organize and streamline my story; Daphne Merkin, who restored my flagging spirits when it mattered, and gave me Claire's number.

I'm also indebted to Ruth Abram, Arlene and Alan Alda, Susie Cohen, Lynn Povich, Selma Shapiro, and Steve Shepard, for pausing their own busy lives to give me feedback on the book's content or cover design. Special plaudits to Carolyn Hessel, the doyenne of modern Jewish literature and my personal fairy godmother, who volunteered to read the manuscript at the eleventh hour, made several brilliant suggestions, and caught a half dozen typos that the rest of us missed. Thanks to my cousins Judy Kahn Sadoff, Priscilla Darvie Donohue, Joel Kahn, and Simma Chester for their indispensable help with Halpern family history; a special round of applause to Pris for sending me precious childhood photographs I never knew existed; to my cousins Wendy and David Bar-Yakov, Ivor Sargon, Simon Sargon, and Babette Eckstein for filling some blanks in Cottin family history; to my nephews and niece, Stephen, Donald, and Cyral Miller, and my nephew Avram Gropper for their memories of my parents, and theirs, Betty and Bernie Miller, and Rena and Murray Gropper, respectively.

To the many friends who shared their secrets on the record or pseudonymously, you have my enduring appreciation for your time and trust.

Finally, a deep bow to the esteemed writers, artists, scholars, and friends who agreed to read the manuscript in advance and gave *Shanda* the generous endorsements that appear in the first few pages of this book and on its cover.

ABOUT THE AUTHOR

Letty Cottin Pogrebin, co-founder of *Ms.* magazine, is a nationally acclaimed writer, activist, and public speaker. The author of twelve books, she has also published articles and essays in numerous print and online periodicals, including the *New York Times, The Nation*, and *Huffington Post*. She is a co-founder of the National Women's Political Caucus and the *Ms.* Foundation for Women; a past president of the Authors Guild and Americans for Peace Now; and has served on the boards of the Harvard Divinity School Women in Religion Program and the Brandeis University Women's and Gender Studies Program. Among her many honors is a Yale University Poynter Fellowship in Journalism, a Matrix Award for excellence in communication and the arts, and an Emmy Award for her work as consulting editor on the TV version of Marlo Thomas's *Free to Be... You and Me*. Pogrebin lives with her husband in New York City and Stockbridge, Massachusetts.

lettycottinpogrebin.com
Facebook.com/letty.pogrebin

DISCUSSION QUESTIONS

1. Among the animating themes in *Shanda* are fear of shame, the "ruinous impact" of public disgrace, and the burdens of secrecy. Do those issues still resonate in this era of hyper-sharing? What role do shame and secrecy play in your life?

2. While writing this book, Pogrebin happened upon a trove of deeply personal letters exchanged between her parents more than eighty years ago. That discovery greatly expanded her purview of the past and sometimes challenged her own memories. Were you to write a memoir, what written materials would be available to you? Since long-form letter writing has largely been replaced by slap-dash texts and inartful emails, do you think future biographers and historians will be hobbled by a paucity of original documents and will readers suffer the consequences?

3. The author writes, "Guilt is the by-product of our actions toward others; shame is the by-product of our judgment of ourselves. Guilt says, 'I did a bad thing'; shame says, 'I am a bad person.'" How would you define the difference between guilt and shame? Which of those emotions is more familiar to you personally?

4. Pogrebin delves into many secrets that her immigrant Jewish family considered shameful—failed marriages, poverty, mental deficiency, certain physical conditions, infractions of Judaism, to name a few. What do you consider shameful today?

5. Revisiting her sexual assault in the 1960s by a famous playwright, Pogrebin admits, "Now, in 2022, I'm ashamed of having sugarcoated my ordeal in Brendan Behan's hotel room, reducing it to a breezy anecdote, and I'm embarrassed by how blithely I transformed an aggravated assault by a powerful man

into a 'sticky sexual encounter.'" In this age of #MeToo, how do you regard her experience in that hotel room and her reaction to it? If you've survived something similar, what did you do about it?

6. *Shanda* describes Holocaust survivors who hid their wartime traumas from their children and grandchildren; she also describes Jews in America who secretly felt ashamed that millions of their fellow Jews went to the ovens "like sheep." What was your response to those stories?

7. Pogrebin shows how fear of shame can overpower self-interest and self-respect. How did you react to the request by the "comfort" women's grandchildren that the old women stop seeking justice from their Japanese tormentors? How about the decision by "Ruby" not to expose her father's violent incest? What needs to happen for survivors to feel safe admitting such secrets? Is public exposure of the perpetrator necessary before survivors can attain justice and achieve closure?

8. The scene at the pool party when Faye arrives is a familiar one. Do you consider yourself a "sizeist?" Have you ever been body shamed? Have you ever been a secret eater? Binger? Purger?

9. In her chapter, "Motherguilt," Pogrebin, a staunch feminist, social justice activist, and mother of three, confesses, "Whether the focus of my work outside the home was on women, Jews, or Israel, it sometimes led me to shortchange my role as a mother." If you're a parent, do you feel you've achieved a satisfactory work/family balance? If not, how weighed down are you by motherguilt? (Or fatherguilt?)

10. The author writes about public shame, the shame of nations, and candidly describes her progressive politics and her condemnation of Israel's treatment of the Palestinians. If you disagree with her views on that Middle East conflict or any other political or religious issue discussed in the book, does it color your feelings about her or her story?

11. For more than thirty years, Pogrebin sought her mother-in-law's love and approval and felt ashamed of her failure to get it.

Have you ever blamed yourself for a comparable rejection? Did the mother-in-law's deathbed apology redeem her in your eyes?

12. Every immigrant and every ethnic group has its own version of Pogrebin's story. Did someone Americanize your family name? Was anyone in your family ashamed of their ethnic, economic, or religious origins to the point where they denied or altered their identity? Do you fault that person for falsifying who they are, or do you credit them with adaptation, assimilation, and reinvention?

13. If you're an Ashkenazi Jew, did you relate personally to the author's description of her family's inclinations regarding shame and secrecy? If you're not an Ashkenazi Jew, discuss how your heritage and experiences have differed.

14. Letty Cottin Pogrebin wants to be free of all secrecy but not of all shame. Do you share that goal? How close are you to achieving it?

15. Given that one person's secrets often involve other people, are you obligated to get the approval of those who may be implicated when your secret is made public? Is it possible to rid yourself of your secret without violating their right to privacy?

16. If you were casting "Shanda: the movie" who would play Letty? Bert? Their kids? Betty? Rena? Jack? Ceil? Nathan? Jenny? Aunt Tillie? Uncle Al? Jeffrey? Simma? The boy with the broken hand? Dr. Spencer?

GLOSSARY

Author's note: In Yiddish and Hebrew, "ch" is not pronounced as it is in cheese, but like a heavy, guttural combination of "h" and "k."

afikoman. The last thing eaten at the Passover Seder. The middle of three matzahs on the seder table, the afikoman is broken in two early in the service, the larger piece wrapped in a napkin, hidden by the seder leader, and meant to be found by the children, whose reward is a special sweet or a silver dollar.

aliyah. The honor of reciting the prescribed blessings before and after the seven or more Torah portions that are read in synagogue at Sabbath morning services.

amidah. The standing devotional prayer.

Ashkenazim. Jews of Eastern European lineage.

ayin ha'ra. The Evil Eye.

balabusta. A woman who is an accomplished homemaker.

bat mitzvah. (lit. Daughter of the Commandments) A coming-of-age ceremony for Jewish girls and women.

bimah. The raised platform in a Jewish sanctuary where stands a Holy Ark containing the Torah scrolls, and a reading desk from which the Torah is chanted.

bubeleh. (lit. little grandmother) Term of endearment.

bubkis. (lit. turd) Nothing.

busha v'charpa. (lit. shame and disgrace) Majorly shameful behavior.

challah. Traditional yeast bread enriched with egg, typically braided, and eaten at Jewish ceremonial meals.

chas v'halila. God forbid!

cherem. That which is proscribed or shunned. Refers to exclusion from the Jewish community for acts or words considered heretical by the community.

chillul hashem. The desecration of God's name by Jews whose words or deeds reflect badly on the Jewish people, Judaism, and the Divine.

cholent. Traditional overnight stew eaten on the Sabbath by Ashkenazi Jews.

chuppah. The wedding canopy in a Jewish ceremony.

chutzpah. Audacity. Nervy, cheeky, brazen.

derech. Path. "Off the derech" describes an Orthodox person who strays from observance of Jewish laws and customs.

di Goldene Medine. (lit. The Golden Land) America.

d'var Torah. (lit. a word of Torah) A brief teaching, generally about the weekly Torah portion.

fresser. Glutton.

Gemara or Gemorrah. A collection of ancient rabbinic commentaries and discussions of Jewish law. One of the two parts that compose the Talmud, the other being the Mishnah.

get. A Jewish bill of divorce.

gribenes. Crisp cracklings produced by rendering chicken fat (see, schmaltz). An Ashkenazi favorite.

"Had Gadya." One of the songs traditionally sung at the end of the Passover seder.

Hadassah. The Women's Zionist Organization of America.

Haftarah. Readings from the Books of The Prophets.

Haganah. (lit. defense) The Jewish paramilitary force in Palestine before Israel became a state.

Halacha. Jewish law.

Hanukkah. The Festival of Lights commemorating the Maccabees' victory over the Syrian Greeks and the rededication of the Temple in Jerusalem.

Haredim. (lit. those who tremble before God) Ultra-Orthodox Jews.

Hasidic. (lit. pious) Strictly observant Jews who follow the teachings and customs of various esteemed Eastern European rabbis of the eighteenth and nineteenth centuries.

hester panim. The hidden face of God.

hocked mir a tchainik. (lit. banged on my kettle) Hassled me.

Kaddish. The mourner's prayer. Traditionally, Jews say Kaddish for thirty days after the burial of a child, spouse, or sibling, and for eleven months after the burial of a parent. From then on, the Kaddish is recited on a loved one's yahrzeit and four times a year at certain synagogue memorial services.

kashrut. Jewish dietary laws.

ketubah. Jewish marriage contract.

ketsileh. (lit. kitten) Yiddish term of endearment.

kiddush. (lit. sanctification) The blessing said over a cup of sacramental wine on the Jewish sabbath and festivals.

Kiddush Hashem. The sanctification of God's name.

kinnehurra/kinehora. (lit. not the Evil Eye) An exclamation intended to ward off evil.

Knesset. The Israeli parliament.

knippel. (lit. a knot or pinch) A nest egg. A woman's secret stash of money to be used for her own purposes.

kugel/kigel. Noodle pudding

macher. An influential person; a big shot in the community.

mamaloshen. Mother tongue, meaning Yiddish.

matzah. Unleavened bread; a large, square, almost tasteless cracker eaten on Passover.

mazel tov. (lit. good luck) Congratulations.

mezuzah. The small case, containing a tightly rolled up parchment with twenty-two words from Deuteronomy written on it, that Jews affix to the right doorpost of their homes.

mishegas. Craziness.

nachas. Pleasure-filled pride—e.g., what you feel when a child plays an instrument well.

nareshkeit. Foolishness.

Nevi'im. Prophets. A section of the Hebrew Bible.

"Ofyn Pripitchik." (lit. On the hearth) Popular nineteenth-century Yiddish song/lullaby.

parasha/sedra/sidra. The weekly Torah portion Jews read in synagogue.

Passover. The Jewish holiday commemorating the ancient Israelites' liberation from slavery in Egypt.

Rosh Hashana. The Jewish New Year.

Rosh Hodesh. First day of the Jewish month.

sabra. (in Hebrew: prickly pear; in Arabic: perseverance) A native-born Jewish Israeli

Sephardi. A Jew of Spanish or Portuguese descent, or whose family originated from the Middle East or North Africa.

schmaltz. Rendered chicken fat. Basic ingredient of Ashkenazi Jewish cuisine.

Shabbos or Shabbat. (lit. day of rest) The Jewish Sabbath, which begins on Friday at sundown and ends on Saturday night when three stars are visible in the sky (about fifty minutes after sunset).

shalom bayit. (lit. Peace in the home) Describes the Jewish concept of domestic harmony and reconciliation between spouses, the maintenance of which is often viewed primarily as the responsibility of the wife.

shammes. A beadle or sexton in a synagogue.

shanda far di goyim. (lit. a shame before the nations) Misbehavior or wrongdoing by a Jew or Jewish collective that embarrasses the broader Jewish community in front of gentiles.

shiva. The first seven days after burial.

shloshim. The thirty day mourning period after burial

shtetl. A small market town in Eastern Europe, home to Jews and gentiles.

shul. Synagogue.

Shulchan Aruch. The Code of Jewish Law written by Joseph Caro in 1563.

siddur. Jewish prayer book containing daily and sabbath prayers.

simcha. Happy occasion.

Taharat Ha'Mishpacha. Laws of family purity that regulate sexual activity for Orthodox Jews based on the wife's menstrual cycle.

tallit. A fringed prayer shawl.

Talmud. (lit. study or teaching) A compendium of rabbinic conversations, commentaries, arguments, and rulings on Jewish law.

tamei. Ritually impure.

tefillin. Phylacteries. Two small black leather boxes containing parchment slips inscribed with Torah quotations; the boxes, attached by leather straps, are worn by observant Jews on the left arm and forehead during morning prayers.

teshuvah. (lit. return or answer) Repentance. Or, rabbinic opinion. (Context determines meaning.)

Torah. The Five Books of Moses.

traif. Foods forbidden by Jewish dietary laws.

trombenik. Lazy, idle, dissolute, ne'er-do-well.

tsimmes. (lit. a stew) A big fuss.

yarmulke. Skullcap.

yahrzeit. The anniversary of the death of a parent or near relative observed annually by the recital of the Kaddish and the lighting of a memorial candle.

yenta. Colloquial: a gossip; original: gentle, genteel, noble.

yeshiva. Upper-level Jewish religious school.

Yiddishe kop. (lit. A Jewish head) Smart, clever.

Yiddishkeit. The quality of being Jewish; the Jewish way of life, its customs, practices, and the Yiddish language.

Yizkor. A solemn service held in synagogue on certain holy days to memorialize deceased relatives or Jewish martyrs.

Yom Kippur. Day of Atonement. The most sacred day of the Jewish year.

zaftig. (lit. German for juicy) Curvaceous, having a full, rounded figure.